INTRODUCTION TO
CONTEMPORARY
JAPANESE LITERATURE
——Synopses of Major Works——
1956—1970

INTRODUCTION TO CONTEMPORARY JAPANESE LITERATURE

—Synopses of Major Works—

1956–1970

UNIVERSITY OF TOKYO PRESS

Published by
University of Tokyo Press
Tokyo
Copyright © 1972 Kokusai Bunka Shinkokai
All rights reserved
Printed in Japan
by General Printing Co., Ltd. Yokohama

PUBLISHER'S FOREWORD

This is the third volume in a series of introductions to contemporary Japanese literature. The first volume covers the period 1902–1935 while the second volume includes eighty-one authors whose works appeared between 1936 and 1955. This volume includes seventy-two authors whose works were published between 1956 and 1970.

The authors in this volume have been arranged in alphabetical order, a shift from the chronological order used in Volume I and II. Each listing includes a short biographical sketch and a synopsis of one work. Fifteen of the authors included have had their works translated into English. For these authors, only the biographical sketches are given.

The appendix at the end of this volume includes a list of works, publishers and dates of publication for each author.

The Japanese texts were translated by Mr. Ohta Yuzo (Ota Yûzô), research assistant in the Department of Comparative Literature and Comparative Culture at the University of Tokyo. The English texts were revised and rewritten by Mrs. Marianne Patricia Ohta, Lecturer of Rikkyô University, and Miss Margaret Johnson, a research student at the University of Tokyo and now a junior research fellow in the Department of Japanese, Monash University (Australia).

January 1972

KOKUSAI BUNKA SHINKOKAI
(Japan Cultural Society)

EDITORIAL NOTES

1. Responsible for the selection of the authors and works for inclusion was the Selecting Committee consisting of the following people:

Fukuda Tsuneari   Senuma Shigeki
Miyoshi Yukio   Tanaka Chikao
Muramatsu Sadataka   Tanaka Yasutaka
Nakamura Mitsuo   Yamamoto Kenkichi
Okuno Takeo

2. The Introduction was written by Okuno Takeo, one of Japan's best known critics and a professor in Japanese literature at Tama Bijutsu University. For this background, Professor Okuno has relied considerably on his previous book, *Nihon Bungakushi: Kindai kara Gendai e* (History of Japanese Literature: From the Early Modern Period to the Present, Chûôkôron Shinsho No. 212) (Tokyo: Chûôkôronsha, 1970).

3. The Hepburn system, with minor modifications, is used in romanizing Japanese words.

4. For the personal names, the family name comes first according to common Japanese usage.

CONTENTS

INTRODUCTION

1 "*The Third New Generation*"

The works of writers discussed in the sections with the subtitles of "The 'New Burlesque' Group", "Democratic' Literature" and "Postwar Newcomers" in the Introduction to *Synopses of Contemporary Japanese Literature II (1938–1955)* are products of an age where all the established order had collapsed and everything was in confusion in the aftermath of the defeat in war.

The "New Burlesque" writers like Dazai Osamu, Sakaguchi Ango, Oda Sakunosuke and Tanaka Hidemitsu saw in the collapse of the established order, values, and ethics, the disintegration of their own inner selves. They set their own egos into a state of turmoil, hoping to cause an inner revolution and to discover their new selves. Writers of "Democratic Literature" like Miyamoto Yuriko and Nakano Shigeharu regarded the period of confusion after the war as a unique opportunity for a socialist revolution and dreamed of establishing a new society, a communist society by revolution. As for the so-called *après-guerre* writers (or the "postwar Group") like Noma Hiroshi, Shiina Rinzô, Umezaki Haruo, Nakamura Shin'ichirô, Takeda Taijun, Ôoka Shôhei, Haniya Yutaka and Hotta Yoshie, they wanted to grasp the essence of man and society anew, when all the existing order and values had collapsed, and express it comprehensively in their works. At the bottom of these efforts were their war experiences or their experiences of ideological conversion. They managed to create works which are characterized by interest in ideas and by social concern. In this respect they achieved what Japanese writers before them had not been able to do. They then aspired to write ambitious full-scale novels which would be worthy of standing beside the finest modern novels of the Western world, an ambition which no Japanese author since the Meiji period had realized. They thought that after the war conditions favourable to genuine novel-writing had been created.

Postwar Japan, however, was no longer a part of the age immediately following the feudal age. These writers had forgotten that, and tried to produce modern novels comparable to those of 19th century Europe which belonged to a different historical stage. It was probably the peculiar humanistic atmosphere of postwar Japan that induced them to commit such an anachronistic error. They clung to an outmoded ideal, instead of facing the challenge of creating new literature appropriate to the contemporary world. They gradually lost their initial natural spontaneity and their works gradually became empty "romans". One after another these writers fell into a state of stagnation, finding it difficult to write.

About that time the confused period immediately following the war came to an end, and the normal everyday order was reasserting itself. The period of sweet illusions of a peaceful revolution, a new society and so on, came to an end, and people were once again obliged to face a prosaic and cold reality. The ruins of the air-raids were once again filled with houses, straying war orphans were driven away, and cramped boring life started again. People who had been aiming to become rich overnight as black-marketeers, people who had been calling others to revolution as active members of trade unions, and others who had been living as wanderers all became decent salaried men once again, and started thinking about climbing the hierarchical ladder in the firms in which they worked and about the amount of money they would get when they retired. People had thought that society was unstable, and that it might drastically change or even collapse at any moment. Thus they had either been anarchistically living for the moment, or else living in a fantastic idealistic dream. But now they began to think that society was likely to stabilize. Inflation came to an end, and roughly from the time of the outbreak of the Korean War in June 1950, the policies of the Occupation Forces which had so far been progressive underwent a big change, and reactionary tendencies set in.

In such a period of relative stabilization when people once again started to work diligently in their posts writers called the "Third New Generation" appeared on the literary scene. But they did not enter the stage with a flourish. Their appearance corresponded to the changing atmosphere of the society. Hattori Tatsu, a critic belonging to the same generation as the "Third New Generation" writers, enumerated their characteristics as follows:" concreteness, simpleness, closeness to everyday life, conservatism, traditionalism, lyricism, monotony, autobiographical quality in the "I" novel tradition, formalism, amorality, illogicality, uncritical quality, apolitical quality", etc. As this list indicates, these writers looked extremely unpositive, just the opposite of the highly idealistic *après-guerre* writers.

Yasuoka Shôtarô, a representative writer of the "Third New Generation" said in a round-table talk, "We are ploughing the ground which the *après-guerre* writers opened with their tractors. Their method was too high-handed and rough. We would like to plough more carefully... Their works lacked any real literary quality". In saying this Yasuoka sounds modest but confident. The "Third New Generation" writers felt instinctively repelled by the rough unliterary qualities of the ambitious "*après-guerre* literature". They were attracted by the fine artistic qualities of "I" novels of the prewar period or by the shyness or masochism of "New Burlesque" writers. Many readers felt, however, that the valuable start for orthodox novels made by *après-guerre* writers was nullified by the "Third New Generation" writers, and were disappointed. Most people agreed that the "Third New Generation" was an ephemeral phenomenon called forth by the Korean War and would soon vanish. But just as the Japanese economy rapidly recovered, taking advantage of the special procurement boom at the time of the Korean War, and subsequently showed a phenomenal growth, so the "Third New Generation" writers, far from disappearing from the literary scene, continued to grow steadily, and have come to occupy a firm position as the most stable nucleus of contemporary Japanese Literature.

Most of the "Third New Generation" writers were born between 1916 and 1926, and spent their student days in a period when the Marxian ideological movement in Japan had already come to an end. Most of them were drafted into the army as soldiers, some of them when they were still students. Thus they were a war generation whose youth corresponded to the war years. They share an instinctive distrust of ideologies or of politics. It is true that the term the "Third New Generation" is used for mere convenience, and that each writer of this group has his individual characteristics which make it impossible for us to discuss the group *en masse*. On the other hand, it is worth noticing that most of them have been close friends from the days when they were mere literary aspirants, that they have encouraged and stimulated each other in their development as writers, and that they have created a group atmosphere, which is rather rare among postwar Japanese writers.

Yasuoka Shôtarô is the son of an army veterinary surgeon. After being off school for some years, he entered Keiô University. While he was studying there, he was drafted into the army, but contracted T. B. of the bones in Northern Manchuria. During the difficult years following the war, he earned his living by doing irregular jobs for the Occupation Forces and so on. His style of life was like that of a social failure. Among his works are *Aigan* (*Pet,* 1952) and *Inkina Tanoshimi* (*Gloomy Pastime,* 1953) which depict the unpleasant psychological complex of a lazy bad student towards his parents and himself. Yasuoka treats his subjects with humour and masochism. His works often have a poetic atmosphere reminiscent of a fairy tale world, as for example in his *Garasu no Kutsu* (*Glass Shoes,* 1951). Yasuoka's essays characterized by humour, his amateur political discussions and his vivid reports as a non-professional reporter are also quite popular. He won a firm position as an important writer with his *Kaihen no Kôkei* (*View of the Bay,* 1959).

Yoshiyuki Junnosuke is the eldest son of Yoshiyuki Eisuke, a writer of the Neo-Artistic School. When he was a student at Tokyo University, he was a member of the group magazine *Sedai* (*Generation*) issued by students regarded as the intellectual *élite*. While other members were interested in the progressive ideas then in vogue or in politics, Yoshiyuki deliberately ceased to live as a brilliant student and led the life of an idler. He worked as the editor of a pornographic magazine to get money, and associated with prostitutes of the red-light districts. *Genshoku no Machi* (*Primary Colours Street,* 1951) and *Shûu* (*Shower,* 1954) are works which express the complex feelings of the author by depicting his relationships with prostitutes who are excluded from normal respectable society. In *Honoo no Naka* (*In the Flames,* 1955) Yoshiyuki depicted a youth spent during the war and expressed the sentiments of the so-called war generation. His *Yami no*

Naka no Shukusai (Festival in the Dark, 1961) describes the eternal triangle of the hero, his wife and his mistress, and tries to understand the essential meaning of "the home". In works like *Suna no Ue no Shokubutsugun (A Group of Plants on the Sand,* 1963) and *Hoshi to Tsuki wa Ten no Ana (Stars and the Moon are Holes in Heaven,* 1966) Yoshiyuki used experimental techniques to deal with the theme of hidden sexual desire by depicting the various modes of sex in contemporary society. Yoshiyuki is not so good at writing long novels, but he is a master of the short novel form. His fine urban senses, his intelligence and purity which he retains even when depicting a life of dissipation, make the introverted and somewhat nihilistic Yoshiyuki the leading contemporary representative of the aesthetic "art for art's sake" writers.

Shôno Junzô was born in Ôsaka, the son of a teacher. When he was a student at Kyûshû University, he became friends with Shimao Toshio. He was influenced by Satô Haruo and Itô Shizuo and wrote works like *Aibu (Caresses,* 1949) and *Pûrusaido Shôkei (A Pool-Side Scene,* 1954) which depict the ordinary life of common citizens in a sympathetic quiet tone. His early works tended to show facile sweetness, but *Seibutsu (Still Life,* 1960) which depicts a seemingly happy family hiding a crisis showed a greater penetration. Shôno attracted attention for this work which expresses human helplessness and a moving determination to endure it. He has also published *Yûbe no Kumo (Evening Cloud,* 1964–1965), a long novel, *Akikaze to Futari no Otoko (Autumn Wind and Two Men,* 1965) and other short stories in the vein of *shinkyô shôsetsu* (mental life novel). These works suggest the peaceful life of the author in close contact with nature. Shôno's mastery of his restrained style is shown when he records, for example, the conversations of people walking by.

Miura Shumon who is the youngest of the "Third New Generation" writers is a graduate of Tokyo University. While teaching at the Art Department of Nihon University, he published *Meifu Sansui Zu (Landscape of Hades,* 1951), *Semiramisu no Sono (The Garden of Semiramis,* 1952), *Yasei no Yagi (Wild Goat,* 1954) and other stories based on the history, myths and classics of Asia and Europe. Miura, who became recognized through these clever short stories reminiscent of the early works of Akutagawa

Ryûnosuke, is a practical man, who leads a regular life like that of a business man. Probably because of this he was at first not very good at writing "I" novels and works dealing with inner problems, and did not show much progress as a writer for some time. His *Tomo Enpô yori Kitaru* (*A Friend Comes from Afar*, 1961), *Shinwa* (*Myth*, 1963) and *Hakoniwa* (*Miniature Garden*, 1967), works which depict family life and everyday routine through the eyes of a mature common sensical middle-aged man with bitter resignation, however, show that Miura has matured as a writer considerably in recent years.

Agawa Hiroyuki who, upon his graduation from Tokyo University, was drafted into the navy and spent some time as a young naval officer, published, soon after the war, *Nennen-saisai* (*Year after Year*, 1946) and *Rei Sandai* (*Three Deceased*, 1946). The former depicts the author's experiences when he returned from China to Hiroshima, his home town, which had been reduced to ashes by the A-bomb. The latter is reminiscences of his dead Navy comrades. By these work, Agawa was recognized by Shiga Naoya and others. But when the *après-guerre* writers (the writers of the so-called postwar group) started publishing their works, Agawa with his unpretentious "I" novel style works was overshadowed by them and was forgotten. At the time of the emergence of the "Third New Generation" writers, however, he also emerged again as a writer of the so-called war generation with his *Haru no Shiro* (*Spring Castle*, 1952) which depicts the author's experiences in the Navy, *Kumo no Bohyô* (*Gravemarker of Clouds*, 1955) which was the first work to deal with Japan's Kamikaze pilots, and other works. His short stories such as *Gentô* (*Side Lights of a Ship*, 1966) are also in a similar vein to those of other "Third New Generation" writers, and Agawa gradually came to be regarded as one of this group. He also wrote biographical or documentary works such as *Yamamoto Isoroku* (*Yamamoto Isoroku*, 1964–1965).

Endô Shûsaku is a Catholic writer, who graduated from Keiô University, and studied in France in the early postwar years. He wrote *Furansu no Daigakusei* (*Students in France*, 1951–1952) and was active as a critic for a while. In 1955 he published *Shiroi Hito · Kiiroi Hito* (*White People · Yellow People*, 1955), a pair of novels born out of his miserable experiences in

France and of the inferiority complex he felt as a coloured person there. Since then, Endô has published such works as *Umi to Dokuyaku* (*The Sea and Poison*, 1957) which deals with the problem of vivisection, and *Chinmoku* (*Silence*, 1966) a novel about Catholicism and the Japanese spiritual climate set in the period of Christian persecution in early 17th century Japan. All these works are Endô's attempts to arrive at a better understanding of the relationship between the Japanese people and the Christian faith. Endô is attracting attention internationally. His works betray a deep preoccupation with ideas and problems which sometimes makes them too abstract and schematic. In this respect, Endô has a greater affinity to writers of the "Postwar Group" (so-called *après-guerre* writers) than to the "Third New Generation" writers. On the other hand, his humorous novels like *Obaka-san* (*Blockhead*, 1959), his mischievous essays (Endô calls himself Korian, i.e. Fox-Badger-Hut. In Japan foxes and badgers are supposed to have supernatural powers for deceiving human beings.), his behaviour which supplies good material for journalistic circles, and the circle of his friends place him near the "Third New Generation" writers.

Kojima Nobuo was born in Gifu, and studied at First Higher School and at Tokyo University. Among his classmates at higher school and university was Nakamura Shin'ichirô. He was drafted into the army. He issued the group magazine *Dôjidai* (*The Contemporary Age*) with Usami Eiji and others. He had been unknown for a long time, until at last he emerged out of obscurity with the "Third New Generation" writers. Because of the timing of his appearance on the literary scene, he is generally regarded as one of the "Third New Generation" writers, but his works show that Kojima is, like Shimao Toshio, considerably different from other "Third New Generation" writers. His *Shôjû* (*A Rifle*, 1952), *Kitsuon Gakuin* (*School for Stammerers*, 1953) and *American School* (1954) depict the worlds of somewhat crippled people with their funny sides and frustrations. *Kami* (*God*, 1954), *Shima* (*Island*, 1955) and *Hiru to Yoru no Kusari* (*Chain of Day and Night*, 1959) are difficult ambitious novels of a somewhat abstract nature in which Kojima tried to depict the network of human relationships allegorically. Then he published *Henshô* (*Reflections*, 1964) and *Hôyô Kazoku* (*Keep the Family United*, 1965), in which Kojima depicted from a new angle the funny precarious position a man occupies as the husband or father in a home which threatens to collapse in this contemporary age. The last two works show that in his preoccupations Kojima has a lot in common with other "Third New Generation" writers.

Shimao Toshio also shows a certain affinity to the "Third New Generation" writers, especially in *Shi no Toge* (*The Thorns of Death,* 1960) and other works dealing with his sick wife, but because of his other characteristics we will discuss him later in a different section. It is interesting to notice that so many writers, especially writers of the "Third New Generation" produced around this time, works dealing with family problems after the old patriarchal family system, which had been one of the central themes of naturalistic novels and of "I" novels of prewar period, had collapsed. Shimao's *Shi no Toge* (*Thorn of Death*), Yasuoka's *Maku ga Orite kara* (*After the Curtain Falls,* 1967), Yoshiyuki's *Yami no Naka no Shukusai* (*Festival in the Dark,* 1961), Shôno's *Seibutsu* (*Still Life,* 1960), Miura's *Hakoniwa* (*Miniature Garden,* 1967), Agawa's *Gentô* (*Side Lights of a Ship,* 1966), Kojima's *Hôyô Kazoku* (*Keep the Family United,* 1965), Fukunaga Takehiko's *Kokubetsu* (*Farewell,* 1962), Itô Hitoshi's *Hanran* (*Overflow,* 1956–1958) and *Hakkutsu* (*Excavation,* 1962–1964) are all examples of such works. Since the Meiji period, Japanese writers had been producing works criticizing the Japanese family system using the advanced Western countries as their norms. But in struggling to discover the essential meaning of the home and the relationship between man and wife while dealing with various aspects of the disintegration of the home like adultery, wife swapping and generation gap, Japanese writers were now confronted with problems for which the West could no longer supply undisputed norms; the problems connected with the home and monogamy are now the common problems of the world. This is a very fruitful field for contemporary literature. By delving into the problems of marriage and the home, writers might find a clue to understanding man alienated from himself in this unprecedented chaos of the contemporary world, and also to understanding the essence of present social conditions.

Among other writers who show an affinity with the "Third New Generation" writers are Kondô Keitarô, the author of *Kokunanpû* (*Stormy*

South Wind, 1952) and *Umi (The Sea,* 1966) who produces works related
to the sea by depicting the life of fishermen with uninhibited eroticism;
Onuma Tan who writes humorous novels like *Kaichûdokei (A Watch,*
1968) in the manner of the "shinkyô shôsetsu" (mental life novel); Yûki
Shin'ichi, the author of *Aoi Mizu (Blue Water,* 1955) who creates a closed
world of sweet lyricism; Itô Keiichi who writes sentimental war novels
like *Hotaru no Kawa (Fireflies' River,* 1961); and Takeda Shigetarô, the
author of *Fûchô (Trend,* 1954) who writes solid realistic novels in the tradition of writers connected with Waseda University. Although their literary *début* was somewhat later than the authors mentioned above, Miura
Tetsurô, the author of the pure lyrical "I" novel *Shinobugawa* (1960),
Kawamura Akira, the author of *Bidan no Shuppatsu (The Beginning of a
Laudable Deed,* 1962), and Yamaguchi Hitomi, the author of *Eburiman shi
no Yûgana Seikatsu (The Graceful Life of Mr. Everyman,* 1962) are also akin
to the "Third New Generation" writers in their mentality.

Among women writers, Setouchi Harumi, the author of *Natsu no
Owari (Summer's Ending,* 1962) and *Kanoko Ryôran (The Life of Okamoto
Kanoko,* 1962–1964), who boldly depicts female psychology and physiolo-
gy, often in the manner of a confession, and Tsumura Setsuko, the author
of *Saihate (The Remotest Area,* 1964) are close to the "Third New Generation" writers. Other women writers who appeared around this time are
Sono Ayako and Ariyoshi Sawako. Sono is the wife of Miura Shumon.
She first attracted attention by her *Enrai no Kyakutachi (Visitors from Afar,*
1954) and other sophisticated well-written novels. Her *Reimei (Dawn,*
1955–1956) and *Tamayura (For a Time,* 1959) are fine portraitures of life
of contemporary people. Ariyoshi wrote *Kinokawa (River Kinokawa,* 19-
60), *Hi-shoku (Non-coloured,* 1963), *Hanaoka Seishû no Tsuma (The Wife
of Hanaoka Seishû,* 1966), *Izumo no Okuni (Okuni of Izumo District,* 1967–
1969) and other orthodox long novels which are at the same time good
stories and became a long-winded best-selling writer.

The "Third New Generation" writers have inherited the tradition of
modern Japanese literature, especially that of the "I" novel. They are
characterized by a fine artistic quality and a tendency to masochistic confession. They have managed to restore to the right track the course of

Japanese Literature which had, during the supremacy of the "postwar group", deviated from the path towards genuine contemporary literature and was aiming to create anachronistic great "romans". Thus, although not in a very active way, they are forming a contemporary literature which is characteristically Japanese. On the other hand, because of a huge demand for them in this age of mass media, they might fall into mannerisms compromising with the existing modes of literary expression and degenerate into mere entertainers.

Roughly coinciding with the emergence of the "Third New Generation" authors, new writers started appearing in the field of literary criticism, though after a long interval. In fact after the critics who started the group magazine *Kindai Bungaku* (*Modern Literature,* 1946–1964), no new critics worth mentioning had appeared. But in 1954 the magazine *Gendai Hyôron* (*Contemporary Criticism*) was started, and after this many new critics appeared and formed the next generation to those of *Kindai Bungaku* (*Modern Literature*). Among them are Hattori Tatsu who expounded the theory of "metaphysical criticism" in his *Warera ni totte Bi wa Sonzai-suruka* (*Does Beauty Exist for Us?*, 1955) and who committed suicide in 1955; Shindô Sumitaka, the author of *Sengo Bungaku no Kishu* (*Standardbearers of Postwar Literature,* 1955); Sako Jun'ichirô, the author of *Bungaku wa Kore de ii noka* (*Is Literature All Right Like This?* 1957); Okuno Takeo, the author of *Dazai Osamu Ron* (*An Essay on Dazai Osamu,* 1952); Muramatsu Takeshi, the author of *Chôkan Shôsetsu Ron* (*On Quasi-popular Novels,* 1954); Hino Keizô, the author of *Kôshinkoku ni Okeru Gendai no Kadai* (*Present-day Tasks in a Backward Country,* 1954); Yoshimoto Takaaki, the author of *Machiu-sho Shiron* (*An Essay on the Book of Matthew,* 1944); Shinoda Hajime, the author of *Dentô to Bungaku* (*Tradition and Literature,* 1962–1963); Saeki Shôichi, the author of *Nihonbungaku no Uchi to Soto* (*The Inside and Outside of Japanese Literature,* 1969); Takei Teruo, Haryû Ichirô, Hinuma Rintarô, Fukuda Kônen, and Komatsu Shinroku. The critics who first rallied to the magazine *Gendai Hyôron* (*Contemporary Criticism*), however, have split into several competing groups: the 'metaphysical' group of Hattori, Shindô and others; the *Gendai Hihyô* (*Contemporary Criticism*) group, comprising Okuno,

Yoshimoto, Takei and others, which has an existential or political tendency, and so on.

2   The Development of Mass Communication Media in a Mass Society

In January 1956 the Akutagawa Prize was awarded to *Taiyô no Kisetsu*
(*Season of Violence,* 1955), a novel written by Ishihara Shintarô, then an
unknown student of Hitotsubashi University. The selection place swarmed
with newspapermen and magazine reporters, and the next day newspapers
devoted a big space in the social columns page to reporting the event. The
weekly magazine *Shûkan Asahi* (*Asahi Weekly*) issued a special number
(February the 2nd number) on "The Student Writer Who Received the
Akutagawa Prize". *Taiyô no Kisetsu* (*Season of Violence*) became a bestseller, and sold more than 300,000 copies. Ishihara's novels were made into
films one after another. Sometimes Ishihara himself worked as a producer
or appeared on the screen as an actor. A hair style called "the Shintarô
cut" became popular. The word *Taiyôzoku* (literally meaning "sun-
tribe") which owed its origin to the title of Ishihara's novel *Taiyô no
Kisetsu* (*Season of Violence*) was widely used. Among literary circles a controversy over *Taiyô no Kisetsu* (*Season of Violence*) was waged in which
Satô Haruo, Kamei Katsuichirô, Funabashi Seiichi, Usui Yoshimi,
Nakamura Mitsuo, Yamamoto Kenkichi and others took part. Scandalized PTA's and Eirin (Committee for Regulating Ethical Standard of
Films) also contributed to enhance the repercussions *Taiyô no Kisetsu* was
creating. A single novel finally developed into a big social issue! Many
youths all over Japan who did not even know the name of Natsume
Sôseki or Shimazaki Tôson idolized *Shinchan,* as they called Ishihara
Shintarô, and became his enthusiastic fans. It was the first time in Japanese
history that a writer had become such a "star". After the publication of
Taiyô no Kisetsu (*Season of Violence*), writers and their works came under
the increasing dominance of the mass communication media which developed phenomenally in the postwar period.

Why is it that Ishihara's *Taiyô no Kisetsu* (*Season of Violence*) caused such a great repercussion? Of course it is mainly due to the quality of the novel itself, to its remarkable freshness. When this novel appeared in 1955, it was already ten years since the end of the war, and Japanese society was entering a relatively stable phase. Leftwing circles and student movements rapidly lost their influence after the anti-American riots in Tokyo on the 1st of May, 1952 (so-called "Bloody May Day"). The standard of living was rising rapidly, but young people had lost their dreams and clear aspirations in life, and were feeling frustrated. The number of juvenile delinquents who did not know what they really wanted increased, and people were looking forward to something shocking. Just at this time *Taiyô no Kisetsu* (*Season of Violence*) appeared—a novel which laughs at existing timid conservative morals of adults, which, unsentimentally and with youthful energy, asserts the authenticity of sexual instincts and the new sexual behaviour, and which seems to be groping for something passionate beyond good and evil. Although adults were shocked and scandalized, it is no wonder that young people found in this novel, written in an unsentimental vigorous style, a genuine literary expression of their generation and enthusiastically supported it. On the other hand, without the conscious efforts on the part of the mass communication media to manipulate and magnify the initial impact this novel had made, it would not have created so many repercussions. The interesting personality and behaviour of Ishihara Shintarô were other factors which helped bring about the unprecedented commotion which surrounded this novel. But the appearance of Ishihara's *Taiyô no Kisetsu* (*Season of Violence*) was in fact a symbolic event announcing the arrival of a new epoch for literature, an epoch in which literature is increasingly made to serve the purposes of the mass communication media. It also signified the arrival of the age of the mass society. The new 6-3-3-4 educational system adopted after the War, (six years of primary school, three each of junior and senior high school, and four of university), the creation of many local universities, the rise of women's status and so on all contributed to the phenomenal increase in the literate population and reading public. Also the appearance of many so-called *chûkan shôsetsu* (*quasi-popular novels*) made literature more familiar to common people. There was also an extraordinary development of mass communication media after the war. Many weekly magazines were started, commercial broadcasting began, and TV sets were beginning to be accessible to common people. All these factors combined to produce phenomena characteristic of the mass society in various places.

After the war Shishi Bunroku, Ishikawa Tatsuzô, Ishizaka Yôjirô, Yoshikawa Eiji and others achieved popularity with the novels they published in newspapers and weekly magazines. Matsumoto Seichô who arrived on the literary scene after them and who was awarded the Akutagawa Prize for his unostentatious *Aru "Kokura Nikki" Den* (Some Notes on "Kokura Diary", 1952) opened a new horizon for detective stories with his *Ten to Sen (Points and Lines, 1957–1958)*, *Me no Kabe (Wall for Eyes, 1957)* and other works. After this, social detective stories enjoyed a fantastic boom. Matsumoto became suddenly an extremely popular writer, and showed an almost superhuman capacity for turning out novels. After Matsumoto, Minakami Tsutomu who had written "I" novels like *Furaipan no Uta (Fryingpan Song)* and who had been living in poverty changing his jobs often, became suddenly the second most popular writer of social detective stories with his *Kiri to Kage (Fog and Shadow, 1959)* and *Umi no Kiba (Stormy Sea, 1960)*. Following them, many popular detective story writers appeared one after another, for instance Kuroiwa Jûgo, Sano Yô, Yûki Shôji, Niki Etsuko, Takagi Akimitsu, Sasazawa Saho, Togawa Masako, Nakazono Eisuke, Chin Shunshin, Miyoshi Tôru and Kijima Jirô. In the field of novels set in old Japan, writers like Gomi Kôsuke, Shibata Renzaburô (both of them are Akutagawa Prize winners), Murakami Genzô, Nanjô Norio, Shiba Ryôtarô and Yamada Fûtarô wrote fresh intellectual historical novels, novels of swordsmanship, or romances. About this time the relationship between organization and the individual was often discussed, and many writers produced novels connected with this problem. Shiroyama Saburô, the author of *Sôkaiya Kinjô (Kinjô, a Man Who Is Active Behind a General Assembly of Shareholders, 1965)*, created the new genre of economic novel. Genji Keita, Nakamura Takeshi, Toki Yûzô and others wrote novels about the life of salaried men. Nitta Jirô, Sugimori Hisahide and Natsubori Masamoto, authors with a sharp social consciousness, also produced unique novels. It is worth noticing that around this time a new type of literary craftsman like Kajiyama Toshiyuki appeared. Kajiyama became a popular writer for his novels on industrial espionage and by his erotic stories. Gomikawa Junpei's best-selling long novel, *Ningen no Jôken* (*Human Conditions*, 1956–1958), which depicts in a popular style humanistic and heroic acts of people in Manchuria during the war also appeared around this time.

In Japan since the Meiji and Taishô periods, the distinction between so-called *junbungaku* (literature of quality) and *taishû bungaku* (literature for the masses) had been maintained clearly. For example, the Akutagawa Prize was for writers of *junbungaku*, while the Naoki Prize was for writers of *taishû bungaku*. But now it was becoming increasingly difficult to make such a clear-cut demarcation. Minakami Tsutomu who had been regarded as a "popular" writer started to publish unique works of purely literary quality like *Gan no Tera* (*The Temple of Wild-geese*, 1961) and *Goban-chô Yûgiri-rô* (*Restaurant Yûgiri-rô in Goban-chô*, 1962). Osaragi Jirô also wrote serious historical novels like *Pari Moyu* (*Paris in Flame*, 1961–1963). The most remarkable was, however, the case of Yamamoto Shûgorô who had been writing popular historical stories before the war. Like a craftsman who had successfully worked his way up from an apprentice, he published one after another *Momi no Ki wa Nokotta* (*A Fir Has Remained*, 1954–1955), *Ochiba no Tonari* (*The Nextdoor House Surrounded by Fallen Leaves*, 1959), *Aobeka Monogatari* (*The Story of a Fishing Town*, 1960), *Kisetsu no Nai Machi* (*Town without Seasons*, 1962) and *Nagai Saka* (*A Long Slope*, 1964–1966), novels which could compete with the works of any so-called "junbungaku" writers. These novels of Yamamoto which are highly artistic and contain valuable insights into life, deeply impressed a wide range of readers including the intellectuals. The traditional rigid distinction between *junbungaku* (literature of quality) and *taishû-bungaku* (literature for the masses) in Japan had become, all but meaningless after about 1955. Many writers and critics, beginning with Itô Hitoshi who put forward the thesis that so-called *junbungaku* (literature of quality) had undergone a transformation, discussed anew the essence of *junbungaku* and *taishûbungaku*. Among them were Takami Jun, Hirano Ken, Ôoka Shôhei, Hinuma Rintarô and Okuno Takeo. There appeared also scholars and critics like Tsurumi Shunsuke, Tada Michitarô and Ozaki Hideki who seriously studied and discussed *taishûbungaku* (literature for the masses). Among other manifestations of this popularization of literature was, for example, that Takeuchi Yoshimi discussed Nakazato Kaizan and Yoshikawa Eiji who had never received scholarly attention before, and maintained that a real 'national literature' should be established. Hanada Kiyoteru, Sasaki Kiichi and others called for the establishment of a new revolutionary popular art out of the existing popular entertainment, and stressed the importance of creating a genuine audio-visual culture including television. The policy of the Chinese Communist Party which emphasizes the importance of the role of the masses also contributed to the very complicated manifestations of popularization of literature. The development of mass communication media tended to standardize people's literary taste and sense. In the growing mass society, literature showed unprecedented prosperity as far as the quantity of literary products were concerned. But their quality was usually mediocre, as it catered to the standardized popular taste. Even when Japan entered a highly prosperous phase often compared to the Genroku period (1688–1704), real literary masterpieces seldom appeared. Writers became either respectable gentlemen, or a sort of entertainer, and literature began to show signs of degeneration.

Two events of this period merit our special attention. One is the admirable defence of literature Itô Hitoshi and other writers put forward when Itô was prosecuted for obscenity for his translation of *Lady Chatterley's Lover*. The other is the tenacious efforts based on social conscience that Hirotsu Kazuo, Uno Kôji and other writers made to prove the innocence of the defendants of the Matsukawa case. These two were memorable examples of writers influencing the society by awaking its critical spirit.

3 The Establishment of Really Contemporaneous Literature

With increasingly rapid scientific and technological progress, industrial structures, social life, and family life all undergo a rapid change. Mental labour rather than physical labour becomes of primary importance for production. Jobs become highly specialized or technical. As for consumption, all sorts of goods formerly available only to a small number of people become accessible to common people. Communications develop, and the amount of information supplied daily becomes colossal. Leisure activities increase. Through the development of communications and transport the world really becomes one, so that there is no longer any place in the world which is cut off and free from outside influences. The whole world is in an unprecedented situation which our ancestors never knew. To return to Japan, the changes which have taken place since the beginning of the Shôwa period, or rather, since the end of World War II are far greater than those which had previously taken place in a society engaged chiefly in irrigated rice cultivation for the last 2,000 years.

People are leaving agricultural villages and flocking to the big over populated cities. There, however, they feel isolated, their small-sized families being the only real human ties they have. Although material culture has developed considerably, human alienation has deepened. Such rapid changes in the life and consciousness of human beings naturally have a profound influence on literature. To restore a healthy balance to the present age where science and technology have developed disproportionately, art and literature have a very important role to play. Spirited young writers are groping for a new literature. Especially the novel, the product of modern times, which was once said to be an almighty art form has to criticize and deny itself, and be reborn as a new novel (even though the new form may be so radically different from the old one that one hesitates to apply the same term 'novel' to it). Otherwise it would not be able to retain real relevance to this present age.

Despite its apparent prosperity in this age of mass communication and mass society, contemporary literature is in danger of losing its autonomy. A small number of young writers like Mishima Yukio were already aware of this danger. They realized that the novel would soon be, not an art form intended for everybody as in former days, but an esoteric experimental art form understandable only to a small number of intellectuals. They were aware that unless the novel chose to be such an esoteric art form, they would not be able to create a genuine contemporary literature. They resisted the standardization of mass society and tried to establish *junbungaku* (literature of quality) really relevant to this age.

Mishima Yukio was born the son of an official in an uptown area of Tokyo. He grew up in a period when Japan was engaging in a series of wars. He was academically an excellent student during his Gakushuin School days, and at the same time was deeply interested in literature. He was strongly influenced by the ideas of *Nihon Rôman Ha* (*The Japanese Romantic School*). In 1944, at the age of 19, Mishima published the first collection of his short storeis, as a sort of will. It also shows clear traces of the influence of the *Nihon Rôman Ha* (*Japanese Romantic School*). Unlike the writers of the postwar group (the *après-guerre* writers), Mishima had never come in contact with Marxism. The revolutionary ideas which influenced Mishima were those of rightwing young officers of the February 26th incident, those of *Nihon Rôman Ha* (*Japanese Romantic School*) and those of Hasuda Yoshiaki, an ultra-rightwing writer. His attitude toward the Pacific War was not that of a critic or of an outsider. For Mishima who had believed in the cause of the war, who had accepted it as a destiny, and who had made up his mind to die for the country and the emperor, Japan's surrender in 1945 was a traumatic experience as if the whole world had collapsed. He received this tremendous blow at the age of 20 when he was still in his formative years. Mishima wrote, "Time had stuck to that mid-summer blue sky". He felt that his life had come to an end on that 15th of August 1945, the day of the surrender. The years after that seemed to him to be somewhat superfluous. The prescience of the world's downfall came to take a deep root in him.

Mishima started to work for the Ministry of Finance, and for a while he continued to publish elaborate aesthetic novels like *Tabako* (*Tobacco*, 1946) and *Yoru no Shitaku* (*Preparations for the Night*, 1948) based on the same techniques as his previous works published during the war. Then he came to realize that all sorts of inhibitions had been taken away from him on account of Japan's defeat in the war, and with a great resolution wrote *Kamen no Kokuhaku* (*The Confessions of a Mask*, 1949). It is a cool, conscious analysis of his libido from early childhood, of the origin of his homosexuality and of the essence of his self. It is written in an unsentimental classical style devoid of romanticism. This was an epoch-making work only possible in the postwar period which had experienced Japan's defeat. He then published *Ai no Kawaki* (*Thirst for Love*, 1950), a psychological novel dealing with his hidden desire, and *Kinjiki* (*Forbidden Lust*, 1951), an ambitious full-scale *roman*, which ridicules the spirit which was holding him in its grip during the war. In it Mishima praised the beauty of the human body and tried to justify male homosexuality, a phenomenon that is on the reverse side of ordinary reality. The profound shock and nihilistic feelings he experienced at Japan's defeat, his protoexperience, found their literary expressions in *Ao no Jidai* (*The Age of Blue*, 1950), *Shizumeru Taki* (*The Submerged Waterfalls*, 1955), and *Kinkakuji* (*The Temple of the Golden Pavilion*, 1956), all of which deal with the destructive behaviour of the youth of Mishima's generation. In these works Mishima tried to express beauty and truth which are ephemeral and would not last. In *Shiosai* (*The Sound of Waves*, 1954) and *Bitoku no Yoromeki* (*Wavering Virtues*, 1957), Mishima showed some danger of making a compromise with popular taste. Then he wrote *Kyôko no Ie* (*Kyôko's House*, 1958–1959), an attempt to summarize, and bid farewell to, his own anarchistic youth which had strived to create a 'utopia' in the ruins of war. After that he decided to live in this boring plebeian age as a practical man convinced of the approaching end of the world.

About this time Mishima realized clearly the difficulty of creating genuine contemporary literature, and he wrote perceptive literary essays. He came to write his novels increasingly for the readers of the world and just for the Japanese. After writing *Utage no Ato* (*After the Banquet*, 1960) and *Utsukushii Hoshi* (*A Beautiful Star*, 1962), a serious satirical novel consisting of political and intellectual discussions about the fall of mankind, he rapidly became a highly nationalistic traditionalist. He wrote *Eirei no Koe* (*Voices of the Dead*, 1966) and founded a rightwing youth group called Tate no Kai (The Society of the Shield). His was, however, an aesthetic nationalism. Mishima was a writer who had learned better than any other Japanese writer the Western way of reasoning and looking at things. This made him clearly aware of the difference between Oriental or Japanese ideas and traditions and thoes of the West, and he could not resist their charms. He wrote *Hôjô no Umi* (*The Sea of Plenitude*, 1969–1971), an ambitious lengthy tetralogy consisting of highly aesthetic novels dealing with the mystical Oriental Buddhistic theme that a person's soul and aspiration in rebellion against the scientific materialistic civilization of the world transcends his individual self and migrates from one person to another over generations. The moment he finished this tetralogy, Mishima Yukio invaded the headquarters of the Self-Defence Force, gave a speech inciting the forces to a *coup d'état* and died in a most sensational manner by committing *hara-kiri*. This suicide, I feel, is not so much an expression of ultranationalism or rightwing conviction as an expression of active nihilism which rebelled against modern civilization. I also think that it is at the same time the tragedy of an art for art's sake writer who had to make a martyr of himself for the spiritual pose which he needed to write *Hôjô no Umi* (*The Sea of Plenitude*) and which turned out to be a trap from which he could not escape, although he had made it himself. By his suicide Mishima communicated to people his conviction that there was something more valuable than life. His suicide which contrasted with the general tendency to value only individual life and material welfare shocked people greatly, and even affected those people who did not approve of Mishima's nationalistic thought. Mishima's suicide also shows what a difficult spiritual adventure it is to write novels in this present age; for a really conscientious writer insanity and death are probably the only alternatives left in the end. Mishima's suicide is the most eloquent symbol of this crisis of literature.

Mishima also published many excellent plays such as *Kindai Nôgaku Shû* (*Modern Nô Plays*, 1950–1955), *Rokumei Kan* (*Rokumei Reception Hall*, 1956) and *Sado Kôshaku Fujin* (*Marchioness de Sade*, 1965). He was at his best in drama.

Abe Kôbô is another writer who is internationally highly esteemed as an *avant-garde* writer. Abe, who was a student of the Faculty of Medicine of Tokyo University, was in Manchuria at the time of Japan's surrender in the war. After considerable difficulties, he came back to Japan penniless. He won recognition as an *après-guerre* writer with his highly abstract difficult spiritual autobiography, *Owarishi Michi no Shirube ni* (*As a Signpost for the Road I Have Come*, 1948). His unique talent attracted attention when he published *Kabe* (*The Wall*, 1951), an allegorical satirical novel reminiscent of Kafka. Abe is a Marxist writer. As his works like *Kiga-dômei* (*Starvation League*, 1954), *Kemonotachi wa Kokyô o Mezasu* (*Animals Are Heading Their Home*, 1957) and *Yûrei wa Koko ni Iru* (*The Ghost is Here*—a play, 1959) show, his works present reality in a light entirely different from a commonsense point of view "by discovering an unexpected subsidiary line as when you try to prove a theorem in geometry" (Abe). From his highly original conceptions, he develops plots unsentimentally and logically as if he were dealing with the laws of physics. His works are unlike anything Japanese writers had produced before him. His *avant-garde* works do not seem to be tied to any nationality or generation, but are cosmopolitan. His more recent works like *Suna no Onna* (*The Woman in the Dunes*, 1962), *Tanin no Kao* (*The Face of Another*, 1964), *Moetsukita Chizu* (*The Ruined Map*, 1967) and *Tomodachi* (*Friends*—a play, 1967), however, manage to create a unique climate of their own. Through extreme situations, they express convincingly and movingly the sentiments of contemporary people who are deprived of the feeling of solidarity with others, and are alienated and isolated. These works which are devoid of any sentimentality have a strange reality and fresh poetry. I think we can expect much more in the future from this most *avant-garde* writer.

Shimao Toshio whose family is from Fukushima but who grew up moving from one place to another—from Yokohama to Kobe, from Kobe to Nagasaki, from Nagasaki to Hakata—is essentially a wanderer. On graduating from Kyûshû University, he was drafted into the army and was stationed in Amami Archipelago as the commander of a suicidal special attack unit. His experiences there had a decisive influence on his future. His experience of receiving the news that the war had come to an end immediately before setting out for a suicidal attack was equivalent to that of Dostoevskii who received a reprieve just before his execution. His *Shutsu Kotô Ki* (*Account of the Departure from the Solitary Island*, 1946) and *Shuppatsu wa tsui ni Otozurezu* (*Departure Never Came*, 1962) are based on this extraordinary experience. In works like *Yume no Naka deno Nichijô* (*Daily Life in a Dream*, 1948) and *Kotô Mu* (*Dream in a Distant Island*, 1946), Shimao tried to shed light on the essence of man and reality by giving

unique expressions to nightmarish fancies cropping up in oppressive everyday reality. Shimao's series of novels depicting dreams are his own inven-
tion and his unique contribution to contemporary literature. They indicate a most promising literary path for the future. When his wife, (daughter of the head of the island where Shimao had been stationed as the commander of the special attack unit with whom he had fallen in love at that
time) became mentally ill, he wrote a series of powerful novels on his sick
wife beginning with *Shi no Toge* (*Thorn of Death*, 1960). These novels deal,
without any embellishments, with the relationship between man and wife,
deprived of all inessentials, and ask the meaning of home, and of the naked
reality of man and woman. They impressed readers deeply.

Shimao emerged on the literary scene as one of the writers of the Post-
war Group. Temperamentally, however, he is nearer to the "Third New
Generation" writers, and has a big influence over them. Thus he is a sort of
mediator or unifier of the Postwar Group and the "Third New Genera-
tion". He is also influencing more recent newcomers. He lives on Amami
Ôshima Island in the Ryûkyû group and is trying to interpret Japan as
Japonesia. He is one of the most earnest *junbungaku* writers of present-day
Japan.

Inoue Mitsuharu is close to the above-mentioned writers in age as well
as in his works. He spent his childhood in Lushun, in Kwantung Leased
Territory. He worked at a coal mine and at a factory in Kyûshû, but studied by himself and passed an examination which qualified him as an
equivalent of middle school graduates. He was a right-wing revolutionary
youth during the war. When the war ended in Japan's defeat, however,
Inoue was awakened to a completely different new view of the world.
Desiring a real emancipation for himself and others, he worked hard as a
member of the Communist Party. His own experiences of poverty-
stricken life acted as a driving force behind him. He was, however, expelled from the Communist Party when he wrote *Kakarezaru Isshô* (*An Unwritten Chapter*, 1950) and, earlier than others, criticized from inside the
inhumanity within the Party. He wrote one after another works based on
the sentiments of the so-called war generation (the generation which had
its youth during the war) like *Sôtô no Washi* (*Two-headed Eagle*, 1952),

Gadarukanaru Senshi Shû (*War Poetry of Guadalcanal,* 1958), *Shisha no Toki* (*The Time of the Dead,* 1959–1960) and *Chi no Mure* (*The Crowd of the Ground,* 1963), and dealt with problems basic to Japanese society—the emperor system, socially discriminated communities, A-bombs, Koreans, prostitutes, suicide pilots, right-wing people, workers at American military bases, the Communist Party and former coal mine workers who have become unemployed and so on. He relates all these problems to corruption within his own soul, and persistently delves into them. His works are written in Sasebo dialect, and remind one of a thickly painted picture. Probably he is a little too prolific. But his works which never tire of dealing with earthly realities and which are somewhat like Buddhist pictures showing the law of retribution are so full of vitality that we are induced to say in admiration, "Only Inoue can write them."

Kôno Taeko who was born in the same year as Inouye Mitsuharu experienced the war in her formative years. She wrote about her unusual experiences during the war in her works like *Hei no Haka* (*Within the Walls,* 1962) which depicts how mobilized girl students secretly pet a little boy who strayed into their dormitory as if he were a puppy until he is killed by mistake. Among her other unique works are *Yôji-gari* (*Boy-hunting,* 1951) which deals with sexual complexes arising from war experiences and *Kani* (*Crabs,* 1963) dealing with the psychology of sadism and masochism.

Yoshimoto Takaaki is a poet, thinker and critic belonging to the generation of Mishima, Abe and Inoue. He was born the son of a shipwright in Tsukudajima in downtown Tokyo. His father had come from Kyûshû. After graduating from Tokyo Industrial University, he wrote philosophical poems like *Koyûji to no Taiwa* (*Dialogue with Proper Time,* 1952) and philosophical critical essays like *Machiu-Shiron* (*An Essay on the Book of Matthew,* 1954). His ideas are based on unique syntheses of tradition and novelty. He discussed the war responsibility of leftwing writers, and criticized Marxism. He had published *Takamura Kôtarô* (1957), *Gengo ni totte Bi to wa Nani ka* (*What is Beauty in Language?,* 1961–1965), *Kyôdo Gensô Ron* (*On Common Illusions,* 1968) and other unique essays based on discussions of basic principles. As a sharp critic, he is exerting a profound influence on anti-Communist Party revolutionary youths and students. He is a lonely tenacious thinker, but we must not forget other thinker-critics like Hashikawa Bunzô, the author of *Nihon Rôman Ha Hihan Josetsu* (*Introduction to Critical Discussions of the Japanese Romantic School*, 1960), Murakami Ichirô, Tanigawa Gan, Tsurumi Shunsuke and Shibusawa Tatsuhiko.

4   Artistic Achievements

The emergence of the "Third New Generation" writers and the experimental efforts and partial success of Mishima Yukio, Abe Kôbô and others in establishing genuine contemporary literature had a great influence and stimulative effect on established writers. Several major writers who had been pursuing their own artistic path made another step forward, and wrote masterpieces one after another to crown their lifelong efforts. Tanizaki Jun'ichirô who had completed *Sasameyuki* (*The Makioka Sisters*, 1943–1948) and who seemed to have given a final expression to his admiration of Japanese classical beauty by writing *Shôshô Shigemoto no Haha* (*The Mother of Captain Shigemoto*, 1949–1950) did not, however, enter the world of quiet Japanese simplicity in his old age. Instead he published *Kagi* (*The Key*, 1956) and, using almost *avant-garde* techniques, dealt with the abyss of human sex and the beauty and secrets of female body. This novel caused a big literary controversy, and was widely discussed. Then he wrote *Kasanka Mangan Sui no Yume* (*A Dream of Manganese Peroxide Solution*, 1955), a masterpiece of extraordinary beauty, and in his late 70's he completed *Fûten Rôjin Nikki* (*Diary of a Mad Old Man*, 1961–1962), a novel dealing with the problems of sex and death in old age. This novel is the culminating expression of Tanizaki's fetishistic adoration of the female body (especially of the feet) and of his psychological masochism. Both were already present in *Shisei* (*Tattoo*) published in 1910. In *Fûten Rôjin Nikki* (*Diary of a Mad Old Man*) the hero wants to engrave the footprint of the woman he adores on his tombstone like the footprint of Buddha engraved on a stone in a temple in Nara. Then, after his death, he can rest under the foot of the beautiful woman. That is his idea of paradise. In this masterpiece cravings for beauty and sexual satisfaction are elevated to a faith stronger than death. It is no wonder that Henry Miller praised Tanizaki highly in the preface to the German translation of *Kagi* (*The Key*) and said, "Tanizaki is the most masculine writer of the twentieth century" and that Sartre commented on *Fûten Rôjin Nikki* (*Diary of a Mad Old Man*) and said that "it is the first novel of the world which has directly dealt with the problem of sex in old age".

Murô Saisei who had once been a major innovator in modern Japanese poetry showed remarkable activity in the last phase of his life. He emerged suddenly from the stagnation of the early postwar years, and published *Onnahito* (*Women,* 1955), *Waga Aisuru Shijin no Denki* (*The Life of my Favorite Poet,* 1958) and *Anzukko* (1957), a long novel centering around his daughter which depicts his own life and the fate of women. Then he published *Mitsu no Aware* (*Moving Sweetness,* 1959), in which a goldfish is transformed into a girl and plays with an old writer, and *Kagerô no Nikki Ibun* (*The Women of Kagerô Diary,* 1958–1959) which is an artistic sublimation of his longing for his real mother who was taken away from him for ever from the beginning. These two novels are exquisitely beautiful and rich in imagery, and together with *Ware wa Utaedo Yaburekabure* (*I sing, but in a Devil-may-care Mood,* 1962), a record of his valiant struggle with a fatal illness, impressed people deeply. Murô Saisei explored a new frontier of Japanese literature, and achieved what is in the van of contemporary world literature.

Kawabata Yasunari who had been absorbed in the world of Japanese traditional beauty and had published works like *Yama no Oto* (*The Sound of the Mountain,* 1949–1954) and *Senba-zuru* (*A Thousand Cranes,* 1949–1951), wrote in the 1960's *Nemureru Bijo* (*House of the Sleeping Beauties,* 1960–1961) and *Kataude* (*One Arm,* 1963–1964). Probably he had received a big stimulus from Murô Saisei's works in his last years. Using such fanciful conceptions as loving unconsciously sleeping girls and as caressing a woman's borrowed arm, Kawabata expressed his longing for virgins in a bold surrealistic manner. Kawabata Yasunari became in 1968 the first Japanese to receive the Nobel Prize for Literature. The internationalization of Japanese Literature after the War and Kawabata's high aesthetic achievement had combined to make this possible.

Masamune Hakuchô also wrote in his last years, works like *Kotoshi no Aki* (*This Autumn*, 1959) and allowed us a glimpse of his serene old age. Nogami Yaeko, another long-established writer, vividly depicted early figures in the modernization of Japan in her *Hideyoshi to Rikyû* (*Hideyoshi and Rikyû*, 1962–1963) when she was well over seventy years old.

The 30's of the Shôwa period (1955–1964) were marked by a remarkable activity on the part of women writers. Harada Yasuko's *Banka* (*An Elegy*, 1955–1956) became a great best-seller. Sono Ayako, Ariyoshi Sawako and Setouchi Harumi became famous as talented women. But even more remarkable than their activities was the prolific work of Enji Fumiko who had started writing in the prewar period but who had been suffering from poor health for a long time. She emerged again by publishing *Shu o Ubau Mono* (*The Vermilion Pilferer*, 1955–1969), an autobiographical work which reminds one of Mishima Yukio's *Kamen no Kokuhaku* (*The Confessions of a Mask*, 1949), and *Onna-zaka* (*The Female Slope*, 1949–1957) which depicts the tenacity and revenge of an oppressed woman. Then she wrote *Yô* (*Enchantress*, 1956), *Nisei no En, Shûi* (*The Two Worlds, Gleanings*, 1957), *Onna-omote* (*Woman's Mask*, 1958) and other works with great energy, and created an uncannily beautiful world of sadism and masochism based on her good knowledge of the literary classics of the Heian period. In these works Enji shed light on the eternal curse latent in women. Uno Chiyo who was famous as the wife of several well-known people wrote novels like *Iro Zange* (*Confessions of an Amorous Life*, 1933–1935), *Ohan* (1947–1952) which is reminiscent of the world of *Jôruri* drama, and *Kaze no Oto* (*Sound of Winds*, 1969) which describes aesthetically the life of a masochistic woman. Mori Mari, a daughter of Mori Ôgai, published *Koibitotachi no Mori* (*The Forest of Lovers*, 1961), *Kareha no Nedoko* (*Bed of Withered Leaves*, 1962) and other genuine tasteful aesthetic novels, which are real rarities in Japan. Sata Ineko, known as a writer of the Proletarian School, depicted in works like *Haiiro no Gogo* (*Grey Afternoon*, 1960) and *Sozô* (*A Plastic Image*, 1966) clashes between the Communist Party and the private personal life of its members. Hirabayashi Taiko published *Sabaku no Hana* (*Flowers of Desert*), an autobiographical novel about the first half of her life centering around politics and love. Because of these women writers, this decade really looked like "a little Heian period", a period of refined aestheticism.

Ishikawa Jun who is respected and loved by writers like Abe Kôbô, Fukunaga Takehiko and Ôe Kenzaburô as a forerunner of the *avant-garde* literature of today emerged out of relative silence which had lasted for a while, with his long novel *Aratama* (*Violent Soul,* 1963–1964) which deals with a miracle that an infant buried in the ground is transformed into a lump of black energy and rages in the criminal part of the contemporary society. After that he continued to write again strangely youthful works like *Shifuku Sennen* (*Millennium,* 1965–1966) and *Tenma Fu* (*Ode on a Heavenly Horse,* 1969) which are based on the synthesis of the author's learning with his active curiosity toward the present age. Takami Jun in his last years conceived the idea of writing a series of novels which might be titled *Shôwa* (*The Shôwa Period*) dealing with recent history, and published *Iyana Kanji* (*Disagreeable Feeling,* 1960–1963) and *Gekiryû* (*A Raging Torrent,* 1959–1962). Itô Hitoshi attempted a thorough analysis of egoism accompanying sex and death on the part of contemporary man in his trilogy, *Hanran* (*Flooding,* 1956–1958), *Hakkutsu* (*Excavation,* 1962–1964) and *Henyô* (*Transformation,* 1967–1968), and created a vision of rich old age.

In the field of the traditional "I" novel, the works of Ozaki Kazuo, Kanbayashi Akatsuki, Kiyama Shôhei and Amino Kiku express their authors' serene inner life with humour. These novels are now acquiring a sort of rarity value and also becoming highly regarded again as the most natural expression of the life in harmony with nature which every Japanese secretly longs for as his spiritual starting-point. Ibuse Masuji who had always written humorously about the life of common people without ever showing any interest in politics and whose works had been loved by many people, published *Kuroi Ame* (*Black Rain,* 1966) which depicts very realistically the disasters caused by the atomic bomb in Hiroshima; Ibuse had been at the time of the A bomb drop in a place not far from Hiroshima and had acquired first-hand-knowledge about its horror. Since *Kuroi Ame* (*Black Rain*) is written without any particular ideological bias, it moved people all the more strongly.

Niwa Fumio, a major figure in the present literary scene of Japan, published *Shinran*, an ambitious novel about the founder of the *Shin* sect which believes in salvation through the benevolence of Amida Buddha. Funabashi Seiichi wrote *Aru Onna no Enkei* (*A Distant View of a Woman*) are *Kage-e Nyonin* (*Portrait of a Lady*), using his knowledge of the literary classics of the Heian and Edo periods. Ishikawa Tatsuzô wrote *Ningen no Kabe* (*Human Walls*) which deals with the problem of Japanese education. Although Niwa, Funabashi and Ishikawa are still very productive, they do not appeal so much to younger readers, and it seems that their age is passing away. Inoue Yasushi who belongs to their generation but who started writing novels only after the war is, however, attracting a wide range of readers by his historical novels like *Tenpyô no Iraka* (*The Tiled Roofs of Tenpyô*, 1957), *Tonkô* (*Tun-huang*, 1959) and *Aoki Ôkami* (*Blue Wolf*, 1960), and by his modern love novels and "I" novels like *Tsuki no Hikari* (*Moonlight*).

During this period writers of the Postwar Group who had freed them-selves from the vain dream of writing orthodox modern "romans" also produced impressive works of contemporary literature. Ôoka Shôhei, the author of *Furyoki* (*War Prisoner's Memoirs*) and *Nobi* (*Fires on the Plains*), wrote *Kaei* (*Shadows of Flowers*) which depicts the ephemeral love and death of a bar hostess. Then he again took up the themes connected with his war experiences, and wrote *Reite Senki* (*An Account of Battles in Leyte Island*) and *Mindoro Tô Futatabi* (*Mindoro Island Again*, 1969). Umezaki Haruo who had begun his literary career by publishing *Sakurajima*, a novel which depicts a critical situation near the end of the war had been writing humorous novels about the life of common people in the manner of the "I" novel. Immediately before his death he wrote *Genka* (*Hallucination*, 1965), a masterpiece which deals with a related theme to that of *Sakurajima*, and which crowned his lifelong efforts as a writer.

Noma Hiroshi dealt with the problems of Marxism and Buddhism in the long novel *Waga Tô wa Soko ni Tatsu* (*My Tower Stands There*, 1961). He completed the lengthy autobiographical novel *Seinen no Wa* (*The Circle of Youth*, 1947–1971) which deals with his own youth. Takeda Taijun tried to write comprehensive novels of an Oriental type and produced *Mori to Mizuumi no Matsuri* (*The Grove and the Lake Festival*, 1957) and

Kizoku no Kaidan (Degrees of Aristocracy, 1959). Haniya Yutaka dreamed of creating metaphysical novels on a grand scale. Nakamura Shin'ichirô obstinately continued to produce Western-style "romans" like *Koi no Izumi (Fountain of Love,* 1962). Fukunaga Takehiko wrote novels like *Sekai no Owari (The End of the World,* 1959), *Bôkyaku no Kawa (River of Forgetfulness,* 1964) and *Kaishi* (1967) and, using all sorts of new techniques, tried to write love novels with depth. Thus the 1960's were in a sense a decade in which writers of the Postwar Group who had been converted to writing up-to-date novels bore their first fruit in the new direction.

Serizawa Kôjirô completed a lengthy novel, *Ningen no Unmei (Human Destiny,* 1962–1968), which depicts an intellectual living in a tumultuous age comprising World War II. Critics like Usui Yoshimi and Nakajima Kenzô have started writing long autobiographical novels.

As for big critical works of this period, we should name Honda Shûgo's *Monogatari Sengo Bungaku Shi (Story of Postwar Japanese Literature,* 1958–1963), Kamei Katsuichirô's *Nihonjin no Seishin Shi Kenkyû (Studies in Japanese Intellectual History,* 1959–1966) and Itô Hitoshi's *Nihon Bundan Shi (History of the Japanese Literary World,* 1952–1969). The latter two works are the authors' real lifeworks. Unfortunately both of them were still incomplete at the time of their authors' deaths.

The above-mentioned were the hard-won fruit of modern and contemporary Japanese literature after Japan had gone through the stormy period of the Shôwa era.

As the winning of the Nobel Prize for Literature by Kawabata Yasunari indicates symbolically, Japanese literature which had since the Meiji period developed through successive trials and errors, struggling its way through the complicated tangle created by modern Western literature from which it continuously borrowed, the traditional Japanese view of literature and feudalistic reality in Japan, at last managed to free itself from local narrowness and backwardness and became international. Japanese writers can now compete with writers of the world on an equal footing. In order to express complicated contemporary situations or the alienated self, Japanese writers can no longer depend on Western writers as examples. Thus the inferiority complex of Japanese writers towards Western literature has gradually disappeared. They have to tackle with present-day reality themselves. Formerly many Japanese writers had also had a complex about communism and socialist revolution which kept working on their conscience. But through seeing the realities in actual socialist countries and communist parties in the world, this complex also disappeared, and writers can now deal with political themes freely in their works without feeling undue diffidence. Liberation from these two complexes which had been underlying Japanese literature was most important in making Japanese literature of this period more international than before. Willy-nilly, Japanese writers had now to open the path for contemporary literature themselves. They too have become frontiersmen.

5   The Emergence of New Writers

Let us see in the last section of this introduction what writers have e-merged since the publication of *Taiyô no Kisetsu* (*Season of Violence*) in 1955. Ishihara Shintarô who made a brilliant literary *début* with *Taiyô no Kisetsu* (*Season of Violence*), or shall we say, who was thrown into the turmoil created by mass communication media and found himself treated as a "star", which was an unprecedented phenomenon in the history of Japanese Literature, however, was not spoilt by all this. He published *Shokei no Heya* (*The Punishment Room*, 1956), *Kanzennaru Yûgi* (*Perfect Play*, 1957), *Kiretsu* (*The Crack*, 1956–1957), *Funky Jump* (1959) and *Shi no Hakubutsu Shi* (*Natural History of Death*, 1963). Some of them are literary experiments in depicting completely amoral situations. Others are efforts to depict extreme situations beyond good and evil, creating physical pain or fear of death in order to search human truths there. Ishihara, however, developed his interest increasingly in the direction of discovering and constructing new morals. This factor was already latent in *Taiyô no Kisetsu* (*Season of Violence*) itself. After writing *Chôsen* (*Challenge*, 1959–1960), *Kôi to Shi* (*Action and Death*, 1964) and *Ôkami Ikiro Buta wa Sine* (*Live, Wolves! Die, Pigs!*, 1960), he turned his interest to political life. Finally he ran for election to the House of Councillors as a Liberal Democratic Party candidate from the national constituency, and was elected with the highest poll. He is now a young politician standing for up-to-date nationalism and new conservative political ideals.

With his dramatic *début* with *Taiyô no Kisetsu* (*Season of Violence*), Ishihara succeeded Mishima Yukio who had been the literary spokesman of the young generation for ten years after the war. He definitely over-shadowed other young writers like Ishizaki Haruhisa, Kawakami Sôkun, Katsura Yoshihisa, Sakagami Hiroshi, Fukai Michiko and Iwahashi Kunie who, as successors of the "Third New Generation" writers, were trying to express the unstable sentiments and wild manners of the genera-tion whose youth and self-awakening coincided with the confused postwar years. The most noticeable among them is Yamakawa Masao, who with lyricism and intellectual clarity, depicted the sentiments of adolescent boys growing into adults in the years immediately after the war in somewhat nihilistic works like *Entotsu* (*Chimney,* 1954), *Hibi no Shi* (*Daily Death,* 1957), *Ai no Gotoku* (*Like Love,* 1964) and *Saisho no Aki* (*The First Autumn,* 1964). This young promising writer was, however, killed in a car accident. Yamakawa's works have a certain affinity to writings of such cultured writers as Tsuji Kunio and Kita Morio. (We will discuss them later). The appearance of Ishihara Shintarô also stimulated young talented women writers like Sono Ayako, Ariyoshi Sawako and Harada Yasuko, who pro-duced many clever sophisticated works and were also active in the mass communication media.

In 1956 Fukazawa Shichirô was awarded the First Chûô Kôron New Writer's Prize for his strange work *Narayamabushi-kô* (*The Songs of Oak Mountains,* 1956) and thus made his literary *début*. Fukazawa who was born in 1914 was at that time already over forty years old. His works which are in close contact with the indigenous culture and life of common people had a great impact on the literary circles as a fresh contrast to the cultured sophisticated modern literature since the Meiji period which continued to dominate after the war. Fukazawa was born in Yamanashi Prefecture and did not have any higher education. He is in a sense akin to the talented painter Yamashita Kiyoshi whose general intelligence was subnormal. Fukazawa's works have a vague similarity to the works of Kida Minoru, the author of *Kichigai Buraku Shûyû Kikô* (*Journey Around Madmen's Vil-*

lage, 1946) and to the humorous works of Ibuse Masuji, but Fukazawa's works have something more intuitive, instinctive and naive. He continued to publish unique works like *Tôhoku no Jinmutachi* (*A Tale from Tôhoku,* 1957), *Fuefukigawa* (*The River Fuefuki,* 1958) and *Shomin Retsuden* (*The Biographies of Common People,* 1962–1969) which give expression to the instinctive and subconscious world of the common people of Japan. His *Fûyrû Mutan* (*An Elegant Fantasy,* 1960), a satirical novel with some wildly fantastic elements, which, when it was published in 1960 immediately after the anti-security treaty riots, was accused by right-wingers of disrespect toward the Imperial family. This event finaly led to the so-called Shimanaka Incident in which a right-wing youth invaded the house of President Shimanaka of Chûô Kôron Publishing Firm which had published the novel, and killed one and injured another of his family. That such a writer as Fukazawa appeared probably attests to the tendency of the present age to produce mutations.

Kaikô Ken, Ôe Kenzaburô and Kurahashi Yumiko are among writers who continued what Ishihara Shintarô had started as a champion of the real postwar generation. Ishihara used the body regarded as an end in itself and a healthy unsentimental "decadence" as weapons in his rebellion against established morals, ideas and values. These new writers inherited the fruit of Ishihara's struggle, developed it further in its social and intellectual implications, and created new epoch-making contemporary literature. They grew up under the influences of the *après-guerre* writers, and tried to continue these authors' interrupted efforts in the right direction— i.e. that of genuine contemporary literature.

Around 1957 and 1958 Japanese literature appeared to be entering a fruitful age: two promising young writers Kaikô Ken and Ôe Kenzaburô appeared almost simultaneously, and were competing with each other, when they were joined by Etô Jun, a young promising critic. Kaikô Ken was born in Ôsaka and had published some works in the magazine *Kindai Bungaku* (*Modern Literature*). He attracted attention for his *Panikku* (*Panic,* 1957), a novel dealing with an extraordinary plague of rats due to the fact that some bamboo grasses flowered and bore fruit after 120 years' interval. This novel is allegorical in a double sense. Then, competing against Ôe

Kenzaburô, he won the Akutagawa Prize for his *Hadaka no Ôsama* (*Naked King*, 1957). His position as a promising young writer became firm when he published *Nihon Sanmon Opera* (*Threepenny Opera of Japan*, 1959), a novel which depicts the anarchistic sentiments and remarkable vitality as well as the resistance to the authorities on the part of lower-class people of Ôsaka in the confused years after the war. This work is written in a colloquial style in Ôsaka dialect. After that he became increasingly involved in political and social issues, and found fulfilment in actions rather than in writing. He made trips overseas, participated in the peace movement, and followed the army in Vietnam and wrote reports. He still wrote fine works like *Mita, Yureta, Warawareta* (*I Saw, I Vibrated, and was Laughed at,* 1963), which is a caricature of himself, and *Kagayakeru Yami* (*Shining Darkness,* 1968), but on the whole he shows a tendency to avoid facing the difficulties of contemporary literature and to escape into actions although not in the same fashion as Ishihara Shintarô.

It is Ôe Kenzaburô who, more than any other new writer, impressed readers as opening up a new frontier and creating something entirely new. Ôe was born and brought up in a village in Ehime Prefecture. When he was a student of the Department of French Literature of Tokyo University, he attracted attention with *Kimyôna Shigoto* (*A Strange Job,* 1957) and *Shisha no Ogori* (*Lavish are the Dead,* 1957) which depict with cruel humour the fatigue of the senseless labour of the present day and the fretfulness of lonely youths. He was awarded the Akutagawa Prize for *Shiiku* (*The Catch,* 1958). This novel deals with the fictional relationship between boys of a mountain village and a captured Negro soldier during the war, symbolizing a crack in the contemporary age. Then in *Me-mushiri Kouchi* (*Tearing Buds and Shooting Children,* 1958) he astonished readers with his success in evoking the world of childhood to perfection. Using concepts similar to those found in French Literature and a style reminiscent of translations of Western novels, he depicted the indigenous customs, complicated present-day realities of Japan and so on from an entirely new angle, and turned what he saw into resonant sentences. In his works, ideas are often expressed in surprising concrete imagery at once rich and grotesque. After that, he published problematic works like *Warera no Jidai*

(*Our Age*, 1959), *Seinen no Omei* (*Bad Name of a Youth*, 1959–1960), *Sakebi-goe* (*Cries*, 1962), *Seiteki Ningen* (*Obsessed*, 1963), *Nichijô Seikatsu no Bôken* (*Adventures in Everyday Life*, 1963–1964) and *Kojintekina Taiken* (*A Personal Matter*, 1964), and depicted Japanese youths who are "imprisoned" and alienated in the present age. A strong hope for the future and a violent fretting lie behind these novels. In contrast to usual interpretations of human history which emphasize production, labour, politics and so on, Ôe thought that the concept of "sexual man" had a central significance. From this angle, by investigating the essence of sex and decadence, Ôe tried to subject the present civilization to fundamental criticism, and to discover new possibilities for mankind. In *Hiroshima Nôto* (*Notes on Hiroshima*, 1964–1965) and other essays, Ôe expressed rather stereotyped political opinions as a conscientious progressive intellectual. In his long novel, *Man'en Gannen no Futto-bôru* (*Football Played in the First Year of Man'en*, 1967) Ôe tried his utmost to depict subtly the complicated political aspirations of his contemporaries and the indigenous ways of thinking in Japan which he could not very well express in essays. Ôe Kenzaburô is now struggling hard to make another step forward. Together with Mishima Yukio and Abe Kôbô, he is one of the most representative young Japanese writers who is trying to express the essence of the present age, using fully the new experimental techniques of contemporary literature. He is also internationally recognized.

Etô Jun who made his literary *début* roughly at the same time as Ôe Kenzaburô with his *Natsume Sôseki* which he published serially in the magazine *Mita Bungaku* (*Mita Literature*) defended the works of young writers like Ôe in his powerful literary essays published in *Dorei no Shisô o Haisu* (*Slavish Ideas Should be Rejected*, 1957) and *Sakka wa Kôdôsuru* (*Writers Act*, 1959) and came to be regarded as a representative critic belonging to the young generation. He gradually moved to a more conservative common-sense position, however. By the time he published *Kobayashi Hideo* (1960–1961) he had become critical of Ôe. Etô is now active as an important orthodox critic of present-day Japan.

Kurahashi Yumiko is a writer who is even more radically *avant-garde* than Ôe Kenzaburô, and who is producing unique abstract novels unlike anything ever seen in Japanese Literature. She was born in Kôchi Prefecture. When she was studying as a postgraduate student in the Department of French Literature of Meiji University, she published *Parutai* (*Communist Party*, 1960) which exposes the inhuman unrevolutionary nature of a communist party through sharp intuitive critical eyes, and which attracted immediately attention. Then she published *Hebi* (*Snake*, 1960) *Kon'yaku* (*Betrothal*, 1960), *Kurai Tabi* (*Gloomy Journey*, 1961), *Seishôjo* (*Holy Girl*, 1965), *Yôjo no Yôni* (*Like a Witch*, 1964) and other works based on the techniques of anti-realism or what Haniya Yutaka calls "reducing realism". They are bold experiments in grasping the essence of contemporary man's thought metaphysically and abstractly. Like Ôe's works, they are sometimes full of outspoken sexual descriptions, but they are somehow very feminine and convincing. She went to the United States to study, and remained silent for a while. Now she is active again. Her recent works termed "anti-tragedy series" like *Sumiyakisuto Q no Bôken* (*The Adventures of Q, the Sumiyakist*, 1969) and *Suikyô nite* (*In a Drunken State*, 1969) deserve attention as works in the van of contemporary literature. She is a writer with a unique literary talent.

The works of the so-called *Junsui Sengo Ha* (*Genuine Postwar Group*) writers represented by Ishihara, Kaikô and Ôe have a remarkable affinity to the writings of authors belonging to the generation of "angry young men" in England and other countries. What is worthy of emphasize, however is, that these Japanese writers did not imitate young writers in Europe and America. They tackled contemporary realities in Japan independently, and tried to give adequate literary expression to these realities. In so doing they created similar works to those of young American and European writers, because the contemporary world is facing very much the same basic problems everywhere. At the time of the revision of the Security Treaty with the United States, many of these young Japanese writers took an active part in the movement against it. Ishihara, Ôe and others formed the Society of Young Japan, and discussed the problem. After this, individual differences in their thinking and aspirations became clarified.

There are quite a few writers who have dealt with actual social and political problems of the present age like Kaikô Ken. For instance, Inoue Mitsuharu with his indigenous vitality depicted the bases of Japanese society, while Oda Makoto, who was born in Ôsaka, was greatly influenced by *après-guerre* writers like Noma Hiroshi. He wandered around the world recording his impressions in *Nandemo Miteyarô* (*I will Observe Everything*, 1961), and also wrote the novel *Gendaishi* (*The Contemporary History*, 1969), and novels in colloquial Ôsaka dialects. He is now presiding over the Society for Creating Peace in Vietnam, and is active as an internationally known anti-war intellectual. We should also name Iida Momo who published soon after the war *Rei Jikan* (*Zero Hour*, 1949). He was active as a member of the Communist Party and also published a unique novel in a chatty style, *Monomi yo, Yoru wa Nao Nagaki ya* (*Guard, Is It Long Till Sunrise?* 1961). Takahashi Kazumi studied Chinese Literature at Kyôto University. He depicted the inner sufferings of intellectuals in *Hi no Utsuwa* (*Vessel of Sorrow*, 1962), *Yûutsunaru Tôha* (*Melancholic Fraction*, 1965) and other novels, and was popular as a conscientious progressive writer, inheriting the main current of the *après-guerre* writers. His death by cancer at the age of forty which seems to have been hastened by his worries over university strifes shocked students and other young people as much as Mishima Yukio's suicide. We should not forget, either, Matsugi Nobuhiko, the author of *Hikaru Koe* (*Shining Voice*, 1966), Ôshiro Tatsuhiro, the author of *Kakuteru Pâti* (*Cocktail Party*, 1967) which depicts the contradictory situation of Okinawa, Ri Kaisei, the author of *Mata Futatabi no Michi* (*The Road to Once Again*, 1969) and Komatsu Sakyô, the author of science fiction works like *Nihon Apatchi Zoku* (*Japanese Apache Tribe*, 1964) based on fantastically original conceptions.

As for writers who aspire to create contemporary literature or literature of the future which is of more genuine literary quality by bold *avant-garde* literary experiments, no really promising new authors have appeared since Ôe and Kurahashi. For example, Uno Kôichirô, the author of *Yami no Ue* (*Hunger of Darkness*, 1961) and *Geishin* (*God of Whales*, 1961), declared himself to be a writer of the genuine postwar generation tackling directly the problems of the body, but he ended up writing decadent novels on sexual manners. Shibata Kakeru who depicted the failure and boredom of contemporary youth in *Saredo Warera ga Hibi* (*Our Days, However*, 1963) is now in stagnation. Only the appearance of many women writers constitutes an interesting phenomenon. Kanai Mieko, the author of *Kimyôna Hanayome* (*Strange Bride*, 1970) is writing boldly experimental works reminiscent of Kurahashi Yumiko. Mori Makiko, the author of *Mitsuyaku* (*A Secret Promise*, 1969) and Tsushima Yûko, the author of *Aozora* (*Blue Sky*, 1969) seem to be quite talented. Ôba Minako, the author of *San-biki no Kani* (*Three Crabs*, 1968), attracted attention suddenly with her description of the nihilistic sentiments of modern man in the setting of a foreign land. Kuroi Senji, the author of *Jikan* (*Time*, 1969) which deals with modern enterprises and life in big apartment houses, Gotô Akio and Saki Ryûzô are among the new writers who combine the tendency of Kaikô with that of Ôe, but we don't know enough about them yet.

Another major current of young writers today is that which comprises writers slightly older than the generation of Ishihara, Kaikô and Ôe and which may be termed the "Intellectual Group" or "Cultured Group". It is a group of urban aesthetic writers who have a certain similarity to Yamakawa Masao who died young. Around the time of Japan's surrender unlike Inoue Mitsuharu, who belongs roughly to the same generation as they, but who cast his eyes downwards into the bottom of the earth symbolized by a coal mine, they, with Mishima Yukio, watched the sky above the ruins with nihilistic sentiments.

Kita Morio, the second son of Saitô Mokichi, was studying at Matsumoto Higher School situated near the Japan Alps around the time of Japan's surrender. He depicted his experiences of that time in works like *Iwaone nite* (*On the Rock Ridge*, 1956), *Reibai no Iru Machi* (*A Town with a Medium*, 1956) and *Ha-ari no Iru Oka* (*A Hill Where There Are Winged Ants*, 1960). They are works permeated with nihilistic boredom which, however, are written with clear sensibility. Kita received the Akutagawa Prize for *Yoru to Kiri no Sumi de* (*In the Corner of Night and Mist*, 1960) which is based on his experiences as a psychiatrist although the setting of the novel is Germany under the Second World War. He also wrote *Yûrei* (*Ghosts*, 1954), reminiscences of his childhood containing childhood myths, and *Nire-ke no Hitobito* (*People of the House of Nire,* 1964) which depicts the history of his family over three generations from the Meiji period. It is written with humour in an intellectual sensuous manner. These two works show him at his best. Kita is also widely read and cherished for his humorous essays in the tradition of Natsume Sôseki—like the series whose titles all begin with "Dokutoru Manbô" (Dr. Sunfish).

Other writers of this group are Nada Inada, another psychiatrist, who wrote *Bôshi o* (*My Hat,* 1959) and other refined essays; Maruya Saiichi, the author of *Toshi no Nokori* (*Life's Remainining Year,* 1968), who with his knowledge of English Literature is trying to write contemporary novels like Joyce's; Tsuji Kunio, a writer with good knowledge of French literature, who is aiming at producing genuine artistic novels and who is the author of *Kairô nite* (*In the Corridor,* 1963); Ogawa Kunio who has an interest in the biblical world and who has produced such refined works as *Gehena Kô* (*Port Gehenna,* 1969); Kaga Otohiko who wrote *Furandoru no Fuyu* (*Winter in Flanders,* 1967) which deals with the insanity of a Japanese student abroad through the eyes of a doctor; Furui Yukichi, Hoshi Shin'ichi who opened up a new frontier with short short stories like *Jinzô Bijin* (*An Artificial Beauty,* 1961) dealing with themes similar to those of science fiction; Yoshimura Akira, the author of *Senkan Musashi* (*Warship Musashi,* 1966) who is trying to write non-fiction novels; Kashiwabara Hyôzô, Tabata Mugihiko, Yamazaki Masakazu, Yamada Tomohiko, Moriuchi Toshio and Kiyooka Takayuki. These writers' range of vision is not restricted to Japan, they are trying to learn artistic secrets from the various literatures of the world. This is a new tendency, although it may escape the notice of many people. At the same time as these writers, a group of new critics has emerged and has started searching for the right direction for contemporary literature. Among them are Akiyama Shun, Isoda Kôichi, Matsubara Shin'ichi, Kamei Hideo, Tsukimura Toshiyuki, Ueda Miyoji, Oketani Hideaki and Takenishi Hiroko.

Literary magazines with a long tradition like *Shinchô* (*New Trends*), *Bungakukai* (*Literary Circle*), *Gunzô* (*A Group*) and *Bungei* (*Literary Art*) which are major organs for the publication of Japan's serious literature have been in recent years dominated by the works of new writers and new critics

such as those mentioned above. New writers have never had such wide op-
portunities to publish their works before. Although the demand for new
works is so great, supplies do not keep pace with it, which means that even
the immature works of new writers can often find a ready market. This
however also indicates that with the proliferation of new theories of what
constitutes good literature, the magazines are becoming more receptive to
the various experiments of new writers.

Due to her rapid economic growth, Japan has entered a period of an unprecedented material prosperity often called *Shôwa Genroku,* and people's
leisure activities have increased tremendously. On the other hand, the
society, by giving priority to industry and by ignoring human values has
deepened the alienation of human beings. Due to the development of the
information industry, society has also become more tightly controlled. In
such a situation, movements and thoughts which negate all the established
values and authorities, and which try to free mankind from the present
industry-centred society, have spread, as is seen from the recent university
strife caused by student radicals. In the 1970's contradictions in contemporary society will deepen further. Japan is becoming increasingly a mass
society, a fact which first became noticeable at the time of the publication
of *Taiyô no Kisetsu* (*Season of Violence,* 1955). Mass communication media
are developing extraordinarily, and information and entertainment flood
through audio-visual media like television. It is quite natural that, in such
circumstances, all sorts of new phenomena are occurring in literature:
many of the new types of entertainers are trying their hand in literature,
many writers are becoming something of a "star" or an entertainer, the
distinction between *jun-bungaku* (literature of quality) and *taishû-bungaku*
(literature for the mass) is becoming obscure, and literature is increasingly
dominated by mass communication media. From the midst of such a mass
society, entirely new types of writers are emerging e.g. Nosaka Akiyoshi,
Itsuki Hiroyuki and Shôji Kaoru. Nosaka has invented a unique style
reminiscent of frivolous popular novels of the Kansai Area. He depicts
human decadence masochistically and tries to deal with psychological
complexities like those of war orphans, incest and so on in aesthetic novels.
Among his works are *Erogotoshi-tachi* (*The Pornographers,* 1963), *Hotaru*

no Haka (*The Grave of Fireflies*, 1968) and *Honegami Tôge Hotoke Kazura* (*Uncanny Vines of the Honegami Pass*, 1969). Itsuki showed his talent as a storyteller in novels like *Saraba Mosukuwa Gurentai* (*Farewell, Young Hoodlums in Moscow!*, 1966). He is now trying to create a new type of social novel which is both romantic and serious. Shôji depicted the frivolous smartness of contemporary youths in works like *Akazukin-chan Ki o Tsukete* (*Be Careful, Little Red Riding Hood*, 1969) which are characterized by the skilful use of a fluent intellectual style. The appearance of these writers is symbolic of the chaotic state Japanese Literature is in at the moment, groping its way for the future.

Japanese Literature is no longer a special literature developing in isolation, nor is it the literature of a backward society which merely imports and imitates the modern literature of advanced societies. Whether it likes it or not, its task is that of a member of contemporary world literature; it is to create a new contemporary literature which can cure human alienation in this age. Of course, since Japan is geographically far away from Europe and America, the present centres of world literature, and since Japanese Literature is written in an isolated language called Japanese, it will be long before it wins world-wide appreciation. Nevertheless Japanese Literature with its long history can only develop further as a part of present-day world literature. Without realizing this severe yet hopeful situation that Japanese Literature is in, we can no longer understand its essence.

To sum up, in the years immediately after the war, we first witnessed the revival of the long established writers, who produced the last masterpieces of modern Japanese literature ("modern" in the sense of coming between the feudal age and the contemporary age), as well as the groping for contemporary literature on the part of the writers belonging to the "New Burlesque" Group. Then there came the birth of contemporary literature with new techniques and new contents through the efforts of the *après-guerre* writers. This new literature, however, fell into the anachronism of attempting to revive the 19th century "romans" in Japan, and in the literary world at large quasi-modern novels in the form of quasi-popular novels and novels of manners were in vogue. It was the "Third

New Generation" writers who restored this anachronistic trend back to the aspirations of new contemporary literature prevalent in the early Shôwa period (1935–1944). The appearance of new writers like Ishihara Shintarô, Ôe Kenzaburô and Kurahashi Yumiko and the works of such writers as Mishima Yukio, Abe Kôbô, Shimao Toshio, Kojima Nobuo and Inoue Mitsuharu established the right direction for the new Contemporary Literature. It was a revival of *junbungaku* (literature of quality) which risks the danger of not being understood except by a small number of intellectuals. It was this conscious resistance against the tide of standardization in the midst of a growing mass society from the time of the publication of *Taiyô no Kisetsu* (*Season of Violence,* 1955), which was the start of authentic Contemporary Literature.

A series of literary controversies were waged after the movement against the revision of the Security Treaty with the United States in 1960. (Among these are a controversy over "the degeneration of junbungaku" in which Itô Hitoshi, Hirano Ken and Takami Jun participated; a controversy over the thesis that the achievements of postwar literature are illusory in which Sasaki Kiichi and Yamamura Shizuka figured as important personages, and a controversy about the relationship between politics and literature which was waged between Okuno Takeo and Yoshimoto Takaaki on the one side and Hariu Ichirô and Takei Akio on the other side.) These controversies eliminated former complexes towards modern European Literature, and freed literary people from connected taboos. They made it clear that Japanese Literature was about to enter the age of new contemporary literature which was distinctly different from postwar literature up to that time.

During the past 100 years since the beginning of the Meiji period, Japanese literature consciously cut itself off from the popular literature of the Edo period, imported modern Western literature at a tremendous rate, and by assimilating it established in the special climate of Japan a narrow but unique modern literature of its own centering around "I" novels. Of course it is obvious that this literature was based on various traditions of Japanese Literature which could claim 1000 years of history, even if consciously it was indebted only to Western Literature. As soon as it attained literary maturity in the democratic atmosphere of the Taishô period, it had to witness the passing away of the modern age in world history. From the end of the Taishô period, the groping for a new contemporary literature was expressed in two competing slogans, namely "literature for revolution" and "revolution of literature". Various attempts were made during the tumultuous years which witnessed the Pacific War. In the fifteen years following the war, two major complexes within the Japanese literary circles, namely a literary complex towards orthodox modern Western novels and an ethical complex towards Marxism based on modern humanism both vanished, and Japanese Literature, with a correct understanding of the harsh realities of the age, has just fulfilled the basic conditions necessary to establish autonomously an authentic contemporary literature which is not without connections to Japan's cultural past.

The historical significance and value of Japanese Literature since the Meiji period up to the present will be determined by the future of contemporary Japanese literature in the context of world literature. The history of Japanese literature as a part of world literature has just begun, and we do not yet know what sort of development it will show.

Abe Kobo

It was in 1950 that Abe Kôbô's *Akai Mayu* (*The Red Cocoon*) was awarded the Prize for Postwar Literature. At that time, Abe had already published *Owarishi Michi no Shirube ni* (*As a Signpost for the Road I Have Come*), in 1948. This was an existential work unlike anything written by traditional Japanese writers.

To understand his works, we must remember that he was brought up in Manchuria, and that the deserts were familiar to him there. He came to associate reality with the image of a desert, and reality was conceived as fluid, like shifting sand, and not at all stable and solid. His works are often attempts to show the "absurdity" of reality and to point out the discrepancy between the fixed names we use, and the real nature of human beings and other things. His strong interest in surrealism also strengthened the peculiar individuality of his works. Abe was awarded the Akutagawa Prize for *Kabe* (*The Wall*) in 1951. Since then, he has been very productive, and published *Kiga-dômei* (*Starvation League,* 1954), *Kemonotachi wa Kokyô o Mezasu* (*Animals are Heading Their Home,* 1957) and many other works. In this essay, I would like to discuss some of his most representative works written after 1955.

We live in an age in which we try to foresee our future by using computers. But how would we react, if we were told that a catastrophe was awaiting us? Abe's *Daishi Kanpyô-ki* (*Inter Ice Age 4,* 1959 translated by E. Dale Saunders, Alfred A. Knopf, New York, 1970; Tuttle, Tokyo, 1970) is in a sense an attempt to answer such a question. In it he shows our age in a panic, foreseeing the end of one geological age. The abnormal activity of submarine volcanos shows that there will be an immense tidal wave, and the whole surface of the earth will be covered by water. Abe depicts, very imaginatively, people confronted with such a problem. The only solution would be to create a new type of human being, an aquatic human being. Although this is possible, some people are repelled by the idea. They feel that to allow the creation of aquatic men would be to deny themselves, making themselves mere living fossils of the past. To such an objection one character answers, "We must endure it". In this novel, the present human-centred value system is turned upside down, and aquatic man is characterized by his "singular coolness". In this novel, the future confronts us with a problem.

The hero of *Suna no Onna* (*The Woman in the Dunes*, 1962 translated by Sauders, E. Dale, New York, A. Knopf, 1964) is a man who is imprisoned in a hole in a dune. It is impossible to escape. However he realizes that he is gradually becoming a better man, as he lives with a woman who inhabits the hole. He acquires the courage to try and overcome the seemingly impossible situation he is in. In this novel, fluid unpredictable sand becomes a symbol of reality. "If you are on the side of the sand, everything with a shape is vain. What is certain is only the flow of the sand which denies every shape", says the hero. This is a symbolic statement which expresses most clearly Abe's refusal to settle down in reality, to have a home in it, a refusal which characterizes Abe's thought from the beginning. He looks at the reality of everyday routine, not from the inside, but from the position of their very opposite, unreality or abnormality. For Abe, order is merely something imposed on experience, and logic is simply an abstraction which cannot fathom reality. *Suna no Onna* (*The Woman in the Dunes*) shows most concisely the actual absurd state of reality, using the metaphor of a man struggling with the sand. This is the reason why the novel has become world-famous.

Tanin no Kao (*The Face of Another*, 1964, translated by Saunders, E. Dale, New York, A. Knopf, 1966) has, as its hero, a man who has received a horrible keloid scar all over his face due to an explosion of liquid air during an experiment: he has lost his own face. In order to regain the love of his wife who is repelled by his ugly scarred face, he makes a mask of plastic, and tries to seduce her, pretending that he is not her husband. The novel depicts the process of his self-recovery, and also gives expression to Abe's criticism of modern civilization. The hero has in a sense lost his identity, but he regards this as something quite common among people living in this age. He thinks that love is stripping off each other's mask.

This is a bitter irony aimed at our age. Starting from the problem of a human face, Abe tries to analyze human existence itself. In this novel, Abe contrasts a real face with a mask. Similar procedures are seen throughout his works. Abe is deeply aware of the discrepancy between things and their names: many names or words have lost every connection with that which they are supposed to represent.

Mukankei na Shi (*Irrelevant Death*, 1964) and *Chinnyûsha* (*Intruders*, 1952) deal with a similar theme. The former depicts a man who one day finds the corpse of a person who has no connection whatever to him. He does not know what to do in this absurd situation, and attempts all sorts of things in vain. Whereas in *Chinnyûsha* (*Intruders*), it was a group of strangers which intruded into the routine world and a man was exploited by a strange family who one day invaded his room, in this novel, it is a corpse which intrudes into the routine world. Here the hero willy-nilly comes to be related to a thing which should have no connection with him. The uncanniness of such an event is powerfully evoked in the novel. Abe wants to show that such an event really could occur. This is why Abe says that everyday life has no meaning, unless logic and pattern are imposed upon it.

Abe's play, *Tomodachi* (*Friends*, 1967) deals with a similar theme to that of the two novels just mentioned. The hero of the play is a man, a deputy section chief of a certain commercial firm, who rents a flat because he is going to get married. One day, a strange family with eight members (grandfather, father, mother, two sons, and three daughters) whose job, they say, is to deliver love and friendship to lonely people, just as to "rethread a broken necklace", comes thronging into his flat and forces him to live with them. Neither the police nor the landlord takes his complaint seriously. He is put into a cage for allegedly trying to escape. The eldest son steals his fiancée, and he is finally killed by the second daughter. After his death, the family leaves for their new destination. As we have seen, this play has more or less the same theme as *Chinnyûsha* (*Intruders*) and *Mukankei na Shi* (*Irrelevant Death*), and it was awarded the Tanizaki Jun'ichirô Prize.

Another play by Abe, *Bô ni Natta Otoko* (*The Man Who Turned into a*

Stick, 1969) is a critique of the tightly controlled nature of modern society where man has lost his individuality and becomes a mere cog in the wheel, a "stick".

In summary, Abe Kôbô's works are based on an existential understanding of reality. He regards reality as shifting appearance. He points out the discrepancy between names and the reality which they denominate, and directs sharp satire at modern civilization by parodying the absurdities which arise from that discrepancy.

Agawa Hiroyuki

Agawa Hiroyuki was born in Hiroshima in 1920. As soon as he graduated from the Department of Japanese Literature of Tokyo University in 1942, he was drafted into the Navy. He engaged in the communications and information business in China as a sub-lieutenant. After Japan's surrender, in 1946, he went back to Hiroshima which had been devastated by the atomic bomb, and found that his family was bankrupt. Later he went to Tokyo and became a journalist. His first work was *Nennen-saisai* (*Year by Year,* 1946) which depicts the miseries of war and the joys of living in the relating of the story of a soldier who returns from abroad to Hiroshima reduced to ashes. For some time Agawa lived in obscurity, because his works went against the current of the day which welcomed those centring on ideas. However, in 1952 he was awarded the Yomiuri Literary Prize for his novel *Haru no Shiro* (*A Castle in Spring,* 1952) which tells the war experiences of a student soldier. Next, in *Ma no Isan* (*Devil's Heritage,* 1952, translated by Maki, John M., Tokyo, Hokuseido, 1957) he discussed A-bomb victims, and in 1955 he published *Kumo no Bohyô* (*Gravemarker of Clouds*) which depicts the thoughts and feelings of a World War II "suicide pilot". All of these above works established him as a writer.

Kumo no Bohyô (*Gravemarker of Clouds*) has as its hero a Navy officer who was drafted while still a student. He suffers a lot, trying to find out how he can live as an intellectual in the midst of war which forcibly nullifies the bloom of youth. He is killed in battle. The author depicts the hero in a straightforward fashion, feeling a considerable empathy with the student fighter. As a piece of war literature this novel is extremely realistic. These novels which depict youth chased by death, the suffering caused by the A-bomb, and the cruelty of war are nevertheless written in the beautiful style characteristic of Agawa, a style which is realistic but not pedantic, and which is both lyrical and rhythmic. This quality which is not found in many abstract ideological pieces of war literature makes Agawa's work deeply interesting.

In 1955 he was given a grant by the Rockefeller Foundation and spent one year in the United States. He wrote of his experiences in the United States later in *Kariforuniya* (*California*, 1958–59).

After this he published a series of fine "I" novels such as *Aoba no Kageri* (*The Shade of Leaves*, 1960), *Saka no Ôi Machi* (*The Town of Many Hills*, 1960) and *Gentô* (*Side Lights of a Ship*, 1965). His *Yamamoto Isoroku* (1964–65) has also attracted attention as a work which has opened up a new area in biographical literature.

Yoru no Namioto (*The Sound of Waves at Night*, 1957) the synopsis of which is given above, is a psychological study of a woman who lost her husband during the miserable days of the war, and of her father during the needy years following the war. It tells of how she comes to love a married man with children who gives her moral support. It is a highly artistic work which awakens in us a love for our fellow human beings because of the warm sympathetic gaze with which the author looks at human life.

Agawa is an author who carefully shapes his deep observations of life into well constructed novels. He is still quite active as a writer.

AGAWA Hiroyuki
Yoru no namioto *(The sound of waves at night)*
Published in *Shinchô*, May 1957.

(Synopsis) Only at night can you hear at the house of Kitagawa Makie
the sound of waves which, though at first monotonous, if you listen carefully, is rhythmic and highly interesting with a slight variation each time.
It is twenty years since Makie lost her husband, and it is seven years since
her father died. She has already passed her prime and her looks are not
what they used to be. She is awakened from her shallow dreams by the
oppressive sound of waves. It is a beautiful spring morning. A memorial
service for the seventh anniversary of the death of her father, Kentarô, is
to take place at the temple that day.

When he was young (around 1923), Kentarô opened a western-style
restaurant in Tokyo, which proved a success. Hamamura and Seikichi,
both from the same province as Kentarô, worked faithfully for him, and
Kentarô's restaurant gradually acquired the reputation of being a good
honest place to go. However, Kentarô lost his wife when his restaurant
was at the height of its prosperity. She had caught pneumonia as a result of
working too hard. At the time, Makie was eighteen years old, and her
sister Kazuyo fifteen. The neighbours were expecting that Makie would
marry Hamamura whom her father trusted, and would inherit the restaurant. From her childhood Makie had liked to be spoilt by Hamamura, and
Hamamura had also been kind to the beautiful Makie. However, to everyone's surprise, Kentarô adopted a quiet diligent salaried man called Tasaku,
and Makie married him. This was because Kentarô, in accordance with
the will of his wife, desired Marie to live peacefully and securely as the
wife of a salaried man without the ups and downs which usually accompany the running of a business. Not so long after the marriage,
Hamamura and Seikichi both took a wife. Makie's sister, Kazuyo, also got
married and went to live in Ôsaka. All of them were initially happily married. However, while Makie was pregnant, her husband was drafted into

the army to fight against China. He met a sudden death in a landing operation on the central coast of China, leaving Makie a widow at the age of
twenty-four. Then she gave birth to Akio, her eldest son. As World War
II grew more violent, and the shortage of goods more severe, it became
difficult for honest Kentarô even to stock materials, so that his restaurant
was virtually closed. Finally both the restaurant and his residence were
burnt down in an air-raid. After the war the Kitagawa family lived in
hired rooms in a poor part of Tokyo. Hamamura, who had become head
cook of the K. Hotel, looked after them. Kentarô died a lonely death in
extreme poverty. His property, which did not amount to much, was
placed under Hamamura's care despite the machination of ambitious
Minesaburô, Kentarô's younger brother, to take it over. Makie, with
Hamamura's help, built a new house in Kentarô's home village where she
went to live modestly with Akio, her son, who at that time was a university student.

When the story opens, Kazuyo, Makie's sister, has arrived at the new
house from Ôsaka. Kazuyo thinks that Makie looks younger than before.
While they are chatting animatedly, Ofude, a distant relative, arrives to
help. Also having lost her husband in the war, she lives alone with her
daughter who is insane. She manages with great difficulty to make both
ends meet by working as a day labourer, locking her insane daughter in
the house each day. When Makie sees Ofude who looks quite worn out
with the care of living, she is reminded of the changes of fortune which
have occurred to many people during the ten years or so of the war
period. She feels that, although she too is living alone with her child she
is more fortunate than Ofude. At the same time, she feels an intense
loneliness. Then Hamamura and Seikichi arrive. The people concerned
with the anniversary celebration are, more or less, all present, so the party
proceeds to the temple. When the memorial service is nearly over, Minesaburô, Kentarô's brother, arrives late. After visiting Kentarô's tomb, they
all return to Makie's new house to a modest feast. They drink saké and
indulge in reminiscences of Kentarô. Only Minesaburô says hurtful things,
without restraint. At this point he finds his purse is missing. He suspects
that Ofude, who was left in charge of the house, has stolen it, but while he

is teased by Kazuyo and pacified by Hamamura, a taxi-driver arrives with the purse which he had found lying on the seat of his car. A little embrassed by this, Minesaburô hastily drinks saké, gets drunk, and goes, taking leave of Hamamura with an ironical remark. The others also leave one by one, until Hamamura and Seikichi, who fell asleep after getting drunk, are the only guests who remain. After calculating the expenses of the day, Hamamura is about to leave the house with Seikichi to return by taxi, when Makie, thanking him for his help for the day, comes near him, helps him to put on his coat, and removes a piece of waste thread from the collar of his coat. Kazuyo notices that it is done naturally as if Makie were Hamamura's wife.

That night, while they are both in bed, Kazuyo remarks to Makie that their father should have married Makie to Hamamura and had them inherit his restaurant. She also says that the reason why Makie looks so young must be that she is in love with Hamamura. Makie confesses that, although she knows that it is impossible that she will ever be united with Hamamura who has a wife and children, she does not have sufficient energy to live without his support. She starts crying, and Kazuyo, who has a warm sympathy towards her sister's love, cries with her. She then proposes to Makie that they go to Tokyo on the next day, watch a *Kabuki* performance and visit the grave of Tasaku, Makie's late husband, consoling Makie by saying that Tasaku would forgive her for loving Hamamura. Makie just cries and cries. The night goes on quietly. The distant sound of waves rises and falls again and again.

Akimoto Matsuyo

Akimoto Matsuyo was born in Tokyo in 1911. When she was young, she did not think of becoming a writer, but shortly after the Second World War, she came to know Miyoshi Jûrô, a dramastist, and under his influence, she aspired to the same art. Since then she has continued to write one-act plays showing the tenacious powerful realism which she learned from Miyoshi. *Reifuku* (*Full Dress*, 1949) which she published at the age of thirty-eight, established her as a dramatist. This play is about children who gather to hold a remembrance ceremony for their dead mother. In a realistic detached manner it manages to evoke from the fragmentary words of the children the image of a mother who was full of life and energy. This play, which marks Akimoto's starting-point as a dramatist is already coming to be known as a modern classic, a master-piece among postwar one-act plays. After *Reifuku*, Akimoto started writing plays with two or more acts. Among them are plays like *Mono Iwanu Onnatachi* (*The Silent Women*, 1955) and *Muraoka Iheiji Den* (*The Life of Muraoka Iheiji*, 1960), which uses as its subject-matter the story of the ill-fated women who fell victim to the exploitation of the South Sea Regions before and during the war. These plays are not the usual heavy tragedies one might expect from those of the genre. Their focus is rather on the robustness of these women who lived optimistically with a greater energy than most men have. At the same time, by depicting the joys and sorrows of people on the bottom tier of society, they manage to throw light on the mechanics of politics. Akimoto's interest in the life of the common people has gradually led her to study folklore, and she has published two great masterpieces on this in recent years: namely, *Hitachibô Kaison* (1964) and *Kasabuta Shikibu Kô* (*An Investigation on Lady Scab*, 1969). Each of them uses an old popular provincial legend as its source and depicts people who fell victim to the rapid modernization of Japan. The author shows a warm sympathy towards these people, but at the same time the plays are animated by the author's rigorous critical spirit. Her aim is to show, through these people at the "bottom" of society and through their ethos, the contradictions created by the modernization of Japan, and to indicate how they might be overcome. It is not surprising that these two plays have called forth responses from beyond the theatrical field.

Akimoto is anything but a prolific dramatist. It is also seldom that she gives public utterance to her opinions about social or political matters, but when she publishes a new play, it always testifies to her steady development as a dramatist. She has also written some good T. V. drama.

AKIMOTO Matsuyo
Kasabuta Shikibu kô—a play in three acts.
(An investigation on Lady Scab)
Published in Bungei, June 1969.

(Synopsis) (Act I) The present. Toyoichi (thirty years old) is the eldest son of a small-time farmer of a poor Kyûshû village. Roughly one year ago, he was injured in a gas explosion at the small coal mine where he was working away from home. The after effects of gas poisoning reduced him to the mental level of a small child. His mother, Isa, finds her only consolation in looking after him; his wife Terue, however, is an energetic woman who opposes his mother in everything. She regularly goes to village meetings and she is rumoured to be in love with a youth who is very active at such meetings.

One day a group of pilgrims headed by a thirty-year-old nun, Chishûni, whom they revere as the head of their sect arrives in the area. Chishûni maintains that she is the sixty-eighth descendant of the famous Heian poetess, Izumi Shikibu. Her followers try to induce Isa, Toyoichi's mother, to accept their faith, but she firmly refuses. In the evening, Isa quarrels violently with Terue who no sooner has come back from one meeting than she wants to go out to attend another. Toyoichi, reminded of the gas explosion by the smell of the charcoal fire which Isa has lit, becomes wild, and rushes out of the house. The singing of the pilgrims is heard in the distance.

(Act II) The pilgrims arrive at the dilapidated community centre on the hill. They have joined the pilgrimage to escape from heavy miseries and problems. They engage in harmless conversation and try to console one another. Toyoichi who rushed out of his house has been following the pilgrims. He peeps at Chishûni from behind the shrubbery of the community centre garden, and is absorbed like a child by her beauty. He believes that she is a living Buddha and wants to serve by her side. In spite of the misgivings on the part of her followers, Chishûni allows him to join the pilgrimage. Isa comes hurriedly in search of her son, and finds him among the pilgrims. She cannot change his childish determination to serve Chishûni so she decides to travel with the pilgrims to the headquarters of their sect far away in the south. Terue also comes to fetch her husband, but the only thing she can do is to repeat her arguments with the pilgrims. She cannot prevent Toyoichi and his mother from setting off with the pilgrims. While the invocatory chanting of the pilgrims rises to an emotional crescendo, Chishûni and Terue look fixedly into one another's eyes.

(Act III, Part 1) It is afternoon, several days later. In front of the headquarters which is in a deep valley, Chishûni, dressed in white with her beautiful long hair hanging down, is caressing and making fun of Toyoichi as if he were a puppy. He crawls on the ground, presses his face on her foot and kisses it. She plays with his face with her toes, and then kicks him down on the ground, laughing a low dry laugh. A man called Yumenosuke who is somewhat mentally retarded has been watching this scene. He follows the two into the hall and attacks them. He binds Toyoichi with a rope, swings him from a tree, and Toyoichi falls into the valley. Yumenosuke then presses Chishûni to have sexual intercourse with him. Toyoichi's voice calling for Chishûni and the voice of Isa searching for Toyoichi echo in the valley.

(Act III, Part 2) It is about noon of the next day. In the building situated halfway up the mountain, which the believers use for devotional purposes, Chishûni is relating the legend of the founder of their sect to a large crowd of believers. According to the legend, Izumi Shikibu, born roughly 1000 years ago into a noble family and reputed to be the greatest poet of the day, was famous for her extraordinary beauty and passed a gay life until she lost her child. It was then that she came to understand the transience of the world, and wandered around many provinces saving helpless common people from their misery. She took all the diseases of the people on herself, and finally came to this mountain far down in the southern part of Japan. Following this narration, a representative of the pilgrims tells how Toyoichi has fallen down into the valley and come to his senses. He calls it a modern miracle and praises Buddha for the protection of Toyoichi.

However, Toyoichi, sane at long last, explains that it is his mother who has saved him. Witnessing her son regaining his memory completely, Isa cries out wildly for joy.

(Act III, Part 3) The next morning Toyoichi is trying to discuss a difficult passage in the Buddhist scriptures with Chishûni. However, she has lost all interest in him since he came to his senses. She answers him very coldly. Infuriated by her words, he once again loses his senses. Terue who has heard the news of Toyoichi's recovery arrives in great haste. When she finds an insane Toyoichi, however, she again attacks Isa. Isa has lost every hope in reality and in faith, and advises Toyoichi and Terue to go home. As for herself, she has decided to remain in the mountains. Nearby the believers are noisily putting on show a picture titled *Toyoichi and His Mother* which beautifully expresses the story of the "miracle".

(Act III, Part 4) One year has passed. The building for devotion where *Toyoichi and His Mother* is on exhibition is crowded with people who have come to see this famous picture. Old Isa, wearing torn dirty clothes which look as if they are covered by scraps is working silently on as a house-keeper. The mountain is lit up by the evening sun, and from it the singing of pilgrims is heard again just as it was before.

Amino Kiku

Amino Kiku was born in 1900 in Azabu, Tokyo, the eldest daughter of her family. Her father was running a saddlery. She grew up in a traditional Tokyo environment. She graduated from the English Literature Department of Japan Women's University which was at that time the highest educational institution for women. Among her classmates were women like Miyamoto Yuriko, a lady much ahead of their time, whose interests included the "women's liberation movement". However, far more important for her than the blue-stocking movement was her encounter with the writer Shiga Naoya whom Amino came to revere. This was really a "once in a lifetime" encounter, and acted as a permanent influence upon her.

Her works are characterized by a calm style devoid of every decorative element and pervaded by a thoroughgoing realism. Using such a style she has calmly depicted in "I" novels her real mother who was sued by her father for adultery and from whom she was separated at the age of six; her three stepmothers; the destinies of her half brothers and half sisters born of different mothers; and her own unhappy married life and subsequent divorce. Among her prewar works are Mitsuko (*Mitsuko*, 1926) and *Kisha no Naka de* (*On the Train*, 1940). Despite the modest number of her prewar novels, their quality won her recognition as a writer. During the postwar period Amino was twice awarded the Women's Literary Prize: the first time for *Kin no Kan* (*Golden Coffin*, 1947) and the second time for *Sakura no Hana* (*Cherry Blossoms*, 1961).

There is nothing ostentatious or striking about her work. She conscientiously pursues her art, unperturbed by the changing fashions of the time. Amino is highly esteemed as a unique writer. In *Ichigo Ichie* (*Once in a Lifetime*), summarized below, Amino is projecting herself into the actor Danzô who was, like her, unpretentious and lived quietly. Her long autobiographical novel *Yureru Ashi* (*Trembling Reed*, 1962) is also attracting attention as a novel which minutely depicts life in Tokyo.

AMINO Kiku
Ichigo ichie *(Once in a lifetime)*
Published in *Gunzô*, November 1966.

(**Synopsis**) On the 4th of June I had an unusually great number of visitors, and I was kept busy from early morning. Towards nine in the evening, the last guest left. I turned on the radio, and suddenly the words "The passenger who jumped in the sea was almost certainly Mr. Ichikawa Danzô" struck my ears.

In the newspapers next morning the suicide of the eighth Ichikawa Danzô made the headlines. Danzô was born on the 15th of May 1882, and was 84 years old. He was the oldest of the leading *Kabuki* actors, but when we saw him on the stage, we did not sense his age. Last year, he tendered his retirement on the grounds of failing health. He gave his retirement performance at the Kabuki-za Theatre this April. On the morning of the first of May he set out on a pilgrimage to Shikoku, a thing which he had been hoping to do for the past twenty years. It was on the way back from this pilgrimage that he threw himself overboard from a ship heading for Ôsaka from Shôdoshima. "Since he died calmly in a beautiful sea after ending his pilgrimage, we cannot call him unfortunate", I thought, but still I could not help feeling extremely sad. Since I was living alone, I did not have to trouble about propriety, and I cried aloud. I was not his personal acquaintance; I was not his particularly enthusiastic fan, either, but I had been interested in him for a long time. To begin with, the name Danzô was the first actor's name I had come across. I was seven or eight at the time. The house of Danzô's father's concubine happened to be in our neighbourhood. During the war, on the recommendation of Mr. Shiga Naoya, my much revered teacher, I read a book entitled *Ichikawa Danzô the Seventh* written by Danzô the eighth. It was a voluminous book. The people depicted in the book were vivid. It was enlightening without being didactic. It had a natural humour. In short, it was a fascinating book. After reading this book, I came to pay greater attention to Danzô on the stage. It was a shame, but I noticed that there was one defect in his art. That is, while he was careful about details and sincerity he lacked what is called *hana* ("flower"). "Even when one has been performing for many years one can still lack in 'flower.'" I thought; "This is quite discovery." At the same time, I could not help being reminded of myself, who had been writing for many years and was still mediocre at my art. Since I had been continuously subjected to the criticism that I lacked literary skill and "fragrance", I could not help sympathizing with Danzô as a person who was suffering from a similar defect, and I tried to discover his good points. Probably this explains in part why I retain a vivid memory of the role Danzô played. In particular, I remember Sen'ei Zenji (Priest Sen'ei), the part he played so well in the new play *Ii Tairô* (*Lord Ii, the Chief Minister*). This was a very suitable part for him. I was deeply moved when the solitary figure of Priest Sen'ei played by Danzô left the stage quietly leaving an old bamboo hat in an empty room of the suburban residence of Lord Ii. On that hat was written *"Ichigo Ichie"* (Once in a Lifetime).

Since I was becoming old, I felt concern for aged actors. When I heard that Danzô was going to receive the Education Minister's Prize for Artistic Achievement which I also had been awarded, I was very glad and felt as if some secret tie was created between us. At his retirement performance this April Danzô played Kiichi Hôgen in *Kiku-batake* and Ikyû in *Sukeroku* wonderfully well, but when Ikyû was killed by Sukeroku, I had felt it somehow ominous, and was sad and unhappy. Like myself, Danzô had been separated from his mother, never to meet her again. I imagined his upbringing from my own lonely childhood. A few years ago I saw him off stage. It was near the Kabuki-za Theatre. He was wearing a suit which showed his good taste. "An actor is an actor even if he is old and his art is conservative", I thought with admiration. I followed him with curiosity. On the way to the Ginza crossroads he stopped at a camera-shop and looked at the display in the window. An old actor and a camera—that combination seemed to me to be quite interesting. However, I suppose he had sensed that I was following him, and stopped just to let me go past.

Danzô's death was heatedly discussed in the newspapers, on TV, in the weekly magazines and everywhere else. All sorts of hypotheses were put forward to explain his death. Danzô's speech and behaviour from the time of his retirement performance was minutely reported. As one ages, one inevitably thinks about one's death. Danzô, who had said in a comic poem that to live long did not pay, wrote a letter immediately before his death in which he said that he was thankful for his longevity. This is consoling for his surviving family as well as for us. On autumnal equinox day, I went to see a memorial exhibition for Danzô held at the Theatrical Museum of Waseda University. The exhibition hall was rather empty. When I saw the last photograph of Danzô's unshaven face, I became sad and tears started coming to my eyes. I took a bus for home, and watched the world from the window, but even then, to my embarrassment, the tears would not stop.

This novel *Ichigo Ichie* (*Once in a Lifetime*) could hardly be called a short novel if judged by European and American standards. By those, it would rate as an essay. However, in Japan, there is an unique genre called "Shinkyô Shôsetsu" (Mental life novel) or "Watakushi Shôsetsu" (The "I" novel) which lies somewhere between an ordinary short novel and an essay, and a work like *Ichigo Ichie* (*Once in a Lifetime*) which hides a welter of emotions behind the facade of a casual style is traditionally highly evaluated. As the title of the novel suggests, behind *Ichigo Ichie* (*Once in a Lifetime*) is the idea, similar to that of Matsuo Bashô, that if you meet someone soul to soul even once in a lifetime, such a moment of encounter is the most valuable, the most worthy in that it contains the essence of a lifetime's experience. In this sense, Japanese readers find this novel moving.

Ariyoshi Sawako

Ariyoshi Sawako was born in Wakayama City of Wakayama Prefecture in 1931. Her father was working for a bank. She spent her childhood in Java to which place her father had been transfered. In 1952 she graduated from the Department of English Literature of Tokyo Women's Christian College. In 1956 she published *Jiuta* (*Jiuta Ballad*) in the January number of *Bungakukai* (*Literary Circle*). Through the merits of this work, Ariyoshi became runner-up in the selection for Akutagawa Prize winners. In the same year she also published *Masshiroke-no-ke* (*Pure White*) in the October number of *Bungei* (*Literary Art*), and thus began her writing career. In 1957 Ariyoshi became runner-up in the Naoki Prize selection for her *Shiroi Uchiwa* (*White Fan*) which was published in the June number of *Kingu* (*King*), and her reputation as a woman novelist adept at depicting the world of entertainers and artists rose quickly. In 1959 she went to the U.S. to study. From January to May 1960 *Kinokawa* (*The River Kinokawa*) was published in serial form in *Fujin Gahô* (*Women's Illustrated Magazine*). This novel depicts the life of a woman who lived through the Meiji, Taishô and

Shôwa periods. The author finds in the heroine, who believing in the virtue of stoic submission, devoted herself to the prosperity of her family, an elegance which is beautiful. In *Kôge* (*Incense and Flowers*, 1961–1962) Ariyoshi depicted the life of a geisha, and in *Sukezaemon Yondai Ki* (*The Four Generations of Sukezaemon*, 1962–1963) the vitality of tradition which runs through certain old families of Kishû (approximately, the present Wakayama Prefecture). *Hi-shoku* (*Non-coloured*) which Ariyoshi wrote during 1963 and 1964, deals with a subject which has an international significance, namely, the Negro problem. In this novel, Ariyoshi tells us how Japanese women married to Negroes have to endure a miserable life in the U.S. Obviously Ariyoshi is making good use of the knowledge she acquired directly while she studied in New York. This work is rather unique in that a Japanese woman novelist is writing about the fates of Japanese women abroad. However, this is not the only reason why it attracts out interest. Its universal appeal comes from the fact that it shows how deep-rooted racial prejudices are. Ariyoshi also published *Aritagawa* (*The River Aritagawa*) in 1963 and Hidakagawa (*The River Hidakagawa*) in 1965. With *Kinokawa* (*The River Kinokawa*), they form a series of novels which treat subjects related to the three main rivers of Kishû. After finishing them, Ariyoshi, who is a Catholic, went to China to study Nestorianism at Peking University. After returning to Japan, she published *Hanaoka Seishû no Tsuma* (*The Wife of Hanaoka Seishû*). This is a novel which portrays the life of a surgeon of Kishû (who, by using the anaesthetics he invented, performed the first successful breast cancer operation in the world), and the lives of his wife and mother. This novel was received with enthusiasm. In Japanese literary circles, Ariyoshi has a reputation as a good story-teller with a rare knowledge of human nature, who can deal with a wide range of subject-matters.

ARIYOSHI Sawako
Hanaoka Seishû no tsuma *(The wife of Hanaoka Seishû)*
Published in *Shinchô,* November 1966. Published in book form by
Shinchôsha, February 1967.

(Synopsis) In the villages along the River Kinokawa, which runs north-
wards, people have talked, from generation to generation, about a marriage which took place around the middle of the Hôreki period (1751–
1763). The marriage in question was that of Otsugi, daughter of the
Matsumoto family, a big landlord dwelling in Chôno-machi, Ito-gun, and
Hanaoka Naomichi, a poor doctor of Hirayama, Nate, beyond the river.
Otsugi was famous for her beauty and talent from her childhood. That she
married Naomichi was due to the following circumstances. When Otsugi
became of marriageable age, she caught a terrible skin disease. The
Matsumoto family took her to many doctors, without sparing money, but
none of them could cure her. When Naomichi heard that Otsugi was suffering from the seemingly incurable disease, he crossed the River Kinokawa and visited the Matsumoto family. He assured them that he could
cure her. However, as a reward, he asked them to give her to him in marriage when she was cured. Although he was a completely unknown
country doctor they were at such a loss as to what to do about their
daughter's disease, that they accepted his terms, and left her treatment to
him. Otsugi was completely cured, and married to Naomichi. Since
Naomichi had cured an "incurable" disease, it would have been quite
natural if his reputation as a doctor had shot up, and all sorts of tales about
his skill had spread far and wide; but nothing of the sort really happened.
This was partly because the people living in his neighbourhood were
rather fed up with his love of big talk, and partly because Otsugi was so
wise and beautiful that people were envious of him.

There was a village called Ichiba-mura which bordered on Hirayama.
Imose Sajibei, the powerful headman of this village, had a daughter called
Kae. It was when she was eight years old that Kae first saw Otsugi. Her

nurse, Tami, had often told her how beautiful and wise Otsugi was; finally she asked the nurse to take her to the neighbouring village and peeped into the garden of the Hanaoka family. At that moment Otsugi was watering the plants in her garden. From that time on Kae felt adoration and longing for Otsugi. Her young heart worshipped Otsugi as if she were a divine being. This "religious adoration" became stronger and stronger as she grew older.

Otsugi bore Naomichi a son. When he became old enough, this son, Unpei (later called Seishû), went to Kyoto to study Dutch medicine. While he was studying at Kyoto, Otsugi visited the Imose family. She found in Kae a suitable prospective bride for her son, Unpei, and asked them to give Kae to Unpei in marriage. Tae's father, Sajibei, was first opposed to the marriage; he thought that the social positions of the two families were too different. However, Kae was only too glad to marry Unpei, the son of Otsugi, whom she respected so much. In the second year of Tenmei (1782), on an autumn day, Kae was given in marriage to the Hanaoka family. Since Unpei was away in Kyoto, studying, it was a wedding without the bridegroom. In lieu of Unpei a medical book handed down from the family ancestors was placed in the bridegroom's seat.

In order to support Unpei while he was studying in Kyoto, Otsugi produced hand-woven cotton at her home. As soon as Kae became a member of the Hanaoka family by marrying Unpei, she joined Otsugi in her work. When Naomichi died, Unpei who had returned from Kyoto after finishing his training, became the head of the Hanaoka family. Using his knowledge of Dutch medicine, Unpei planned to conduct surgical operations on patients after administrating an anaesthetic. In order to test anaesthetics, he first experimented on cats and dogs. However, his research finally reached the stage where in order to progress, he was obliged to begin experimenting on human beings. "Since I am always near him, it would be very stupid of me if I didn't realize that all Unpei can do now is to experiment on human beings. I am his mother I will be the subject for his experiments", Otsugi declared one day. To this Kae replied in an excited voice, "I have long since made up my mind that I will be used for his experiments" "Of course, you won't.", said Otsugi. "I would be too ashamed to show myself in public if I let my precious daughter-in-law suffer from a possible accident". "No, it would be me, your daughter-in-law, who wouldn't be able to show her face in public. How could I live peacefully if I let my precious mother-in-law take an anaesthetic which might prove harmful? Please, let me take the responsibility!" On the surface, this conversation between the mother-in-law and Kae suggests a beautiful rivalry in selflessness. In fact her mother-in-law's voice made Kae feel as if sharp stakes had been driven into her body. Seishû (Unpei's professional name) could not decide between the offer of his mother and that of his wife. In the end it was decided that both of them should take part in the experiments. First Otsugi received the anaesthetic. When she came out of her unconscious state she was perfectly all right. However Kae, to whom Seishû had given a stronger anaesthetic, lost her sight. After such sacrifices, anaesthetics harmless to human beings were invented, and for the first time in the world Seishû conducted a successful operation for breast cancer on a patient subjected to general anaesthesia. It was thanks to the devoted cooperation of his mother and his wife that Seishû achieved this feat. And behind their devotion lay the cold rivalry of a mother and a wife over their influence on Seishû. In the twelfth year of Bunsei (1829), Kae went to her eternal rest, closely following her mother-in-law. At her death, her eyes and lips were tightly closed.

Endo Shusaku

Endô Shûsaku is a Catholic writer, and occupies a unique position in the history of Japanese Literature. In Japan there are less than 900,000 Christians, Protestants and Catholics combined. He is one of the writers forming the "Daisan no Shinjin" (Third New Generation) group. However, unlike Yoshiyuki Junnosuke (1924–   ) and Yasuoka Shôtarô (1920–   ) who also belong to this group, Endô has shown from the beginning a marked inclination towards abstract thinking. He was introduced to Hori Tatsuo by Yoshimitsu Yoshihiko, a Catholic philosopher, and came to know Hori and his circle, people well versed in European Literature. Later Endô wrote *An Essay on Hori Tatsuo* (1956). This shows that his position is quite unique among the "Daisan no Shinjin" (Third New Generation) group. After his return from France, where he studied from 1950 to 1953, he wrote *Aden made* (*Till Aden,* 1954) and the next year he wrote *Shiroi Hito* (*White People*) and was awarded the Akutagawa Prize. Since then he has written a great variety of books, including, *Umi to Dokuyaku* (*The Sea and Poison,* 1958) and *Chinmoku* (*Silence,* 1966). He has persistently dealt with his central problem, that of literature and religion, in these works.

Among works published after 1955, *Aoi Chiisana Budô* (*Green Little Grapes*) is a novel that centres on Lyon in the postwar period. A German ex-soldier, Hanz, who has lost one arm, comes to visit a Japanese called Ihara. Together they look for the French girl, Souzanne, who had rescued Hanz. The "green little grapes" she gave to Hanz acquire a symbolic meaning in the novel: these "grapes" are nowhere to be found unless you make them yourself.

Umi to Dokuyaku (*The Sea and Poison,* 1958) is set in Japan. It is concerned with the vivisection of American prisoners of war at the medical faculty of F University towards the end of World War II. A timid assistant called Suguro takes part in the experiments, suppressing the voice of his conscience. The sea in the title is probably a symbol of what makes him forget his conscience, and poison stands for what destroys his conscience. In this novel the author relates vivisection to the problem of the absence of God. God is present only as an almighty judge, revealed in Suguro's later suffering from pangs of conscience, "Nobody knows the day fixed for punishment, but it will surely come". This is an ambitious work. That Endô has dealt with problem of conscience in a novel which, unlike his previous works, has Japan as its setting, is very significant. Endô was awarded the Shinchô Literary Prize for this novel.

Otoko to Kyûkanchô (*Three Men and a Starling,* 1963) does not centre on Endô's preoccupation with literature and religion. It is a work which reveals another side of Endô, Endô as a humorous writer. In a hospital room where three male patients are living, an old man arrives with a starling. Since he is immediately confined to bed, these three men look after the bird. When the old man dies, they are at a loss what to do with it. This work is not heavy or solemn, and shows a pleasant delicacy of touch. *Ryûgaku* (*Studying Abroad,* 1965) consists of three chapters, *Rûan no Natsu* (*Summer in Rouan*), *Ryûgakusei* (*A Student Abroad,* 1965) and *Nanji mo Mata* (*You, too,* 1964), which are quite independent of one another. They are stories of defection or failure of Japanese students, who have suffered from the difference in intellectual climate between Japan and Europe. The first chapter has a contemporary setting, and has Kudô as its hero. The second chapter has Araki Thomas, who went to Rome in the 17th century, as its hero. The third chapter has again a contemporary setting, and a scholar called Tanaka, who studies Sade, as its hero. The problem of cultural difference is raised: for example, in the first chapter, Kudô reflects, "Japan is different from Africa and the Congo. People here don't know anything about Japan. .... In my country there is a climate in which Christianity can never take lasting root".

Chinmoku (*Silence,* 1966, translated by Johnston, William, Tokyo, Tuttle, 1969) is a novel which deals with the apostasy of Catholics (such as a Japanese called Kichijirô) in 17th century Japan. The novel to a large extent takes the form of letters written by a Catholic missionary, Father Rodorigo, who comes to 17th century Japan where Christianity is banned and where the intellectual climate is unfavorable to it anyway. God has kept silent in the face of the tortures, deaths and the blood shed during the twenty years' of persecution. Why? This poignant question is central to the novel: Christ himself cried out on the cross, "My God, why hast thou forsaken me?" This novel portrays, among others, Feleira who finally betrays his faith after years of missionary activity in Japan, Kichijirô who plays the part of Judas Iscariot in the end, and Rodorigo who finally tramples on the image of Christ. Endô shows, however, that God was not silent and indifferent to these people after all, but that he suffered with them. Such a theme is developed against the ambiguous intellectual climate of Japan. The unique merit of this novel lies in the fact that Endô has directly tangled with the central problem of faith, centring on the figure of the apostate Rodorigo, and using accurate historical material with great

imagination. In this novel, a drama takes place, arising from the clash between the clear-cut dualism of European thinking and the marsh-like
ambiguous tolerance of Japanese thought. *Chinmoku* (*Silence*) was awarded
the Tanizaki Jun'ichirô Prize.

The play, *Bara no Yakata* (*A House Surrounded by Roses,* 1969), is also set
in Japan. The action takes place in a Catholic church in Karuizawa during
World War II. The theme of the play is the conscience of Christians during
the war. As in *Chinmoku* (*Silence*), the problem is individual conscience in
its historical context and is focused on the problem of faith. A Swiss missionary, Father Ussan, cannot give satisfactory advice to a student who has
been drafted into the army and is distressed. This priest cannot stand the
feeling of his inadequacy, and commits suicide immediately after he has
listened over the radio to the Emperor's announcement of the cessation of
war. The other characters involved in the play are a nihilistic writer, and a
girl who loves the student. As far as the structure is concerned, the play is
really well-made. One conspicuous thing about the characters is that they
are all passive in the face of reality and just endure. This shows the unique
nature of Endô's understanding of Christianity. In a sense, *Bara no Yakata*
(*A House Surrounded by Roses*) is a variation of *Chinmoku* (*Silence*) on a
smaller scale.

Endô's approach so far has been dualistic. He places Catholicism on one
side and the intellectual and spiritual climate of Japan, which he regards as
a spiritual marsh, on the other. However, this sort of dualistic approach is
more difficult in Japan than in Europe, because from olden times, the
Japanese have been receptive to many different ideas quite regardless of
their logical contradicion of one another. This explains why some people
are not very satisfied with Endô's interpretation of the material he has used
in his novels, for example, in *Chinmoku* (*Silence*). Ôoka Shôhei (a writer)
has said, "The motives for apostasy which Endô gives the priests of
Chinmoku (*Silence*) are not convincing enough to overcome the secular
criticism that it is a mere illusion to justify the cowardice of apostates".
Another person, Sasabuchi Yûichi finds Rodorigo "arrogant" because he
compares his own suffering, which leads to apostasy, to the sufferings of
Christ. I also feel that it is necessary for Endô, in order to develop further

as a writer, to examine this dualistic approach more closely. It is possible that a different image of God from that existing in Europe, arising from the different spiritual climate of Japan, may also be a sound and valuable concept.

Enji Fumiko

Enji Fumiko was born in 1905 in Asakusa, Tokyo. Her father Ueda Kazutoshi was a professor of Tokyo University and a famous expert on Japanese. Because of such a family background, she read Japanese classics from her childhood. She was particularly influenced by the decadent aestheticism which dominates the novels, woodprints and plays of the late Edo period, and liked to indulge in daydreams of a sensual nature. She enjoyed strange sadistic and masochistic daydreams from her early childhood, a characteristic linking her with Mishima Yukio. Their writing also shows certain similarities. They later became sympathetic supporters of one another. Enji entered Japan Women's University but left it without graduating from it. She was interested in the theatre, and through it she came to be associated with the leftist movements then in vogue. In 1928 her first play *Banshun Sôya* (*A Noisy Night in Late Spring*) was staged at the Tsukiji Little theatre. In 1930 she married Enji Yoshimatsu who was a newspaper reporter. She then gave up writing plays and turned to writing novels. However, in the prewar period and during the war she did not publish much. It was after she had developed cancer of the womb, and had been deprived of her sexual ability through an operation that she became really productive as a sensuous aesthetic writer. Her realization that she had become "a strange monster who is neither woman nor man", as she put it, removed rational restraint from her and made freer literary expression possible. Her long novel *Onna-zaka* (*The Female Slope*, 1953–1957) depicts the life of an intelligent woman who, as the wife of an influential official of the Meiji Government, has endured her husband's lewd polygamous life and who takes revenge on him shortly before her death. It is a powerful work. Her long autobiographical trilogy beginning with *Shu o Ubau Mono* (*The Vermilion Pilferer,* 1955) depicts the life of an intelligent and sensual woman who, although unsatisfied with her husband, still continues the life of a housewife. In the background of the novel is depicted the destiny of Japan marching toward the Second World War. In 1970 Enji was awarded the Tanizaki Jun'ichirô Prize for this novel.

Enji has written intellectual realistic works such as the ones mentioned above. They are impressive works. However, her best novels are those, such as *Yô* (*Enchantress,* 1956), *Nisei no En. Shûi* (*The Two Worlds, Gleanings*), *Onna-omote* (*A Woman's Mask,* 1958), *Futa-omote* (*Two Matching Faces,* 1959) and *Namamiko Monogatari* (*Tale of an Enchantress*), which create a unique artistic world of fantasy and mystery by combining images taken from classical Japanese literature with the somewhat perverted sensuality of contemporary men and women. She has created in these works a unique type of woman whose strong ego prevents her from being wholly absorbed by the men to whom she is strongly attracted physically, who hates men spiritually, who dominates men not by any action but by her ability to possess other people as a spirit, and takes revenge on them.

Enji is the most cultured aesthetic woman writer of present-day Japan, and is still very active as a writer.

ENJI Fumiko
Namamiko monogatari *(Tale of an enchantress)*
Published in *Koe,* January 1959–January 1961.

(Synopsis) *Tale of an Enchantress* opens with the sentence, "During the reign of the Emperor Ichijô, there were two empresses."

The Emperor Ichijô married at the age of eleven the eldest daughter of Michitaka, the Lord Keeper of the Privy Seal. His new empress, Empress Teishi, who had just reached her 16th birthday, had inherited her mother's artistic nature. She was excellent at poetry, calligraphy, and at playing the harp and the cither. However, she was a modest person and had no wish of showing off her unusual ability. She was a person who combined in herself the brightness of early cherry blossoms with the subdued fragrance of plum blossoms. She behaved with indescribable grace. Probably because he was feeling shy towards the empress who was five years older than himself, the young emperor, even when they went to bed together, just talked with her in a leisurely manner. However, before long, her slim graceful neck, hands, legs, and her graceful demeanour, which reminded him of a willow tree, started exerting a strong sensuous hold on his mind. He started saying things like, "I like sleeping, leaning my cheek against Teishi's cool round snow-white breasts which contain red buds like those of a peony", without blushing. Michinaga who had been appointed by his brother Michitaka to the post in charge of looking after the Empress had been keeping a close eye on her. When he heard this remark of the young Emperor, Michinaga realized that he himself had been made extremely curious about, or almost attracted, by the Empress. He thought that she must be an exceptionally beautiful lady. It was quite natural that for the Emperor Ichijô, Teishi, who had been his first woman, remained his most beloved woman throughout his life. Michinaga who had a great thirst for power and who was hoping to marry his own daughter to the Emperor some day observed the Emperor and Teishi carefully. He wanted his own daughter to be loved by the Emperor more than Teishi.

Michinaga in due course became the Civil Dictator. He tried various schemes to alienate the Empress Teishi from the Emperor. When the Emperor's mother Higashi-sanjô-in was haunted by a ghost, it was rumoured that it was the live ghost of Teishi. When the Emperor visited his afflicted mother, he saw that the ghost who had possessed a medium cursed his mother in a tone of voice which was exactly like that of Teishi. The gestures of the possessed medium were also reminiscent of Teishi. The Emperor found the scene very uncanny, but when he saw Teishi's innocent face, his doubts about her were dispelled, and their relationship became even more affectionate and intimate. The medium, Miwa no Ayame, had in fact imitated the Empress Teishi's voice and behaviour using the information she had acquired from her sister Kureha who was a lady-in-waiting at the palace. Everything had been planned by Michinaga. Michinaga came to realize that he could not alienate Teishi from the Emperor. He was afraid that Teishi's brothers, Korechika and Takaie, might ascend to power once Teishi gave birth to a prince. He exiled both of them, taking advantage of a trivial fault they had committed. Korechika and Takaie resisted the order, using the Empress Teishi, who was staying at her parents' house to give birth to a child, as a hostage, but finally they were forcibly separated from Teishi and banished from the capital. Overwhelmed by sorrow, Teishi cut off her hair, sent it to the Emperor, and became a nun. The Emperor's sorrow knew no end. Michinaga was worried lest the Emperor's sorrow lead to an unexpected outcome, and he hurriedly changed the place nearer to the capital than the original one. Although Teishi had become a nun, the Emperor missed her so much that she finally returned to the palace as the Empress. The Emperor loved her even more strongly than before. Teishi had lost all her supporters. Noblemen would not dare to come near her because they were afraid of the power and disapproval of Michinaga. She was really isolated. The helplessness of her position, however, made the Emperor pity her and love her even more. After having given birth to a princess, Teishi bore a prince.

Michinaga made his daughter Shôshi, who had only just become twelve years old, an Imperial consort. The ceremony for her bridal entry into court was full of splendour. Michinaga made Shôshi an Empress, too. Although Teishi was nominally an Empress one rank higher than Shôshi, all the courtiers flocked around Shôshi. There were few people who supported Teishi and a desolate atmosphere prevailed in her palace, but the Emperor continued to love Teishi who had been his consort for almost ten years. When he played the flute accompanied by Teishi's harp, his flute-playing sounded different and conveyed the ecstasy of perfect love. Mickinaga again started scheming to alienate Teishi from the Emperor. Soon the Empress Shôshi started being haunted by a ghost. It was again rumoured that the ghost was the live ghost of Empress Teishi which came to curse Empress Shôshi every night. At the time Kureha, Teishi's lady-in-waiting had suddenly disappeared. When the Emperor visited Shôshi, the ghost possessed the medium, and said, "I am always in love with His

Majesty, but I have not the slightest wish to curse Empress Shôshi." This medium was Kureha. Michinaga's plan was to make her feign before the Emperor the possession of the live ghost of Teishi and have her utter curses on Shôshi, but this time the live ghost of Teishi really possessed Kureha for the first time. Michinaga's plan was baffled by Teishi's devoted love to the Emperor.

Soon Teishi gave birth to her third child, and died immediately afterwards. Emperor Ichijô lamented her death bitterly, and payed an unprecedented Imperial visit to her parental house to see her corpse. Indeed Empress Teishi was the only woman of the age who could with her beauty and attractive personality withstand the power of Michinaga.

Fujieda Shizuo

Fujieda Shizuo was born in 1908 in Skizuoka Prefecture. His real name is Katsumi Jirô. He is a practising eye doctor at Hamamatsu, Shizuoka Prefecture. During the war he worked as the chief eye specialist of a Navy hospital. While he was a student of the Eighth Higher School in Nagoya, he became good friends with Hirano Ken and Honda Shûgo who were to become leading literary critics of postwar Japan. It was Fujieda who first kindled a strong interest in literature in his two friends who were living in the same school boarding house with him. Fujieda himself, however, did not change his original intention to give preference to medicine rather than to literature, entered Chiba Medical School, and for a long time concentrated on his activities as a doctor. Fujieda's favorite author was Shiga Naoya, and he regarded masculine moral "I" novels as the highest form of literature. After the war, in 1947, encouraged by Hirano, Honda and others he published his first novel, *Michi* (*Road*). He was already forty years old. After that, in his spare time, he continued to write novels at a slow pace, and published them in the magazine, *Kindai Bungaku*, with which Hirano and Honda were associated. The solid realistic quality of Fujieda's writings and a unique "medical" way of looking at things attracted the attention of the journalistic world. He gradually came to be regarded as one of the important writers of serious literature in Japan although there was nothing showy about him. Recently he has published bold experimental novels which indicate that he has made great progress as a writer.

To deal briefly with his more recent works *Iperitto Gan* (*Mustard Gas and Eye Disease,* 1949) which deals with the problems accompanying the production of poisonous gas during the war and *Inu no Chi* (*Blood of a Dog,* 1957) which takes its subject matter from a medical experiment, are memorable for evoking an uncanny atmosphere using a neat style and orthodox technique of writing. Fujieda has also written *Kyôto Tsuda Sanzô* (*Tsuda Sanzô, the Assassin*) which depicts the failure of an idealistic youth who attempted to assassinate the Russian crown prince then visiting a rather hostile and gloomy Japan. This novel is a solid realistic novel.

Fujieda who had been a typical "I" novel writer with a strong moral concern, began in his old age to use the techniques of the "I" novel in a parodying manner and started to produce, instead of moral "I" novels like those of Shiga Naoya, works which express boldly repressed perverted sexual desire or abnormal sexuality. Among them are *Kûki Atama* (*Air Brain*) and the serial *Gongu Jôdo* (*Seeking to Enter Paradise*) which depicts the problems of death, Buddhism and sex from the point of view of an old man, in a manner which is at once both stoic and decadent. Fujieda is a strange writer in whose works the physiological realism characteristic of a doctor, subconscious sexual desire and guilt feeling, and Confucian stoicism are combined and present a unified whole.

FUJIEDA Shizuo
Kuki atama *(Air brain)*
Published in *Gunzô,* August 1967.

(**Synopsis**) It was already dark when I arrived back at the tiny station after going pinetree viewing. During the train journey I was aware that a dry sound of a moth beating its wings had started echoing in my head as the train vibrated. I was also aware that the upper half of my field of vision had started becoming indistinct. I thought that my usual symptoms had begun to manifest themselves. When I opened the front door of my house, I was able to recognize M, the big-eyed girl, as I had expected to do. I sighed, and shoved her out of my way. I hastened to the surgery, took out the apparatus for sending air into the head which I had invented, and started disinfecting the syringe, which was hardly one millimetre long in diameter. This syringe had to be fitted into the head of the apparatus.

I invented this apparatus, taking my inspiration from a device used to cause artificial pneumothorax. The idea is that you insert the syringe along the eyeball into the bottom of the brain, pump in air between the pituitary gland and the optic nerve and create a cavity. First I paralysed the conjunctiva, and made the difficult insertion which required great skill, and then I turned on the air. My vision blacked out, my senses became dull, and pure ecstasy started spreading from behind my ears. Oh, how I detest that rotten part deep down in my skull which is trying to induce me into the shameful world of upper-half blindness.

It was roughly three years after my wife's illness had begun that my field of vision became rather strange. It was towards the end of the war and I was working at a naval hospital. It was an age when everything was abnormal. I did not take the strangeness of my vision seriously. I just regarded it as a symptom of overtiredness. At that time I was in love with A, a nineteen-year-old nurse. We made love in the air-raid shelter or in the X-ray room. Since A had attained a high degree of sexual maturity despite her young age, she could give me wonderful pleasure. Fascinated by her passionate body, I made love to her almost every day. A soon started coming to our meeting place without wearing pants. After making love to her, I would feel that I had done something really substantial and good. After the war, it no longer remained a secret that A was my mistress. Our relationship continued until my sexual appetite began to ebb conspicuously. Defeated by A's body, I escaped to the house of my wife's parents.

Before long, I opened a surgery in a medium-sized city along the Tôkaido highway. Then I came to have an affair with B, a twenty-five-year-old war widow. However, B soon began to despise me for my poor sexual performance. I wanted to regain my sexual ability by some means or other and to conquer her with my body. I started to search for suitable means. B came to approach me only when the upper half of my visual field was blacked out, that is, only when my sexual appetite was abnormally aroused. I started to collect literature on sex starting from the oldest texts. I also started studying tonics, trying to get useful information from my fellow doctors. In my study I came across a funny Chinese phrase which taught me that human excrement was a cure for low sexual ability in men. Following the ancient method, I made various medicines from human waste. On the pretext that I was doing some valuable research, I placed a lot of bamboo pipes inside the toilets of a junior high school.

Chinese medicine did not mislead me: in one year's time I could collect from these bamboo pipes "golden juice" which was as clear and beautiful as morning dew. Trembling with joy and a certain anxiety, I tasted a few drops of the gemlike juice. Immediately the upper half of my field of vision was blacked out. That night my spirit and my penis sang and danced about for joy, and B squeaked like a monstrous bird. I conquered B completely and I lived happily for three years. Then I noticed a strange thing. B was beginning to emit a faint smell of excrement from her skin, although she was becoming more and more beautiful and charming. Soon I could no longer endure the smell, and started to keep away from B. I also threw away the medicine.

One night at a cabaret show, I was watching B, when my body started floating upwards like a bubble until I became stuck against the cold ceiling. I could look down and see the whole of the large interior of the cabaret. Every sound vanished, my skull became empty, the upper half blindness was gone, and a feeling of joy and satisfaction began to surge up in my heart. When your mind becomes free, you can see everything. The experience of empty headedness on that night led me to invent air-therapy for the brain. Thanks to this therapy, I have been liberated from sex and have attained spiritual fulfilment similar to the enlightenment talked of in Zen Buddhism. I am intending to fill every part of my brain with air, and ascend to Heaven as an air-brained man.

Fukazawa Shichiro

Fukuzawa Shichirô occupies a very peculiar position among Japanese writers. Apart from the fact that after quitting a middle school without completing the course he became an apprentice in a chemist's shop, and that he has been a guitarist who had wandered all over Japan, he is very unusual among modern Japanese writers in that he has produced novels which were inspired by his intimacy with the world of folklore and tradition. What we find in his novels is neither the self-consciousness of an "I" novel writer, nor the struggles with feudalism typical of an intellectual. In short, his novels are not primarily concerned with modern problems. Rather, they depict, from the point of view of the common people, the world of local traditions and taboos which he found in Yamanashi Prefecture where he was born.

Narayamabushi-kô (*The Oak Mountain Song,* 1956, translated by Keene, Donald, "The Old Woman, the Wife and the Archer", pp. 3–50, New York, Viking, 1961), which was awarded the Chûô Kôron New Writers' Prize in 1956, is interesting for its uniqueness. It is based on the tradition of abandoning old women. In a mountain village of Shinshû (present Nagano Prefecture) where Orin, the heroine of the novel, lives, there is a custom, due to the shortage of food, that when one becomes seventy years old, one has to leave for Oak Mountain beyond the seven valleys and three ponds. Orin is now sixty-nine, and is making preparations for this. Since her eldest son has managed to find his second wife, there is nothing left for her to desire. Encouraged by her, her eldest son unwillingly and half-weeping carries her on his back, and climbs the mountain along the dark path. At Oak Mountain, there are piles of corpses and bones, and some birds are preying on them. After making her son go, Orin sits stoically behind a rock. It has started snowing. Looking like a white fox in the snow, Orin repeats the *Nenbutsu* (a short invocation to Buddha), while gazing fixedly into space. This is a rough outline of the novel. It goes without saying that the novel gave a strong impetus to the Japanese literary world to be concerned afresh with problems like "What are the indigenous ways of thought of Japan?" and "What are the traditions of Japan?" It is very significant that the author's detached descriptions have once again brought some hidden basic elements of Japanese thought into general consciousness.

The next year he wrote *Tôhoku no zummutachi* (*A Tale from Tôhoku*, 1957). The hero of this novel is a man called Risuke. In his village second-born, or third-born sons are called "yakko" (servants) and are not treated as full-fledged human beings. Risuke is one of them. On top of that, he has very bad breath. Everybody looks at him with contempt. In his village, they say that if you eat a mushroom called "rikôbô" (the wise one), you will be cured of every type of disease. Risuke is looking for this mushroom. When the owner of the "triangular residence" in the village dies, he leaves a will which says that his wife should receive every *Yakko* of the village as a bridegroom for a night. This is meant to be an atonement for the sin of his father who had killed a *Yakko*. In fulfillment of his will, the wife calls one *Yakko* to her house every night, but somehow Risuke's turn never comes. This distresses Risuke. His elder brother takes pity on him, and says that he will offer his own wife instead. However, it is not Risuke's sister-in-law who comes to him, but an old woman of the village. She says she will spend a night with him to console him. Just like *Narayama-bushi-kô* (*The Oak Mountains Song*), this is a work which tries to depict some characteristic features of Japanese indigenous culture.

Next, Fukazawa published *Fuefuki-gawa* (*The River Fuefuki*, 1958). This novel depicts the vicissitudes of a farmer's family, nicknamed "Gitchon Kago" (Gitchon Basket), which lives at the side of the River Fuefuki which flows between Kôfu and Isawa. The events depicted in the novel take place during the sixty or seventy years which cover the birth of Takeda Shingen (a general, 1521–1573) and the death of Takeda Katsuyori (Shingen's son, 1546–1582). There are a lot of deaths depicted in the novel, and its plot is altogether ruthlessly un-sentimental. The idea of the migration of souls which it uses is also worth noticing.

Fukazawa published *Fûryû Mutan* (*An Elegant Fantasy*) in 1960. This work, however, scandalized many right-wing people who thought that its treatment of the imperial family showed a grave lack of respect. This even resulted in a terrorist action, making a political issue of the novel. Afterwards Fukazawa returned to his life of wandering.

In 1968, Fukazawa published, after a long silence, *Yôjutsuteki Kako* (*The Magical Past*). Unlike his previous works, it has a contemporary setting, and in this respect its world is neither that of ordinary folklore nor of local tradition. The hero of this novel is a man called Kinji who has recently been expelled from the house by his wife. He stands absent-mindedly, looking down at the wintry town which looms before him in the fog, remembering past days. When he was working as an assistant of the automobile driver who owned the only automobile in town, Kinji drove the car without a driving licence, and injured a coach-horse. He had to pay damages. Afterwards he happened to meet a woman in a bar who was the daughter of the coach-owner's neighbour. He came to be acquainted with her and finally married her. Kinji's father did not like this daughter-in-law, and attributed their marriage to the curse of *batô kannon*, the guardian deity of horses. After Kinji was drafted into the army, his wife was killed in an air-raid. Kinji married again, this time to a woman who had looked after his younger brother at the house of an army comrade where he had stayed after riding there on horseback. On his wedding day, Kinji's father saw, on the glass of a sliding-partition, the shadow of Kinji's second wife which was like a horse's shadow. When Kinji's son by his second wife grew up, he caused a traffic accident. When Kinji went to the police station to settle the matter, he saw the shadow of a horse's head on the frosted glass there. He realized that it was the shadow of his wife. When he told his wife this, she became angry with him, and told him to clear out. Now he was looking down at the lights of the city, remembering all these things.—This is a rough outline of the novel. Although it has a contemporary setting, it contains one strange factor, that is, the connection between horses and human beings. The reason why this novel centres around the figure of *batô kannon*, the guardian deity of horses, is that the author wants to transpose the world of folklore and magic on to the realistic surface of a novel. That Kinji's wife suddenly becomes rebellious and tells Kinji to clear out when he has mentioned the shadow of a horse he saw at the police station, means that she is also a supernatural being, as Kinji comes to realize. This novel takes the reader into a weird world somewhat like that of a ghost story before he has time to realize it. It is a sort of contemporary folktale, somewhat akin to an orally transmitted story.

In order to understand the ideas expressed in Fukazawa's works, we must remember his intimacy with the local traditions. At the same time, we must not forget that he is an excellent guitarist, if we want to understand the form of his novels. In his dialogue with Kaikô Ken (a writer), Fukazawa has said, touching on the forms of music, "In music one melody usually appears twice in succession at the opening. Then comes another melody. At the end, however, the first melody appears again". Fukazawa added that he had used such a musical form in *Narayamabushi-kô* (*The Oak Mountain Song*). Fukazawa Shichirô's works have a close tie with the ancient forms of oral literature (as opposed to written literature). This is readily understandable, when we remember that he plays a guitar to accompany folksongs, and that he writes novels as if they were folksongs. In this lies the key for understanding his writing. This is also the reason why he is now farming, playing the guitar and writing novels as if they formed one mode of life.

Fukuda Tsuneari

Fukuda Tsuneari was born in Tokyo 1912, and graduated from the English Literature Department of Tokyo University. He started writing plays even before entering the university. He was also keenly interested in D. H. Lawrence. Roughly from the time of his graduation, he turned to literary criticism. His critical essays on the proletarian literature of that time or on the "Ich Roman" (or the "I" novel in vogue in modern Japan), essays which he published one after another, are based on the author's solid knowledge of Modern European Literature. These essays won him wide recognition.

After the war, he continued to be active as a unique critic. His criticism was not restricted to the field of literature. He wrote social criticism too. His critical spirit can also be seen in his plays. *Saigo no Kirifuda* (*The Last Trump*, 1948), *Kitty Taifû* (*Typhoon Kitty*, 1950), *Ryû o Nadeta Otoko* (*The Man Who Stroked a Dragon*, 1952), *Gendai no Eiyû* (*A Hero of Modern Time*, 1952) and others, are a series of satirical comedies which are distinguished by wit and paradox reminiscent of Aldous Huxley. In 1956 he published *Meian* (*Light and Darkness*) which is a modern verse play somewhat in the style of T. S. Eliot. This play occasioned a controversy over verse drama. (In fact, his plays have provoked many controversies in the theatrical world of postwar Japan).

After that, he started to translate the complete works of Shakespeare into modern Japanese. He was stimulated to undertake this work after seeing performances of Shakespearean plays in England during his tour abroad. It took him roughly ten years to complete his translation; the complete works of Shakespeare in Japanese were then published in fifteen volumes.

While he was working on this translation, he wrote a modern-style *Hamlet*. He also published two historical plays, *Akechi Mitsuhide* (1957) and *Arima Ôji* (*Prince* Arima, 1961), using *Macbeth* as his model, and tried to create ties between traditional *kabuki* actors and the actors of modern drama. He was always a pioneer. In 1963, he left the theatre group Bungaku Za, and established the Gendai Engeki Kyôkai (The Contemporary Drama Association). He also established a theatre troupe called Kumo (Cloud) attached to this association. Ever since, he has been enthusiastically engaged in theatrical activities. He has also been trying to foster an exchange of ideas and experiences with foreign producers.

Recently his utterances, literary and social, have been addressed to an increasingly wide range of people. In the theatrical field, he has started a troupe called Keyaki (Zelkova-tree) which is intended for a wider circle and thus has a relatively high degree of popularity.

Among his recent plays are a comedy *Okumanchôja Fujin* (*The Millionairess*, 1967) which is an adaptation of Bernard Shaw's play of the same title, *Wakatte Tamaruka!* (*You Can't Understand It!*, 1968) which is based on a current event, and *Sôtô Imada Shisezu* (*Hitler Is Still Alive*, 1970), an excellent comedy, which satirically depicts the false image people have of tyrants by transferring the discussion of genuine works and fakes from the field of art into the political field.

FUKUDA Tsuneari
Sôtô imada shisezu—a play in three acts.
(Hitler is still alive)
Published in *Bessatsu Bungei Shunjû*, Summer 1970.

(Synopsis)   *Time*: the present.
The Place: a room of the flat where a mysterious woman in her forties called Fujii Yumeko and a German man called Adolf Bormann, who is almost seventy years old, are living together.
(Act I)   One morning, a middle aged man who says that he is a reporter called Mizumaki comes to this flat. He surprises Yumeko who answers the door by saying that he would like to see Adolf Hitler, the Führer of the Third Reich of Germany. They start arguing about the last days of Hitler. Mizumaki is not only well versed in the Russian documents testifying to the last days of Hitler made at that time, he also knows that Yumeko lived in Shanghai during the war, that she escaped to Austria via Hongkong shortly before Japan's surrender, and that it was there that she came to know Bormann, an ex-bodyguard of Hitler, who had escaped from Berlin. Mizumaki asserts that Bormann was disguised as Hitler in order to protect the Fuhrer during the last few years of the Nazi regime. He also maintains, using rhetoric characteristic of him, that it is in such a counterfoil that people can find an apt symbol of the great Fuhrer whom they

will adore for ever. He discloses that he is an official of a secret society called the F. A. (Führer-Anbetung), a society of people who adore Hitler. Then he introduces his comrades, the members of the F. A., who have been waiting outside the door.

The six members of this society, among whom is a German woman called Helga, have been performing a series of plays with the collective title *The Führer Game* once a week under Mizumaki's direction. In this, Hitler, Göring, Göbbels and his wife, Eva Braun, Mussolini and others appear. The group wants to develop this into a world-wide movement headed by Bormann. Bormann, who has been having occasional fits of the "Führer disease", now comes to be convinced by the skillful suggestion of Mizumaki that he really was Hitler's "dummy", and this saddens Yumeko. Then one of the members brings news that he has met a man called Hermann Schmidt, who says that it was he who acted as Hitler's stand-in. Bormann solemnly declares that he is going to interrogate him to see whether this is the truth or not. Everybody salutes him in the Nazi style.

(Act II)   After the members of F. A. leave, Yumeko entreats Bormann to go to a quiet place to cure himself of illusions of grandeur, but Bormann is too absorbed in acting Hitler to listen to her. Then Mizumaki arrives with Schmidt, and the two "dummies" confront one another. Each of them furiously tries to prove that it was he who acted as Hitler's dummy. At one stage Schmidt seems to be winning with his representation of Hitler, but at this point Mizumaki says that an impostor who is casual enough to look like the genuine person is much more genuine than a genuine person who is theatrical enough to look like an impostor, and thanks to this remark Bormann comes to be acknowledged as the genuine dummy and symbol of Hitler. The confrontation of the two "dummies" is gradually assimilated into *The Führer Game* and finally even Yumeko begins to take a part in this play. Mizumaki's plan has succeeded completely.

(Act III)   On the evening of the same day, the members of the F. A. discuss the parts they are going to take in *The Führer Game* to be performed that evening. Meanwhile Bormann, his wife and Schmidt, who have been given sleeping pills, are asleep. The aim of performing *The Führer Game* this particular evening is to show that Bormann is in fact the real Führer. *The Führer Game* on this occasion consists of four acts describing the main events in the last four months of Hitler's life. When everyone has finished dressing up, Bormann, who is dressed up as Hitler, and Yumeko, who is dressed up as Junge's wife appear, and the ingenious play begins.

This play first depicts the tragedy of Hitler as a nihilist who adores motherhood; then it shows how the news of Roosevelt's death was received as an indication that the Nazis would enjoy a miraculous reversal of fortune as their ancestor, Friedrich the Great, had done. After that, the play proceeds to show scenes depicting the declaration to defend Berlin to the last and the treachery of Göring. The last scene is going to show Hitler's marriage to Eva and his suicide on the 29th of April 1945 at the air-raid shelter of his official residence. The contents of this scene are as follows:

Bormann is afraid of being killed as a Hitler substitute and he tried to escape with Junge's wife (Yumeko). However, the real Führer (played by Schmidt at Mizumaki's direction) appears and commands them to commit suicide with him. Bormann, who is acting as stand-in for Hitler in Hitler's marriage to Eva, discloses to her in the midst of the wedding that he is only a stand-in. Then Eva drinks poison because of her betrayed love for Hitler and dies, and Bormann shoots to death Hitler played by Schmidt.

When the play is over, Mizumaki says that the real person would not conform to the image people have of him to the extent that his imitator and stand-in would, and therefore, that Bormann, whose representation of Hitler does not conform to their image of Hitler perfectly, must in fact, be the real Hitler. He makes the others perform the climax again to confirm this point. Thus Mizumaki has succeeded in creating a perfect embodiment of Hitler—a symbol of the desires of the mass. Now Bormann as the real Führer, phoenix-like, gives a speech on the world-wide mission of the German people, and the members of F. A. answer by chanting his slogans. In the background is heard a broadcast advertizing a special sale.

Fukunaga Takehiko

Fukunaga Takehiko was born in Fukuoka Prefecture in Kyûshû. When he was in a middle grade of primary school, his family moved to Tokyo. He entered the First High School, and then studied at the Department of French Literature of Tokyo University. Ever since his high school days, his poems, novels and literary criticism have appeared in various magazines. He was interested in Baudelaire, Mallarmé, Rimbaud and Lautréamont and studied them in depth. Since he had suffered from poor health since childhood, he escaped military service. After graduation, he worked for the Japan-Italy Association and the Japanese Broadcasting Corporation. He became a pupil of Hori Tatsuo who was living in Karuizawa, and even during the war years he was absorbed in studying literature of the "art for art's sake" type, which rose above the petty concerns of the world. Because of this he acquired an extensive knowledge of literature, particularly of Western literature. This was rather rare among the Japanese writers of his generation. During the war, he formed, together with Nakamura Shin'ichirô, Katô Shûichi and others, a group called *Matinée Poétique*, and studied various forms of Japanese poetry and experimented with regular rhymed verse. After the war, this group published a collection of essays titled *1946 Bungakuteki Kôsatsu* (*Literary Observations of the Year 1946*), and Fukunaga attracted attention for his vast erudition and for his sharp power of analysis. In 1946 his first book, *Tô* (*Tower*), was published. In this work Fukunaga experimented with various techniques of writing, and expressed gloomy ideas about life; with this he made a brilliant entry into the literary arena as a postwar writer. He got T.B., however, and was obliged to spend seven years as a patient. During this period he worked on his long novel *Fûdo* (*Climate*) which depicts the fate of a painter with his love and loneliness. He completed it after working on it for ten years and published it in 1952. The seven years Fukunaga spent to recover his health gave him the ability to look at reality from the point of view of

the dead, and led him to write *Kusa no Hana* (*Flower of Grass*, 1954), a long
novel; *Meifu* (*Hades*, 1954), which together with *Yoru no Jikan* (*Hours of
the Night*, 1955), and another work, forms a trilogy dealing with the consciousness of darkness; and *Haishi* (Abandoned Town, 1960) which depicts a decaying town in Fukunaga's native area and expresses his mental
state through it. *Sekai no Owari* (*The End of the World*, 1959) brilliantly
evokes a schizophrenic image of the fall of the world. Although Fukunaga's works are gloomy and dark, there is something lyrical and sweet
about them. At the same time, they are well-told stories. Especially among
young women, Fukunaga has enthusiastic supporters. His essays on love
and loneliness are also widely read. Fukunaga writes poems, too. He is
also a scholar who has published works of real academic merit, such as,
Bôdorêru no Sekai (*The World of Baudelaire*, 1947) and *Gôgyan no Sekai* (*The
World of Gauguin*, 1961). Fukunaga, who is well versed in world literature, and who has such wide interests, (including the writing of detective
stories), is a real dilettante in the good sense of the word. He is a conscientious champion of art for art's sake, who is trying to keep the Japanese
artistic tradition alive in the context of the Western style modern literature
of Japan.

Fukunaga Takehiko
Bôkyaku no kawa (*River of forgetfulness*)
Published by Shinchôsha in May 1964.

(Synopsis) I am writing this down because I am in this room and because I have discovered something here. I do not know whether that
something is my past, or a way of living, or a fate. I may have discovered
a story. This room is the room of a shabby flat. I could almost call this
room my room, but not a hundred per cent so. The woman disappeared
somewhere, but even after that I often come to this room to idle away
the time. I am the president of a company which I founded after toiling
for many years after the war. Business is not bad, but I have definitely lost

that energy and vitality which I had ten years ago, that is, before my wife
fell ill. I often forget the present and find myself in the gray muddy stream
of time past. This state of affairs started on the morning following that
stormy day when, getting out of my car, I looked up at the ten-storied
building in front of me. Every window of the building became an eye,
and looked at me. "Have you forgotten? Can you live without remembering it? We are watching you", these windows said innocently.

I remember myself as a robot, who was running as fast as possible in a
shower on a battlefield in the South Seas Area. I was running to give the
last cup of water to another robot, my fellow soldier, before he died. He
was a lively fellow and would say, "I will return to Japan alive by any
means, since my beloved wife is waiting for me there." When I reached
the place where he was, however, I found that he was already dead with
both his eyes wide open. I wonder what he saw at the moment of his
death. I should have died in his stead.

I found a young woman writhing in pain in the heavy rain on that
stormy night. She was an utter stranger, but somehow she reminded me
of the woman I had loved but from whom I had cowardly run away. My
regret for having done so induced me to help this woman whom I did
not know. I placed her in my car, and drove her to a flat. Her pains did
not subside. I called an ambulance by public telephone, and accompanied
her to a hospital. She said that I was a kind person. My wife and my
daughters, Misako and Kayoko, think that I am cold-hearted, so why did
I show such kindness to a stranger on that stormy night? The memory of
the sanatorium where I spent some of my student days comes back to me.
I had taken part in a left-wing movement but things had not gone well
and I was thinking of starving myself to death there. "Why don't you
eat anything? It's not good for you", a young nurse reproached me in a
singsong voice, and looked at me with her beautiful big eyes. This innocent nurse who had come from a lonely village on the Japan Sea coast
gave me new hope in life. I loved her. We walked together along the path
of a grove when the leaves of the trees had turned to autumn colours. We
embraced each other in the annexe of a farm-house which had originally
been a silk-worm-rearing room. She said to me, "I love you. I wish I

could die while I am in your arms. I will surely die when you have gone."
The day for me to leave the sanatorium finally came. I firmly promised
her to marry her. I told her that I would come to fetch her without fail
and that I would never let her go home without marrying me. I was in
earnest. I really promised to marry her without any intention of breaking
my promise. When I came back to Tokyo, however, I found that another
match had been arranged for me by my parents. They were opposed to
my marrying the nurse. I could not very well ignore the wishes of my
adoptive parents who had kindly brought me up. I wrote to the girl, explaining the circumstances, and apologizing to her. She did not reply. A
week before my wedding I went to the sanatorium to see her, but I was
told that she had quit her job long before and had gone home. I went to
visit her home. It was in a tiny fishing village. The seashore was covered
with stones. I could not find her in the house where I had expected to see
her. A woman who looked like her mother sternly looked at me and said
that, unable to bear the shame of having become pregnant, she had thrown
herself into the sea and had died.

It seems that by killing her my true self also died, although I was not
killed in the war and have already lived another thirty years. I tried to love
my wife but I could not. When my first son was born, only to die shortly
afterwards, my wife said that I was a cold-hearted person. My daughters
also seem to hate me. The woman whom I helped on that stormy night
said that I was a lonely person. She has also gone away somewhere. I wonder if she is leading a happy life.

I came to this room and searched the pockets of my coat and took out
one tiny stone. It is the stone which I picked up near the spot where she
died: after visiting her home, I had wandered around the cliff from which
she had jumped into the sea. When I held the stone in my hand again,
thousands of thoughts which had then crossed my mind swarmed back
to me, after so many years. This stone is a symbol of my guilt, of my
shame and of my miserable life. I held it in my hand silently for some
time, and then threw it into the ditch. The water rippled gently for a
while, and then became still again.

(Note) This is a chapter from *Bôkyaku no Kawa* (*River of Forgetfulness*).

Bôkyaku no Kawa (*River of Forgetfulness*) consists of seven chapters in which one member of a family (the hero of the chapter here summarized, his daughter Misako, Kayoko his wife, and others in turn) discloses the secrets and doubts of his innermost heart in a first-person narrative.

Funabashi Seiichi

Funabashi Seiichi was born in Honjo, Tokyo. His father, son of a Confucian scholar, was a professor of Architecture of the Technology Faculty of Tokyo University. His mother was the daughter of a business man. In Funabashi, who was the eldest son, puritanic Confucian *Yamanote* (high-class residential area of Tokyo) elements from his father and artistic, more relaxed *shitamachi* (the merchants' and craftsmen's area of old Tokyo) elements from his mother coexist side by side. Temperamentally he was attracted to the atmosphere surrounding his mother and her family. Funabashi was brought up as the son of a wealthy family. He loved the theatre from his childhood, and aspired to be a dramatist. Through his theatrical activities, he also came in touch with the progressive political ideas of that time. He graduated from Mito Higher School, and then from the Department of Japanese Literature of Tokyo University. At first he wrote modernistic plays. In 1933 he became a member of the group magazine *Kôdô* (*Action*). In 1934 he published the novel *Diving*, purported to champion a literary movement in Japan which would correspond to the movement in France pleading for bold action headed by André Malraux. This attracted much attention. However, the fundamental characteristic of his work seems to lie in his persistent interest in female bodies, as *Bokuseki* (*Miss Dry-as-Dust*, 1938), indicates. His strong point lies in depicting sex and the body in an aesthetic manner. As the war approached, he was frowned upon by the authorities, and could no longer deal with his favorite themes of sex and the body freely. During the war, he concentrated on writing *Shikkaiya Kôkichi* (*Kôkichi, the Dyed-cloth Salesman*, 1945), a masterpiece which depicts the tenacious devotion to his craft on the part of a humble craftsman. After the war, oppressive restrictions on writing were abolished. Society was ready to welcome erotic novels and sensuous uninhibited novels. Funabashi published erotic novels such as *Susono* (*The Base of the Mountain*, 1947) and *Yukifujin Ezu* (*Life Scenes of Lady Yuki*) one after the other, and showed himself to be a real master of this sort of writing. He became one of the most popular writers of Japan. However, it would be a mistake to regard Funabashi merely as a writer of erotic novels with an aesthetic flavour. He is a writer who has a solid knowledge of Japanese classical literature. He also has an uncompromising critical spirit and a strong curiosity about reality. He is an aesthete like Tanizaki Jun'ichirô and Kawabata Yasunari, but he is not fully satisfied with being an aesthete. He is typical of the writers who started writing in the 1930's. Like many of them, he cannot accept the age he lives in and be content in it. He has a vigorous critical spirit, and accordingly his works abound in satirical touches. *Aru Onna no Enkei* (*A Distant View of a Woman*, 1963), which depicts a contemporary scene against the background of the world of Japanese classical literature of the Heian period, *Kagee Nyonin* (*Portrait of a Lady*, 1962) which depicts a writer of popular fiction of the Edo period, and *Sukina Onna no Munekazari* (*The Brooch of the Beloved Woman*, 1967), are among his more recent works which have created a synthesis out of his aestheticism, classical learning and critical spirit.

Funabashi, together with Niwa Fumio, the realistic writer, is one of the most representative writers of present-day Japan. For all his critical spirit, essentially he is an "art-for-art's-sake" writer like Mishima Yukio.

FUNABASHI Seiichi
Aru onna no enkei (*A distant view of a woman*)
Published in *Gunzô*, May 1961.

(**Synopsis**) When the equinoctial week came, Tsunako visited the grave of Iseko, her aunt. Iseko's grave was in the graveyard of a tiny temple in an old castle town, M. It was two or three hours' journey from Tokyo. Tsunako had loved Iseko more than her real mother. Iseko was thirteen years her senior, and was the younger sister of her father. Iseko died when she was barely thirty years old. When Tsunako was only a primary school-girl, she was already very much attached to Iseko. She adored her, and imitated her. Tsunako's father Kutani Shûkichi had been an official of the Prefectural Administration, but was at that time a librarian, and was leading a fairly comfortable life as a salaried man. He liked Iseko, his real sister, more than his wife. Iseko had a delicate neck, and her body was voluptuous. She was a real beauty. She was also well versed in Japanese classical literature of the Heian period. Tsunako used to follow Iseko around all the time, and she was worried about the existence of Izuminaka Monya, the young president of a munitions factory, whom Iseko loved.

When she was nine years old, Izuminaka stole a kiss from Tsunako at a mountain hotspring resort. He told her not to tell anybody about it. The kiss gave Tsunako a sweet ecstasy which was to have a decisive influence on her future life. Tsunako thought that she could not allow her adored Iseko to marry such a lewd person as Izuminaka. Tsunako hated Izuminaka who would probably some day be Iseko's husband. Izuminaka was a father of a child by Tokiko, a geisha girl whose geisha name was Tarômaru. He had been hiding this from Iseko, and when she found out she became hysterical. She threw away all modesty as an intelligent woman, and passion-ately pressed Izuminaka to marry her. Izuminaka was now deeply attracted by Iseko, and they indulged in coarse love-making which even geisha girls would not be willing to do. However, irresolute Izuminaka, black-mailed by Tokiko with suicide, finally married Tokiko. At the same time he kept telling Iseko that she was his only true wife, and continued to make love to her. After the war, when her marriage was arranged by her brother Shûkichi, Iseko committed suicide at the Nekonaki hotspring resort. It was a tremendous blow to Tsunako.

Tsunako met Izuminaka by the side of Iseko's grave. Tsunako had grown up and become a beautiful woman very much like Iseko. Tsunako hated Izuminaka as the person responsible for Iseko's death, but at the same time she could not forget the ecstacy his kiss had aroused in her when she was nine years old. Izuminaka was now a member of the Diet and was an influential politician. Through his mediation she had several interviews with a view to marriage, but every single man she met seemed to her to be less attractive than Izuminaka. Izuminaka, who was a born philanderer, boldly tried to seduce Tsunako. Tsunako's father, Shûkichi, became really upset when he knew this, and desperately tried to dissuade Tsunako from having anything to do with him. However, Izuminaka was now far above him in social status, and Shûkichi could not do anything positive to stop Izuminaka from seducing Tsunako. Tsunako was invited by Izuminaka and his wife Tokiko on a trip to Kyôto to collect mushrooms. During this trip, Tsunako was first seduced by Tokiko, and then by Izuminaka, and she fell for Izuminaka. Overcome by Izuminaka's strange attractiveness, Tsunako, who could not believe his promise to divorce Tokiko and marry her, decided to be content even to be his concubine. Although their relationship was kept secret as Tsunako wished, Izuminaka fulfilled none of his promises.

Izuminaka who was leading a busy life would call Tsunako twice or three times a month to a hotel or to a *machiai* (a place where guests usually send for geisha girls). Sometimes they had a rendezvous at some resort place. Izuminaka was absorbed by Tsunako's charming body. Tsunako did not always accept his love-making. For the slightest reason, she would get excited or her excitement would cool down. When Izuminaka called her "a bitch" or "a slut" in the bedroom, she felt bold and thought that no matter how much she was humiliated by him she would not care. Sometimes Izuminaka entreated her to spit in his face.

Tsunako's parents were half mad when they came to know of the relationship between Izuminaka and Tsunako. Shûkichi was particularly upset that not only his beloved sister Iseko but also his own daughter had fallen victim to Izuminaka. Tsunako, however, forgot everything else when she actually saw Izuminaka and was captured by his charm. She was treading the same path as her aunt Iseko had trodden before her. Tsunako left her parents' house, and came to live in a high-class flat which Izuminaka had rented for her. However, Tokiko kept interfering and finally, persuaded by her parents, Tsunako returned to her parents' house without notifying Izuminaka, and was confined in the house. She read Iseko's diary, and knew that Iseko whom she had adored had had affairs with other men. She was disillusioned. Izuminaka would not leave Tsunako alone. He tried persistently to get her back. Overcome by his seductive charm she once again, with an excited heart, started meeting him secretly.

Haniya Yutaka

Haniya Yutaka was born in 1910 in Hsinchu, Taiwan, where his father was working, and lived there until he became a first-year student of middle school. Although his family register is in Fukushima Prefecture, there is nothing in any of his works which reminds us of Fukushima Prefecture. This is because he spent the whole of his childhood in Taiwan.

In 1927 he entered the preparatory course for Nihon University. He was interested in anarchism, which induced him to take part in a leftist farmers' movement. He was arrested in 1930, and gave up his study at the university. In 1931, he became a member of the Japanese Communist Party, and again took part in a farmers' movement. He was arrested in 1932, and spent more than a year in solitary confinement.

In 1933 he renounced communism and was released from prison. Until Japan's defeat in the war, he was engaged in writing for an economics magazine company. His experiences in these youthful years—participation in a labour movement, solitary confinement, renouncement and release from prison—are an endless source for Haniya's writing.

He established the literary group magazine *Kôsô* (*Conception*) with others, and published in it his aphorisms. *Fugôri Yueni Ware Shinzu—Credo, quia absurdum—(I Believe Because It Is Absurd To Believe—Credo, quia absurdum—)*, and a novel serialized from 1939 to 1941. In the postwar period he became connected with the group magazine *Kindai Bungaku* (*Modern Literature*) whose first number appeared in January 1946. In this magazine he published his long novel *Shiryô* (*Ghosts*) which attracted much attention. However, because of Haniya's heart disease and intestinal tuber-culosis, only the first part was written, and it is still incomplete. It is also a difficult work. Nevertheless it is said to be one of the greatest masterpieces of postwar Japanese literature. This novel attempts with the help of bold imagination to analyze the concept of "a vast single tone which rever-berates throughout the universe". It uses a complicated cumulative tech-nique brilliantly and the main idea is developed very impressively.

After spending several years fighting against illness, Haniya resumed writing in 1955. He wrote literary and political criticism, at which he was quite productive. Around the time of the movement against the Security Treaty with the United States (signed and ratified in 1960), he was the re-presentative of one type of thinking among the postwar generation.

Since then he has concentrated on fiction. His long meditation during his illness has added depth to his writing. His effort to scrutinize the very fountain of life, unfettered by time and space, has found a more attractive literary expression in his recent works. In 1970 he was awarded the Tanizaki Jun'ichirô Prize for *Yami no Naka no Kuroi Uma* (*A Black Horse in the Darkness*).

HANIYA Yutaka
Shin'en *(Abyss)*
Published in *Gunzô*, October 1957.

(Synopsis) I am suffering from a strange dizziness which I myself name "a fainting fit with consciousness". When I am sitting in an armchair, absorbed in thought, suddenly I notice that there is something wrong with the floor on the left side. It starts slanting. Then an invisible disturbance runs through the floor, and it begins shaking. A transparent crack runs across the floor, and suddenly a dark funnel-shaped abyss appears. When I have watched it for a few seconds, I feel a sudden dizziness as if something in my skull were falling into that abyss. My doctor told me that it was probably due to some trouble in my semicircular canals. "But even if we know for certain that there is something wrong with them, we will not be able to decide whether, to speak figuratively, the keeper of the room is dead, or the line is cut off, or something is wrong with the bell itself", the doctor had said. However, I thought it was possible to interpret it in an entirely different way, and replied roughly as follows: "In my semicircular canals, there is an entirely different keeper. The canals are connected by a different line, and a different type of bell is ringing. My dizziness is accompanied by a powerful sense of existence and an attractive sense of freedom. I even have a strange impression that only I am facing naked reality, unveiled. We, human beings, are brought up in different environments and so our experience of freedom is probably very varied".

The doctor asked me to meet a certain patient. I followed him up a gently graded spiral stair case. He took me to the special ophthalmic consultation room, but he left the room immediately. When I am in this state of "a fainting fit with consciousness", everything moves like a tiny shadow-picture dreamily. In such a state I met an old friend of mine who had gone underground several years ago and whose whereabouts were unknown. This man told me that he had contrived to get certified as a mentally ill patient to be used for special research by the doctors, and had been hiding here for several years, as he had been so directed by the party. However one morning they began treating him as a dissenter. He told me that he had attended an inquiry commission that day and had said to the commission, "In an organization people are often accused of certain faults and expelled. But quite often these faults are invented to expel them. Their 'faults' do not come first, but the will to expel them. This much is obvious".

I suggested to him that probably the champions of that foolish commonplace he had pointed out—namely that the members do not really control the organization they belong to but that the organization controls the members—could be defeated by using the logic of the dead. He answered as follows: "The dead who neither misuse anything nor are exploited by anybody are the most suitable destroyers of stiff political hierarchy. Since they are in their graves or in 'empty nothingness' where no measure means anything to them any longer, they can be a match for any opponent however evil and cunning. But the dead cannot enter the world of time".

"I was unwittingly aiming to be like one of the dead", he said, and added that one should not be fascinated by the idea of a suffering "gorilla who had become an observer" —of a "gorilla" who tired of struggle and who clasped his knees together, and looked downcast. He said that one should go back to the political arena with fighting gorillas that had vigorous arms and legs.

With firm steps he walked down the corridor, turned at the end and disappeared from my sight. I met the doctor in front of the spiral stairs. I noticed that his expression had completely changed. I asked him if the inquiry commission had decided what action was to be taken against this old friend of mine. He answered that due to the decision of the commission he was to stay here for ever for the same reason as he came to hide here several years ago, and hinted to me that a gas would be employed which would drive him into genuine insanity, after he had been allowed to breathe it in unwittingly for some time. Watching the doctor descend the stairs, I, in a state of "a fainting fit with consciousness", continued to see some sort of revelation.

Hotta Yoshie

Hotta Yoshie was born in 1918 in Toyama Prefecture. His family was an old family of the district, and his father was a shipping agent. Hotta was the third son. In his childhood Hotta wanted to be a musician, but he later contracted an ear disease and had to give up this idea.

In 1936 he entered the Faculty of Law of Keiô University, but did not read books connected with his speciality. Instead he was absorbed in reading literature and in 1940 changed his major subject to French Literature. During his student days, he joined the group magazine of poetry, *Arechi* (*Waste Land*), and other group magazines and published his poems in them. He was mainly under the influence of the French symbolists. After graduation he worked for the Japan Cultural Society. It was war time, and Japan was closed to the rest of the world, but by working for the Japan Cultural Society, Hotta could keep in touch with what was going on abroad and deepened his interest in China. In the meantime he joined the magazine *Hihyô* (*Criticism*) run by Yoshida Ken'ichi and others, and published poems and essays on poetry in it. In 1945 he went to China, where he was requisitioned by the publicity department of the Kuomintang, and remained until 1947 when he returned to Japan. His experiences in China had a decisive influence on Hotta's social consciousness and on his view of literature. After he had returned to Japan, he published, one after another, novels like *Sokoku Sôshitsu* (*Fatherland Lost*, 1950) and *Haguruma* (*Cogwheel*, 1951) which deal with subjects related to China. In 1951 he published *Hiroba no Kodoku* (*Solitude in the Plaza*) which depicts the feeling of crisis on the part of intellectuals who try to fight with the contradictions of the age. Through this novel Hotta came to be regarded as a writer who was opening a new horizon for Japanese Literature by introducing many social elements. He established himself as a representative contemporary writer dealing with the problems of intellectuals.

Hotta is a writer with an international perspective. He tries to shed light on sinister structures of politics by posing ambitious themes like war and revolution or society and man. His sharp critical spirit penetrates into the life of intellectuals. He has published impressive works dealing with the predicament of contemporary man. Among these are *Jikan* (*Time*, 1953) which depicts the Nanking massacre through the eyes of a Chinese; *Yoru no Mori* (*Forest at Night*, 1954) which deals with the rice riots of 1918 and the expedition of Japanese troops to Siberia in the same year; and *Kinenhi* (*Monument*, 1955) which tries to depict Japan during World War II comprehensively. *Kibukijima* (*Kibuki Island*, 1956) is a work born out of Hotta's contact with the indigenous culture of common people and sheds light on the form of Christianity which was preserved in a distant island. This work shows that Hotta's interest has enlarged to the bottom of Japanese society. His long novel, *Uminari no Soko kara* (*From the Bottom of the Rumbling Sea*, 1960), which deals with the Shimabara Rebellion of 1637-8 is, in its theme, related to *Kibukijima* (*Kibuki Island*). Among his other works is *Shinpan* (*Judgement,* 1955).

HOTTA Yoshie

Uminari no soko kara *(From the bottom of the rumbling sea)*
Published in *Asahi Journal,* September 1960—September 1961.

(Synopsis) More than 37,000 people, young and old, who were mostly farmers, marched to the ruins of Hara Castle. They silently brought in several thousand *koku* (one *koku* = 4.9629 bushels) of rice and several hundred guns to this ruined castle which could hardly be expected to serve as a fortress. They constructed huts and dug ditches around the ruined castle. Among them were some village headmen and unemployed *samurai* who were the leaders of the farmers. These people had been suffering from hunger and heavy land-tax. They had also been persecuted for their Christian faith. But now they were rising in revolt. "We have burnt our boats", murmured Kyûemon, the headman of Arima Village. In the ruins of the castle a banner bearing the words, "Blessed be the Holy Sacrament of the Eucharist!" was fluttering in the wind. In the centre of the banner was a picture of the holy grail being admired by angels. It was a painting by Yamada Uemonsaku. Uemonsaku had been induced by others to take part in the revolt, and was one of its leaders. He was, however, sceptical about the outcome of this revolt, and his position was delicate. His two sons, Wasaku and Gonnosuke, had been taken as hostages as a proof that he would remain faithful to the cause of the rebels. "I will be a Christian again, but I am not sure whether this revolt is reasonable", he had thought to himself. When he became a leader commanding 500 farmers and was entrusted with the task of communicating with the enemy forces through letters tied to arrows, his consciousness as a painter revived. Was not his job to paint the living outside world? He missed his old *atelier.* "We should not make Uemonsaku another Judas Iscariot", thought Ôhara Gen'emon who was aware of what was going on in Yamada Uemonsaku's mind. The office of communicating with the enemies through letters tied to arrows was a very important one, and the success or failure of this task might have a decisive influence on the outcome of the impending battle. Ôhara Gen'emon wondered what could be done. The revolt which had originally been a farmers' revolt became increasingly a Christian one, whose participants were increasingly united by their faith. At the same time, the news of the revolt of the farmers who had burnt down villages and also the castle town of Shimabara, had reached Edo, the political centre of Japan of that time, and been passed down to other places. Itakura Shigemasa and Ishigaya Sadakiyo were entrusted with the task of suppressing this revolt, and the army commanded by them started marching toward Hara Castle. The revolt was already termed a Christian revolt by the authorities. The farmers wore white robes to meet the government forces, and were busy preparing for battle. The commander of the rebelling farmers was an unsophisticated 17- or 18-year old youth called Shirô. Gradually his personality came to possess electrifying power. He preached to the people, "Heaven and the earth were both created by God, and every human being is equal before God." The farmers prayed with him, but Uemonsaku could not give up the idea of living as a painter. Toward dawn a letter announcing the beginning of battle was attached to an arrow and shot in to the enemy camp, and sounds of shooting were heard. Uemonsaku wrote in the letter, "Since my sons are taken hostages, I cannot escape from here however much I want to." He was so much obsessed with the idea of painting again. The first attack made by the government forces under Itakura Shigemasa ended in failure. Itakura consulted with other generals many times and decided to attempt to break into Hara Castle. In the ruins of the Castle, Shirô knelt on the ground and prayed to God. The farmers fought bravely, dyeing their white robes with blood. Itakura's army suffered great casualties, and was repelled. The government forces were permeated by a tense atmosphere at the unexpected strength of the farmers. The sons of Uemonsaku had already been set free, but Uemonsaku was waiting for a reply to the letter attached to an arrow he had sent. Uemonsaku as well as Gen'emon were aware that only annihilation was waiting for the rebelling farmers. The government forces commanded by Itakura had already completely surrounded the ruins of Hara Castle. Itakura Shigemasa, however, was also in a very difficult situation due to increasing dissatisfaction with him on the part of the ministers of the Edo government. Risking his death, Itakura ordered his army to launch a general offensive on the enemies. Sensing the enemy plan, Shirô wore his armor for the first time. The farmers all became tensed up. Uemonsaku reflected on the fact that he was betraying the rebelling farmers. He did not, however, have any feeling of guilt. The general attack began at midnight, and a severe battle followed, in which Itakura Shigemasa was killed, while the rebels also started to show signs of exhaustion. Shocked by the cruelty of the battle, Uemonsaku was induced to meditate on the nature of reality. The attacks on the rebelling farmers became more and more violent. "What is the use of dying here?"— Uemonsaku could not bear the misery of martyrdom. The farmers were losing vigor on account of food shortages. It was before the commencement of the second night attack that Uemonsaku received a reply from the enemy camp. His betrayal, however, was detected, and his family was slashed to death. The rebelling farmers were killed one after another during the course of the cruel battle until the castle was taken. Uemonsaku survived. The farmers were all put to death in silence.

Ibuse Masuji

As is well known, Ibuse Masuji's works show a power of accurate observation and an interesting sense of humour. His powers of observation may be related to the fact that, as a boy, he aspired to be a painter, spent much of his time sketching, and also travelled about looking for interesting things to sketch. He looks at things with an un-sentimental eye, realistically and in detail. Whoever he chooses to depict, no matter whether it is a common man or an important historical figure, he shows that, if seen from a larger point of view, which commands the whole of human existence, men are pathetic, funny, struggling to live fully in the midst of routine. This shows that behind his sense of humour lies a unique sense of resignation. This seems to be the reason why we often see a mixture of cynicism and love in his works.

To deal with his post-war works, *Yôhai Taichô* (*A Far-worshipping Commander,* 1950, translated by Shaw, Glenn W., *Japan Quarterly,* Vol. 1, No. 1, 1954, pp. 53–73, and also by Bester, John, in *Lieutenant, Look East and Other Stories,* Tokyo, Kôdansha International, 1970) depicts with pathos the tragedy of an ex-lieutenant of the army who was injured during the war. *Honjitsu Kyûshin* (*No Consultations Today,* translated by Seidensticker, E. and Shaw, Glenn W., *Japan Quarterly* Vol. 8, No. 1) published in the same year, depicts humorously the life of the common people who ignore the notice "No Consultations Today" and come to the surgery. The events are seen through the eyes of a doctor. Ibuse received the first Yomiuri Literary Prize for this work. He was also awarded the Japan Academy of Arts Prize for *Hyômin Usaburô* (*Usaburô, the Castaway,* 1956). From the works he has written since then, *Chinpindô Shujin* (*The Curio Dealer,* 1959) and *Kuroi Ame* (*Black Rain,* 1966, translated by Bester, John, Tokyo, Kôdansha International, 1969) are worthy of discussion.

The hero of *Chinpindô Shujin* (*The Curio Dealer*) is a fifty-seven year old man called Kanô Natsumaro. He was a teacher of a middle school before the war, but has become a curio dealer since the end of the war. He is good at finding rare articles and he has been given a special nickname because of this. He is proud of it, and regards himself as a connoisseur. From time to time, he makes a mistake and buys a fake, but he picks up genuine masterpieces too, and gazes at them for hours. Then he finds a rich patron called Kutani, rents a big house, and opens a high-class Japanese restaurant. He uses tableware of first-class quality. He goes to buy the materials for cooking himself. However, gradually he comes to quarrel with the forty-year old woman called Ranranjo who is well experienced in running Japanese restaurants and whom Kutani has sent as an adviser to Kanô. Kanô is a thorough man who wants to have everything his own way in the restaurant, but he is timid, and does not know how to tackle the adviser. The employees also feel hostile towards this woman and before long go on strike. The strike, however, is stopped by the combined manoeuvrings of Kutani and Ranranjo, and Kanô is expelled. He becomes a curio dealer once again, and ardently tries to pick up lucky finds every day. In the novel, Ibuse depicts with humour and pathos how the curio dealer's idealistic and naive view of life is undermined by the hard reality, represented by Kutani and Ranranjo. In the figure of the curio dealer, who is deceived by "fakes" throughout his life, and yet obstinately pursues his dreams, Ibuse's cynicism and love, two elements which are inseparably combined in his writing are movingly expressed.

Ibuse first started writing *Kuroi Ame (Black Rain)* under the title *Mei no Kekkon (The Niece's Marriage)*, and changed the title in the middle. The subject of the novel is the experience of the atomic bomb victims of Hiroshima, and the novel is written, as is not rare with Ibuse, in diary form. A man called Kanma Shigematsu lives in a village called Kobatake-mura which is some distance away from Hiroshima. He is worried about his niece, Yasuko. Although outwardly there is nothing really wrong with her, people suspect that she was affected by the atomic bomb and is suffering from an atomic disease. Because of this suspicion, she has so far not been able to get married. Shigematsu wants to prove that his niece was not exposed to direct radiation after the atomic explosion. In the novel the niece's diary and Shigematsu's diary appear side by side. A note written by his wife Shigeko, titled "Hiroshima diet during the war", and the notes of a doctor are also produced in the novel, and between them, they build up a horrible picture of suffering from the day the atomic bomb was dropped, to the final Japanese surrender. At the end of the novel, contrary to the expectations of the reader, the niece suddenly suffers from the outbreak of an atomic disease, and there the novel ends. This novel, starting from something as ordinary as the marriage problems of a niece, gradually delves into the appalling suffering caused by the dropping of the atom bomb on Hiroshima, which has become a part of Japanese consciousness. In this novel, Ibuse Masuji abandons his usual position of an outsider or a person who looks at life obliquely, and deals with his subject directly. On the other hand, we can perceive no forced theatrical effects on his part. He just makes us feel the overwhelming accumulated weight of the facts, which he collected from various sources and from the view-point of various people. There is no hasty and direct political criticism. The inhumanity of using an atomic bomb is clearly shown by the mere weight of the facts, incorporated into this fiction. In this novel, we are aware of the eye of a keen observer who has tried, without losing his normal composure, to look directly at a fateful historical event and the destiny of individuals who were involved in that event, which was to them unavoidable. The ancient Greek notion of Fate pervades the atmosphere of the novel. At the same time, we feel that the reason why Ibuse was able to draw this hellish picture of the sufferings of people after the atomic explosion, without losing his composure, was partly because he viewed it with the same passive resignation he has shown towards unusual calamities beyond human control in *Aogashima Taigaiki* (*Aogashima Tragedy*, 1934) and *Gojinka* (*The Sacred Fire*, 1944). Therefore, it is possible that his attitude towards the atomic bomb calamity, expressed in *Kuroi Ame* (*Black Rain*), is not fundamentally different from his attitude towards natural calamities. The novel may be an angry one: the inhumanity of using an atomic bomb seems to be amply revealed through the sheer weight of the facts recorded; however, these facts may have been produced with the resignation to fate characteristic of Japanese sensibility. If so, what Ibuse Masuji has presented in this novel, which was awarded the Noma Literary Prize in 1966, is the view of a nihilist observer who reacts with the traditional Japanese resignation to fate. In this sense Ibuse is a spiritual descendant of Kamo no Chômei, the 11th century author of *Hôjôki* (*An Account of My Hut*), who had a traditional penetrating understanding of the transience of the world.

Iizawa Tadasu

Iizawa Tadasu was born in Wakayama City in 1909 as the second son of Iizawa Takio, then the governor of Wakayama Prefecture. His father was an important figure in connection with the Ministry of Home Affairs who was later to become, consecutively, the Mayor of Tokyo, a member of the House of Peers, and Privy Councilor. Iizawa has made full use of this unique family background in his plays. In 1930, Iizawa entered *Bunka Gakuin* to become an interior decorator. However, while studying at this school, he joined the theatre group *Teatoru Komedi* (Théatre Comédie) and his interest in the theatre developed. He started writing plays. When his comedy, *Fujiwara Kakka no Enbi-fuku* (*The Swallow-tailed Coat of his Excellency Fujiwara*), was published in 1932, he won general recognition as a dramatist. In 1933, one of his oil paintings, which he had submitted for selection for the Nika-kai (an association of Western style painters) Art Exhibition was accepted, and his wish to become a painter was very strong, but, following his father's advice, he joined the Asahi Newspaper Company. After that, he lived as a journalist and wrote plays in his spare time. *Pekin no Yûrei* (*The Ghosts of Peking,* 1943) and *Chôjû Gassen* (*The Battle of Birds and Beasts,* 1944), both of which were written during the war, contain criticisms of the state and social satire. He also started writing radio drama during the war. The post-war play, *Sukiyabashi no Shinkirô* (*The Mirage at Sukiyabashi,* 1949), is a fine piece of writing, full of fantasy and poetic sentiment. Later he also wrote good radio and TV drama for children. He was very versatile, and also produced puppet picture books.

In 1959 he left the newspaper company and started to live wholly by the power of his pen. He published many novels of "manners" as well as humorous novels. As a playwright he published *Konronzan no Hitobito* (*People at Mt. Konron,* 1951), *Nigô* (*The Mistress,* 1954), *Yashi to Onna* (*Coconuts and a Woman,* 1956), *Mugaina Dokuyaku* (*Harmless Poison,* 1965), *Gonin no Moyono* (*Five People called Moyono,* 1967), *Akushu . Akushu . Akushu* (*Yet Another Handshake,* 1969) and many others, all of which are comedies of quality. The main characteristics of his comedies are originality of ideas, skillful building-up of suspense, humorous dialogue based on the author's deep understanding of human nature, unexpected endings and satire of the present state of things, characterized by the author's dislike of vulgarity. He has also written several modern *kyôgen* comedies. All his comedies show a penetrating power of observation and critical intelligence. Iizawa

was awarded the Prize for Broadcast Productions in 1958, and the
Yomiuri Literary Prize in 1968. He is known as one of the representative
comic dramatists of modern Japan.

IIZAWA Tadasu
Mô hitori no hito—a play in three acts. *(One more emperor)*
First performed by the theatre group Mingei in February 1970. Published
in *Bungei,* March 1970.

(Synopsis) *Place*: The play takes place partly in the underground air-raid
shelter of the house of Prince Kashii, and partly in the house of Sugimoto
Jun'ichirô in downtown Tokyo.
Time: Shortly before and after Japan's defeat in World War II (From 1944
to 1946).
(Act I) World War II is nearing its end. It is becoming clear that Japan
will lose the war. Events show that the war is becoming increasingly
unfavourable to Japan. Prince Kashii (his first name is Tamenaga) is a
dandy and a unique Imperial Prince. He does not like the eminence of
strutting militarists, and he continues to live gracefully in the same old
fashion in the splendid underground air-raid shelter of his house.

The Japanese army is defeated in a series of battles in the South Sea Islands, and Saipan Island falls into the hands of the enemy. Prince Kashii
anticipates Japan's final defeat in the near future. When the mistress of a
Japanese restaurant which he had frequented comes to see him in search of
work, he advised her to leave Tokyo and live in the country. He also tells
his children to be prudent and not to sacrifice their lives senselessly in their
youthful impetuosity. Then, without warning, a retired lieutenant-
general called Ozawa Ikunoshin comes to his house. He is a man who was
injured in battle on the Malay front and lost one leg. He says that he
wants to discuss a certain matter in strict secrecy. Ozawa then tells Prince
Kashii that the reason why Japan is being defeated in battle at present is
that Japan is reigned over by an emperor of a false Imperial Line, namely

that of the Northern Dynasty. This surprises Prince Kashii. Lieutenant-general Ozawa continues, and asserts that, unless Japan is governed by an Emperor who comes from the true Imperial Line of the Southern Dynasty, Japan will not win the war. Prince Kashii says he is afraid that this may develop into a political issue and advises him not to go too far in the matter.

Sugimoto Jun'ichirô was formerly a shoe maker. He lost his job due to the changed economic state of things during the war, and is now a factory worker. Because of his obstinate artisan spirit, he is disliked by his neighbours and is treated as if he was an unpatriotic person. He and his wife Saku have a son called Masaru, who is an engineer. However, Masaru is drafted into the army. Sugimoto loves his son, and wants him to marry the girl he loves before he departs for the front. To get money for the wedding he sells cherished family treasures which have been handed down from generation to generation.

(*Act II*) The antique objects which Sugimoto sells bear a chrysanthemum crest very much like the Imperial crest. When this is discovered, Sugimoto is interrogated by the police. Later, at his poor downtown house, Sugimoto receives a visit from lieutenant-general Ozawa who has become convinced that these objects prove the existence of an Imperial Line of the Southern Dynasty. lieutenant-general Ozawa says to Sugimoto, "You are the true Emperor." Sugimoto is taken aback by these unexpected words, but hoping that it might help to secure the safe return of his only son, at an early date, he decides to act the part of "the true Emperor".

One night, lieutenant-general Ozawa calls at Sugimoto's house with Prince Kashii. Prince Kashii is against the war policy of the present militaristic government. He is against the idea of continuing the war and having the decisive battle in Japan itself. What he wants is to put an end to the war peacefully and as soon as possible, his only condition being that the emperor system be preserved. For this purpose, Prince Kashii wants to use Sugimoto who is alleged to be the descendent of the Southern Emperors. This is the reason why he visits Sugimoto. However, on that night, there is a big air-raid, and Sugimoto's house with all the "evidence" is burnt down.

(*Act III*) In the summer of 1945 an atomic bomb is dropped on Hiroshima. Japan is forced to decide whether she is going to accept the terms of the Allied Potsdam Proclamation unconditionally. The residence of Prince Kashii also has been destroyed during an air-raid, and only the underground air-raid shelter remains. Lieutenant-general Ozawa comes to visit Prince Kashii with Sugimoto. Lieutenant-general Ozawa says that it is high time to proclaim Sugimoto as the rightful Emperor and to clarify the concept of power in the state. Sugimoto in a faltering voice just asks Prince Kashii to use his influence to have his son, Masaru, returned home soon. During Nagasaki that very day reaches Prince Kashii. Prince Kashii makes up his mind that Japan must accept the terms of the Potsdam Proclamation, and rejects lieutenant-general Ozawa's proposal. Angered by Prince Kashii's rejection of his proposal, lieutenant-general Ozawa kills Prince Kashii and his son with his sword, and then commits ritual suicide and dies.

The war is over. Sugimoto, whose house was burnt down during the war, is now living in a makeshift hut. At last his son, Masaru, demobilized, comes home. Sugimoto has managed to obtain orders for shoes again, and he is optimistic about the future. Whenever he remembers the nightmarish experiences of the war years, he feels that he is utterly fed up with the idea of war. Out of the ruins, the new energetic life of the common people begins again, in peace.

Inoue Mitsuharu

Inoue Mitsuharu was born in 1926 in Lushun (present Luta) in Kwantung Leased Territory. His father was a potter with the temperament of a master-artist who produced "Imari" ware, but he went on a wandering journey in Northern Manchuria and became missing. When Inoue was four years old, he was also separated from his mother. He returned to Kyûshû with his grandmother and lived in Sasebo. When he was twelve years old, driven by poverty, he and his grandmother moved to Sakito Island outside Sasebo Port, where there was a coal mine. He worked there as a boy coal miner. Since this coal mine was on an island, and formed an isolated community, most of the workers employed there were Koreans, and the working conditions were so bad that the workers were not much better than slaves. Inoue thus grew up, seeing day after day the inhumane treatment and the exploitation of workers that existed in an imperialistic capitalistic society. At one time, he was detained in prison on suspicion of having instigated Korean boy workers to seek national independence. Around the beginning of the Pacific War, he managed to pass an examination which qualified him to proceed to a higher educational institution including a university. He had studied by himself. After this, he left this hellish island.

Inoue held emperor-centred revolutionary ideas coloured by fascist or national-socialistic ideas. After the war, he came to know Marxism which denied the emperor system and was greatly influenced by it. He entered the Communist Party, and while still young became one of the leaders of the Communist Party in the Kyûshû area. He was also active as a romantic revolutionary poet. However, his works, *Kakarezaru Isshô* (*An Unwritten Chapter*, 1950) and *Yameru Bubun* (*The Sickened Part*, 1951) which criticized the unrealistic and inhumane elements within the Japan Communist Party, started off a big controversy, as a result of which Inoue left the Party. Although he became isolated by leaving the Party, he continued his activities as an independent orthodox Marxist and criticized the Japan of that time which was becoming a military base for the United States Army then engaging in the Korean War.

Among his works are *Sôtô no Washi* (*Two-headed Eagle*, 1952) which tells of the author's experience as a right-wing youth during the war and which also deals with the problem of homosexuality, *Nagagutsu-jima* (*Boot-shaped Island*, 1953) which is based on Inoue's experience as a coal miner, *Kyokô no Kurên* (*Fictitious Crane*, 1960) which depicts the thoughts and feelings of youth immediately after the war, *Shisha no Toki* (*The Time of the Dead*, 1960) which depicts the consciousness of a suicide pilot who has been subjected to social discrimination because he was born in a so-called outcast community, and *Chi no Mure* (*The Crowd of the Ground*), summarized below, which depicts the miseries of A-bomb victims. Thus Inoue has been producing works which are the result of a frontal attack upon the most important problems of contemporary Japan: this is why he enjoys strong support from youths interested in ideas, especially *Zengakuren* students.

What strikes us about Inoue as a writer is that he is never tired of dealing with the worst aspects of Japanese society, the skeletons in the cupboard. This is obvious from a list of the subjects he treats in his works: these include—the war, defeat, coal mining, former coal mine workers who have become unemployed, Korean people, ostracized communities, the A-bomb, suicide pilots, American military bases, the right-wing, leprosy, the emperor, prostitution, incest, and age-long rivalries among potters who are connected by ties of kinship. He uses Kyûshû dialect in his works, and his words are powerful and remind us of vivid oil paintings. Inoue, however, is not merely a realistic writer whose works evoke interest by the' sheer novelty of their subject-matter, he has also been seriously concerned with the question, "Why do I write?", and has attempted bold technical experiments. Inoue who aspires to constant never-ending revolution has always an air of imperfection, but that is not to be regretted in an author of his nature. He is a writer who has very high potentiality and promise.

INOUE Mitsuharu
Chi no mure *(The Crowd of the Ground)*
Published in *Bungei,* July 1963.

(Synopsis) An old woman appeared at the back door of Unan Chikao's surgery. It was Tsuyama Kanayo whose job was to sell pigs' white contorted intestines and blackish purple hearts. When Unan saw her, he remembered Shu Hôko, a Korean girl, who had been his classmate when he was a first year pupil of the higher elementary school. When he was sixteen according to the old Japanese way of counting age (that is fourteen or fifteen years of age), one summer day he had pressed against himself the body of Shu Hôko who was in charge of safety lamps. It was in a place where mining timber was kept. She smelt of batteries, and she became covered with mud, because he was so dirty.... Kanayo was complaining about her own grandson to Unan's mother. "Three or four years ago, they pulled down the Catholic cathedral at Uragami, didn't they? Nobuo stole the head of a christian statue which was lying on the ground, and dashed it into pieces. The police arrested him for that, but I don't understand why he should have been blamed for destroying a fragment of what Americans had destroyed of their own accord. His mother died suddenly because of the effect of the A-bomb in the second year after it was dropped, but Nobuo was quite all right, and we had been feeling so relieved. But unfortunately after he started going to school, his heart became wild."

Nobuo who had been detained in prison for some time as a suspect on a rape charge, and who had just been released, was remembering the time when he had dashed the head of a statue of Mary into pieces. After being barked at by a dog, he had thrown the stolen head away. At that moment the head had looked like the head of an A-bomb victim. He had felt as if the many corpses of Catholic believers at Uragami who had been killed by the A-bomb were swarming to him, demanding Nobuo to give back the head to them. Outside the Fukuchi family house Nobuo heard a harsh voice saying, "You cannot get away by remaining silent, Tokuko. If you don't get a written statement from the rogue so that he won't cause you any more trouble in the future you will be a laughing-stock for the rest of your life."

Unan went to examine Yasuko whose legs were soiled by blood because blood kept coming out of a cut. When Unan suggested that she might be suffering from an atomic disease, her mother obstinately denied it. When a faith-curer came from an area called Kaitô-shinden where an ostracized group of people among whom were many A-bomb victims lived, she also told him that her daughter had no atomic disease, and repelled him.

In the evening of the same day, Unan Chikao was pouring whisky into his heavy stomach, and was remembering that a fellow member of the Communist Party had died of malnutrition on a shutter used as a stretcher.

His thoughts were interrupted by a girl who came and asked him to write a certificate that she had been raped. It was Tokuko. When she came out of the surgery, Nobuo, who had been following her and waiting for her outside, stopped her and said, "Hey, you! When on earth did I rape you?" "Wait a minute! I will explain, if you were interrogated by the police on my account. Before I start, I want to ask you a question. Don't you know a person in Kaitô-shinden who always wears a glove on his left hand to hide a keloid scar?" "Do you mean Miyaji?", Nobuo asked her. "Is his name Miyaji? Yes—it must have been him".

Unan was sent for by Yasuko's family again and went in the ambulance with Yasuko to the City Hospital; Yasuko's bleeding had not stopped. He then returned to his surgery and was about to fall asleep, when a policeman came from the police station and told him that a murder had taken place in Kaitô-shinden. After Tokuko had been to Kaitô-shinden by herself to negotiate with the Miyaji family for compensation and had been repelled by them, her mother, Matsuko, had gone there and banged on the door of the Miyaji household. Miyaji's father had told her, "You're as unreasonable as your daughter. You come to our house all of a sudden and accuse my son of raping your daughter. But he hasn't had anything to do with your daughter. I can't understand how you could invent such a groundless accusation. You are from the outcast community, aren't you? Probably that's why you are so shocking". Matsuko had answered, "Did you then make a plaything of my daughter, thinking that you could do anything to a person from a so-called outcast community with immunity? Don't you know what people say about this area, Kaitô-shinden? If we are outcasts, you are even more so. You are outcasts whose bleeding would not stop." Stones had whizzed through the air at her one after another. One stone had hit her hard on the forehead as she was crouching down to protect herself.

"I shouldn't have said that it was Miyaji", thought Nobuo absentmindedly, and dropped to the ground the stone which he had been holding tightly in his hand. He was not sure whether the stone was the first one he had picked up or the second one.

Inoue Yasushi

Inoue Yasushi began his literary career rather late, but once he started writing seriously, he very quickly acquired a large number of readers. He is rather unusual in this respect. Before he started writing novels professionally, he had been a newspaper reporter. In addition, he was particularly well versed in art, and produced a steady output of poetry. He published *Ryôjû* (*The Hunting Gun,* translated by Yokoo Sadamichi and Goldstein, Sanford, Tokyo, Tuttle, 1961) and *Tôgyû* (*Bullfight*) in 1949. These two novels made him famous overnight. His writings are roughly divided into three categories. The first category comprises works which are poetical and lyrical. *Ryôjû* (*The Hunting Gun*) belongs to this group. Other works belonging to this group include, for example, *Tsuya no Kyaku* (*Guests at the Wake,* 1949), *Hira no Shakunage* (*The Azaleas of Hira,* 1950, translated by Seidensticker, Edward, *Japan Quarterly,* Vol. II, No. 3, 1955, pp. 322–248) and *Aru Gisakusha no Shôgai* (*The Counterfeiter*). They depict the lonely consciousness of modern man, which rejects any attempt of other people to penetrate it. Works belonging to the category are characterized by a hero who has to be for ever engaged in energetic action to feel that he is living, and who falls a prey to nihilism as soon as he stops being involved in action. *Tôgyû* belongs to this type, as do *Kuroi Ushio* (*Dark Tide,* 1950) and *Shatei* (*Firing Range,* 1956). *Hyôheki* (*Wall of Ice,* 1957) is one of the most representative works of this type. In *Shatei* (*Firing Range*) and *Hyôheki* (*Wall of Ice*) appear women who are idealized and adored by the male characters, but such idealization finally brings tragedy. The third category consists of historical novels which are quite akin to the second group except that they are much broader in scope. Some of Inoue's historical novels use material taken from Japanese history. Among these are *Fûrin Kazan* (*Wind, Forest, Fire, Mountain,* 1954) and *Yodo-dono Nikki* (*The Diary of Lady Yodo,* 1960). Others draw their substance from the histories of other Asian countries. *Tenpyô no Iraka* (*The Tiled Roofs of Tenpyô,* 1957), *Rôran*

(1959) (*Lou-lan,* translated by Seidensticker, Edward, *Japan Quarterly,* Vol. VI, No. 4, 1959, PP. 460–489), *Tonkô* (*Tun-huang,* 1959), *Aoki Ôkami* (*Blue Wolf,* 1963) and *Fûtô* (*The Wind and the Waves*) are among these. Somewhat unique among his historical novels is *Oroshiyakoku Suimu-tan* (*Castaway in Russia,* 1968), a historical novel with a theme akin to that of *Hyômin Usaburô* (*Castaway Usaburô,* 1955) by Ibuse Masuji. This novel depicts the fate of Japanese who are cast ashore on one of the Aleutian Islands. It is worthy of attention also that after writing a series of historical novels, Inoue recently wrote *Tsuki no Hikari* (*Moonlight,* 1970) which centres on the character of an aged mother and which reads rather like an "I" novel. In this essay, we shall concentrate on the historical novels Inoue wrote after 1958.

Rôran (*Lou-lan*) took its inspiration from *The Wandering Lake* by Sven Anders Hedin (1865–1952). It is reported that the author of the book excavated the mummy of a young girl. From this, Inoue's imagination created the heroine of this novel, the beautiful queen of Lou-lan who committed suicide. Lou-lan is a country in East Turkestan which is said to have existed long ago. This novel depicts in an epic manner, the rise and fall of this tiny country, Lou-lan, which was situated between two big powers, Han and the Huns, and also the disappearance of Lake Lop in the desert, Lake Lop in which a dragon revered as a god by the people of Lou-lan lived.

Tonkô (*Tun-huang*) is the name of a town which was situated at a strategic point to the west of China. Inoue's novel, *Tonkô* (*Tun-huang*), depicts the decline of this town during the Sung period. Its hero is a young man absorbed in studying for the state examinations to qualify as a public servant. One day he sees a woman from East Turkestan in the capital, and from that time on he is attracted to Tun-huang. Finally he goes to Tun-huang as a general. This is a novel which depicts the fateful encounter of history and man and the downfall of the capital.

Aoki Ôkami (*Blue Wolf*) is a novel which depicts the life of Genghis Khan, the great conqueror. Inoue shows how Ghengis Khan became the head of his nomadic people, how he unified Mongolia after repeated battles with other nations, and how he lead a great expedition as far as Europe.

This novel provoked a prolonged controversy between Ôoka Shôhei (a writer) and Inoue as to what constituted a good historical novel, and the controversy made the novel even more famous.

Yodo-dono Nikki (*The Diary of Lady Yodo*) is a historical novel in a Japanese setting, and depicts the life of Lady Yodo or Chacha who was the daughter of Asai Nagamasa, and was destined to become the concubine of the man who had destroyed her family, Hideyoshi. She finally committed suicide in the burning Ôsaka Castle.

Fûtô (*The Wind and the Waves*) is concerned with the history of the Mongols' attempts to invade Japan seen from the Korean point of view. Korea (at the time under the Kokuryô dynasty) had become the base for the attempted invasions of Japan by Kublai Khan. The Korean people spent a gloomy period lasting several decades because of Korea's geographical nearness to Japan, which would not acknowledge herself a tributary state of the Mongol Empire (Yuan). Two kings of Korea, their ministers, generals and rebel forces play a part in this novel, which depicts a period of national crisis in Korea. The title "fûtô" or "wind and waves", symbolizes the emperor of the Mongol Empire who causes storms and all sorts of tidal waves in the national history of Korea. The miserable fate of a small country depicted in this novel is a theme which is quite relevant to the contemporary world.

Oroshiya-koku Suimu-tan (*Castaway in Russia*) tells the story of seventeen Japanese people who are cast ashore on one of the Aleutian Islands. After ten years' time, after experiencing all sorts of problems, only three of them manage to return to Japan. However, one of them dies of illness upon arriving back in Japan. The story this novel tells is a gloomy one. The personalities of the characters are well depicted. Among the seventeen castaways are a youth, who is attracted by a Russian widow and becomes a naturalized Russian citizen, and another youth who has to have his frost-bitten leg amputated. Even those who have managed to return to Japan cannot return to their homes because the national isolation policy of the Tokugawa government prevents this. As people who have been abroad, the returned castaways have to live in confinement for the rest of their lives. Kôtarô, one of the returned castaways, says, "We are now in a penal island: if we look on our prison life in that way, it is no longer so intolerable. . . . Once you are in a penal island, you should not question anything." Inoue Yasushi depicts the life of these castaways with restraint. The author feels sympathy with them and is deeply concerned about their fate, but his feeling does not come to the surface in a naked form. He conveys a sense of the darkness of human fate in a factual tone. What we see depicted in this novel is not the relationship between man and politics but the drama of the fateful encounter of man with history. This is shown in full relief despite, or rather because of, the emotionally restrained style. *Tsuki no Hikari (Moonlight)* is, as mentioned above, a novel written in the manner of an "I" novel. The mother, who is eighty-six years old, is at first sight quite healthy, but in fact she is senile, aged, and cannot distinguish illusion from reality. She wants to go back to her native village. She converts her desire into action and leaves the house to go there. The drama between her and the son, who looks for her, strikes the reader as uncanny despite the fact that nothing really extraordinary happens as far as outward things are concerned. The mother imagines that she is twenty-three years old, and that she is walking in the moonlight looking for her son whom she imagines to be one year old. The real son, and the son of her senile imagination and the reversion to the past in the illusions of the mother create a fascinating contrast. At the bottom of this novel is the understanding that human beings are lonely. With such an understanding the author surveys the life of the mother in reverse, backwards to her birth.

No matter what type of novel Inoue writes, the voice of unavoidable human loneliness is always there. Heroes, men of action, or beautiful heroines all express human loneliness. This sometimes makes his novels too lyrical. On the other hand, this is quite understandable since Inoue was originally a poet, and wrote poetry before he started writing novels.

Ishihara Shintaro

Ishihara Shintarô was brought up in the Shônan area (to the west of Tokyo) near the sea, and accordingly his works abound in images of the sea, and are also full of the brightness and the active people we associate with the sea. Among the people who went to the same junior high school as he, was Etô Jun, now a literary critic, who was one year behind him. As a boy, Ishihara was absorbed in sports and oil painting. Later, he entered Hitotsubashi University. In 1954 his first work, *Haiiro no Kyôshitsu* (*Grey Classroom*) was published, and was followed in 1955 by *Taiyô no Kisetsu* (*Season of Violence*, translated by Milles, John G. and others, in *Season of Violence and Other Stories*, Tokyo, Tuttle, 1966). These established him as a writer. That he won general recognition is not merely due to the fact that the latter work was awarded the Akutagawa Prize: there was something fresh and novel in his strong belief in the goodness of the body, and in the practical nature of his thought. He was different from both the writers of the "dai-ichiji-sengoha" ("The First Post-war Group") and the "daisan no shinjin" ("Third New Generation" Group). The uncomplicated affirmation of self expressed in Ishihara's work appealed to many young people of his own generation. He came to be known as the representative writer of the "junsui-sengoha" (Genuine Post-war Group). The timing of *Taiyô no Kisetsu* (*Season of Violence*) was also significant. The year 1955, in which this novel appeared, was a time when Japanese society was beginning to enter a more stable phase: it was more than ten years after the war, and the Korean War was over. The affirmation of the body in the novel found an immediate echo in the life-affirming feeling of young people. This was a historical turning-point in feeling: people were no longer completely preoccupied with the problem of making a living: they were beginning to pursue leisure activities for their own sake. It was Mishima Yukio who expressed his support for Ishihara's writings earlier than anybody else. It is clear that Mishima's aspiration to transform his fragile "intellectual's" body was influenced by Ishihara's affirmation of the body. Mishima said of Ishihara, "When Mr. Ishihara talks about action, body, and the fulfillment of life, as he frequently does, it is clear that he doesn't believe in mere social customs, or in social phenomena as such. . . . Because the reality he believes in as the ultimate thing, moments of fulfillment of life, should be so powerful, concrete and simple as to be able to reject any abstract preconception". Mishima was basically right in saying this although to some extent he was perhaps reading his own thought into Ishihara's work.

Tsugawa Tatsuya, the hero of *Taiyô no Kisetsu* (*Season of Violence*) is a student boxer. He says, "I will do what I like best in the way that I like best". He behaves as a man of action who denies the existing order or existing values. He comes to know Hideko, a girl from a bourgeois family, who came to watch the boxing matches: she has treated his wounds. Although Tatsuya has known many women, he is impressed by the freshness of Hideko who throws herself directly and porwerfully at him. He feels mingled hostility and love towards her, somewhat like the feeling he has towards a worthy opponent in the boxing ring, and he sleeps with her. Tatsuya's only belief is to experience oneself in action. He sails a yacht with Hideko and experiences the wild excitement of love for her on the yacht or in the sea. The nature of his love for her is best expressed in the words: "For human beings, love cannot be a sustained emotion. Perhaps it flashes violently in the instant when two bodies are united". The excitement he felt for Hideko gradually dies as they repeat their meetings. When it is discovered that she is pregrant, he orders her to get an abortion. Hideko enters a hospital to get an abortion, but afterwards dies of peritonitis. Tatsuya goes to her funeral but when he sees a photograph of Hideko smiling at him as if to provoke him, he throws an incense-burner at it, and rushes out. He goes to his boxing gymnasium. While he is practising using a punch-bag, he sees a vision of the smiling face of Hideko, and strikes at it in excitement. This is roughly the plot of the novel. In this nihilistic novel, affirmation of the body and the emptiness after fulfilment are expressed in the concrete language of daily living. The novel also embodies the idea of negating love which has been born of physical fulfillment by a violent cruel action.

Such a fulfillment of self through action is more directly depicted in a later work, *Kiretsu* (*The Crack*, 1958). The hero of the novel is a student writer, Tsuzuki Akira. There is a night-club where a man called Fifty is working as a head-waiter. There he sleeps with a woman whose name he does not know. He also meets an actress, called Izumi Junko, there. Fifty introduces him to a boxer called Kamijima. Other characters include Asai, an ex-soldier who is now a professional murderer hired by a right-wing politician; a professional wrestler who has an affair with Junko; and a climber who is Akira's friend. Using these characters, Ishihara depicts the chaotic state of contemporary society—a society abounding in murders, physical desire, lust for power and money. However, Akira himself is unable to become another "crack" in this chaos. The style of the novel is intentionally confused, trying to convey directly the confused state of society. Here action cannot give the sense of fulfillment it is supposed to produce. The higher the expectation of fulfillment, the greater the disappointment. Love, except as physical attraction, is also impossible. What Ishihara probably wanted to describe in this novel are various actions and the impossibility of being completely fulfilled by them. Whether this novel shows a high degree of literary perfection is open to question.

The hero of *Kôi to Shi* (*Action and Death*, 1964) is a man called Minagawa. For his love, Falida, he joins the Suez Volunteer Corps, swims through the sea at night carrying explosives, and experiences intense moments of fulfilled life. When he returns to Tokyo, however, he is lost in promiscuous relationships with various women—in the ocean of sensuality. The contrast between Suez and Tokyo, between love for Falida as a genuine fulfilment of life and the barren violent world of sex in Tokyo, is the subject of the novel. However, despite Ishihara's intentions, the style is without vigour, and the novel has no clear focus in theme. We cannot help regarding this novel as an ambitious failure.

As we have seen, the underlying "philosophy" of Ishihara's novels, from the outset, is affirmation of the body and a strong yearning for fulfilment through action.

We can easily understand that Ishihara, just like Mishima Yukio, could not be contained within the boundary of literature, and moved into the field of politics. He is now part-politician. This is an entirely logical development. Ishihara, in a dialogue with Akiyama Susumu (a critic), said: "After all, the important thing for a human being is what concerns himself, his own existence—an ontology". In this dialogue he tried to explain his present position by quoting Gide's words: "I will tell you what a passion is, Nathaniel. When I die I want to die as a man fully content or as a man in the blackest despair". This is quite significant. He is the opposite of an Ôe Kenzaburô who sees thought and imagination as an end in themselves, and believes that the writer's task is to write. Ishihara will probably go on living as a practical man directly converting his ideas into action, however his career as a writer has not yet come to an end.

Ishikawa Jun

Ishikawa Jun first came into contact with the world of literature through translating some French authors. He was interested, for example, in Anatole France, André Gide and Paul Valéry. He published his first work, *Kajin* (Fair Lady) in 1953 at the age of 36. It was the time when the fashion of "Proletarian Literature" was on the wane. Using boldly imaginative settings and burlesque disguises, Ishikawa tried to depict the anxiety of the intellectual. His works of this period include *Hinkyû Mondô* (*Dialogue on Poverty*, 1935) and *Fugen* (*The Merciful Bodhisattva*, 1936). The latter, which depicts rebirth through despair, was awarded the Akutagawa Prize. This was probably because it showed great sensitivity and precision in delineating the troubled consciousness of an intellectual. In the field of criticism, Ishikawa wrote *Mori Ôgai* and tried to express his views about art. In the post-war period, he published, among others, *Ôgon Densetsu* (*The Golden Legend*, 1946), *Taka* (*Falcon*, 1953) and *Shion Monogatari* (*Asters*, 1956, translated by Keene, Donald, in *Three Modern Japanese*

Short Novels, pp. 119–172, New York, Viking, 1961). This essay concentrates on *Shion Monogatari* (*Asters*) and two other works published after it. *Shion Monogatari* (*Asters*, 1956) is set in the last Heian period. The hero's name is Takayori. He was born into a family of bards, but abandons this family art. Desiring to control the world by power, he goes to a faraway district as governor. There he meets a man called Heita, a sculptor of Buddhist images, who seems to ignore his quiver of power with all its arrows of knowledge, death, and magic. Takayori has to overcome him. He shoots off the head of a Buddhist image in a storm and Heita dies, but he himself is killed by hurtling to the bottom of a valley. After his death, to witness to his fateful act, the song of the ogres reverberates over the fields and mountains. This story, which shows that despite repeated discouragement and death, an individual encounters the moving force of history, is one of the best Ishikawa has written.

After this, Ishikawa wrote *Hakutô-gin* (*Lays of the White-haired*, 1957), *Shura* (*Asura*, 1958) and *Kitsune no Ikigimo* (*The Fox's Liver*, 1959). After these he published a play called *Omae no Teki wa Omaeda* (*Your Enemy is Yourself*, 1961), which was received with enthusiasm. This is a play in three acts, and the action takes place in a seaside hotel. At the bar of the hotel three guests are sitting. They are going to start a dubious enterprise together. Watari is the man with the ideas; Sahara was formerly a political reporter; Motomura is in charge of accounting. They want to get concessions in connection with the new island to be created near the seashore, but they do not easily agree as to the details. In the background we hear the song of a mad female guest. As a rival to the three men, an old man appears who is the head of Idogumi, a construction firm. He also wants to get concessions. Among other characters in the play are a young couple who are staying in the hotel and the manager of the hotel who plans to make a profit out of the two competing groups of concession hunters. They all engage in complicated intrigues, one against the other. At the end of Act II, the hotel is destroyed by an explosion. In Act III, we find that a new hotel has been built. The planned new island has also been constructed. The plan of the three men we met in Act I has been realized, and Watari is now a company president. However, he had, in the mean time, become quite like his old rival, the head of Idogumi, and appears with the same stick in his hand. The man from the couple who appeared in Act II appears in Act III again. Although the mad woman who appeared in Act I is supposed to have been burned to death with the hotel, we still hear her song with its constant refrain, "Your enemy is yourself". At the end of the play, a professional murderer called Kaji Tarô appears, and kills Watari with a dagger. In Act I, Watari cloaked his demand for concessions in an idealistic guise, but when a company is established on the island, and, with it, an order convenient to himself, Watari, who has acquired power, becomes just like any member of the political group he was initially against. It is then that he is murdered. The professional murderer, Kaji Tarô, who appears at the end clearly acts as a mouthpiece for Ishikawa's idea that "Every sort of order is wicked". This play may be regarded as an allegorical play. That he has not incorporated political ideologies directly into the play, shows Ishikawa's flexibility of thought.

Shifuku Sennen (*Millennium, 1967*) is another masterpiece. In this novel revolutionaries appear who, at Nagasaki, have come into contact with Christianity and with a view of civilization which came originally from Holland. The main characters are a man called Kôgen who is skilled in producing hand-printed cotton, a Shinto Priest called Kamo Naiki who uses a white fox, Matsudayû who is a master of dwarf-tree cultivation, a man called Jagatara Ikkaku who is a master of disguise and who is now in prison, and Hanaki Shuma, a disciple of Egawa Tan'an (a pioneer in gunnery in Japan). Kamo Naiki, the Shinto priest, plans to bring about a millennium on earth. He induces Kôgen to cooperate with him. Kôgen has a disciple called Yojirô whose real father is Kiroku, the leader of the beggars. Kamo tries to use these connections. His idea is to make a Christ of Yojirô and get help from the paupers. Matsudayû, who secretly believes in Mary, plans to build a Notre Dame Cathedral in Edo. Hanaki Shuma becomes Matsudayû's follower. The novel depicts the miscarried revolution in Edo from the year 1858 to 1864. Eventually, Kôgen who has dropped out of the crusade organized by Kamo Naiki, and who has become a prophet in the wilderness, dies in misery. Kamo Naiki, who has tried to become a pope and a Christ himself, sacrificing Koroku and Yojirô, also meets his well-deserved death. Matsudayû in the mean time has become a merchant engaging in trade with the West. The riot in Edo which Ikkaku had tried to create evaporates because of the indifference of most people to it.

That Ishikawa Jun, as a "burlesque" writer belonging to the so-called *burai-ha* ("Outlaws' Group") hides a sort of nihilism at the bottom of his writings can be seen from the words he puts into the mouths of various characters in this novel. For example, one character says, "What I expect from a villain is basically a manifestation of his villainous nature. Even if he leads a dissolute life, or disrupts the social order, it is entirely in accordance with his nature. No need to be surprised". Again, we find words like "A good-for-nothing is after all a good-for-nothing. . . . An idler is an idler wherever he goes" or "If I have a wish, this is just my wish, which I know is quite impossible to realize". Just like *Omae no Teki wa Omaeda* (*Your Enemy is Yourself*), this novel shows how those who dream of creating an order are destroyed by their very dream. It is obvious that this has an allegorical significance for the modern world. Ishikawa has said, "Since I expect only despair at the end of all human endeavour, I know of no disappointment or resignation in the process of living". This assertion clearly shows that he is different from Dazai Osamu and Oda Sakunosuke, writers belonging to the same *burai-ha* ("Outlaws' Group"), who ended up by committing suicide or by ruining themselves. Even in despair, Ishikawa does not cease to be a detached observer. This is the reason why his works mirror reality so accurately.

Ishikawa Tatsuzo

Ishikawa Tatsuzô established himself as a writer when he received the Akutagawa Prize in 1935 for his novel *Sôbô* (*People*) which depicts a group of Japanese emigrants in Brazil.

His works can be divided into two categories. To one belong such works as *Sôbô* (*People*) or *Ikiteiru Heitai* (*Living Soldiers*, 1938) and their main characteristic is that they are based on a thorough investigation of the subject matter. Thus *Ikiteiru Heitai* (*Living Soldiers*) is a novel somewhat reminiscent of the reports of a war correspondent, and depicts, among other things, typical soldiers, intellectual soldiers, and (Buddhist) army chaplains. This is regarded as a masterpiece of war literature.

To the second category belong works labelled "seitai-mono", or novels concerned with "modes of life". They try to grasp the relationship between individuals and society by observing people's various styles of living. At the same time, they try to avoid becoming merely "novels of manners" and attempt to explore human motivation on a deeper psychological level. In the post-war period, works of this second type became dominant, and Ishikawa wrote such novels as *Nozominaki ni Arazu* (*Not Without Hope*, 1947) and *Doro ni Mamirete* (*Soiled by the Mud*, 1949).

If we were to choose from the history of Japanese literature writers similar to Ishikawa, we would probably name Kikuchi Kan (1888–1948) and Yamamoto Yûzô (1887–   ). Ishikawa's intention is to write works based on his strong sense of social justice. In other words, he tries to represent the voice of "common-sense", and deals with his subjects in a broad journalistic manner. *Shijû-hassai no Teikô* (*Resistance at Forty-Eight*: translated by Nakayama Kazuma, Tokyo, Hokuseidô, 1960) is a novel which belongs to the second category (mentioned above). The hero, Nishimura Kôtarô, is forty-eight years old and the assistant manager of a fairly big insurance company. He is depicted as a good-natured, sensible, middle-class citizen. He has a wife whom he married more than twenty-odd years ago, and a twenty-three year old daughter called Rie. His home is respectable and peaceful, if not exactly happy. However, Nishimura's inner peace is disturbed by the idea of approaching retirement. In him there grows a desire to experience something interesting and intense, quite unlike the peaceful but mediocre life he has been leading. One day he goes on a company excursion to Atami, a hot-spring resort. To idle away the time on the train, he begins to read Goethe's *Faust*. While he is reading it, a young company employee called Soga comes to him and, like Mephistopheles, tempts him—to conceal his whereabouts or become a "missing person". (Incidentally, such cases of missing persons have become so common recently, more than ten years after the publication of this novel, that a special word, *"jôhastu"*, which literally means "evaporation", has been coined for it.) That night Nishimura slips away from the group and wanders around Atami for three hours with Soga; this gives him a brief experience of being a "missing person", and encourages him to break away from the normal routine of his life. After his return to Tokyo, Soga introduces him to Marte's House, a bar, where he comes to know a simple girl called Yuka, for whom he feels a strong love, deciding on the spur of the moment to have with her a last adventure in love, and risking his last remaining hopes and youth on her. His daughter, Rie, in the meantime, has fallen in love with a man called Kei, who is younger than she is, and elopes with him, ignoring the objections of Nishimura and his wife. Nishimura has to acknowledge their relationship in the end, realizing that his daughter is already pregnant. His wife, Satoko, is also won over to their side by becoming aware of the deep love Kei has for her daughter, and she starts making baby clothes for the coming grandchild. The thought that he will soon become a grandfather makes Nishimura feel acutely that he is in the twilight of life. He feels miserable. One snowy day, giving a plausible reason for his absence to his wife, he goes to Atami with Yuka. It is not that he is free from guilt and the realization that what he is doing is immoral, but it has become clear to him that he can no longer bear the mediocre routine of his life. He knows that he will have to return home in the end but he cannot help trying to escape. On that night, however, when Nishimura tries to embrace Yuka, she resists him violently and says "Forgive me ...." in an affectionate tone as if making a heartfelt apology. Nishimura is touched by her and understands her feelings. He feels guilt and remorse and thinks of resigning himself to everything. He catches pneumonia after returning from Atami. When he recovers he realizes that his own possibilities in life have come to an end. In one month's time, he starts going to work again, and picks up the mediocre routine of his life. He thinks of the remaining life he has as a gift which he wants to accept with greater humility. In the spring of the same year the wedding ceremony of his daughter takes place and the young couple, blessed by all, begin their new life, while, for Nishimura and his wife, only a lonely old age awaits. When being toasted, Rie's face glows beautifully but tears trickle down Nishimura's cheek and his eyes are closed.

What is the main idea which this novel tries to express? It depicts the unsuccessful attempt of a man in his late forties to regain the unique joyousness and vitality of youth, which is like divine grace. It uses Goethe's *Faust* as a framework. It shows how the psychological instability of middle age comes to the surface or can come to the surface as fundamental dissatisfaction with the cruel routine of everyday existence. In presenting this theme, the author shows keen insight into the mental climate of the early 30's of the Shôwa period (1955–1960), when society was just entering a stable and peaceful phase. In this novel, the hero, Nishimura, finally returns to a "sensible" attitude, resigning himself to circumstances, although at first he struggled to open a new vista in his otherwise unexciting life in which only death is waiting for him. Perhaps this sort of "common sense" end is just what made this novel appeal to so many people when it was published as a newspaper serial. On the other hand, whether this is admirable or not is another problem, and it is open to question. For literature represents by no means merely the voice of sound commonsense. On the contrary, literature must also represent the "Outsider's" point of view to society. All the same, this work is very relevant to our age. In this novel, Ishikawa Tatsuzô has anticipated, as early as 1956, the problem of seemingly groundless "Jôhatsu" or "Escape" of people in their forties, a problem which has become very common in recent years, and which is an eruption of irrational impulses in this rational and all the more tightly controlled society under peace. Although the hero just returns to a position of "sound common sense" at the end of the novel, the problem the author anticipated has a contemporary relevance, which is even greater now than when it was first published.

Ito Hitoshi

Itô Hitoshi (*alias* Sei) was born in 1905 in Hokkaidô. His father was a low-ranking military officer from Hiroshima who later settled down in Hokkaidô and became a teacher and a village clerk. At that time Hokkaidô was still an underdeveloped part of Japan. Itô grew up with his many brothers and sisters in a seaside village, and became a sensitive lyric poet. When he was twenty years old, he published the first collection of his poems under the title, *Yukiakari no Michi* (*Snow-lighted Path*). He studied at the Tokyo Commerce (now Hitotsubashi) University, though with some financial difficulty. He was interested in *avant-garde* literature of the period after World War I. He was a hard-working man, and translated Joyce's *Ulysses,* and Lawrence's *Lady Chatterley's Lover* into Japanese. He was the first person to introduce new modes of poetry and novel-writing to Japan. He advocated "neo-psychological literature" which was based on the stream-of-consciousness technique which Joyce had used. Itô himself published experimental novels such as *Kanjô Saibô no Danmen* (*A Phase of Emotional Life*) and *Seibutsu Sai* (*The Festival of the Living,* 1932). During the pre-war period he also published *Yûki no Machi* (*The Street of Demons,* 1937) and *Tokunô Gorô no Seikatsu to Iken* (*The Life and Opinions of Tokunô Gorô* 1940–1942). The former depicts the suffering and weakness of Japanese intellectuals who were trying to establish their freedom and individuality by precariously picking out a course between left-wing politics and fascism. It is written in an imaginative manner with some masochistic touch. The latter caricatures prewar Japanese intellectuals; the satirical sketches in this novel remind us of British satirical works. Itô was the most intellectual Japanese writer of the time.

After the war he published *Narumi Senkichi* (1950) which humorously caricatures the helplessness of Japanese intellectuals, including the author himself. Underlying it, however, is bitter critical spirit. This work was a starting point for postwar Japanese literature. *Shôsetsu no Hôhô* (*The Meth-*

ods of Writing Fiction, 1950) and *Shôsetsu no Ninshiki* (*Understanding Novels*), which Itô published after the war, are excellent scholarly attempts to arrive at a systematic understanding of modern Japanese Literature by comparing it with Western Literature. These critical works have furnished a basis for all subsequent critical discussion of modern Japanese Literature.

It is quite ironical that this most gentlemanly and highly moral writer was prosecuted for public indecency for the publication of his unabridged translation of Lawrence's *Lady Chatterley's Lover.* Although the entire literary world of Japan defended him, the case ended in a verdict of guilty. Through the experience of this trial, however, Itô's works gained in maturity and depth, and he has since become a best-selling author. Among his later works are *Hi no Tori* (*Fire-bird,* 1953) which deals with the relationship between art and life; *Hanran* (*Overflow,* 1958) which depicts an organic chemist who has suddenly become an executive of a big company and his inner and outward reactions to this change, *Hakkutsu* (*Excavation,* 1964) which shows the futility of contemporary man's egoism; and *Henyô* (*Transformation* 1964) which deals with the discovery of the richness of sex in old age. Through these works Itô has maintained his position as one of the leading writers of contemporary Japan. At the same time he has also written *Nihon Bundan Shi* (*A History of the Japanese Literary World*) in twenty volumes. It is a unique book. It is highly readable, but at the time is very scholarly and is well founded on accumulated facts. Itô continued to be a university teacher. He also showed his competence in practical matters, and contributed greatly to the founding of the Library for Modern Japanese Literature.

Itô was on the one hand very introspective, masochistic and shy, but at the same time he was rational, practical and competent as a member of society and as a scholar. His talent was shown not so much in his many laboured novels as in his literary criticism and essays which are at the same time both theoretical and well-substantiated by facts. Itô, who died in 1969, was the first highly intellectual contemporary man of letters Japan has produced. He was also very versatile. He contributed a good deal towards making Japanese Literature internationally appreciated. He became a candidate for the Nobel Prize for Literature. Since his death, *Itô Hitoshi Zenshû* (*The Collected Works of Itô Hitoshi*) in twenty-two volumes, has been published by the Shinchôsha Publishing Company.

Itô Hitoshi
Henyô (*Transformation*)
Published in *Sekai*, January 1967–May 1968.

(Synopsis) Taken by Kurata Mansaku, I, Tatsuta Hokumei, had come for the first time to Izumigawa with its conspicuous white-walled castle tower when I was twenty-two years old. The time of which I write, I had come to the city to attend a ceremony marking the unveiling of a literary monument to this friend. The monument was made of obsidian, and its width was greater than its height. On its front was engraved a passage from Kurata's writing, and on its back was carved a nude woman I had drawn. That picture had been used as an illustration for *Chimata no Hana* (*Beauty in the Street*), Kurata's representative novel. Although it was commonly regarded as an illustration drawn for the novel, in fact it was the other way around. I had drawn the picture using Kobuchi Utako as my model. Stimulated by my picture, Kurata wrote the novel about his relationship with Utako. Kurata suddenly became the favorite of the age with *Chimata no Hana* (*Beauty in the Street*), and began writing with great zest and energy, which in the end exhausted him and cost him his life. He died at the age of forty-seven in the midst of his fame. The unveiling ceremony was conducted by Maeyama Sakiko, Kurata's elder sister, and her daughter Akiko. That night the Maeyama family invited the people present at the ceremony to a party. Maeyama Sakiko had been making a living as a teacher of Kyôto dances during the postwar period. She was already over sixty, but her chubby figure was still very attractive. I placed my bed beside hers, and for two nights listened to her night-time confessions about her life. When I spent the summer in this city with Kurata during my student days, one night, Sakiko, who had only been married a short time tried to seduce me. Pretending to be sleeping, I responded to her invitation. She was the first woman I slept with. That secret has kept us close ever since. When I was young, I imagined that a man of sixty would have no desire for women. When I reached that age, I realized that things were entirely different. I was strongly attracted by the feminine charm of Sakiko who was over sixty. That memory from my youth also played a part in this.

I married a woman who had been my colleague when I was a young teacher. She was the type of woman I liked. I painted my pictures using her as a model for a long time, until her beauty faded. Then I started looking for another model, and this tormented her. During the war I stopped painting for a while. Then she became healthy, and worked with great vitality again. However when,, prompted by an inner urge, I started painting again after the war, and became recognized as a painter, her health deteiiorated. She went to a sanatorium for lung diseases. Since I did not want to give her anxiety or cause her jealousy, I tried to avoid relationships with model girls. It was about this time that I met Kobuchi Utako at a bar. She was a little plump, but the expression of her eyes and mouth were irresistible to me. I asked her to become my model, and soon we became intimate. However, I was so much afraid that my wife would come to know this and that her illness would worsen that I did not stop Kurata Mansaku getting acquainted with Utako at my studio and falling in love with her. I almost welcomed it when Utako became Kurata's woman. My wife died shortly afterwards, however. Kurata became a popular writer through writing erotic novels, in which the heroine was based on Utako. He soon came to have an affair with another woman. Utako opened a bar with the money she received from Ichikawa, a toy wholesaler. Then she gave birth to a girl, Masako. After Kurata's death, Utako was made much of by journalists as the widow of Kurata, and her bar was frequented by many writers and journalists. Maeyama Sakiko asked me to investigate whether Masako was really Kurata's child as Utako had said, and I went back to Tokyo. I went to Utako's bar and met her again after a long time. As I repeated my visits, our old relationship revived. Unlike her former self, Utako had become a woman who was passionate and forward in love-making.

Maeyama Sakiko suddenly became dangerously ill. She wanted to see me once more before she died. When I received this news, I hastened to Izumigawa and was at her bedside until she died. A human being who shared a secret with me as far back as forty years ago, and who lived up till now, was about to leave the world. The weight of this fact moved me deeply. In the train on the way back to Tokyo I opened a newspaper and read that Utako had been found dead with Ichikawa in her flat. It seemed to me that Ichikawa had forced Utako to be his companion in suicide. I offered to adopt Masako who was the daughter of two of my closest friends, and Masako came to live in my house. My intimate friends had died one after another. There was only one friend left to whom I could tell everything and get sympathy and understanding: that was Uehara Setsuko, who had been a good friend of my deceased wife. I visited her, and we consoled each other for the misfortunes we had suffered in life.

Kaiko Ken

Kaikô Ken was born in Ôsaka in 1930, and graduated from the Faculty of Law of Ôsaka Municipal University. He took various part-time jobs during his student days, and even after graduation, often changed jobs: he worked for a bookshop selling foreign books, an English conversation school, a firm dealing on foreign liquors and so on. At one time he edited a public relations magazine. In his spare time he wrote novels, and won recognition for his *Panikku* (*Panic,* 1957). This short story depicts the enormous energy and insanity of a plague of rats which had increased unusually, and the corruption of the local authorities who were pressed hard to devise some means to deal with the situation.

This allegorical technique expressing the timely theme of "organization and the individual" was also used by Kaikô in his next novel *Hadaka no*

Ôsama (*Naked King*, 1953). In this work the stereotyped behaviour of a group of judges of a children's painting contest is caricatured through a contrast with a picture by a child who has expressed his world straight-forwardly.

For *Hadaka no Ôsama* (*Naked King*) Kaikô was awarded the thirty-eighth Akutagawa Prize, and established himself as a writer. After that, he continued to depict the contradictions of organized society and an over-flowing vitality of common people living in it. In *Ryûbôki* (*Account of Wandering*, 1959) Kaikô shed light on the relationship between the rulers and the ruled against the background of the construction of the Great Wall of China, in *Nihon Sanmon Opera* (*Threepenny Opera of Japan*, 1959) he depicted a beggars' community in the former site of an army arsenal in Osaka, and in *Robinson no Matsuei* (*Robinson's Descendants*, 1960) he de-picted the miserable struggling life of a group of farmers who settled in Hokkaidô. Kaikô's radius of action extends beyond the boundary of Ja-pan. For example, he went to Israel to attend the trial of Eichmann, and also went to Vietnam to observe the war. He is the author of *Betonamu Senki* (*Vietnam War*) and other *reportages*. Kaikô is one of the so-called *junsui sengo-ha* (pure postwar group) writers who grew up mostly after World War II. Kaikô was nourished also by postwar Japanese literature in his formative years.

KAIKO Ken
Panikku *(Panic)*
Published in *Shin Nippon Bungaku*, August 1957.

(Synopsis) In the autumn of 1956, exactly 120 years' since 1836, bamboo grasses bloomed all at once and bore fruit. Nobody was harvesting the fine fruit, and it covered the autumn fields thickly. This was the cause of the subsequent panic.

All sorts of rats living in this area gathered to eat the fruit of the bamboo grass. They made a network of under-ground tunnels through the tangled roots, and while the thick bamboo grass shrubberies protected them from being detected by kites and hawks, the complicated underground tunnels protected them from snakes and weasels, and the abundant food resulted in a phenomenal increase of the number of rats.

Shunsuke who was working at the Forestry Section of the Prefectural Administration Office had predicted this even before flowering of the bamboo grass. Cooperating with technical officials in the Research Section, he devised countermeasures, and handed in his plan to his superior. His main idea was to burn off the ground covered by the bamboo grass, but his proposal was simply ignored, and the paper he had handed in, lay idly in the chest of drawers of the section chief. Meanwhile a corruption case around the newly built administration building had been detected and in the personnel changes which followed it, Shunsuke's section gained a new section chief, a repulsive-looking man with a fairly bald head, a weak stomach, and bad breath. He had been working at the Supply Section which was said to be the source of the corruption case. He did not know anything about the jobs of the Forestry Section, and did not take Shunsuke's worries about rats at all seriously. Corruption was hushed up, and the section chief was still attending secret meetings at a Japanese restaurant as before. Shunsuke could not help feeling how deep-rooted the corruption in the Prefectural Administration Office was. Due to repeated scandals, the countermeasures to prevent the rats' increase which Shunsuke had devised with others were even more forgotten. Then came the winter. In the bamboo grass field covered with snow, the rats were steadily increasing.

When the spring came, exactly as Shunsuke had predicted, a multitude started gnawing cypresses, cedars, larches and other valuable planted trees, and completely damaged them. They also ate up seeds sown in the wheat field, and no sprouts came out of the ground. Rats, as if they were underground water, came swarming about the ground. Hunger seemed to have changed their nature completely, and they became so wild that they even attacked human beings or tried to eat the cheeks of a human baby.

The Forestry Section rallied around Shunsuke, and set up a committee to fight the rats. They delivered rat-poison to people living in the area, bought weasels and snakes, and freed them in the field and hills. They laid special snares for rats. In fact they tried everything they could think of to destroy them, but no matter what they tried, it was all useless before the fantastic number of rats, which not only caused great damage in the countryside, but also finally created panic in the towns. The chief of the Research Section, an agronomist, said to Shunsuke who was cracking his brain to curb the seemingly uncontrollable damages which the rats were causing, that the great efforts made to curb the rats would simply mean so much waste of energy. When the section chief asked Shunsuke why he was wasting his energy on this hopeless matter, Shunsuke, undisconcerted, answered, "It kills time all right". Shunsuke was aware that what was behind his passionate efforts to destroy rats was a sort of intellectual satisfaction of a sort of pleasant excitement one could get from a mock warfare.

All the pupils of the primary schools and junior high schools of the area were mobilized for rat hunting. The smoke rising from the piles of caught rats being burnt reminded one of Auschwitz.

The number of rats, however, did not show any sign of decreasing. Wicked merchants sold the same weasels twice by catching them after they had been let loose. Some farm houses were completely ravaged by rats overnight, and there were even cases of infants being bitten to death by them. Rumours of epidemics spread, and psychological panic deepened and became critical. This finally developed into a big political issue. Voices denouncing the corruption of the prefectural administration were raised openly, and a movement to recall the governor was started. Shunsuke's report which he had handed in to his section chief came to light, and soon he found himself regarded by the public as a hero, as a prophet to whom others would not listen, as a symbol of active conscience.

One day the chief of Shunsuke's Bureau and the chief of his section invited him to a Japanese restaurant. The chief of the Bureau told him that they were going to mobilize the primary school children once more, and that after that the committee to curb rats' damages would be disbanded, and that they would announce that the rats had been annihilated. Scared by the spreading panic, they had thought up the idea of pretending that the multitude of the gray animals were mere illusions and did not exist. It was an old political trick. They tried to divert the attention of people from what was pressing them hard by declaring that it was a mere illusion. After the Bureau chief had gone, the section chief said to Shunsuke, "You have been promoted to a post in the central bureau in Tokyo". Shunsuke was miserable, and felt hurt by the hypocrisy of his superiors.

That night the multitude of rats suddenly started moving. They were seized by insanity. Driven by a huge blind power, they just continued running. In the direction of their march was a lake, but they did not change their course. They just jumped into the lake one after another, and were drowned. The force which had devastated 100,000,000 m² of planted trees, causing 600,000,000 yen worth of damages, was finally mysteriously wasted, and the underground organization of rats was destroyed. Shunsuke was seized by a strange sort of excitement and inertia.

Kanbayashi Akatsuki

Kanbayashi Akatsuki is a writer of "I" novels which are no longer very fashionable today. He has said, "I started writing novels as if I was writing a personal testament". His life has not been a very happy one. For example, his wife became mentally ill, and he had to nurse her for a long time only to lose her in the end. However, Kanbayashi is not an "I" novel writer like Dazai Osamu who committed suicide. No matter how painful his life is, Kanbayashi has always tried to live. This does not mean, however, that he has uncritically accepted everything in his daily life. For example, although his aged parents are living alone in Kôchi Prefecture, his native place, he refused to live with them. This was because he did not like the idea of a routine life. Explaining his relationship towards his parents, he wrote in a recent novel, *Onme no Shizuku* (*Tears from your Eyes*) "I lost my wife more than ten years ago, and I have not yet married again. If I marry again, I know full well that my parents will be very pleased and relieved, but I have not complied with my parents' wish. This is because to me living is more important than pleasing my parents and setting their minds at rest. When I think about it, from the very moment I started writing, I have not compromised in this respect. Even now, I am trying not to be prevailed over by my affection towards my parents, I am refusing to do this as a weakening of my mental power, and am going to return to Tokyo. No matter how unhappy my parents may feel about it, I refuse to pay attention". Kanbayashi has been like that throughout his literary career.

Onme no Shizuku (*Tears from your Eyes*) depicts how "I", a mediocre writer living in Tokyo, visits his parents' home after two years' absence and lives with his parents for a while. His father is 78 years old, and is half blind due to a cataract. The mother works all day long, although her back is bent with age. The only thing his father, who is sick and confined in a twilight world all day, enjoys is to listen to the radio. "I" imagines that his father is living in a hell of loneliness. Since he is neglected by his wife and daughter, "I" drinks saké with him and listens to his complaints and his reminiscences attentively. The father is grateful to the son who, unlike his wife and daughter, does not mind his argumentativeness, and who listens to him attentively even when he disagrees with him. Sometimes, the father is overwhelmed by the anger, long repressed in his heart, and denounces the present age which damns everything in the past as feudalistic. "I" gradually comes to feel that if he lived with his parents, that would make them happy. However, in the end, he decides to return to Tokyo, reflecting on the fact that he was able to begin a literary career only because of his refusal to follow such a feeling. The night before his departure, "I" advises his father not to quarrel with his family too much, when "I" is drinking with him. When "I" watches his father's face, he is stricken with pity for him. He remembers Bashô's poem, which was written after seeing the statue of the aged blind priest Ganjin at Tôshôdaiji Temple; especially the line, "I would like to wipe tears from your eyes", and thinks that although his father's eyes are not filled with tears, he would at least like to shave his unshaven face. When he has done that, his father suddenly looks cheerful and even childlike.

Kanbayashi's works can be roughly divided into two groups. One

group deals with his life in Tokyo. The other group deals with his visits to
his parents. In fact, during his life as a writer, he has visited his parents'
house many times. This novel *Onme no Shizuku* (*Tears from your Eyes*)
naturally belongs to the second group. The first and second groups of his
works represent respectively Kanbayashi's suffering and rebirth. Only
repeated movement precariously from one to the other keeps him from
becoming a writer abandoned to despair like Dazai. This repeated movement from Tokyo to his native home shows where this "I" novel writer
draws his power to recover from despondency.

This first group of his works dealing with his life in Tokyo is, as already
mentioned, dominated by the theme of suffering. Among the works
which depicts the suffering of his sick wife is *Sei Yohane Byôin nite* (*At St.
John's Hospital,* 1946). He has also written about his own suffering.
Kanbayashi had a stroke in 1952, and some of his works are based on his
experiences following that. He recovered from this, but in 1962 had a
second stroke. *Shiroi Yakatabune* (*A Stately White Barge,* 1963, translated
by Carlisle, Warren, *The Japan P.E.N. News,* No. 17, 1966) was dictated
by Kanbayashi in sick-bed, and deals with his illness.

In *Shiroi Yakatabune* (*A Stately White Barge*), the hero, "I", has a stroke
in the public baths, and is taken home. His dreams, illusions, and reality
intermix in this novel. At one point, he dreams that his father has died, and
he sobs in his dream. At another time, he dreams that his mother dressed
entirely in white has come to see him. Since he cannot see her face, he
imagines that only her soul has come to visit him. Then he regains consciousness and discovers that a woman called Mrs. Ishitani, his attendant
nurse, is by his side. He dreams again, and, in his dream, Mrs. Ishitani
shows him around in a white barge. In his native area, there is a tradition
that when you die, a white barge will come to fetch you. This dream is
connected with that. While he lay dreaming, he seems to have unconsciously embraced Mrs. Ishitani. She tells him that and adds that this has
convinced her that his nerve centre is intact. After three months he leaves the
hospital. He can now return to the world which has looked like a different
planet from the hospital window. As he descends the stairs of the hospital,
the atmosphere of the ordinary outside world becomes more and more

distinct. He feels as if he has returned from outer space. He passes along familiar roads and arrives home.

This novel, which uses the imagery of death, appearing in dreams, illusions and flashbacks, has managed to attain a depth beyond the docile realism of an average "I" novel. It is quite justifiable that Kanbayashi was awarded the Yomiuri Literary Prize in 1965 for a collection of his works, the central one of which is this novel. As we have seen at the beginning, Kanbayashi started writing novels as if he was writing a personal testament. What sustained such a resolute attitude of his at the beginning was his "pure passion", as he himself said. In retrospect, his family life was a continuous suffering, but he did not want to lose his initial simple purity through the cares and worries of living. He wanted to be purified through his sufferings, rather than to be crushed by them. In both *Onme no Shizuku* (*Tears from your Eyes*) and *Shiroi Yakatabune* (*A Stately White Barge*) the two elements of suffering and purity are discernible. It is by keeping his eyes steadily upon these two elements that Kanbayashi has managed to keep his spiritual balance.

Kawabata Yasunari

Kawabata Yasunari distinguished himself at an early age by writing *Jûrokusai no Nikki* (*Diary of a Sixteen-Year-Old*). This was published in 1924, and featured his grandfather who had very little time left on earth. It clearly witnesses to Kawabata's fine sensibility and to his gift of accurate observation. *Izu no Odoriko* (*The Dancer of Izu*, 1926) appeared in English translation in *Atlantic Monthly* 195, pp. 108–114, 1955, and through its fresh youthful lyricism, firmly established him as a writer. Kawabata appears in literary history as a member of the *Shin Kankaku-ha,* or New sense school of writers. Yokomitsu Riichi and Nakagawa Yoichi are also placed in the same school. However, although they all show an almost pathologically keen sensuous appreciation of reality, Kawabata is different from them in that he has been deeply affected by Oriental nihilism and behind his works is the idea of purified death and eroticism. In this connection, it is significant that Kawabata says in his *Bungakuteki Jijoden* (*Literary Autobiography*, 1934), "I believe that the classics of the East, especially the Buddhist classics, are the greatest works of literature in the world". Since World War II, he has deepened his thinking, especially that concerning the Japanese sense of beauty. Kawabata's words, "Since Japan has surrendered, the only thing left for me to do is to return to the traditional sorrow of spirit of the Japanese people", are important to any understanding of his works. One might use the phrase, "purified eroticism". Behind Kawabata's love of women is not only sexual fantasy, but also unconscious longing for his young mother whom he lost when he was three years old. This is why, in his works, sexual fantasies appear not in a realistic way but in an extremely abstract form. Among his postwar works are *Senba-zuru* (*A Thousand Cranes*, 1951, translated by Seidensticker, E. G., New York, A. Knopf; London, Secker and Warburg, 1959) *Yama no Oto* (*Mountain Sounds*, 1954), *Nemureru Bijo* (1961) (*House of the Sleeping Beauties*, translated by Seidensticker, E. G., and published in *House of the Sleeping Beauties and Other Stories*, Tokyo, Kôdansha International, 1969), *Koto* (*The Ancient Capital*, 1962), *Kataude* (*One Arm*, 1964, translated by Seidensticker, E. G., and published in *House of the Sleeping Beauty and Other Stories*, Tokyo, Kôdansha International, 1969) and *Kami wa Nagaku* (*Long Hair*, 1970). I would like to concentrate on discussing these works in this essay.

Nemureru Bijo (*House of the Sleeping Beauties*) is a story about an old man called Eguchi who has already lost his sexual ability and who is introduced by his friend to a secret inn where he can sleep beside a perpetually sleeping beauty. The theme of an old man's sexual fantasies is similar to that of Tanizaki's *Fûten Rôjin Nikki* (*Diary of a Mad Old Man*), but Kawabata does not treat the subject with the obsessive interest Tanizaki shows. In this novel, the desire and resignation of the old man appear in a nihilistic light, always haunted by the shadow of age and death. The secret inn the old man, Eguchi, visits is a secret place of enjoyment for old men who are approaching their death. Eguchi visits the place five times. Lying by the side of a sleeping beauty, he remembers his experiences with the various women he has met in his life. He regards these sleeping beauties as buddha-like existences who cure him of nightmarish memories of vice and immorality. Those old men who have died in this inn have usually been carried out unobtrusively. At the end of this novel, the sleeping beauty Eguchi has lain beside suddenly dies, and is carried out. In this novel, the image of a young mother hides behind the image of a woman. This novel depicts the height of abstract eroticism in delicate beautiful Japanese language. The image of death only intensifies the effect of eroticism in the novel.

Koto (*The Ancient Capital*) depicts the beautiful twin sisters, Chieko and Naeko, who have been for a certain reason brought up separately. As background, the customs, the festivals and the nature of Kyoto are drawn. Chieko and Naeko meet for the first time when Chieko goes to see the cedars in the hills to the north of Kyoto. After this, they start visiting each other. Hideo, son of the owner of a weaving-shop, who has been chivalrous to Chieko, gets to know Naeko and proposes to her. Naeko feels, however, that she is loved merely as Chieko's copy and hesitates to accept his proposal. One winter night, Naeko visits Chieko. Chieko asks Naeko to live with her, but Naeko, who does not want to obstruct Chieko's happiness, declines. That night they sleep in the same room side by side for the first time. The next morning Naeko returns through the snow to her house. In this novel, the loneliness of the two women who have been brought up separately despite the fact that they are twins, and the nature which surrounds them, make a striking contrast. Looking at the cedars, Naeko says, "Why has mankind come into existence? It's really dreadful, isn't it?" These words show symbolically that this novel is not merely a novel depicting Kyoto, but that it is also a nihilistic novel.

The hero of *Kataude* (*One Arm*) borrows the arm of a certain girl for one night. He brings it back to his flat, and sleeps with it. The details of this novel are particularly sensuous and beautiful. Comparing the nails of the girl's arm and his own nails, the hero says, "A woman is always trying to overcome being a human being even in her nails". When he wakes up in the morning, he notices something uncanny at his side. When he looks carefully, he discovers that it is his own right arm. Startled, he

takes off the girl's right arm from his shoulder, and places his own there.
Here the novel ends. The plot is not so important in this novel. The novel
is sustained by the working of various images about a woman which
occur to the hero. These images constitute the beauty of the novel. In this
respect, this novel is similar to *Nemureru Bijo* (*House of the Sleeping Beauties*).

The hero of *Kami wa Nagaku* (*Long Hair*) is an old man who is seventy-
eight years old. He has lost his wife, and is now leading a lonely life with
his chauffeur, the chauffeur's wife, and a cat. One day he finds in the
reader's column of a newspaper a poem which roughly says that a black
hair draws an abstract picture over a white shirt. This poem reminds him
of a woman called Haruko with whom he once had an affair and who is
now running a small restaurant. He also remembers her daughter Hisako,
a geisha girl, with whom he spent a night at Kawana Hotel at the request
of the mother "to make her a woman". He remembers Hisako's hair
which was wet with tears. The combination of an old man and a young
girl is similar to that in *Nemureru Bijo* (*House of the Sleeping Beauties*), but
the latter is throughout filled with sexual fantasy of an extremely abstract
nature, whereas this novel depicts the hero's real contact with a girl.

In these works, Kawabata Yasunari has created "decadent literature
which has a perfect formal beauty and which has a fragrance reminiscent
of the rotting smell of over-ripe fruit" (Mishima Yukio's words). Here is
a world of perfect sensuous refinement, coloured by Oriental nihilism. It
is not too much to say that Kawabata's works represent the culmination of
Japanese sensibility.

Kinoshita Junji

Kinoshita Junji was born in 1914 at Hongô, Tokyo. He went to middle
school and to higher school at Kumamoto, the home of his family. He
graduated from the Department of English Literature of Tokyo Univer-

sity in 1939, and continued his studies as a postgraduate student. While he was a student, he studied, in particular, Shakespeare, under Nakano Yoshio's guidance. At the same time, he was interested in the new movement in the theatrical world of that time, and wrote a rough draft of *Fûrô* (*Wind and Waves*) before being drafted into the army. This historical play, which was published in a finished form in 1947, is set in Kumamoto, in the early Meiji period, and portrays discontented ex-samurai, students of the School of English Studies, and a band of Christians, among others. During the Second World War, following the suggestion of Nakano Yoshio, Kinoshita read closely the Japanese folktales collected by Yanagida Kunio. He organized a study group with Yamamoto Yasue, an actress who had belonged to the Shin Tsukiji Gekidan (New Tsukiji Troupe) which had been disbanded on order of the authorities, and started writing plays based on folk tales. In 1946, the year after the end of the war, he published *Nijûniya Machi* (*Twenty-two Nights of Waiting*) and *Hikoichi Banashi* (*The Tale of Hikoichi*). In 1949 he published *Yûzuru* (*Twilight Crane*, translated by Scott, A. C., New Directions, New York, 1956). With these works he created the genre of folk tale plays and successfully established himself as a playwright.

In 1949 he wrote *Yamanami* (*Mountain Range*), a play in a modern setting, for the Minshû Geijutsu Gekijô (Popular Art Theatre). This play depicts how the personality of a woman, who conducts surveys and research on agricultural techniques and on the social structure of farming villages, flowers through her experience of love. In folk tale plays such as *Yûzuru* (*Twilight Crane*), *Akai Jinbaori* (*The Warrior's Red Coat*) and *Onnyoro Seisuiki* (*The Rise and Fall of Onnyoro*), Kinoshita has tried to deple. In plays with a modern setting—for example, *Yamanami* (*Mountain Range*), *Kawazu Shôten* (*The Ascension of the Frogs*) and *Higashi no Kuni nite* (*In the East Country*)—Kinoshita's main concern has been to cast light on the tragic conflicts underlying the thought and behaviour of Japanese intellectuals during the modern period.

Besides his activities as a playwright and translator (he has translated, for example, some of Shakespeare's plays), Kinoshita founded a theatrical group called Budô no Kai (The Grapes) with Yamamoto Yasue, and

wrote his plays for this group. He has also been deeply interested in problems connected with China and Asia, and has expressed his views about
these on various occasions. Since 1962 starting with *Ottô to Yobareru
Nihonjin* (*The Japanese called Otto*), he has been writing his plays for the
theatrical group Mingei. He has also been experimenting in widening the
possibilities of the Japanese language with the group presided over by
Yamamoto Yasue. From *Ottô to Yobareru Nihonjin* (*The Japanese called Otto,
1962*) to *Shinpan* (*Judgement, 1970*), Kinoshita has constantly been dealing
with the problem of individual responsibility in the context of complicated
contemporary history, and also with the problem of inherited sin.

KINOSHITA Junji
Otto to yobareru nihonjin (*A Japanese called Otto*)
Published in *Sekai,* July—August 1962.

(**Synopsis**) (Act I) Shanghai in the early 1930's. A German man called
Johnson is a member of the intelligence department of the Comintern. He
wants to find out whether the Japanese army in Manchuria is preparing an
invasion of Siberia. He is looking for a Japanese who will spy for him. He
discusses the matter with an American woman called Mrs. Sung, and
chooses a Japanese called Otto, a correspondant of a Japanese newspaper.
Otto, however, recommends a Japanese reporter called Lin. Otto is a
gourmet as well as an ambitious man. He shows great ability in analyzing
the political situation from a Marxist point of view, and is not very keen to
engage in trivial spying activities. He loves his wife. At the same time, he is
in love with Mrs. Sung who is a talented and somewhat masculine-looking
woman. In due course Otto is called back to Japan by his newspaper. Otto
tells Mrs. Sung that he is going back to Japan. Johnson tries to induce him
to stay in China, and says that it would be a mistake for him to separate
himself from Johnson's group. Otto replies that his fatherland is Japan.
(Act II) In the middle 1930's, Tokyo. Otto who has returned from China

is active as an editorial writer for his newspaper and also as an expert on China. Segawa, his friend, who studies philosophy, has been stigmatized as an apostate, and is having a hard time trying to make his living as a philosopher. Otto is free from such worries, and enjoys a brief period of peaceful uneventfulness. Then Lin, whom he met during his stay in Shanghai, comes to him, and asks him if he has not heard anything from Johnson. Finally, Johnson smuggles himself into Japan and establishes a spy ring staffed, among others, by a Japanese painter called Joe who was born in Okinawa and a woman called Kinamida who emigrated to the United States as a farmer. Johnson has summoned them from the United States. The spy ring contacts Otto, and Otto makes an instant decision and agrees to spy for them. This is what he has been meditating about for several years. Otto is fully aware that what he is going to do violates not only Japanese national law, but also international law once the war has started. However, in this unfortunate situation, in which loyalty to the state and the free pursuit of the truth clash, Otto cannot help choosing the latter. He decides to co-operate with the organization in order to establish basic human rights and to emancipate human beings. At this point, Mrs. Sung, who still remembers her love affair with Otto, comes to Japan to see him on her way home from America. Johnson is quite worried that she might distract Otto's attention from the important task he has to fulfil, but Otto promises him that he will not even exchange letters with her in the future. (Act III) Tokyo in the early 1940's. When Otto started cooperating with Johnson, he had the vision of his beloved country Japan uniting with the U.S.S.R. and new China to create a league of liberated Asian nations, but Johnson, who has no fatherland, thinks that his job in Japan is over when it has become clear that the U.S.S.R., the fatherland of Socialism, will not be attacked by Japan because Japan has decided to expand towards the South. When Otto, who is now a supernumerary of the Cabinet and wants to help the present prime minister avoid the imminent war with the United States and to save his fatherland asks for Johnson's cooperation, Johnson just answers that the present prime minister does not have the power to overcome the danger of entering war against the United States. Johnson says that he will leave Japan within the week. Unable to come to any agreement but with firm friendship, Johnson and Otto part from one another. The present Cabinet's negotiation with the United States comes to a deadlock, and a military government is likely to be formed soon. To Otto's office comes Segawa who wants to discuss his plan to follow the army as a war correspondent. He is followed by Lin who asks Otto to find a job for him. Discussing the current situation with them, Otto, feels the difficulty of his position. "Well, I have become isolated, but even single-handed I will try to support Japan", Otto whispers to himself. (Epilogue) The Japanese called Otto is arrested, his spying activities have been detected. The public prosecutor, who was his classmate in high-school, tries to persuade Otto to make a written declaration of his conversion. Otto's first declaration which he wrote after his arrest is a logically constructed statement of his communist convictions, but the public prosecutor tells him that he will have to express his patriotic feelings more lavishly and make it quite clear that he is quite different from an ordinary communist. His advocate also emphasizes to Otto the importance of a show of patriotism. Otto, who has kept silent all the while, says at the end that he has acted as an honest Japanese and that he believes that what he has done was right.

Kita Morio

Kita Morio whose real name is Saitô Sôkichi was born in Aoyama, Tokyo. His father Saitô Mokichi, a psychiatrist, was at the same time the greatest *tanka* poet of modern Japan and also a student of *tanka* poetry. Kita who was his second son was greatly influenced by his father from his childhood. Kita's long novel *Nire-ke no Hitobito (People of the House of Nire)* uses his own family as a model. His grandfather who was born in Yamagata Prefecture in the northern part of Japan came to Tokyo, and established Aoyama Mental Hospital. It is he who adopted Mokichi and later married his daughter to him. In *Nire-ke no Hitobito (People of the*

House of Nire) appears a character called Shûji. The author's own childhood is projected to him. Kita, who was brought up as the son of a respectable family of the *Yamanote* (uptown) area of Tokyo, was interested in insects from his primary school days, and his knowledge about insects was almost as great as that of a specialist. During the war, obeying his father's wishes, Kita decided to be a doctor. He studied at the Science Section of Matsumoto Higher School, and then at the Medical Faculty of Tôhoku University. After graduation, he became a psychiatrist, and then took an advanced medical degree. During his student days, however, he was strongly interested in literature. He admired the works of Thomas Mann, and behind his father's back he secretly started writing novels. After writing some studies like *Hyakugafu* (*A Hundred Moths*, 1950) and *Bokushin no Gogo* (*The Afternoon of a Faun*, 1952), which show the influence of Dazai Osamu, he published *Yûrei* (*Ghosts*, 1954) at his own expense. This long lyrical novel depicts early childhood which is the "mythical age" of an individual. Kita explores the subconscious world of the child. This novel is quite beautiful. In 1956 he published unique short stories such as *Iwaone Nite* (*On the Rock Ridge*) and *Haari no Iru Oka* (*A Hillock of Winged Ants*), which are a mixture of fantasy and nihilism. Kita received the Akutagawa Prize for *Yoru to Kiri no Sumi de* (*In the Corner of Night and Mist*, 1960) which depicts the tragedy of a psychiatrist who conducts research concerning mentally retarded children in Nazi Germany during World War II. After this he became well-known as a writer. In the same year, he published an essay *Dokutoru Manbô Kôkaiki* (*The Voyage of Dr. Manbo*) which is based on Kita's experiences as a ship doctor on board a ship sailing through the oceans of the world to conduct an investigation on tuna. This work is full of sophisticated intellectual humour of good taste and is a rare bird in Japanese literature. This book became a bestseller. After this, Kita published a series of books whose titles all began with the words "Dokutoru Manbô" (Dr. Sun-fish). Among them are *Konchûki* (*Insects*) and *Seishunki* (*Youth*). *Nire-ke no Hitobito* (*The People of the House of Nire*), an ambitious work which depicts the destiny of Japanese people throughout the Meiji, Taisho, and Shôwa periods, focusing its attention on a family running a mental hospital, has also here and there humorous and lyrical touches which are characteristic of Kita. After writing this novel, Kita continued writing steadily. The long novel *Shiroki Taoyakana Mine* (*Graceful White Peak*, 1966), which is based on Kita's experience while participating in the expedition to Karakorum, is one example of his recent work. His somewhat naive sense of humour and his genuine poetic spirit appeal to people, and there are enthusiastic readers of his works among a wide range of people including both primary-school children and intellectuals. All of his works continue to sell well.

Kita Morio
Nireke no hitobito (*The people of the house of Nire*)
Published in *Shinchô*, January–December 1962.

(Synopsis) In the kitchen at the back of Nire Hospital, they were busy preparing the lunch. There were three cauldrons for cooking rice, each of which could hold nearly thirty kilograms of rice at a time. They were used to prepare meals for the hospital staff and their family dependants of whom there were roughly 100 persons, and for the patients, of whom there were over 330. Old Isuke who had been cooking rice there for fifteen years gave the signal, and the long job of putting rice into bowls began.

The building in Aoyama with its two nameplates, "Nire Hospital" and "Imperial Mental Hospital", looked really impressive when seen from the front. One saw rows of Corinthian style columns and seven towers encircling a central clock tower. This impressive white-walled building was built in 1904. When it was completed, the neighbours were really surprised, as if the black ships had appeared again. The building was really a wonder, which only a genius like Nire Kiichirô, the hospital director, could have created. He had used indiscriminately all sorts of architectural styles which he had seen abroad.

Nire Kiichiro was born as the fourth son of a ruined village headman in Yamagata. He disliked life in his native village and ran away. Nobody knew his whereabouts for a long time, but one day he suddenly re-appeared as a doctor of mental illness. Even his name had been changed from Kanazawa Jinsaku to Nire Kiichirô. He married Hisa, daughter of a wealthy landlord, and built the huge hospital in Aoyama. The hospital had been prosperous. It was now fifteen years since it had been founded. This year, Kiichirô had been elected to the Diet. On the hospital foundation day, every member of the staff received a souvenir during a dignified commemorative ceremony. All the members of the Nire family—Hisa, Kiichirô's wife; Tatsuko, his eldest daughter; and other members of the family—always came to this ceremony and sat in a dignified row. Kiichirô had acquired wealth and fame in his own life time. He behaved with an arrogant air, but he never scolded people. He conceived big plans and steadily converted them into reality. He was a worldly-minded genius. His method of examination was a mysterious one. He examined his patient's head with a stethoscope and looked into his ear "to see the brain". Nevertheless, he won the confidence of his patients and his reputation as a doctor was very high.

He had two sons, Ôshû and Yonekuni. Ôshû kept failing his examinations without being a bit dismayed. Yonekuni was an eccentric who entered an agricultural college. Kiichirô also adopted Tetsukichi, a brilliant man from his native area, and Zaôyama Tatsuji, an extremely tall man, as his sons, and nominated Tetsukichi, who had become Tatsuko's husband, as the next director of the hospital. His beautiful second daughter, Seiko, fell in love with a teacher of English. She was virtually disowned, and died. His pert third daughter, Momoko, was made to marry a doctor when she was still a student, but later rebelled. Tetsukichi, who was a scholar-type person, found the theatrical atmosphere of the Nire family uncongenial. He went to Germany and spent all his time in study. The Nire hospital which was left unburnt at the time of the great Tokyo earthquake in 1923 was burnt down in 1924 by an accidental fire when Tetsukichi was on his way back to Japan. Old Kiichirô, undismayed by this misfortune, bought a large piece of land in Matsubara, Setagaya, in the suburbs of Tokyo, and was planning to build a new hospital, when he suddenly died of apoplexy. The whole burden of running the big Nire hospital fell on Tetsukichi, the adopted son. He experienced all sorts of hardships to which he had been unaccustomed, such as borrowing money from an usurer. However, assisted by Katsumata Hidekichi, the deputy director, he managed to build up a huge hospital at Matsubara.

The hospital in Matsubara which was managed by Katsumata and Ôshû prospered. Tetsukichi, gradually became a mere nominal head of the hospital, with no real authority. He was always compared with Kiichirô, his adoptive father, and it was often to his disadvantage. Tetsukichi devoted himself to writing *The History of Psychopathology*, and found there the joy and meaning of his life. His wife, Tatsuko, lived separately in Matsubara. Their three children, Shun'ichi, Aiko and Shûji, grew up, dividing their time between Aoyama and Matsubara. They grew up during the brief period of peace at the beginning of the Shôwa period, their interests commanded by airplanes, romantic films and dreams of love. Various things happened in the Nire family, but from the long-run point of view, it was an eventless life. Then the war broke out. This war which involved the whole of Japan was also very destructive to the Nire family. The Nire hospital, fruit of many people's labour, was burnt down during an air-raid, and Tetsukichi was killed. Yonekuni and Shun'ichi went to fight in the war. Beautiful Aiko had her face burnt by an incendiary shell. Everything was ruined, and then the war ended. Amidst the ruins of war, only Tatsuko remained undismayed. She scolded her apathetic children and made up her mind to rebuild the Nire hospital which had been the pride of Kiichirô, her great father.

Kiyama Shohei

Kiyama Shôhei was born in 1904 in Okayama Prefecture. He entered Tôyô University, but left it before completing his course. He started working as a poet and published two collections of poems, *No* (*Field*) and *Mekura to Chinba* (*The Blind and the Lame*). In 1933 in collaboration with

Dazai Osamu and others, he started the coterie magazine *Kaihyô* (*Seal*), and the next year he also started the magazine *Aoi Hana* (*Blue Flower*) with Nakahara Chûya, Dan Kazuo, Dazai and others. In 1935 he became a member of the editorial staff of the magazine *Nihon Rôman-ha* (*Japanese Romanticists*). *Jinzô no Haru* (*The Spring for Jinzô*), was published in the August edition of *Waseda Bungaku* (*Waseda Literature*) in the same year. It is an idyllic short story which depicts with humour a poor primary schoolboy of a mountain village. *Kôhone* (*A candock*), which he wrote next, is a novel of medium length. The hero of the novel happens to meet a woman whom he once loved. She is returning to her native place with the bones of her late husband. He stays with her at a mountain hot spring resort, and comes back without anything special happening between them. This novel is slightly sentimental, although it has a faintly humorous quality about it. *Ujigami-sama* (*The Guardian God*), published in the March number of *Bungei* (*Literature*) in 1943, is an excellent work which, somewhat in the manner of a travel diary, depicts a family who returns to their native village after a long absence and visits the guardian god of the place.

Kitayama went to Manchuria during the second World War, and became a supernumerary employee in charge of publicity activities, in the Agricultural Land Bureau at Hsin-ching (Ch'and-ch'un), the capital of Manchoukou. He was drafted into the army there. Spending one year in Ch'and-ch'un after the end of the war, he finally returned to Japan. His hard experiences in Ch'ang-ch'un during the postwar period were used as material for *Tairiku no Hosomichi* (*The Narrow Road of Asia*) and *Mimigakunon* (*A Smattering of Knowledge*), Kiyama started writing the former in 1947; it was published in 1962 by Shinchôsha (a publishing firm). Its hero is an honest old soldier of the Japanese army. Through a series of flashbacks, his tragi-comical journey through Manchuria and China is depicted, and the colonial scenes of that time are elaborately painted. It belongs to the category of War Literature, but, because of the author's inborn cheerful carefree disposition, the gloomy subject, similar to that of Noma Hiroshi's *Shinkû-chitai* (*Vacuum Zone*), does not depress the reader. The latter was published in the October edition of *Bungei Shunjû* (*Literary Years*) in 1956. It realistically depicts the life of a fragile middle-aged man in Ch'ang-ch'un Manchuria, who tries to escape being made a prisoner of war. He is very afraid of becoming a prisoner of war, but he speaks to the Russian soldiers he meets on the street using his smattering of Russian. The good nature of the hero makes this novel pleasant reading. *Tairiku no Hosomichi* (*The Narrow Road of Asia*) was awarded the Education Minister's Prize for Artistic Achievement in 1963. Kiyama died on the 23rd of August, 1968.

KIYAMA Shohei
Mimigakumon *(A smattering of knowledge)*
Published in *Bungei Shunjû,* October, 1956.

Although it is no more than mere smattering, I know some Russian words—words like "Hallo!", "Hey!", "One, two, three, four", "Fool!" or "comrade". Apart from these individual words, I also know some expressions which I have mastered after some practice—for example, ("Ya nye Ôchen Zdorôf"). This expression roughly means, "I don't feel well" or "I am sick". The reason why I once learned Russian avidly, which I still retain in my memory to some extent, is that eleven years ago in Ch'ang-ch'un Manchuria, Russia was beginning to round up Japanese people as prisoners of war. According to a rumour, the commander-in-chief of the Japanese army in Manchuria was already imprisoned somewhere in Russia, at Chita or Khabarovsk, and had given false information about the number of men under his charge. It was quite natural that the memory of a person of that age should sometimes play him false, but I was not very happy with the idea of becoming a prisoner of war as a victim of the commander's infirmity. Besides, I was already forty-two years old, and needed spectacles.

On the 16th of August 1945, the day after the war had come to an end, I went out to the town of Ch'and-ch'un by myself. After drinking wine at a Manchurian restaurant, I came to the entrance of the Kodama Park named after General Kodama Gentarô who had been the chief of staff of the Japanese army in Manchuria at the time of the Russo-Japanese War. Suddenly I noticed that the statue of General Kodama, which had been erected there, was headless. While I was staring at the headless statue, two Russian soldiers came from the other side of the road with guns hanging from their shoulders. This was the first time that I had seen Russian soldiers. When I saw them, I crossed towards them in great haste, stood in front of them and said: "Comrades!" in Russian. They could not understand me at first, but when I had repeated the same words several times, one of them also said "Oh, Comrade!" and smiled at his companions. I was glad that I had been able to make myself understood, but I was at a loss what to say next. Then, it occurred to me that in 1941 Matsuoka Yôsuke, Japanese minister of Foreign Affairs at the time, and Stalin concluded the Russo-Japanese Non-Agression Pact. "Wo (I), Wo (I) Matsuoka", I said, pointing at myself and using a mixture of Chinese and Japanese. Then, I said, "You, You Stalin", pointing at the Russian solidiers. This time I used a mixture of English and Russian. The Russian soldiers smiled broadly, shouted "O, Yaponskiy (Oh, Japanese!)" and shook my hand. I hastily rummaged in my pockets, took out my cigarette case and offered it to them. They took it, and each of them gave me one piece of Russian cigarette in return.

The cold winter came again that year to Manchuria. It was rumoured that Russia would soon send Japanese prisoners of war back to Japan, but this was not done for a long time. Since the M Bureau where I was working as a supernumerary employee had been dissolved, I did not know how to earn my living. It so happened, however, that a friend of mine who had been my colleague at the M Bureau, started a *tempura* (fried food) business using the money which he had got by selling his wife's clothes and it was agreed, in January, 1946, that I should be in charge of selling the *tempura*. On the first day of business I was hurrying to my friend's house with the turnover for the day, after fulfilling my assigned rôle with considerable difficulty, when somebody shouted, "Hey, you! Stop!" in Japanese. Without turning back, I knew it was the Manchurian policeman whom I had just passed. I pretended that I had not heard anything, and took several more steps before I was grabbed by the arm by the policeman who had come after me: he had been looking for Japanese to be sent to Siberia as prisoners-of-war. The year before, I had been summoned as a prisoner-of-war, but thanks to the kindness of a female officer who had taken pity on me because of my poor health, I had been allowed to go back on the same day. "To be picked up by a Manchurian copper at the end of the war and sent to Siberia is .... unreasonable! If I am sent, I will freeze to death".—Such thoughts passed through my mind. When we arrived in front of the police station, I wanted to go to the bog. Relieving myself on the spot, I watched for a chance to escape, and managed to break away. I arrived back at my lodgings safely. I rested there for an hour or so, waiting until my heart stopped galloping. Then I asked a woman staying at the same place to lend me her four-year-old daughter for a hundred yen, and went out with the girl on my back. Since I gave the woman one hundred yen, the profit of the day was gone, but I thought that I should at least take the rest of the money to my friend, otherwise he would not be able to lay in the stock for the next day. I should add in explanation that I borrowed the child because they almost never took somebody with a little child on his back as a prisoner of war.

Ko Haruto

Kô Haruto was born in 1906 in Kumamoto Prefecture. He graduated from the Department of English Literature of Meiji Gakuin (a private college in Tokyo). At first he wanted to be a painter, but while he was still a student he came under the influence of Senke Motomaro, a poet who wrote about the life and feelings of the common people. Kô also started writing poetry. Among the collections of his poems which he published at his own expense are *Kô Haruto Shishû* (*The Collected Poems of Kô Haruto*, *Suichû no Kuwa* (*A Mulberry in Water*, 1938). In various literary circles he was taken note of as a writer of humanitarian poems. In 1925 he published his first novel, *Kage no Tochi* (*Shaded Ground*). During World War II, he was mistakenly thought to be a communist. He was detained at a police station for a long period, and was interrogated closely. He was released in 1945—shortly before Japan's surrender. After the war, he experienced great poverty and deprivation. He published somewhat autobiographical short novels in which he used his own experiences as raw material, and won a reputation for being a good writer.

There is nothing grandiose or ostentatious about his novels. They are, just like their good-natured poetical-minded creator, fragile little things which are yet permeated with poetical sentiment. Behind his works lies the strength of a man who stakes his existence on each moment and always lives with his whole might. This creates a solid feeling of reality which gives a quiet weight to his works. The author uses in his work only what he has come to believe, by experience and reflection, to be of the "essence" of life. He also writes with great care.

Furo-oke (*Bathtub*, 1966), summarized above, was reprinted in his collection of short stories, *Ichijô no Hikari* (*A Streak of Light*) which was published in 1968. This collection includes in addition to *Furo-oke* (*Bathtub*) seven short stories including *Akegata no Kyaku* (*A Visitor at Daybreak*, 1948) and *Shimon* (*Fingerprint*, 1949), which are all based on the author's own experiences during the gloomy period of the war and the immediate postwar years, forming a continuous whole. In *Furo-oke* (*Bathtub*), the author has expressed with melancholy and humour the moving efforts of a weak unmanly man who can barely endure living in the cruel inhumane society of wartime, and the charm of his bright affectionate wife who gives him support through her devotion. *Furo-oke* (*Bathtub*) is in itself complete, but to understand it and the characteristics of the author better, one should also consider the other works included in the collection, *Ichijô no Hikari* (*A Streak of Light*). This collection was awarded the Yomiuri Literary Prize and attracted the attention of many lovers of literature.

Most of Kô's works are more or less autobiographical, but he has also written *Shijin Senke Motomaro* (*The Poet Senke Motomaro*, 1957) which is the fruit of Kô's love for his teacher Senke; and *Ushinawareta Sokoku* (*Lost Fatherland*, 1959) which deals with the Sorge case (Sorge is the name of a German person who was arrested in 1941 on the suspicion of spying in

Japan for Soviet Russia). These novels also deserve special attention for their uniqueness.

Ko Haruto
Furo-oke *(Bathtub)*
Published in *Shin Nihon Bungaku,* February 1966.

(Synopsis) I am looking for a bathtub. I don't have a bath at home. I used to go to the public bathhouse in my neighbourhood, but now I hesitate to go there because I know that the owner of the public bathhouse and his wife do not like my coming. This is because I have scabs all over my body.

I spent four months, that is, from March to July of 1945, the year of Japan's surrender, in a police cell. During this period I was confined in an unhygenic place and I could not take a bath. That is how I have come to get these scabs. The reason why I was arrested was that I had books and pamphlets which were banned at that time for ideological reasons. They jumped to the conclusion that I was a villain who belonged to the comintern and who had been active for the Communist Party. I was released from the police cell shortly before Japan's surrender.

After that I boiled water at home and washed myself thoroughly every day. However, after the public bathhouse, *Matsu no Yu (Pine Bath),* re-opened, I started going there, first covering my body with mercuro-chrome. That I was covered with mercurochrome shows how severely I was suffering from malnutrition and its inevitable side product: lack of resistance to disease. Since I pretended that I had been in a hospital instead of saying that I had been in a police cell, people looked at me with some sympathy. A doctor came to examine me once, but he never came again on the pretext that there was no medicine. It was shortly after the war, and the shortage of goods was acute. Poor people were ignored. Hiroko, my wife, burnt vice-bran to get oil, painted the oil on my body, and applied bandages thereafter. It was quite effective in treating the scabs. Among the people I saw at the public bath, there were some whose bodies were also painted all over with mercurochrome, but their number gradually decreased.

After three years had passed, my scabs seemed to have gone, but they erupted again within about two months. This reminded me once more of the time I had been in the police cell. The police cell had been a real den of fleas and lice while I had been there. Even during air-raids, unlike other criminals, the ideological offenders were not allowed out of their cells. Hiroko, my wife, was kind enough to send in to me food and other things for my use quite often. Even N., the policeman who was investigating my case, was impressed by this. It was thanks to my wife's devotion that I remained alive in the police cell. N. told me that the famous philosopher, Miki Kiyoshi, had been arrested. Hiroko, not being afraid of receiving rebukes from the jailer, inserted coloured leaves or other leaves of plants or trees of the season into the lunchbox she sent in to me. It was to keep me in touch with nature. My wife's devotion moved the jailer, and he came to allow her to be at my side while I took a meal. My wife had an unusual talent for procuring food, and, although in dire economic straits, always found food for me. It was roughly a month after the end of the war that I heard that Miki Kiyoshi had died in prison, his entire body almost rotting alive with scabs.

At the public bath, *Matsu no Yu,* they did not refuse to let me take a bath, but I hear that they received protests from other customers. After my scabs erupted again, I wanted by hook or by crook to build a bathroom in my house. Hiroko asked a gardener in our neighbourhood to build a bathroom for us. He answered that he would build it if we could find a bathtub. In such a confused age, he must have thought, that it was next to impossible for us to get a bathtub. This consideration seems to be the reason why, on the surface, he said "yes" to our request. I walked around in vain looking for a shop which sold bathtubs. I asked a coffin-maker if he could make a bathtub for us, but, as I had expected, he said "no". Since the gardener despised us, dwellers in a tenement house, I wanted to revenge myself on him for this, and obstinately continued my search for a bathtub; but it was without success.

One day, when I came near Mejiro Station, I remembered the woman novelist, Miyamoto Yuriko, of the Proletarian School. All of a sudden, I remembered how I had felt happy when she once treated me kindly and how I had been annoyed when I found her cold to me later. I lost interest in continuing my search for a bathtub and came home, but at home I was surprised by the good news that Hiroko had found a new bathtub at a farmer's house in our neighbourhood. The gardener was sent for, but he would not believe the news, and I got so angry that I ordered my wife to fetch the bathtub straight away, without caring that there was fit place to put it in our house.

When the bathtub arrived the next morning, I put it in the alcove of our tiny house. Even the gardener could not help admitting that it was a fine bathtub. I slept by the bathtub, and did my writing in front of it. When a guest came, I explained that, since it was the most valuable thing in my house, I could not put it anywhere else. It seemed that the fresh smell of the wooden bathtub was more effective than any medicine for my scabs. A great number of them fell off my body. In ten days' time, the bathroom was completed.

Kojima Nobuo

Kojima Nobuo is one of the "Third New Generation" writers who followed the "First Postwar Group" writers. Most of the "Third New Generation" writers (Yasuoka Shôtaro, Yoshiyuki Junnouke,s Shôno Junzô, Endô Shûsaku and others) appeared on the literary scene around 1955. Kojima received the Akutagawa Prize in 1954 for *American School*. At first, however, Kojima was not like Yasuoka and Yoshiyuki for whom the only reality is sense data, who make light of ideas, and whose works often represent the views of an outlaw or villain. His early works showed a rather complicated sense of humour, but they did not necessarily show Kojima at his best. The basic character of his works gradually changed.

Hoshi (*Stars*, 1955), *Shima* (*Island*, 1955) and *Ai no Kanketsu* (*The End of Love*, 1956) show that Kojima was attempting literary experiments and that his works were beginning to deal with abstract ideas, unlike his previous satirical works. However, Kojima's experimental works did not receive the recognition they deserved, and he remained in relative obscurity for a while, continuing his persistent efforts to explore and analyze human relationships in society, especially family relationships. It was only after *Henshô* (*Reflections*, 1963), which subtly portrays the psychology of a man who has just lost his wife, that his works came to be appreciated. In this essay, three works are discussed: namely *Henshô* (*Reflections*), *Hôyô Kazoku* (*Keep the Family United*, 1965) which is generally regarded as Kojima's best novel, and *Onoborisan* (*Guests from the Country*, 1970).

The central subject of *Henshô* (*Reflections*) is the psychology of a man who has lost his wife and who is debating whether he should remarry or not. It has hardly any plot. The hero of the novel ponders on his real reaction to his wife's death. He asks himself: "Aren't you thinking that you are lucky?" or "Isn't your real feeling one of relief?" In the novel, there are various female characters, and his relationships with them reveal the complicated nature of his reaction to the death of his wife. There is also a young man called H., who comes to live in the same house with the hero. He serves as a contrast to bring out the psychology of the middle-aged hero in full relief. This novel, therefore, centres on the hero's thoughts and feelings about various women who are compared to his deceased wife, and also around his sexual imaginings. In this sense, the novel is not one representing the general school of realism. It seems to be dominated by the idea that only one's consciousness is real.

Hôyô Kazoku (*Keep the Family United*) is another of his novels in which the man-and-wife relationship has a central significance. The hero is a university teacher, called Miwa Shunsuke, who has studied in the U.S. His wife, who is two years older than he, commits adultery with an American soldier who has been visiting their house. Then she develops breast cancer and is hospitalized. After an operation she comes home, but has to be re-hospitalized. Finally she dies. After her death, the hero has some arranged interviews with prospective brides. The minor characters of the novel include Yamagishi, the hero's junior in school, who in the meantime has come to live in his house, and a housekeeper who keeps coming and going from the beginning to the end. After the death of his wife, there is no longer any centre in his newly-built house. His daughter and his son start doing what they like without restraint. At the end of the novel his son runs away from home.

Throughout the novel, the hero always has a strong desire to be the head of his family. On the other hand, he thinks that he himself has a "powerful freedom". He wants to control the whole family, but always without success. He has to witness its gradual disintegration. He is aware that his family is falling apart, but, with all his desire to be the head, to be the centre of his family, he cannot stop this process. The hero is not only aware of the disintegration of his family, he is also aware of the disintegration within his own self. He says, "I am an insecure man, full of pain". His own disintegration deeply affects the disintegration of his family. His inner disintegration is what prompts the unrestrained selfish behaviour from his wife, his son, his daughter, and the maid.

In a sense, the author depicts the disintegration of the old family system in postwar Japan in this novel. Although the hero aspires to be the moral centre of his family, because of the disintegration of his own ego, the family gradually collapses from inside. This process is depicted through the somewhat masochistic eye of an intellectual, and it gives the novel a significance which is not merely literary. It expresses very eloquently one aspect of the intellectual climate of postwar Japan. This is probably the reason why this novel was awarded the first Tanizaki Jun'ichirô Prize.

The hero of *Onoborisan* (*Guests from the Country*) is also a university teacher. His son is going to get married, and he invites his younger brother and his wife to his house to attend the wedding. This brother is a weak person, while his wife is talkative and impudent. When the hero is importuned by his brother, he cannot refuse to give him money. His brother has not fully recovered from injuries he received in a traffic accident. Besides, he was induced to take part in the business enterprise of his wife's brother and lost a great deal of money. Altogether, he has been very unlucky. His wife also had to be hospitalized. It is only to attend the wedding that she is out of the hospital. All these things are disclosed in the miserable slow conversation between the brother and his wife, which the hero listens to attentively. Only innocent Mariko, the daughter of the brother, gives relief to this otherwise very gloomy novel which depicts a couple in adversity. The novel treats a family relationship, namely, the relationship between the hero's family and his brother's family. Although this is a very ordinary and common-place subject, this novel has a sinistre atmosphere. This is mainly because the gloomy foreboding the brother's wife has about the future is quite convincing. She says, for example, that her husband has the seal of death on his face, and that he may die quite soon. Then she says that, since one's brothers are the first responsibility one has to bear, she hopes to receive help from her brother-in-law and his family. "If my husband dies, I hope your wife will also be kind enough to start working to help us", she says, clinging to the hero's family. Towards the end of the novel, Mariko is accidentally locked in the toilet. When she cries out, her father says, "I will come right away", and gets up. This is where the novel ends.

From *Henshô* (*Reflections*) to *Onoborisan* (*Guests from the Country*), family problems have been a constant theme of Kojima's novels. What is a family? What is the naked reality beneath the veneer of routine relationships? Kojima has been trying to answer such questions by depicting the real thoughts and feelings of people involved in rather depressing family relationships. In his novels we do not meet people with the feudal consciousness which made all the members of a family rally around one powerful head in prewar Japan. Even if such bonds have been broken, however, something seems to be left of the old problem of family ethics in a hidden form.

Kojima has been trying to analyze the problems of family ethics. Family relationships are still the focus of his later nihilistic novels.

Kono Taeko

Kôno Taeko, the eldest daughter of her family, was born in Ôsaka. Her father was a merchant who owned a long-established wholesaler's shop dealing with mushrooms and other goods. Thus, Kôno was brought up in a merchants' world, which was dominated by old customs and mutual obligations among its members, but which was quite rational as far as business was concerned. When she was about ten years old, her family moved to a middle class residential area in the suburbs. Among the wealthy merchants it was, at that time, in vogue to separate the family residence from the shop. In her new home, Kôno came into contact with the "modern intellectual atmosphere". From her high school days, she started reading literary works avidly. When she was fifteen years old, the Pacific War broke out, and gradually the liberal atmosphere disappeared from her world. She entered, partly to avoid requisition, Ôsaka Women's College, and tried to continue her studies of English Literature. However, soon they ceased to give classes at the college, and Kôno, together with other students, was sent to a factory producing military uniforms, and worked in a group under the strict supervision of military men. Her experiences in that inhuman environment were later depicted in her work, *Hei no Naka* (*Within the Walls*, 1962). In this work, girl students who are cut off from the outside world and who are in a state of confinement, together hide and protect a little boy who has been separated from his parents during an air-raid and strayed into the factory. Prompted by their maternal instinct the girl students pet the boy, but he is killed on account of a tiny error. All this comes to light in the end, and develops into a serious affair. *Hei no Naka* (*Within the Walls*) is a fine novel which sheds light on the inhumanity of war from a unique angle. Kôno's war experience in her youth exerted a great influence on her later life. After the war, she had various ambitions, but she had to suffer the severe frustrations of a reality which would not allow her to realize her aspirations. She ignored her parents' opposition, tried to work her way towards becoming a writer, and wrote novels. However, partly because she fell ill, she did not receive recognition as a writer for fifteen years and lived in obscurity. It was by receiving the Akutagawa Prize for *Kani* (*Crabs*) in 1963 that Kôno managed to establish herself as a writer. As *Yôji-gari* (*Boy hunt*), summarized below, indicates, she has been dealing with the theme of perverted sexuality, female sadism and masochism, with discernment and sensibility. She has also managed to avoid falling into unrealistic unrestrained fantasy unlike many other writers dealing with sexual perversion. Her works are given substance by the realistic evocation of the everyday life of couples or cohabitants in actual society. To describe some of her other works, *Saigo no Toki* (*Time of Death*), starts from the question "What happens if I die tomorrow in a traffic accident?" and from "the other side of death" tries to define the nature of an ideal couple. In long novels such as *Fui no Koe* (*Unexpected Voice*), *Kusaikire* (*Steaming Grass*) and *Kaiten-tobira* (*Revolving Door*), she deals with the theme of sex in women who are working and married. She depicts the complexity of the problems connected with sex by depicting sexual perversions and even murder, and pursues the question of how to realize the instinctive sexual happiness proper to a human being. Kôno's works are characterized by a physical sensibility peculiar to women, steady realism in describing everyday life and persistent, almost religious, devotion to her theme.

KÔNO Taeko
Yoji-gari *(Boy hunt)*
Published in *Shinchô*, December 1961.

(Synopsis) Of all human beings, Hayashi Akiko disliked girls of three to ten years of age the most. She could not stand the thought that she had also been such a girl once. On the surface, life had been very nice for her when she had been at that age, but she had felt nauseated and accursed as if she was destined to walk inside a low long tunnel indefinitely or as if mucus were oozing out all over her body. Whenever she saw a girl of that age with her white skin, chubby body, girl-like hairstyle and high monotonous voice, she was reminded of that inner gloom, that nausea she had experienced, and she looked away. Her feeling towards the girls of that age was akin to the repulsion she felt towards small creatures like snakes or frogs. However, strangely enough, she had come to entertain a special liking towards boys of the same age. Although she was childless, she was often induced to do things like buying a cute boy's suit she saw at a department store. After having bought one, she would look for an acquaintance of hers with a boy of corresponding age so that she could give the suit as a present.

Until several years ago she had been a chorus girl in an opera company. When she had graduated from the music school, she had been regarded as promising. She had tried to become a prima donna, but had ended up as a chorus girl. However, the knowledge of Italian which she had acquired for the sake of opera had proved to be very useful to her. She was now earning her living by teaching Italian to her juniors, by translating Italian fashion magazines and by dealing with the correspondance of a compressor manufacturing company as a part-time employee. Usually she did not visit the opera company she had left, but when she thought that a shirt-blouse she had bought at a department store would become the son of a company member, she would go to the dressing room to see him. She could not bear to miss the sight of the boy struggling into the shirt-blouse wriggling his cute bottom in the effort.

In the compressor company there was a man called Sasaki who was two years younger than Akiko. One day, he told her that shortly after the war when he had been a student he had had to help during a childbirth. It was at this time that Akiko came to be really attracted to him. She sensed a certain cruelty on his part from the contents of his story and from the way he told it, and it excited her. Sasaki was the type of man she liked. Sasaki, who was a bachelor also wanted to have a woman around whom he did not have to take too seriously. For Akiko he was the best of all possible choices. United by the affinity of their personalities, they started living together.

One evening when Sasaki came back, after a long absence, from a business trip Akiko was busy making preparation for love-making, employing the many aids to enhance the excitement of the act she had learnt. Sasaki noticed a vinyl rope for hanging out washing, and started bending it in the middle. This rope had metal fittings at both ends. Akiko entreated him to whip her making sure that the metal fittings struck her. Both of them liked the sound human flesh produced under flagellation. The more they got excited, the greater the sounds they produced. That night Sasaki finally pulled the rope tight around Akiko's neck and her throat seems to have produced a tremendous noise. The wife of the keeper of the flats came to warn them and said, "We would not like to be responsible for any death . . .". Other people living in the apartment house all knew their peculiarities, but the noises they made that night were quite out of the ordinary. After love-making that night, Akiko fainted and remained unconscious for nearly thirty minutes.

When Akiko was by herself, she often daydreamed in bed. Once she daydreamed about a boy of seven or eight years of age and his father in his thirties. The father scolded the boy in a very gentle tone of voice and chastized him. He slapped the boy across the face. He tore his clothes off and whipped his bottom with a belt made of crocodile's skin. He hit him with a stick. Blood ran down the stick, and trickled down the boy's thighs. He pressed the boy's back on a burning hot tin roof. He tied the boy's hands and suspended him from a tree, and struck him in his belly. The boy's belly was torn open and his beautiful violet intestines started flowing out. He freed the boy from the tree, and swung him round as if he was a kite. Akiko became really rapturous in her daydream and began to sweat. At three o'clock, she went to the public baths. Her body was covered with scratches and bruises. Hiding them with her towel, she walked to the bath. Taking a bath, she looked around to see if there was not a little boy in sight. She wished that a boy would come. Whenever she found a boy, she would play with him for a long time. On the way from the public baths, she was lucky enough to find a little boy near a greengrocer's shop in an alley. The boy, who was about three years old, was eating a slice of red water-melon. "Is it nice?", Akiko asked him. She wanted to have a bite of the slice which had been untidily gnawed by the boy. "Give me a bit, love" she said. That water-melon which had been soiled by the sweat, saliva and dirty hands of the boy, was lukewarm and was like a lump of flesh. She nibbled at it, and cherished it in her mouth.

Kurahashi Yumiko

Kurahashi Yumiko was born in Tosayamada, Kôchi Prefecture in Shikoku. Her father was a dentist, and was an influential person of the area. Kurahashi was the eldest daughter. Kôchi Prefecture is situated on the Pacific side of Shikoku, is remote from Honshû (the main island of Japan) and the capital Tokyo, and is an area with strong local traditions. This area, however, often produces revolutionary personalities who affect the whole of Japan. Kurahashi grew up in the country, and at his father's command, studied at a school whose curriculum was related to dentistry; however, she acquired a good knowledge of contemporary literature and philosophy, beginning with satire, and of Japanese and world classics through her own private reading. She then entered the Department of French Literature of Meiji University. While she was studying in the graduate section of the department, she entered a short story, *Parutai* (*Communist Party*) in the Meiji University Newspaper literary competition, and was awarded the President's Prize. This fresh intellectual work immediately attracted attention from literary and journalistic quarters, and this unknown girl student was stormed by requests to write novels and literary criticism. During the years following this, *Hebi* (*Snake*, 1960) which vividly and sensuously tells the story of how a man becomes pregnant through mental stimulus, *Hinin* (*Outcast*), *Kon'yaku* (*Betrothal*, 1960), *Ningen no Nai Kami* (*God without Man*), a satire on a tyrant resembling Hitler, *Dokonimo Nai Basho* (*Not of This World*) which is based on Kafka's literary theory, *Kurai Tabi* (*Gloomy Journey*, 1961) which is a sort of Japanese imitation of Butor, and other works, were published one after the other. These works are brilliant, intellectual and ambitious. Kurahashi said that in her works she intended to express a certain view of the "essence of things" through her imagery. She is probably the first philosophical *avant-garde* writer of Japan. In many of her works a twin brother and sister called K and L appear as the central characters: they are usually joined by Q, a lover, and S. who fights against the corrupt state of society. Thus the structure of her novels is often schematic, abstract and metaphysical. The imagery is, on the other hand, bold and unrestrained. It is most feminine, physical and taken from everyday existence. Kurahashi is a talented writer who has defied all the existing theories and techniques behind novel-writing and created *avand-garde* literature which is at once intellectual and sensuous. After writing *Sasoritachi* (*Scorpions*) and *Seishôjo* (*Holy Girl*, 1965) which deal with motives such as incest between father and daughter or brother and sister, the murder of one's mother, and cannibalism; and *Yôjo no Yôni*, (*Like a Witch*, 1965), which fundamentally deals with the problems involved in being a novelist; she did not write anything for a while due to her marriage and a period of study in the United States. She is now actively writing again. Among her recent works are *Sumiyakisuto Q no Bôken* (*The Adventures of Q, the Sumiyakist*) which satirizes revolutionaries in the large-scale fictional world of her fantasy; *Kakô nite* (*At the Mouth of a River*), and *Shiroi Kami no Dôjo* (*The Little Girl with Grey Hair*, 1969), two "anti-tragedy" novels which use *motifs* taken from Japanese classics and Greek tragedy while using a contemporary setting; and *Yume no Ukihashi* (*The Bridge of Dreams*), a long novel. Kurahashi like Ôe Kenzaburô, is receiving enthusiastic support from young intellectual readers for her novels and for her bitingly satirical essays. She is one of the most representative young writers of contemporary Japan.

Kurahashi Yumiko
Parutai *(Communist party)*
Published in *Bungakukai,* March 1960.

One day you asked me whether I had made up my mind at last. I answered that I had. You began to explain that to enter the Party was to subject one's personal life, including of course, the question of love, to Party principles. Your glasses were shining too much for me to see the expression of your naked eyes behind them. The clacking of your teeth almost made the bad alignment of your jaws and teeth visible, and, without realizing it, I let out an animal-like laugh, whereupon you took hold of my hands and squeezed them. As usual, your hands were warm and damp. If I remember rightly, the room we were in was comfortably furnished but unpleasant. After being taken by you to this room, in a mammoth building called "The Hostel", where the "students", while separated from one another by walls, lived a strong community life, I was aware of a strange sense of unreality. Up until this time, it would not be an exaggeration to say that I had loved you with an almost perfect love. We had confessed our love to each other. You, the Party member, weeping copiously, had declared before the "comrade" students that we would love each other, and we had received the students' blessing. You emphasized the great importance of correctly drawing up a "curriculum vitae", one of the documents necessary in order to obtain permission to enter the Party, and explained with great enthusiasm that it was to be written. However, as I had almost no interest in my own past, certainly not enough to pick out the details of my past diligently, dress them up in fine language, put them in logical sequence, and moreover, relate them to my motive for wanting to join the Party. That required just too much effort for my liking. Despite your eager persuasion, I put off writing my "curriculum vitae" from day to day. I felt the past put restraints on me, and, moreover, that it was too much of a bind to have to substantiate all these details. I wanted to escape from the past and reach out towards the future. I wanted to give my loyalty to the Party and to have my freedom limited by the Party simply to gain a greater freedom. You pointed out that my argument showed a dangerous tendency to rely on my own intuition, and that I had not sufficiently grasped the stern "inevitability" of revolution. I cut you short. I had no wish to hear such rubbish. One does not enter the Party because "revolution" is inevitable, but because one chooses "revolution", I said. We started to quarrel. "Why the hell can't you understand?", we both yelled at almost the same moment. Without settling our quarrel and healing the split, we worked together. We, the subordinates of the "harbour School Settlement" group, mainly concentrated on visiting the factories in the industrial city of K, helping the "workers", and setting up "study groups" for them. One day I touched the strong, hardened muscles of a "worker" who attended the group meeting, and had intercourse with him with a perfectly clear consciousness of what I was doing, and feeling as if he and I were animals of a different species. Around the beginning of the rainy season I finally managed to finish writing my "curriculum vitae", and sent it to Party headquarters. I expect it was passed from hand to hand, became quite dirty and seedy-looking in the process, and was finally put into the hands of the top officials. In summer, our group was sent to camp on the banks of the M river, in order to train in community living. I sometimes began to feel, however that our commuinty living was like a group of dogs chained up together. At a night meeting of the group, I criticized the Party, which had avoided revolution and expounded an unprincipled service and love of society. On the following day, the Party ordered us to sell Party handouts outside the station. We were arrested. You glowed with praise simply because I refused to reveal anything under torture at the police station, and for the first time called me "comrade". I was convulsed with hysterical laughter; you looked so bloomingly comic. When I revealed the facts to you, that I had become pregnant by one of the "workers", you were almost knocked senseless, and began to cry. I was released, and after an interval of many months, returned to my room again. After scrutinizing the red party-membership card on my desk minutely, I flung it in the waste-paper basket. I decided to start proceedings to leave the Party.

Maruoka Akira

Maruoka Akira was born in Tokyo in 1907. His parents were both *tanka* poets who had been taught by Ochiai Naobumi. Maruoka was the eldest son. In his childhood, induced by his parents, he decided to be a diplomat, and studied French at Gyôsei Primary School in Tokyo. He was also placed under the custoday of a French family and lived with them. He was forbidden to read literature, but unable to bear his loneliness, used to read secretly. It was roughly in 1927, the year when he entered the preparatory course of Keiô University, that Maruoka made up his mind to become a writer. Led by his passion for literature, he became a pupil of Minakami Takitarô, and published *Madamu Marutan no Namida* (*Madame Martin's Tears*, 1930). In this work Maruoka depicted his experiences in Oku-nikkô where he had met his Swiss girl friend, Simone, for the first time. The fresh realism of this work attracted attention, and Maruoka became known as a promising new writer. Then he wrote many works depicting the life of the leisured-class-people in Karuizawa and other summer resorts. *Kôkan Kyôju* (*Exchange Lessons*, 1930) is one example. They are distinguished by their attractive style, a product of a well balanced knowledge of the old Japanese tradition and of western culture. In his *Ikimono no Kiroku* (*The Record of Living Things,* 1936), influenced by Hori Tatsuo, Maruoka tried to penetrate into the subconscious world of man. It is a Western style "roman" coloured by a fine Japanese sensibility. During the war, he contemplated on the irrational absurdity of human life and wrote a series of stories which were later published in *Yônen Jidai* (*Childhood,* 1954),which traced the development of his personality in his childhood. After experiencing an air-raid in 1945 in which he thought he might be killed, the tone of Maruoka's refined works underwent a big change. In 1951 he published *Nise Kiristo* (*False Christ*) which uses as a model Hara Tamiki, a writer who experienced and suffered from the A-bomb.

Maruoka tries to express what he thinks is the true reality of man and his world. He is a man who seeks truth. His originality is derived from the beautiful harmony between the Japanese and Western elements in his culture. After the war he published impressive "I" novels like *Dôjidai ni Ikiru Hito* (*My Contemporaries*, 1953). He also came to deal mainly with the theme of life and death in his works. For Maruoka who had once narrowly escaped his death, it was a natural, though somewhat uncanny, development.

Shizuka na Kage-e (*Tranquil Shadow Picture*) is a masterpiece in this vein. He continued to write similar works until his death in 1968.

MARUOKA Akira
Shizuka na kage-e (*Tranquil shadow-picture*)
Published by Kôdansha in 1965.

(Synopsis) I read in the newpaper that the ferry service from Tsukuda-jima would soon be abolished. This was probably the last ferry service still surviving in Tokyo. Invited by Mr. Fujishita, a photographer, I went with him to see the ferryboats in their last days. When I was a child, I frequently used this ferry to visit the spinning mill owned by my maternal grand-father on Tsukijima. To get there, you had to take the ferry either from Kachidoki or from Tsukudajima, so the name of these two ferries were very familiar to me at one time of my life. My mother once told me that she had often felt as if she were being dragged into dark water on board a ferryboat. My childhood memories about my mother were revived in me. When I remember my mother, it is always through the medium of some-thing else. This is probably because, when I was a child, I was loved by my grandmother and slept in her room, although my mother was in the same house. On the other hand, I do not have any bad memory of my mother. Until my father died, I could not see what sort of person she really was. When I became a third grade pupil of the primary school, I moved to a Catholic school, and started learning French. I had private lessons in French pronunciation, and was quite busy as a child. About that time, I had a repeated attack of cerebral anaemia in the bathroom until I was finally taken to hospital. It turned out that I had nephritis, and I stayed in the hospital for some time. The next year I was hospitalized for pleurisy. My grandmother had died in the spring of that year. I was taken to a university hospital by my mother. I don't think that my father ever came to see me while I was in the hospital. He was absorbed in preparing the publication of a year-book and in devising a Japanese typewriter. I did not have the slightest idea that my father was nearing his death. He went to see a play at Misaki-za Theatre at Kanda, and came back, complaining of a chill, and died in February. I hear that his mind was clear until the end and that he was discussing something with the doctor shortly before his death.

I remember that when I placed my hand on my father's forehead, it was uncannily cold. When my father died, my mother cut her hair short, and wore the hair-style of a widow. Now we could see her real personality which had been hidden behind my father. She behaved much more naturally and freely. Our house, however, was always somehow quiet, since my father was no longer with us. Remembering my father's wish to see me as a diplomat, my mother sent me to a native speaker for French lessons, but I did not become as proficient as she had expected. I was changing gradually. It was beginning to be painful for me to study to be a diplomat as my father had wished. My mother tried to keep me away from literary books, but she overlooked novels written in French. My mother started around this time to write poetry. I entered Keiô University. The next year my younger sister died of typhoid shortly before her graduation from a girls' school. She was 19 years old. I was carried away by violent emotions, and no longer had any wish to become a diplomat. For a while I could not get rid of the illusion that I had killed my sister. When it was gone, I had a strong desire to lead an independent life away from my mother. I was in the third year of the preparatory course of Keiô University when I married. In that year my novel was published for the first time in the magazine *Bungei Shunjû*. When I married, I left my mother's house, and lived separately. I helped in the publication of *Noh* librettos which my father had been planning, and I became also financially independent. After a while I returned to my mother's house since there was nobody to look after her when she became ill. About a month before the outbreak of the Pacific War, my wife entered a sanatorium in Kamakura. My house was burnt down in the last Tokyo air-raid of the war. My wife and I fainted on hearing the strange roar of fire and the sound of collapsing buildings. The next morning when I came to my senses from the cold, I found that we were lying in the garage. During the time immediately after Japan's defeat in the War, men who had outlived the War died one after another. My mother who was living in Matsumoto as a evacuee could no longer endure life in the provinces and came back to Tokyo in the year after the War. I visited Europe in the postwar period. My mother was not happy about my doing a similar job to that of my father. As for me, I tried to be different from my mother. Then my mother collapsed of brain thrombosis, and after several years died of congestive pneumonia. When, after breathing her last breath, she became completely quiet, I remembered with regret that my mother had been a decisive influence on my life all the time.

Maruya Saiichi

Maruya Saiichi was born in 1925 in Tsuruoka City, Yamagata Prefecture. While he was a student of Niigata High School he was drafted into the army under the Students' Mobilization Law. After the war, he went back to school. He entered the Department of English Literature of Tokyo University, and graduated from it in 1950.

He had entered primary school in 1932. In the previous year the "Manchurian incident" had started. The war with China broke out one year before his entering middle school. When he was a fourth year student, the Pacific War broke out. He spent his high school days in the midst of the war. Thus his childhood and adolescence were spent at a time when Japan was engaging continuously in a series of wars. He is one of the youngest members of the so-called "senchû-ha" (Middle War Generation), "an unfortunate generation which can never forget war even in the midst of peace", as Maruya puts it. That he wrote novels like *Sasamakura* (*Pillow of Grass*) and *Himitsu* (*A Secret*) with an evader of conscription as the hero of each, which is rather rare among Japanese novels, must also be because he belongs to this "unfortunate generation".

Maruya wrote a number of other works which deal directly with some aspect of war—among them are *Nigiyakana Machi de* (*On the Thriving Street*) and *Okurimono* (*A Present*). There are also several other works by him, like *Shisô to Mushisô no Aida* (*Between Thought and its Absence*), which use indirectly the war, that pivot of recent history, as a background.

Maruya's first novel was *Ehoba no Kao o Sakete* (*To Flee the Face of Jehovah*), a novel, which he published in serial form in a group magazine *Chitsujo* (*Order*) for eight years from 1952 to 1960. However, he was known as a translator and a critic even before that. After graduating from university, he published fresh vigorous criticism and translations while teaching at Kokugakuin University and Tokyo University.

He translated with others Joyce's *Ulysses*, Graham Greene's *Brighton Rock* and many other literary works. He published *Nashi no Tsubute* (*Have Heard Nothing from Them*), a collection of critical essays in 1966. These essays fully illustrate his knowledge and ability as a scholar of English Literature. However it is after all in his fiction that we gain the clearest impression of the view of literature he acquired through his study of English Literature.

After becoming three times runner-up for the Akutagawa Prize, he was finally awarded it in 1963 for his *Toshi no Nokori* (*Life's Remaining Year*). The general outlook shown in his novels is quite Western. His power to create a convincing world of fiction has given fresh impact to the Japanese literary world.

MURAYA Saiichi
Sasa-makura *(Pillow of grass)*
Published in book form in July 1966.

(Synopsis) Hamada Shôsuke works as assistant section head in the General Affairs section of a university. One day he received notice of the death of a woman called Yûki Akiko. She was his former love, and had also saved his life.

Hamada's curriculum vitae, which is kept in the file cabinet of his section, is somewhat deceptive. He graduated from a higher technical school in 1940, and worked at a small third-rate wireless company until the middle of that September. About the jobs he did after that time, the curriculum vitae remains silent.

One morning around the middle of September of 1940, he left home, supposedly, to join the Third Regiment in Akasaka. However, he ignored the draft order from the state, assumed a false name, Sugiura Kenji, and wandered all over Japan to avoid detection. He did all sorts of jobs. At one time he repaired radios, at another time he was a street entertainer and drew pictures in sand. Finally he became a dependent in Akiko's house. Such things are not mentioned in Hamada's curriculum vitae.

For five years Hamada lived as an evader of conscription. He was in his early twenties. Hamada's curriculum vitae does not say anything about these five years. It was a difficult time. The gendarmerie and the police were not the only enemies he had to deceive. The whole country of Japan, was against him. Stations, ports, towns—all were united against him. However, he managed to escape till the end, and his evasion of conscription was successful.

It was a real miracle that he did succeed. Nobody knows why his evasion of conscription was successful. He does not know himself. Whatever the reason, his "enemies" could not catch him. Japan was defeated in the war. The army was dissolved. The government which was pursuing him fell.

During his flight, his mother committed suicide, but, despite such an unfortunate event, Hamada still believes that the evasion of conscription was the only course of action he could have taken, and that he was right. He did not evade conscription from mere caprice. He deliberated on it for a long time.

At that time, he was twenty years old. Fresh from school, his way of thinking was still that of a student. There were four main objections to conscription. First, he was against the fighting of any war, against the idea of war itself. Secondly, he was particularly against this Pacific War. Thirdly, he disliked any army. Fourth and last, he was particularly against this Japanese Army. His will to evade conscription became firmer and firmer.

> —I am sleeping here
> On this pillow of grass
> Only for a night
> To dream and to depart,
> Longer I cannot stay.

is a poem written around the time of the *Shinkokinshû* (*New Anthology of Ancient and Modern Verse*) completed in 1205. Hamada's life became like that. Frightened even by the sound of bamboo leaves blown by the wind, Hamada, as an evader of conscription, had to be on guard all the time. His flight was painful and full of anxieties.

It was during his wandering that he came to be acquainted with Akiko. He was attracted by this beautiful woman who was older than himself. She was a somewhat strong-willed woman and, though rather nihilistic in outlook, she was not a fool. He and Akiko journeyed together, behaving as if they were man and wife, until they arrived at Akiko's home in Uwajima. Hamada lived in Akiko's home until the end of the war as a dependent, actually a kept lover.

During his flight, he always coped with dangers by being optimistic and making light of them. What else could he do? Again, after the war, in order to endure life as a man with a past, his only resort was to be optimistic.

Although the power of the government, which was his enemy was destroyed, and the war ended, he was still by no means free. This was partly because of his mother's suicide and his father's early infirmity and his younger brother's tuberculosis. However, the chief reason was that his evasion of conscription created unforeseen results all around him. Whenever he comes across such a circumstance, he remembers an experience at Shimonoseki Pier. It was probably in the April of 1942. He walked with a police-detective down the concrete corridor, threatened by his impending interrogation. The corridor was 150 metres long. Another 30 meters, another 20 metres . . . he was almost praying. How relieved he felt when he arrived at the end of the corridor and discovered that the detective could not see through the lies he had been telling him all the time.

"Life is like that", Hamada thinks. "Since the average life-span has lengthened, one has to live to be sixty or seventy, threatened by all sorts of things like retirement, one's wife's complaints, or deafness caused by streptomycine. If one has rebelled against the state, society, the establishment once, one can never repeal that act of rebellion. One has to be a traveller on a dangerous journey until the end".

Masamune Hakucho

Masamune Hakuchô was born in 1879 in Okayama Prefecture. His real personal name is Takao. His family was an old family of the area which could trace its ancestry back 200 years. Masamune was the eldest son. From his early childhood he was physically fragile, and spent his boyhood in constant fear of death and of what comes after death. In 1896 he entered Tokyo Senmon Gakkô, the predecessor of the present Waseda University, but his anxieties due to fragile health would not disappear. He read the writings of Uchimura Kanzô and was gradually attracted to Christianity. He was baptized at the age of 18. After graduation, he gave up Christianity, and became an atheist. The fact that he had once believed in Christianity, however, had a prolonged influence on him and on his view of life.

Masamune entered the Yomiuri Newspaper Company, and published
theatrical reviews in its paper. Then he published novels like *Sekibaku*
(*Loneliness*, 1904) and *Jin'ai* (*Dust*, 1907) and came to be recognized as a
promising young writer. These novels are all expressions of a gloomy view
of life and are somewhat nihilistic. They allow us to have a glimpse of the
author's inner sufferings. After his marriage, his novels became less abstract. He published, for example, *Shinjû Misui* (*Attempted Double Suicide*,
1913) which depicts the follies of everyday life realistically. As for his plays
like *Azuchi no Haru* (*The Spring in Azuchi*, 1926), they ignore the usual
methods of playwriting, and are centred around intellectual discussions
between the characters. This unique method of depicting human reality
was also used in *Sensaisha no Kanashimi* (*Sorrow of a War Victim*, 1946),
published after the war.

The main characteristic of Masamune's novels is that in them the author
is trying to depict naked human reality without bothering about literary
embellishment. Masamune had a wide knowledge of the thought and
literature of the East and the West, and his criticisms based on it were also
quite impressive. His works are characterised by boredom with life and
nihilism. *Kotoshi no Aki* (*This Autumn*, 1959), summarized below, deals
with the time before and after the death of his younger brother Atsuo. It
skillfully evokes the mental state of 81-year-old Masamune with his
nihilistic view of life which he had retained all these years. Three years
later, in 1962, Masamune died of general prostration on account of cancer
of the pancreas. Shortly before his death, however, he returned to the
Christian faith, and destroyed the popular image of himself as an eternal
sceptic.

MASAMUNE Hakucho
Kotoshi no aki *(This autumn)*
Published in *Chûô Kôron*, January 1959.

(Synopsis) October is a pleasant time of the year, but it is rainy. It becomes really nice from November, both for travelling and for staying home. How shall I spend this autumn?

November 1st, 1958: I left home to attend an art festival held at the Kabuki-za Theatre. On the way I dropped in at a radio broadcasting station to get my voice recorded. There I received a telephone call from my home. I was told that the illness of A., my brother, still living at home, had suddenly worsened. I am the eldest son, and A., who is two years younger than I, is the second son. At that time, I had nine brothers and sisters, among whom A. was particularly close to me, since we ate and slept in the same place until about the time I finished primary school. I think I know his physical and mental qualities well. It would not be an exaggeration if I said that of the whole of mankind, A. is the human being whom I know best. Sometimes I see myself in him. I find that unpleasant, but it is a fact. After A.'s digestive system became so bad that he could not exist on a normal diet, he continued to go to a school in Okayama to teach Japanese classics for several years, and it took him one full hour to get to the school by bus. Since he is quite old, there is no hope for his recovery this time, so I naturally had a strong desire to see him once more while he was still alive. I decided not to attend the art festival at the Kabuki-za Theatre, and instead, managing to get a sleeping berth, set out on the train journey home.

In the country, when you die, your neighbours still attend to your funeral. It's an old custom. It is different in the city. I do not have anybody around me who would care to officiate at my funeral. I do not think that an undertaker is enough. If they could take my body to a crematorium without notifying anybody, just pick up my bones and finish, it would not be troublesome, but since I have been decorated, I am afraid that there will be a great fuss. Since I am of an anxious disposition, I worry about my funeral from time to time, and wonder whether I should not return the decoration and resign from the Academy of Arts at some suitable time.

I arrived at Okayama before dawn and took a bus to my native village. A.'s only son lives in the house where I spent my childhood. When I looked around this house, memories of my childhood were vividly brought to mind. A. has cancer, and apparently the doctor thinks that he will soon die. A. looked quite calm lying in bed. It did not look as if he was dying. As I entered, A. did not even look at me. Probably his sight was also bad. He just said in a low voice, "I did not intend to notify anybody". This was virtually all he said. I did not know how to reply. Finally I decided not to say anything. I am not sorry that I said nothing. A.'s consciousness was clear, but he seemed to be completely indifferent to my visit. I had imagined that when one is to part with life, one might tend to become sentimental. It seems to me now that this is some superficial device used by poets and novelists. I left A.'s sick-room silently, and wandered in the direction of the cemetery by the side of a mountain.

I have written about the death of my father under the title *Kotoshi no Haru* (*This Year's Spring*), and I have dealt with my mother's death in *Kotoshi no Natsu* (*This Year's Summer*). If A. dies I should write *Kotoshi no Aki* (*This Year's Autumn*) about his death. I wonder if anyone will write about my death under the title *Kotoshi no Fuyu* (*This Year's Winter*), when I die.

Mishima Yukio

Mishima Yukio published his first work, *Hanazakari no Mori* (*Flowering Forest*) in 1944 and since then has enjoyed the reputation of being a "wonder boy". *Kamen no Kokuhaku* (*The Confessions of a Mask*, 1949) decidedly established his literary fame. (It has been translated into English by M. Weatherby and published in *Modern Japanese Literature*, Pp. 429–438, New York, Grove Press, 1956; Tokyo, Tuttle, 1957; New York, New Directions, 1958.) It deals with a young man's attempt to analyse his own sexual insecurity, and this is done with a shudder of aesthetic pleasure. Jinzai Kiyoshi (a writer) characterized this work as "Narcissism cursed by the spirit of negation". *Kinjiki* (*Forbidden Lust*, 1953, translated by Marks, Alfred H., Tokyo, Tuttle, 1969 title as *Forbidden Colors*) is another of his works dealing with a similar theme.

Mishima was also talented as a playwright, and his *Rokumeikan* (*Rokumei Reception Hall*, 1956), and *Yorokobi no Koto* (*The Joyful Harp*, 1964), enjoyed, among others, a warm reception.

Among works which deal with themes taken from actual contemporary incidents are *Ao no Jidai* (*The Age of Blue*, 1956), and *Utage no Ato* (*After the Banquet*, 1960, translated by Keene, Donald. *Encounter* Vol. VIII No. 1, 1957, pp. 45–51). They both provoked lively discussion.

The work which is regarded to be his greatest masterpiece by most people, including Mishima himself, is his novel, *Kinkakuji* (*The Temple of the Golden Pavilion*, 1956, translated into English by Morris, Ivan, New York, A. Knopf, 1958; Tokyo, Tuttle, 1959). In it Mishima has succeeded brilliantly in making this temple, Kinkakuji, which was in fact destroyed by arson, a perfect symbol of the uniqueness of life and the uniqueness of art. In the novel, a young monk from the provinces who lives in the temple precincts comes to be charmed by the beautiful temple. The temple becomes the symbol of his own ideal life. He dreams of the temple being destroyed by the war; however, when the war comes to an end the temple still stands with its eternal beauty intact. The overpowering nature of the temple's beauty makes him despair and he seeks to find escape and comfort in women. However every time he goes to a woman, the temple pursues him and stands in the way. Expelled from the temple precincts, he finally burns to ashes the temple which was to him eternal beauty itself. This novel is obviously Mishima's masterpiece, and embodies the desire of uniting art and life in their uniqueness.

Kyôko no Ie (*Kyôko's House*) depicts Kyôko and her circle of intimates. The people who frequent Kyôko's house, where she reigns as queen, include Sugimoto, a nihilist who is convinced in the collapse of the world; Fukai, a boxer; Funaki, an actor; and Yamagata, a painter. All of them fail in life. One is shattered by his wife's adultery, another is a renegade to the right wing, and still another commits a love suicide. Yamagata, the painter, suddenly becomes convinced in the world which Sugimoto mentioned following which, he retreats into mysticism. He visits Kyôko, however, before his departure for Mexico, and makes love to her. Then the divorced husband of Kyôko returns to her house. This is roughly the plot of the novel. Some say that the novel is an ambitious attempt to convey the intellectual climate of the period in which it was written; others regard it as a failure.

Yûkoku (*Patriotism*, 1960) is, roughly speaking, Mishima's first attempt to deal with a political theme. Lieutenant Takeyama who is the friend of the young officers involved in the incident of February 2nd 1936, is forced to crush these rebels by imperial command. Agonized by the dilemma, he decides to die and slashes himself to death with a sword after indulging in an orgy of pleasure with his wife. This novel, which expresses desire for purification through death and eroticism, foreshadows Mishima's recent suicide.

In *Utsukushii Hoshi* (*The Beautiful Star*), just as in *Kyôko no Ie* (*Kyôko's House*) people—the Ôsugi family—foresee the end of the world. They clash with a group, headed by a man called Haguro, which frustrates their peace movement, and whose slogan is "Euthanasia for all mankind" through atomic war. Believing that he has been sent by the universe to save the earth, Ôsugi, despite approaching death, succeeds in struggling to the place where a flying saucer from the outside universe has landed. This novel, like *Kinkakuji* (*The Temple of the Golden Pavilion*) and *Kyôko no Ie* (*Kyôko's House*) before it, reflects the strongly eschatological ideas about individuals and the world which Mishima conceived during the war.

Kinu to Meisatsu (*Silk and Insight*, 1964), depicts president Komazawa of the Komazawa Spinning Company, his family, and the strike of his workers. Komazawa, who at first looks obstinate and vulgar, has a beautiful character associated with the old family system rather than with "modern spirit". Despite his defeat through the strike, he forgives everything with fatherly generosity, and dies. This process is depicted beautifully, with tragic intensity. The "Silk" of the title is a symbol of the Japanese sense of beauty. *Mikumano-môde* (*A Visit to the Three Kumano Shrines*, 1965), has a scholar of Japanese literature and his secretary as the central figures of the story. When the scholar visits the Kumano Shrines, he buries a comb at three different places: these combs are inscribed with the character for "ka", "yo" and "ko" respectively. This must have been done because he cherished the memory of a woman named Kayoko. It is not clear whether Kayoko actually loved him or whether she was just a remote figure who fed his imagination. The scholar says that she was really beautiful and tells Tsuneko, his secretary, that she should compose a song celebrating the vision of this woman. This work evokes subtly and deeply the traditional Japanese sense of beauty.

Eirei no Koe (*Voices of the Dead*, 1966), has a meeting of the dead as its subject. A ghost, who has been summoned to the meeting, says to the Emperor: "Why has your Majesty become a human being?" This is the ghost of an officer who had been involved in the "incident of February 2nd 1936" for which he was executed. Then appear the ghosts of the suicide pilots of World War II. They say that they wanted to be one with the Emperor through their death. In short, they say that the Emperor should have remained a God. There is, in this novel, a sense of longing for direct Imperial rule as opposed to the emperor system, which was just a cog in a huge bureaucratic machine during the Tokugawa period; and also as opposed to the "corrupted democracy" and the "humanized" emperor system of the postwar period.

Suzakuke no Metsubō (*Downfall of the Suzaku Family*, 1967), is a play, which ranges over a one to two years period toward the end of the war. The characters include Marquis Suzaku; his son; the maid, Orei; and Matsunaga Ritsuko. The son realizes that Orei is his mother; later he is killed in the war. Orei is also killed in an air-raid. Ritsuko tells the Marquis to die, but he answers that he has perished long ago. The play is based on a play by Euripides, *Mad Hercules*. Interlacing motifs of filicide, murder of one's wife, and love of fate are developed, and the hero's passive loyalty to the Emperor throughout his loneliness and downfall is depicted. The quality of the language used and the atmosphere of the four seasons conjured up in the play are both intensely beautiful.

Mishima Yukio had just completed his large-scale, four-volumed work, *Hōjō no Umi* (*The Sea of Plenitude*) when he stormed the headquarters of the Self-Defence Force which he deemed to have lost its spirit, cried out for the restoration of direct Imperial rule, and committed ritual suicide. The first volume of this last work centres round the tragic love between Kiyoaki, the son of Marquis Matsueda of the Meiji period, and Satoko who was to be given in marriage to a prince of the blood. Later in the novel, Satoko becomes a nun, and Kiyoaki dies. In the second volume, Honda, who was a friend of the late Kiyoaki and who has just become a judge, meets a youth called Iinuma who has the same birth-mark as Kiyoaki had. It is more than a dozen years since Kiyoaki's death. This boy, Iinuma, is deeply attracted by the ideas of the Jinpûren (a right-wing organization of discontented samurai who revered Shintoism, detested foreigners, and opposed the policies of the Meiji government, believing that the government was polluting their "divine land" and its traditions). Iinuma tries to assassinate certain important politicians, without success. Honda, becoming an advocate, defends the arrested Iinuma and secures his release. Later, Iinuma assails a man who controls the business world from behind the scenes, and commits suicide. In the third volume, Honda, who is visiting Thailand where the cloud of World War II is threatening to burst, meets a young princess of the royal blood who insists on asserting that she was a Japanese in her former life. In the postwar period, Honda notices that the Thai princess, who happens to visit Japan, has the same markings on her skin as Hiroaki and Iinuma had. In the fourth volume, Honda, who is now 76 years old, adopts an orphan who also has the same marks on his skin. This child treats Honda cruelly after he has grown-up. He also tries to commit suicide, without success. Finally, Honda returns to the world of the first volume and goes to see Satoko who is still hiding herself in a nunnery. There he experiences the silence of a bright summer afternoon, which is like eternity. Has Mishima embodied the idea of the transmigration of souls in this novel? If so, how should we understand Satoko's denial of the very existence of Kiyoaki at the end of the novel? If this ambitious book, which covers the Meiji, Taishô and Shôwa periods, finally dissolves into nothingness through Satoko's denial, what should we read from it? Despair or nihilism? Mishima left the completed manuscript of this novel at his home on the day when he committed harakiri. His death was not just his final work of art. Mishima said that he wanted to die not as an artist, but as a samurai. Behind such desire, however, we can now sense the despair which invades his last novel.

Miura Shumon

Miura Shumon was born in Tokyo in 1926. He first wanted to be a scholar. He entered the Department of Linguistics in the Faculty of Literature of Tokyo University and studied the language used in Ponape. In 1948 he became a lecturer of the Faculty of Art of Nihon University. His experiences as a student soldier during the war and the confused state of Japanese society after the war induced him to turn to writing. In 1950 he started a literary group magazine *Shin Shichô* (*New Tide of Thought*). In his spare time as a teacher, he started writing works based on historial materials. His first work *Gaki* (*An Inspired Painter*) was published in 1951. For him history and historical figures were the mirror in which the confused reality of postwar Japan could seek its own image and understand itself. *Ono to Batei* (*An Axe and a Groom*, 1952) is based on Darius the Great of Persia. Its style and neat structure are quite impressive. This work was a sort of ironical comment on postwar Japanese society. Miura won recognition among literary circles by these two works, and established himself as a writer. About this time he was also promoted to the post of assistant professor of Nihon University, and married Sono Ayako who was later to become a wellknown woman writer. Miura was not a prolific writer, but he went on writing steadily. He published *Ponape-tô* (*Ponape Island*) in 1956. After this, he no longer wrote any historical novels, but came to publish novels in contemporary settings like *Seruroido no Tô* (*A Celluloid Tower*) which deals with human relations within a university. His intellectual sophisticated style became increasingly coloured by irony and satire. Among his works following *Seruroido no Tô* (*A Celluloid Tower*) are *Jisshi* (*One's Real Child*, 1959) which depicts a cuckold husband, *Shinwa* (*A Myth*), a novel about an ordinary lower middle class family with two children, and *Tsume no Kai* (*Society of Nails*, 1966) which depicts a meeting of former classmates ironically and with self-sarcasm. These novels attest to the author's subtle insights into everyday life, and are characterized by humour and an intellectual quality. In *Hakoniwa* (*Miniature Garden*, 1967), Miura dealt with the disintegration of the everyday world called the home. Miura's interest in finding out the meaning of the home in everyday life led him to treat this subject also in his subsequent novels. In his long novel *Michi no Nakaba ni* (*Halfway along the Road*, 1967) the problem of the home is dealt with in connection with the problem of how to live which confronts the postwar Japanese. In *Oshie no Niwa* (*School*, 1968), the problem of the home crops up in relation to the problem of the disintegration of a university. This novel is based on the author's experiences at the time of university riots in 1968. After this, he quit Nihon University, and is continuing to develop the theme of *Hakoniwa* (*Miniature Garden*).

Miura Shumon
Hakoniwa (*Miniature garden*)
Published in *Bungakukai*, February 1967.

(Synopsis) Kimata Manabu was woken up by the noise of the gate closing. His younger brother Osamu was leaving for his office by car. Since he had forgotten to close the shutters the night before, bright light was streaming in from the window by the side of his mattress. Having stayed up late writing, he wanted to sleep again, and was going to close the shutters, when he noticed that Osamu's wife, Yuriko, was standing quite close to the window. She was looking at the garden plants with her back to him. She was wearing a short skirt, and her back was somewhat bent. Obviously she was not aware that Manabu was watching her. He could see two thirds of her smooth white legs. Lying on his mattress, he took out a pair of binoculars and took a closer look. There were no hairs on her thighs, but he could see the pores distinctly. He felt somewhat guilty, peeping at his brother's wife, but he persuaded himself that it was all right since he thought her body did not look particularly attractive and since he did not feel any carnal desire. He even felt rather superior.

However, when she turned sideways, the line which her back, her seat and her thighs formed became very voluptuous, and Manabu put doen the binoculars and picked up a newly published book; it seemed to him that to feel sexually attracted to one's brother's wife was immoral.

Although, speaking of immorality, Manabu thought, the relationship between his own wife, Sueko, and his brother was somewhat dubious. Of course there was probably no physical relationship between them, but Manabu remembered, that after he had married, Osamu, who had been a student at the time, had always discussed love and other things with Sueko, and had danced with her. Whenever he came home, he had sensed some intimacy between them which was not so different from love. while he was vaguely thinking about such matters, his wife Tokiko came in. "Oh, you are up!", she said. Tokiko had from some time before started to sleep with Kaori, their daughter, who was a junior high school girl. Kaori, who had been her father's pet, started, from the age of puberty to dislike him strongly for being unpleasantly masculine and unclean. From about that time, his wife had started leaving her mattress and bedding without putting them away in the closet after Kaori left for school. Manabu noticed this, and interpreted it as an unobtrusive invitation to sexual intercourse on the part of his wife, but Manabu decided to ignore it this time. They discussed Osamu, their garden, and other matters, drinking coffee together.

At about that time, Osamu was driving his car to the pharmaceutical company where he worked. From time to time, he stopped his car at a bus queue and invited an attractive looking office girl with whom he wanted to eat lunch that day to take a lift. He had a straightforward view about love affairs and thought that they were all a matter of statistical probability. If girls traveled in his car, some of them would not only eat lunch with him but would also spend the night with him at a hotel catering for intimate couples. Osamu, who loved action, was always enjoying adventures and love affairs, although he had a wife, Yuriko, whom he had met while stationed in Europe. Yuriko, daughter of a wealthy family, had come to Europe to study painting and was suffering from unrequited love. Osamu and Yuriko married after their return to Japan.

Shôgo, the father of Manabu and Osamu, was an educator and had been the principal and administrator of a school called Chigyô Gakuin. This school was a unique school which put into practice Dewey's theory of "learning through action". It catered to backward students who disliked study and gave them a unique education. Shôgo was a sportsman, and did not like study himself. He had married a girl called Kinu, who had been the best student of a teacher's training college. Supported by Kinu, he had finished "higher normal" school, and then graduated from Bunrika University. He had probably quite a shrewd business mind. He became the principal of Chigyô Gakuin at the age of 40. Kinu brought up her sons strictly, dreaming of making Manabu the second owner of the school and Osamu its head administrator. However, because of World War II, Osamu was sent to a military preparatory school. When the war ended in Japan's defeat, Shôgo was expelled from the school, and Kinu's dream was not fulfilled.

Tokiko informed Yuriko secretly that on the day of an alumni meeting she had seen Osamu getting into a car with a woman, in front of a hotel for intimate couples.

Manabu was asked by his wife to advise Yuriko on this matter, so he visited Yuriko and talked with her; however, he came to make love to her almost against his will, as if Yuriko had seduced him. Yuriko told him that Tokiko was a fool. Osamu came back late. When he was interrogated about his behavior on the day Tokiko had seen him, he asserted that he had lent his car to his senior, and gone to play mahjong. However, when the women left, he confessed to Manabu that he had in fact enjoyed himself with a woman.

The health of Shôgo, the father, deteriorated. When he was examined, it turned out that he had cancer. The family quarrelled over who should pay the cost of his hospitalization and treatment, and also over the distribution of his property. Tokiko, who otherwise was quite gentle, became quite a different person under the circumstances, eager to defend her own interests. Yuriko, towards whom Manabu secretly entertained tender feelings, did the same. The father eventually died, and the mother started to encourage Manabu to assume the role of head of the family. Then, suddenly, Yuriko disappeared from home, leaving Takeo, her son, with a notice of divorce. The mother, Manabu and his wife, were upset, but Osamu himself was quite calm. Takeo played with Kaori, and his grandmother felt at ease again. Manabu received a telephone call from Yuriko and he took her personal belongings to the flat where she was living alone. Yuriko told him that she had run away because she could not endure being imprisoned in the stifling atmosphere of the Kimata household any longer. She also told him that he was even more alien to her than Osamu, her husband. Osamu left for Manila, his new place of work, alone and full of new hope. He wrote from Manila that he had constructed a miniature garden in his flat to remind him of Japan. A miniature garden—to Manabu it seemed to be a bit symbol of the life of his family.

Miura Tetsuro

Miura Tetsurô was born in Aomori Prefecture in 1931, and studied French Literature at Waseda University. He was the youngest of six brothers and sisters, and spent his childhood under the shadow of family misfortunes. Because of this, he aspired to be a novelist while he was a student. He married a girl called Shino who was working at a Japanese restaurant. After graduation, struggling with poverty, he published *Jûgo-sai no Shûi* (*The Surroundings of a Fifteen-year-old*, 1954), the lyrical work *Punpe to Yunohana* (*A Pump and Sulphur Mud*) and other works. *Roba* (*A Donkey*, 1957) depicts the inner life of an overseas student from Manchuria against the background of the Tôhoku District during the war. It contrasts the distortions of Japan in the War with human warmth and naive human dreams. It brings into relief the sadness of a guileless soul. In this work Miura hit upon a suitable field for his writing, and was awakened to his proper talent.

The main characteristic of Miura Tetsurô as a writer is that he writes in a light rhythmical style about what activates his fine sensibility. His works are also rich in lyrical humour. The desire to overcome the gloomy shadow of his childhood and meet a guileless soul is hidden behind his works. *Shinobugawa* (1960) is based on the author's real experiences, but he had a moving fairy-tale around his ideal love by omitting the sordid details of reality, although the novel is written in the manner of the traditional Japanese "I" novel. Miura was only 29 years old when he wrote this work. *Shoya* (*The Wedding Night*, 1961) is a sequel to *Shinobugawa* and furnishes the background story of the heroine Shino. Miura wrote many other autobiographical novels which form a larger whole with the two above-mentioned works, and delved into the mystery of human fate. Among them are *Haji no Fu* (*Genealogy of Shame*, 1961), *Kikyô* (*Home-coming*, 1962) and *Danran* (*Happy Home*, 1963). In them Miura tells in his fine lyrical style stories of human love, dreams, disillusionment and so on. *Yoru no E* (*A Night Picture*) is a short novel dealing with a geisha-girl living in a gay quarter. *Umi no Michi* (*A Road along the Sea*, 1967) was conceived as a continuation of the theme of *Yoru no E* (*A Night Picture*). It depicts the first half of the life of a mixed-blood geisha-girl, and sheds light on the destiny of women. Miura has kept writing works with the *motif* of a beautiful love of humanity. *Sankaku Bôshi* (*A Three-cornered Hat*) is another example of such works.

MIURA Tetsuro
Shinobugawa *(Shinobugawa)*
Published in *Shinchô*, October 1960.

(Synopsis) I took Shino to Fukagawa. It was shortly after I had come to know her. Shino was born in Fukagawa and was brought up there until she was twelve years of age. I had come to Tokyo the previous spring from a remote part of the Tôhoku District. It is funny that I took her around Fukagawa, and not the other way around. This was because Shino had gone to Tochigi to escape from the air-raids during the war and had never seen Fukagawa since. Fukagawa had burned down in the blitz. As for myself, I used to walk around Fukagawa two or three times a month, since the memory of my brother had endeared it to me. When we passed the timberyard where I had seen my brother for the last time, Shino unobtrusively joined her hands in veneration, facing the water of the reservoir. The whiteness of her delicate neck peeping out of her *Kimono* struck my eyes.

We crossed a bridge with an arch on which was the sign "Suzaki Paradise" in miniature electric bulbs. We walked along back alleys. At one place, Shino suddenly stopped. It was a crowded brothel area. 'This is the place where I was born", Shino said, blushing, but her voice did not show any servility. "My father worked at a shooting gallery in the gay quarter," she added, and looking straight into my eyes she smiled with her whole strength. "That's all right. It's all right", I said hastily, not realizing that my shrill voice was betraying my agitation. Shino's umbrella started trembling.

Shino and I had become acquainted in the spring of that year at a Japanese restaurant called Shinobugawa which was quite near the student dormitory where I was living. Shinobugawa was a high-class restaurant, and I had not dared to enter it. However, on that day there was a farewell party for graduating students there. I got very drunk. I rested my elbows on the counter downstairs, and asked a little woman who had come downstairs for a cup of water. She smiled at me, said "yes", and disappeared down the corridor. This was Shino. From the next day, I went to Shinobugawa every evening. I just drank saké silently by Shino's side, casting my eyes downwards, but Shino enjoyed my company. Even when she was sent for upstairs, she would not go, saying that she was busy, and asking the girl who had come to fetch her to invent some excuse for her. At the end of July, I came to know that Shino had a fiancé. I got agitated and asked Shino about it. She said that one of the patrons of the restaurant was suggesting a match to which she was not willing. I proposed to her on the spot. Towards the end of the autumn, the illness of Shino's father suddenly became worse. Shino went to Tochigi to see him. In the letter she left behind her were the words, "I wish my father could at least see you." I hurriedly followed Shino to Tochigi. I met Shino's father in a building in the precincts of a Shinto shrine. He had left Tokyo during the war, had come here, and remained here. He looked haggard. He asked me to look after Shino, and said to her, "He is a nice young man". The next day, Shino's father died. On the 31st of December of that year, I took a night train from Ueno to visit my home with Shino. When we arrived at my native place, a dry powdery snow was falling. When my mother saw us, her wrinkled face became full of smiles. She opened her arms as if to embrace us, but could not say anything for some time. She was too happy by far. Out of my three sisters and two brothers, two sisters and one brother had committed suicide, and the other brother was missing. Only one sister remained. She was of poor health and had bad eye-sight. I asked my mother if she was pleased with my bride. She said that Shino was a nice girl. I felt glad. I thought that our marriage would be successful. The next day, it rained for a while, but the sky became clear later. In the evening the thirteen day old moon rose in the sky. I dressed myself formally in Japanese style, and our wedding took place. Only five people—my parents, my sister and ourselves—attended the wedding. There were no guests or go-betweens. My father whose body was disabled sang the Nô song of Takasago to celebrate our marriage. That night, following the custom of that snowy area, Shino and I went to bed completely naked. I made love to Shino for the first time. The night was so silent. Only the bells of a horse-sleigh could be heard approaching slowly in our direction.

Mori Mari

Mori Mari was born in Tokyo, the eldest daughter of Mori Ôgai who was one of the greatest writers of Meiji Japan and who also became the Surgeon-General of the Army. Ôgai had something of the stoic *samurai* about him, but towards the author, his eldest daughter, he seems to have been a kind, indulgent "papa". Protected by her father, Mori grew up, innocent and ignorant of the real world. After graduating from Futsueiwa Girls' School, she got married, but because of her inborn romanticism and her strong personality, her first and second marriages both ended in failure. In the mean time, she visited France and other countries, and acquired a personal knowledge of the cultures of Europe.

The author had been living by herself for a long time, including the difficult war years, with some financial difficulty, when in 1957 she published *Chichi no Bôshi (Father's Hat)*, reminiscences of her father written in prose which is at the same time both sensitive and boldly penetrating. In 1958 she published *Kutsu no Oto (The Sound of Footsteps)*, also containing reminiscences about her father. Through these two works her literary talent suddenly came to be recognized. Thus there came into existence a remarkable phenomenon: three of Ôgai's children—Mori, the author, Kobori Annu, her sister, and Mori Rui, her brother, were all writing fine prose about Ôgai and his literature from their respective points of view.

Reminiscences of her father, however, are not the only things the author wrote. In 1961 she published novels such as *Bocchicheri no Tobira (Botticelli's Door)* and *Koibitotachi no Mori (Forest of Lovers)*. *Koibitotachi no Mori (Forest of Lovers)* has a 17- or 18-year-old youth called Pauro, who is narcissistic and masochistic, as its hero, and depicts his love affairs with women older than himself. It gives skilful expression to a voluptuous and languid sensuous style of life. As Mishima Yukio commentated when this work appeared, the figure of the youth called Pauro is attractively drawn. This work is permeated throughout by a European sense of beauty, which is rare in Japanese literature, and one is never confronted by sordidness or the pettiness of everyday life. Despite, or probably because of, the fact that the author was living a rather financially difficult life in a flat by herself, this novel is a product of lively fantasy. She published a collection of her essays under the title *Zeitaku Binbô (Luxurious Poverty, 1963)*. As this title suggests, she has an ability to find something genuinely rich in a seemingly miserable and poor life. The world of love and romanticism she creates, such as that to be found in her *Kareha no Nedoko (Bed of Withered Leaves)*, never fails to fascinate the reader. Mori is a strange writer who always has something of the young literary enthusiast about her.

Mori Mari
Koibitotachi no mori *(Forest of lovers)*
Published in *Shinchô*, August 1961.

(Synopsis) One afternoon a youth came from behind a building, and jumped into a rose-pink car. He had a slim body, and his movement was very quick. He jumped into the car, glanced towards the front, thrust his head from the car window to see the rear, withdrew his head, pressed down the gear lever and drove away. He seemed to be about seventeen or eighteen years of age—surely not yet nineteen. He had beautiful dreamy eyes, but they had a cold light in them.

This youth, Pauro, had been to a university for a year while his parents were still alive, but now he had stopped going there. He was an born idler and had no desire for doing anything which involved any effort. Since he could drive a car, he was working as a driver for a confectionery called *Rosenstein* in Ginza. Gidô had found this job for him. They had met at a bar in Kitazawa, and soon Pauro's life had become closely connected with that of Gidô. Pauro was a man who let things run their own course as long as it was pleasant to him, as if he had no will of his own. Pauro gradually became fascinated by Gidô, and apart from unconscious pragmatic calculations, he came to be attached to Gidô.

Pauro looked extremely lovely and touching in bed when he threw his graceful arms around Gidô's neck, clasped Gidô's face in his pretty hands, and rubbed his cheek against Gidô's. Gidô was captivated by his charm. When he caressed Pauro's curved back gently, in his heart he vowed eternal love to Pauro.

Mrs. Ueda, Gidô's mistress, was already past her prime as a woman. She was forty-eight years old. The feeling of irritation within her was becoming more and more intolerable day by day. Was it caused by Gidô's recent coldness to her, or was it because of the gradual loss of her feminine charm as she grew older? Probably it was both. Now she had stopped looking at herself in the mirror after taking a bath. It was only one year ago that

Gidô's eyes had shone with excitement when he saw her breasts. The nape of Gidô's neck and his healthy-looking thick chest which had until quite recently caused violent desire and joy in her now only provoked her hatred, which was then converted into stinging words from her lips. However, since Gidô was no longer interested in her at all, her words could not in any way affect him. Mrs. Ueda burned with hatred for Gidô.

Gidô had begun to feel danger in Mrs. Ueda's obsessive hatred of him, long before the time she shot him. The next morning after Gidô's death, Pauro wandered around with a broken heart. He looked somewhat like a little orphan. With vigorless steps, he dragged around for a long time, and then leaned against a railing by the river-side and watched the gray water. It was not long before he noticed that a new light had started shining at the bottom of his heart. It was almost uncanny to him that he was recovering from the shock so quickly. Anyway no need to be in a hurry. He had still some remains of the pocket money Gidô had given him. When he looked up, his lips were again beautifully rosy and his whole face was beginning to look fresh again. It would not take long before he could fully regain that proud beauty with which he had been following Gidô like a favorite geisha-girl, until the night of his death.

Muro Saisei

Murô Saisei was born in 1889 in Kanazawa, Ishikawa Prefecture. He left higher elementary school without completing the course in 1901. Working as a waiter among other things, he pursued his interest in literature although poverty-stricken. His first literary efforts were *haiku* poems, *waka* poems and ordinary poems which he sent to various newspapers and magazines. In 1910 he went to Tokyo, attracted by Kitahara Hakushû, a sensuous symbolist poet, and other writers. He became acquainted with poets such as Hakushû Hagiwara Sakutarô and Yamamura Bochô. Living a life of poverty, wandering and decadence, he founded poetry magazines with others of this company, and revealed his extraordinary talent as a lyrical poet.

In 1918 he published two collections of his poems, *Ai no Shishû* (*A Collection of Love Songs*) and *Jojô Shôkyoku Shû* (*Lyrical Melodies*). These are collections of his poems written during this period of poverty, which express the loneliness, longing and sentimentality of youth, and his humane feelings and ideas. All of them are characterized by the fresh lyrical spirit of Murô. Through these two collections of poems, he established himself as one of the leading young poets of the day.

Meanwhile he also started writing novels. This was partly due to the influence of Akutagawa Ryûnosuke, the novelist. His first novel was *Yônen Jidai* (*Childhood*, 1919). It was followed by *Sei ni Mezameru Koro* (*Awakening to Sex*, 1919), *Utsukushiki Hyôga* (*The Beautiful Glacier*, 1920) and *Aojiroki Sôkutsu* (*Pale Haunt*, 1920), all of which are autobiographical novels about adolescence. They depict, using vivid sensuous images which are without intellectual refinement, how a precocious boy experiences sensual awakening. Through these novels he acquired a reputation as a gifted sensuous writer.

After groping his way between verse writing and prose writing, he put an end to writing lyrical poems for the time being by publishing a "farewell" collection of his poems called *Kurogane Shû* (*Iron*, 1932). At the same time he published novels like *Ani Imôto* (*Brother and Sister*, 1934, translated by Seidensticker, E., "Modern Japanese Stories," pp. 144–161, Tokyo, Tuttle, 1962), *Kamigami no Hedo* (*The Vomit of the Gods*, 1934) and *Onna no Zu* (*Portrait of a Woman*, 1935). In these novels he depicted with deep sympathy the rough unsophisticated life of lower class people. They were labelled "literature of revenge" because of Murô's vitriolic attack on the fundamental evils of life and society.

During the Second World War, he showed at one time an interest in the study of Japanese classics of the Heian period. This was to protect his own literary world, and it prepared the ground for a series of later works set in Heian period.

After the war, he was again very active and produced poems, novels, essays and literary biographies identified by the unpolished vigor and sensuous beauty of style characteristic of him. Among the representative works of the postwar period are *Anzukko* (1957), *Tômegane no Haru* (*Spring Through a Telescope*, 1957), *Waga Aisuru Shijin no Denki* (*The Life of my Favorite Poet*, 1959) and *Ware wa Utaedo Yabure-kabure* (*I Sing, but in a Devil-may-care Mood*, 1962).

Kagerô no Nikki Ibun (*The Women of Kagerô Diary*, 1958–59), summarized below, is representative of Murô's novels which use the world of the Heian aristocracy as their setting. One of the Japanese classics of the Heian period, the *Kagerô Nikki* (C. 982 A.D.), a diary of a Heian noblewoman known as Michitsuna's mother, refers briefly to "a woman who lives in an alley in town". Murô gives this woman a name and calls her Saeno. He makes her an embodiment of the type of "eternal womanhood" which fascinates men. In this novel, Murô depicts the instincts of a man who longs for such an "eternal woman", against the background of the polygamic Heian period. It describes, in beautiful prose, the fate of three women who are rivals in love. It deserves to be called a masterpiece.

Towards the end of his life, Murô edited *The Complete Poems of Murô Saisei* which was to include the poems of his whole lifetime. As soon as it was completed, he died of lung cancer in March 1962.

Muro Saisei
Kagerô no nikki ibun *(The women of Kagerô diary)*
Published serially in *Fujin no Tomo*, July 1958–July 1959.

(Synopsis) Shion, the daughter of Fujiwara Tomoyasu, was a beautiful girl. Her beauty, however, had a noble and cold quality born out of her unusually clear intelligence. In the autumn of the year when she became eighteen years old, she became emotionally and psychologically unstable due to the full maturing of her body. She learned to regain her composure by expressing herself in poetry or prose, and by polishing her inborn dignity and virgin nobility.

In the spring of the eighth year of Tenreki (954 A.D.) Shion, now nineteen years old, was courted by Kaneie, the third son of Fujiwara Moro-suke, the Minister of the Right. Kaneie, at that time the vice head of the Grands of the Right, was already married to Tokihime, his first wife, by whom he had a son, Michitaka. Shion was courted as his second wife. (At this time polygamy was quite acceptable.) Proud Shion rejected him by saying that she was not interested in a man who had already got a first wife. In the autumn of the same year Kaneie wrote to her again. Shion answered him by telling him not to write to her again. Kaneie kept send-ing her love poems, and as she sent back poems in reply, she found herself gradually falling in love with him. One evening, Kaneie paid her a sudden visit and courted her. Shion became agitated and, before she had time to regain her presence of mind, found herself embraced by Kaneie. At one stage she wanted to cut their relationship short. However as Kaneie's visits became more frequent, she was gradually won by him, and came to look forward to his next visit. They married, and she came to be called Shion no Ue (*Lady Shion*).

After her marriage, Shion found herself deeply attracted by Kaneie. At the same time, she felt that intercourse with Kaneie was degrading to her dignity and pride because of his shameless handling of her. Kaneie tried to find full satisfaction of his desire by despoiling that which was beautiful and noble. Shion, on the other hand, tried to keep her purity by avoiding his coarse provocation.

Kaneie found the feminine warmth which he missed in Shion in a wom-an called Saeno who lived in an alley in town, and on whom he started to dote. His visits to Shion became less and less frequent. Shion was dis-gusted with her husband who was attracted by a woman as low as Saeno. At the same time, to her own surprise, she had to admit that she was mis-sing him who now only rarely came to see her. In August of the next year, Shion gave birth to a son, Michitsuna. One day she found Kaneie's love letter to Saeno. Her position was somewhere between the first wife and Saeno. It was a difficult position, and Shion was worried. She also felt jealous. At the same time, she felt a strange sense of solidarity with Toki-hime, the first wife, who was also deprived of Kaneie's love. Shion found her consolation in loving her son, Michitsuna. When Kaneie came, she always behaved in a very aloof manner towards him. Kaneie became even more enamoured of Saeno who was almost uncannily beautiful and at the same time obedient. In time Saeno gave birth to Kaneie's child, but it was born dead. Because of this, Saeno suspected that she was fated to be separated from Kaneie. She visited Shion, taking the dead child with her. Shion was impressed by Saeno who had been schooled by a wider experience of life than herself. She learned from Saeno how a woman should behave towards her husband, and when Kaneie came again she treated him kindly.

Saeno's former husband, Tadanari, suddenly turned up, and Saeno realized that she must soon part with Kaneie. Then Kaneie's first wife, Tokihime, came to see Saeno, and commanded her to return the household goods which Kaneie had taken to Saeno's house. She also told Saeno to part with Kaneie. Saeno promised her to part with him when the time to part came. Saeno disclosed this to Kaneie, and he entreated her not to part with him. Saeno also met Tadanari and told him that she did not love him. All Saeno wanted now was to hide herself from the people she knew in order to find peace, and she returned the household goods to Shion and Tokihime. When Kaneie found some of the returned household goods at Shion's house, he missed Saeno and groaned. Shion told him that for the rest of her life she would feel ashamed of having driven Saeno into retreat, but that it was her revenge as a woman. She also told him that a chance for such revenge came only once in one's life. Kaneie felt miserable, and, to console himself, started visiting a lady called Atarashino-no-Hime. Shion wanted to escape from this world of carnal desire, and at one time confind herself in a mountain temple to the west of Kyoto. However, when she visited the house of her father, Tomoyasu, Kaneie arrived unexpectedly and behaved after disturbed fashion. Shion, however, consoled him kindly, and they went to bed together. It was a long time since they had slept together in such an affectionate way.

In their dreams that night, Saeno appeared. She covered Shion's mouth with her hand, and pressed Kaneie to choose either Shion or herself. Shion drew her dagger and threatened Saeno. Kaneie said that he could not choose, and Saeno was about to disappear into the darkness outside, when

Kaneie and Shion both woke up. They noticed in the dark garden a human figure on the point of leaving. Even Shion's dagger was lying on the floor. Shion clung to Kaneie, and told him that she felt it possible that two living women, for want of other means, could become one person to serve a single man. Kaneie murmured that as long as one lived one could never escape from love's passion, and stared into the darkness of the garden.

Nagai Tatsuo

Nagai Tatsuo was born in Tokyo in 1904. His short story, *Kappan'ya no Hanashi* (*The Story of a Printer*) was accepted for publication by *San'esu,* a literary magazine, in September 1920, and his ability was immediately recognized by Kikuchi Kan who had selected the best contribution for that edition of the magazine. Nagai visited Kikuchi in May, 1923 with the manuscript of *Kuroi Gohan* (*Black Boiled Rice*), and this short story was published in the July edition of *Bungei Shunjû* (*The Literary Years*). He together with Kobayashi Hideo, became a member of the staff of the magazine *Seidô Jidai* (*The Bronze Age*). Later, in collaboration with Kobayashi Hideo, Hori Tatsuo, and others, he started producing the magazine *Yamamayu* (*Mountain Cocoon*), and published many of his own short stories in this magazine. In 1927, through the recommendation of Yokomitsu Riichi, he became a member of staff of the Bungei Shunjû Sha (a publishing firm). In 1929, in collaboration with Yokomitsu, Hori, Kawabata Yasunari, and others, he started the coterie magazine, *Bungaku* (*Literature*). His first collection of short stories, *Ehon* (*A Picture Book*) was published by the *Shikisha* (a publishing company) in 1934. He became the chief editor of *Bungei Shunjû* in 1939. In March, 1943, his short story, *Tebukuro no Katappo* (*An Odd Glove*), was published in the magazine *Bungakukai* (*The Literary World*).

By 1944 it was becoming obvious that Japan would be defeated in the

Second World War. Nagai made up his mind that, if necessary, rather than suffer the atrocities the conquerors might indulge in, the four members of his family would die together. He bought cyanide. The experience of this time was described later in his short story, *Aotsuyu*) *The Blue Rainy Season*).

In 1946, he resigned from the Bungei Shunjū Sha. His short story, *Kurumiwari* (*Nutcracker*) was published in the October issue of *Gakusei* (*Student*) in 1948. This work centres on a painter's recollection of his childhood, relating beautifully the emerging character of a boy brought up in a warm family atmosphere. He describes the period from the time when the boy loses his real mother to the time when he gets a stepmother. This story is often printed in text-books of Junior High School children in Japan.

Asagiri (*Morning Mist,* translated by Seidensticker, E.G., *Modern Japanese Stories,* ed. by Morris, Ivan, pp. 302–319, Tokyo, Tuttle, 1962) was published in the August edition of *Bungakukai* (*The Literary World*) in 1949. This work describes an old scholar and his wife coming to a poultry farm to drink the blood of chickens. It is war-time, and there is a desperate shortage of food. Through the description of the old scholar and his wife emerging from the morning mist we are given an impression of a lonely righteousness. The couple are also slightly humorous. In 1950 this work was awarded the Yokomitsu Riichi Prize.

In 1951 *Kaze Futatabi* (*The Returning Wind*) was published in the "Asahi" newspaper (from July 7th to September 30th). *Ikko* (*One,* translated by Seidensticker, E.G., *Japan quarterly,* Vol. VII, No. 2, 1960) was published in *Shinchō* (*The New Tide*) in August 1959. In 1965, a collection of short stories, *Ikko Sonota* (*One, and Other Stories*) was published by Bungei Shunjū Shinsha (a publishing firm), and Nagai, received the Noma Literary Prize for this work. *Aotsuyu* (*The Blue Rainy Season*)—mentioned above —was published in the same year in the November edition of *Shinchō,* (*The New Tide*). Although the story is about a very gloomy subject—family suicide—it has a humorous flavour due to the calmness of the people before death. It is really an excellent short story, depicting Japanese resignation to "fate".

Nagai Tatsuo
Aotsuyu *(The blue rainy season)*
Published in *Shinchô,* September 1965.

(Synopsis) In the house of Mr. Ôta Senzô (77 years old), who had no oc-cupation, four persons, namely Senzô himself, his wife Hide (67 years old), his adopted daughter Harue (51 years old), and Hide's sister, Hayashi Yuki, (72 years old) were found dead by a grocer, Mr. Umemoto Sada-kichi, their relative, who reported it to F Police Station. According to the police investigation, a letter was found under the pillow of Senzô, which said, "We owe 500,000 yen to the Horie Shop. We tried to start an enter-prise and failed. We are tired of living". At their bed-side, they found 49,000 yen for funeral expenses, the birth certificates of the four people and another letter requesting the burial of their corpses. The Police decided that they had commited suicide by taking poison. According to Mr. Umemoto, the discoverer of the dead bodies, the gas man had felt it strange that newspapers were piling up at the entrance and had informed the grocer about this. According to the police investigation, Mr. Ôta had formerly been an office clerk. He was a punctilious man, and had been regular in paying the interest on the 500,000 yen which he borrowed from the Hori Shop in the previous year. This amounted to 22,500 yen every month. Their house, the grounds and all the household effects had been mortgaged because of the debt, and their life was not easy. The above is just what a newspaper report said. What is in the following pages is an account of what Senzô and the others were doing five days before the dis-covery of their corpses, namely, on the night when they committed sui-cide. We will start with the description of Senzô coming home, and fol-low them until shortly before their death.

A little before nine in the evening a train which had started from Tokyo arrived at F Station on the Shônan Line. All the passengers who got off at this station were armed against the rain. It had been raining for two days. Among the passengers who got off was Ôta Senzô. He was carrying an umbrella and a bag. He stopped at the station shop and bought a small bottle of saké which contained two *gô*, or about 0.36 of a litre. Outdoor lamps were shining here and there among the fresh leaves of the trees. Senzô followed a winding path for a while and came to his house which was the last house on that path. When he entered through the side door of the gate, it grated a little. It looked as if this was because of the weight of the thick growth of the trees in the garden, trees which had fully absorbed the moisture and the darkness of the night. The garden had been left for so long without the care of a gardener. Locking the side door, Senzô looked up at the lamp outside the gate, and exposed his face to the fine rain for a while.

"Hello", Harue, his adopted daughter, said welcoming him home and lighting the lamp in the tiny vestibule. She looked cheerful. Following Harue, Yuki, his wife's sister, came and told him about a show which she, accompanied by Harue, had gone to see on that day. Her back was bent with age. She seemed to have enjoyed this show very much, the last one in her life, and looked happy when telling him about it. In the room at the back of the house, his sick wife, Hide, was sitting on her bed and doing up her hair. After having a bath, Senzô sat in a leisurely manner on his wife's bed.

"As we decided yesterday, I am not going to say anything today, but if you would like to say something now, please go ahead", he said to Hide. "Thank you very much for looking after me so long" was her answer. "That's what I should say to you. I have been an unmanly person. Please, forgive me", he replied. "Last night, we promised not to say anything like that, didn't we? Please, don't say any more", Hide said. Senzô continued quietly, "I don't know what to think about all these years. One moment, I think it was immensely long, but in the next moment, I feel that the years flew away so quickly, as if they had been only three months or half a year. Perhaps that's what man's life is like". Then the four people sat round the table. The bottle of saké was opened.

The night wind shook the glazed doors gently, and flew away, taking the bottle, Senzô offered saké to everyone. "Please, drink a little". Holding her saké-cup in both hand, Harue received the saké. Her saké-cup was

trembling. "Daddy!", Harue gasped out. "Neither Mammy nor Auntie. . . ." "Yes, go ahead!" "Neither Mammy nor Auntie has said a word
about our going to die since this morning. I, I can't help admiring. . . ."
She could not continue. However hard she tried, tears gushed out of her
eyes, and she threw herself on the table, crying. This violent outburst was
the only unseemly incident in this otherwise calm household on the night
of their death.

According to the newspaper report, Umemoto Tatsukichi, who had
been present at the post-mortem, had said: "Although I am Senzô's relative, there is no blood relationship between us. My father found this house
for him roughly ten years ago. Harue was a nurse at the hospital in Tokyo
where his wife was hospitalized when she developed a lung disease. That's
how Harue came to be adopted by them, I think. Probably it was Harue
who had obtained the sleeping pills they used. I don't know whether she
was sexually intimate with Senzô". As for the last bit about sexual intimacy, Umemoto seems merely to have been answering the question of a
newspaper reporter. It is a bad habit of newspaper reporters to put question
and answer together and create the impression that such question had
occurred to the person interviewed.

Nakamura Mitsuo

Nakamura Mitsuo was born in Tokyo in 1911. He entered the Faculty
of Law of Tokyo University but soon left it. He graduated from the
French Literature Department of Tokyo University. While he was still a
student, he published an essay, *Guy de Maupassant,* which attracted much
attention. He established himself as a critic with his brilliant study of
Futabatai Shimei. In 1938, he went to France to study on a scholarship
received from the French Government, but the next year he had to return
to Japan due to the outbreak of the Second World War. He worked for
the Ministry of Foreign Affairs, and in his spare time, he completed his

studies on Flaubert and Maupassant and also published critical works on Modern Japanese Literature.

Since the war, he has been very productive as a critic. Among his publications are *Fûzoku Shôsetsu Ron* (*On the Novel of Manners*, 1950) and *Futabatei Shimei Den* (*The Life of Futabatei Shimei*, 1953). The former traces the rise and fall of realism in Modern Japanese Literature in comparison with realism in the literature of 19th century Europe. The latter is a compilation and completion of his studies of Futabatei Shimei. In addition he has published works on many other authors and has also been involved in literary controversies from time to time. His position as a leading critic of the day has become established.

The basic principle underlying his criticism is his distrust of the quasi-modern culture of Japan since the Meiji period. In particular, he points out the distortions in Realistic Literature in Modern Japan by using Modern Realism in Europe as the standard. This is why he feels a great sympathy with Futabatei Shimei who was deeply attracted by Modern Russian Literature and who, at the same time, continued to manifest a patriotic concern about the rapid modernization of Japan during the Meiji period. His sympathy with Futabatei is not only Nakamura's starting point as a critic, it also lies behind the consistent masculinity and sharpness which runs through Nakamura's critical works.

Nakamura has also written novels and plays. They are based on the same critical principle. His play *Hito to Ôkami* (*Man and Wolves*, 1958) mercilessly exposes the ugliness of modern life. His novel *Waga Sei no Hakusho* (*White Paper of My Sexual Experience*, 1963) shows the same malaise by using various literary circles as typical examples of corruption. *Pari Hanjô Ki* (*A Record of Flourishing Paris*, 1960) uses Paris as its setting and clearly depicts, using comic situations, the pettiness and arrogance of Japanese people among whom are university teachers and other quasi-artists who are chosen to represent the modern Japanese state abroad. It is scarcely necessary to point out that behind Nakamura's criticism of modern Japan lies his own stoic self-criticism.

NAKAMURA Mitsuo
Pari hanjo ki—a play in three acts
(A Record of Flourishing Paris)
Published in *Koe,* Number 8 and 9, 1960.

(Synopsis) (Act I) *Time:* One summer in Paris towards the end of the Fourth Republic.
Place: Kishimoto's room on the second floor of a back-street café.

Kishimoto is a young assistant professor of a Japanese university who has been studying Philosophy at the Sorbonne for three years. He has come to be convinced that French thought can be understood only when you understand the life of French people, and now has made up his mind to live in France permanently and to give up his post in Japan. He is now having a casual affair with Taniguchi Atsuko, a *chanson* singer, who appears at a third rate cabaret show; but he is also on intimate terms with Poline, the only daughter of Nishimoto, the owner of the café and a painter, and his French wife Ereine. Nishimoto was once a promising painter, but after settling down in Paris thirty years ago, he has been more or less dependant on his wife, Ereine. All he does is to make reproductions of Utoriro and sell them cheaply to a picture dealer through his friend Hayashi, also a painter.

One evening Kishimoto, who has not been paying his rent and board for the last six months on the pretext that he is now writing his Ph. D. thesis and needs money, quarrels with Ereine. The next morning, Kishimoto goes out to calm his anger. While he is out, Namiki, a graduate student who was once Kishimoto's student, comes to visit him. At Kishimoto's lodgings he meets Atsuko, the singer, who has been staying there since the night before. A casual love relationship develops between them. At that time a warning against the flooding of the River Seine has been issued, and there is an atmosphere of excitement in Paris. When Kishimoto comes back to his lodgings, he notices that something has happened between Namiki and Atsuko. However, Namiki, unabashed, asks Kishimoto to intercede for him, for he has offended Professor Hashiguchi by not going to meet him when he arrived in Paris yesterday. Kishimoto has not been on a friendly terms with Hashiguchi. He consents to Namiki's request, but points out the contradiction between Namiki's devotion to learning and his desire to get on in society. Namiki answers him by maintaing the importance of a realistic attitude.

Nishimoto, the painter who owns the café, sees in Kishimoto his former self, and advises him to go back to Japan, but Kishimoto's determination to live in France permanently is not shaken. The flood warning says that the area where Kishimoto lives will be inundated within thirty-eight hours.

(Act II, Scene I) Two days later, the flood warning has proved to be groundless. Poline finds a stranger in Kishimoto's room in the morning, and there is a great turmoil. However, it turns out that it is only Nakada, a friend of Kishimoto's, who, as a newspaper reporter, wanted to write an exciting account of the flood. He is Atsuko's former lover. Kishimoto, who spent the night on the river bank of the Seine looking at the Paris which he loves, soon returns. Then, unexpectedly Professor Hashiguchi appears. He tells Nishimoto, the painter who owns the café, that he is related to him by marriage, that Nishimoto's mother has died and that, in accordance with her will, he has brought a part of her legacy to Nishimoto. However, Nishimoto who considers the feelings of his dead mother and the calculation of his sister, Professor Hashiguchi's sister-in-law, hesitates to receive it and leaves it aside for later consideration. A little later Nishimoto comes back again formally, dressed in a Japanese *kimono*, which is quite unusual for him, and holds something like a memorial service for his mother in front of her photograph. Poline and others who are present also attend it, Nishimoto places before his mother's photograph the large sum of money which he has finally accepted following the repeated offer of Hayashi, his painter friend. Nishimoto gets drunk. He accuses his wife Ereine, and complains of his own unmanliness to the photograph of his mother.

(Act II, Scene 2) It is the afternoon of the same day. Nishimoto, now in possession of the legacy, offers to pay Kishimoto's rent for him for the time being and asks him to stay on at the lodging house. This is because he knows his beloved daughter, Pauline, loves Kishimoto. Professor Hashiguchi then returns to see Kishimoto. He delivers a message from a certain influential professor, and out of his feeling of superiority as the one who has become a professor first, he advises Kishimoto to go back to Japan. Professor Hashiguchi also woos Atsuko, saying that he would give Namiki, the graduate student, a good post in the future as compensation. At that moment Namiki rushes in with a knife and attacks Atsuko who escapes with only light injuries.

(Act III) It is three months later. The café has been modernized. A party to announce Nishimoto's painting exhibition is going on. At last, Nishimoto has started to paint original works. However, among the reporters, the reputation of his paintings is as low as that of Atsuko's songs. Namiki, after the incident, has been working under Nakada, the newspaper reporter, and now he is absorbed by the Algerian problem. Kishimoto arrives with Poline. Kishimoto has been charged with fraud and has been much talked about. He discloses that police interrogation has lead to the arrest of the picture dealer who had been buying Nishimoto's reproductions of Utoriro as a member of an international forgery group, and that the police are also making inquiries about Nishimoto and Hayashi. This wrecks Nishimoto's hopes of going back to Japan. For a while they discuss the fine distinctions drawn between reproductions and forgeries. The investigation made by Namiki and a French reporter discloses that Professor Hashiguchi was the informer in this case. However, Professor Hashiguchi unabashedly justifies himself by saying that it was a painful measure to rescue Nishimoto from the hands of the forgery group. Atsuko makes up her mind to part with Professor Hashiguchi, Kishimoto decides to remain in Paris and succeed Nishimoto as the owner of the café, which he will run with Pauline. As if nothing has happened, the night is descending again on Paris.

Nakamura Shin'ichiro

NAKAMURA Shin'ichirô was born in 1918 in Shizuoka Prefecture. Soon afterwards his family moved to Tokyo. When he was three years old, his mother died, and he was placed under the custody of her parents who were living in Shizuoka Prefecture. When he was ten years old, he went to Tokyo to live with his father. When he was sixteen years old, his father also died, and he became an orphan.

He went to the First Higher School, and then entered Tokyo University. He graduated from the Department of French Literature. His student days were not very happy ones. His financial position was precarious. He had to support himself by tutoring, although he also had a grant. It appears that his hard student days as well as his boyhood which was characterized by a series of losses, first the loss of his mother and then that of his father, created in the author lasting disgust with the actual world and deep longing for an imaginary ideal world.

His novel, *Shi no Kage no Moto ni* (*Under the Shadow of Death*) was first published serially in *Kôgen* from 1946 to 1947 and later published in book form with some additions. It is the first in the series of five novels which also consists of *Shion no Musumetachi* (*Maidens of Shion*), *Aijin to Shishin to* (*The God of Love and the God of Death*), *Tamashii no Yoru no Naka o* (*Through the Night of the Soul*) and *Nagai Tabi no Owari* (*Journey's End*). When *Shi no Kage no Moto ni* (*Under the Shadow of Death*) first appeared, it was criticized as being a work written for mere fun or as having no connection with the present age.

Concerning this long novel about the author's youth which, it is said, was started in the midst of the war just to amuse himself, the author has said, "I was trying to fill it only with what had disappeared from my world".

Through misfortune and war, he lost his parents, happy student days and happy youth. It is quite understandable that the author who had suffered from a long series of losses, should try to fill this novel with only that which had disappeared from his world.

The author was not drafted into military service. Working as a lecturer of the Tokyo School of Music and as a supernumerary of a marine meteorological observatory, he engaged in writing. He also enjoyed Hori Tatsuo's recognition and favour. In 1942 he started, together with Fukunaga Takehiko, Katô Shûichi, Kubota Keisaku and others, a group called *Matinée Poétique* for literary study, and maintained his resistance against the prevailing literary trends of the age.

After the war, he won recognition as the leading figure among *après-guerre* writers. He was outside and opposed to the main stream of Modern Japanese Literature which ran from Naturalism to the "I" novel, and enthusiastically tried to give a fresh impact to contemporary Japanese Literature by learning from 20th century Western Literature. *Yahanraku* (*Music at Midnight*, 1954) and *Tsumetai Tenshi* (*A Cold Angel*, 1955) are the main fruits of this attempt.

NAKAMURA Shin'ichiro
Ishi no inori *(Prayer of a stone)*
Published in *Gunzô*, March 1969.

(**Synopsis**) Hagie was brought up by the butler and his wife. Her house was a big-beamed old-fashioned country house and its inside was always quite dark. Her parents were already dead when she began to understand what was going on around her. The aged butler treated her as if she were a princess. Her relatives also spoke to her, the heiress of the family, in a very humble manner as if servants were talking to a mistress.

When she entered the primary school, she found that most of the twenty pupils were children of people employed at her house. They treated her respectfully as the heiress of the illustrous Sakata family. The principal and his wife divided the pupils into two groups and each was in charge of one group. They also gave Hagie special attention as if they were her private tutors.

Thus Hagie grew up. Much of her time was spent in melancholic day-dreaming by herself in the back room of her large dark residence. When she went to Tokyo to enter the university, she tried to forget the life she had led in her native mountain village. She wanted to escape from her native village where her life had been that of a prisoner. She wanted to find an ideal world for herself somewhere far away.

She married Yûtarô who was a dependent of a branch of the family. She married him because he was also longing to be free of the gloomy, conservative, intellectually stifling atmosphere prevailing among the whole clan. However, as a husband Yûtarô was disappointing. He could not suppress his instinctive awe in face of Hagie's huge fortune and position as heiress of the family. The inferiority complex arising from this awe was matched only by the obsession to get along in society, typical of a person who has done well at school.

To be a famous man and to obliterate the memory of his humiliating childhood was Yûtarô's sole ambition. His Philistinism made Hagie miserable.

She left their home, and escaped to a mental hospital. She came to regard her life up to this point as her "former" life which had no connection with her any more. She confined herself in a tiny room of the hospital, and lived there undisturbed in her dream of a faraway ideal land.

From time to time, she became uneasy about living such an unreal life, and provisionally returned home. However, in the end she always found herself incapable of tolerating the Philistinism of her husband, and was driven back to the hospital, feeling irritated.

She had been living in the hospital for more than ten years although her illness was not severe, when a man called Sôichi, her kinsman, came to visit her. He was with a girl whom Hagie did not know.

Sôichi was Yûtarô's cousin. He had been Hagie's fiancé, but he had eloped with a girl of dubious reputation. To Hagie, he was merely a shadow from her "former" life, but his appearance and the malicious arrogant behaviour of the young girl who came with him somehow induced her to visit her home unexpectedly.

As Hagie had expected, Yûtarô, her husband, looked unmistakenly perplexed by her sudden return. "Do you want a divorce?", she demanded of him. "Don't be so stupid! If I divorced you, society would condemn and abuse me because you are ill", he answered nervously.

Hagie felt disgusted by this stereotyped reaction of Yûtarô who could only look at divorce, which concerned both of them, from his own selfish point of view. Hagie murmured, "Somehow you look like a TV actor". she felt that her husband acted like a robot, a perfect Philistine, and became discouraged. However, her husband, whom she had hitherto only thought of as nothing but a superficial distorted piece of humanity, suddenly started talking about time and death.

Hagie returned to the hospital, and took a walk along her usual walking route. She came to the side of a pond. She thought that, for her husband death was probably merely another social event, and started meditating about her own unique death. Fixing her glance on the surface of the pond, she felt that she was turning into a stone. "There is no time in a stone. A stone is already dead", she reflected. She wondered if her mind had not already crossed beyond the moment of death and whether she was not living in death. "What misery!", she thought, and unwittingly started praying to something.

Nakano Shigeharu

Nakano Shigeharu was born in 1902 in Fukui Prefecture. His father was a small landowner who worked for the Tobacco Monopoly Bureau, and was half a farmer and half a salaried man. Nakano was his second son. During his childhood he was brought up by his grandparents, whose influence was mainly responsible for his interest in literature. While he was a student of the Fourth Higher School in Kanazawa, he wrote *tanka* and poems in other forms. In 1924 he entered the Faculty of Literature of Tokyo University, and after that became a pupil of Murô Seisei, a poet-novelist, and started publishing leftwing poems and essays on poetry in the literary group magazine *Roba* (*Donkey*). He was also associated with a study group of Proletarian Literature. Nakano's poems had a very strict rhythmical structure, and attracted the attention of Akutagawa Ryûnosuke who thought that they indicated the new direction in which Proletarian Poetry was moving. Nakano became a central figure in the Marxist Literary Movement, and published new views and theories about leftwing art and literature. He had, however, to spend more than two years in prison on suspicion of violating the Law for the Maintenance of the Public Peace. In 1934 he was released on the condition that he would leave the Communist Movement, and started writing again. Even after this, however, he was repeatedly forbidden to write or was subjected to preventive detention. His personal freedom was thus always threatened. *Dai Isshô* (*The First Chapter*, 1935) is the first of a series of novels which deal with the Proletarian Literature movement since about 1927. In this novel Nakano's own defection from the leftwing movement is depicted as a serious setback to the movement. *Hitotsu no Chiisana Kiroku* (*One Tiny Document*, 1936) and *Shôsetsu no Kakenu Shôsetsuka* (*A Novelist who Cannot Write Novels*, 1936) are its sequels.

Nakano's writings are permeated by a sense of beauty characteristic of a poet and by tenacious logic. He first wrote rebellious lyrics, and then important theoretical essays on art, and finally moved to writing novels. *Uta no Wakare* (*Farewell to Song*, 1939) depicts Nakano's own youth autobiographically. This novel, together with *Muragimo* (*The Heart*, 1949), depicts in an objective manner Nakano's complicated youth and his development. In *Nashi no Hana* (*Pear Blossoms*, 1957), Nakano went back to his childhood and birth to discover the origin of his idealistic attitude. *Hagi no Monkakiya* (*The Crest Painter of Hagi*, 1956), summarized below, is an "I" novel which sheds light on Nakano's inner self by depicting his reactions to seemingly common everyday occurrences. Among Nakano's other works is the long novel *Kô Otsu Hei Tei* (*A, B, C, and D*, 1965).

Nakano Shigeharu
Hagi no monkakiya *(The crest painter of hagi)*
Published in *Gunzô*, October 1956.

(Synopsis) I was strolling in the town of Hagi having already finished my business. The aim of my visit to Hagi was to clarify the relationship between two men who had been associating with each other for years obscuring their basic differences. Anyway that business was over. I had no other task, and I was pleased. I just continued to roam about.

Hagi was a tiny quiet town. The water of rivers was clear. I came to a big house. The family living here must be an old respectable family of this area. The nameplate bore a name written in a beautiful calligraphy. "Aha, this is the house of so-and-so", I thought. Beyond that, however, no particular thought occurred to my mind. I did not feel any fundamental hatred. Probably some festival was going on. I noticed a scaffold with a drum on it in the road just in front of the gate of that house. Probably this was an annual custom. I felt something fishy about it. At the same time it created a certain peaceful atmosphere. Since I was on a journey and was freed from usual responsibilities, my attention was caught more by the peaceful atmosphere of the scene. Thus I went on walking. Presently I came to a somewhat crowded place. A big post-office came into sight. I noticed that there was a sweet shop just opposite the post-office. I remembered my daughter who had accused me of never bringing back any souvenirs when I travelled. My daughter was already in the third year of a junior high school, but still I felt sorry for her. When she was a little girl, she would feel unhappy about her father's not going to any work. She seemed to be envious of her playmates in the neighbourhood. Anyway, no matter where I am, I prefer to walk without carrying anything. I entered the sweet shop. Probably I was really in a relaxed mood. Among the articles displayed there, some candied summer oranges caught my eye. Memories of Sumoto in Awaji Island revived in me. At that time life in Tokyo was becoming increasingly difficult because of the war. Sweets had disappeared from shops. Eggs were difficult to get. Our children were waiting for me at home. Their mother had been detained by the police. I was at a loss how to look after our children. Their mother, however, was released towards the end of the year. Just then I received a letter from a friend of mine living in Sumoto on Awaji Island. He invited me to come with my family and stay with him. We went to Sumoto. At a sweet shop at the outskirts of Sumoto, I found candied summer oranges. I bought one, and when we arrived at my friend's house, I displayed it proudly to my friend.

"Could I have this one?", I said to the sweetmeat dealer's wife. She wrapped the bottle carefully. I borrowed a writing brush, and addressed it to my children. Then I entered the post-office. When I placed it on the counter, however, I changed my mind, and decided to bring it back with me. If I sent it by post, it might get broken when they threw it. I bowed silently, and went out of the post-office. The place was fairly lively. I went on walking with a bit of frivolous curiosity.

As I walked, the appearance of the town gradually changed. The houses looked different. The area was now a sort of backstreet slum. Probably the town of Hagi was coming to an end. Then I noticed a tiny shop, where a woman was facing me through the window. She was looking down seemingly absorbed in doing something. Bending her head deeply she was wrestling with something tiny. That reminded me of the postures of a seal-engraver and watch-repairer which I had seen from my childhood. I walked a little nearer. She seemed to be a young woman. I could not see her face properly. Both her mouth and her chin were out of my sight. She was holding a slender writing brush in her right hand. Its tip was really extraordinarily slender. She was holding the writing brush in a way that its tip was slightly nearer to her than the other end. She was holding something like a pot in her left hand. The tip of the writing brush on the right touched the small bottle on the left repeatedly as if she was poking in with a needle. After straining my eyes for a considerable while, it dawned on me that she was painting a crest on a *haori* (a Japanese coat) or something. I felt relieved. As I was walking away, I noticed something like a signboard with "Crest painter" written on it. Underneath was another board bearing the words "The house of a fallen soldier". "Crest painter" sounds like an ancient trade. They must have been having a hard time in these years. I resumed walking hurriedly.

Nakayama Gishu

Nakayama Gishû was born in 1900 in Fukushima Prefecture. After he had graduated from the Department of English Literature of Waseda University, he worked as a teacher of English in Narita in Chiba Prefecture, and other places until he moved to Tokyo to live by his pen. During his life of poverty as an unknown writer, he lost his wife. His path was not smooth. Among Nakayama's classmates at Waseda University was Yokomitsu Riichi who was to become one of the great figures of 20th century Japanese literature. Nakayama had started the literary group magazine *Tô* (*Tower*) with Yokomitsu and others, and had published studies there. After becoming a professional writer, he followed Yokomitsu's example, and wrote many psychological novels. He first discovered his own unique literary style in *Atsumonozaki* (*The Thick-Petalled Chrysanthemum*, 1938). This novel depicts, with bitter suspense, a miserly impudent old man who is a social failure, but will not admit his defeat, and who through his very stubbornness makes something of his life. The portraiture of the man is very vivid. *Ishibumi* (*Stone Monument*, 1939) also depicts the ups and downs of a man who lives his life impudently without losing heart. During the war Nakayama went to Java as a member of the Naval Reporters' Corps, and then made a tour of the South Sea Islands. After the war, he published *Teniyan no Matsujitsu* (*The Last Days of Tinian*, 1948) which is based on his experiences at this time. In this novel Nakayama depicts very realistically the anxieties and agitations and subsequent crushing collapse of an isolated outpost under the shadow of Japan's impending defeat. As for *Sôrenka* (*The Pilgrimage of a Woman*, 1952), its realistic power is even more impressive. It depicts with poignant poetic feeling a woman who wanders at the mercy of an utterly unpredictable fate.

Nakayama's works which depict life's pilgrimage with deep emotion are characterized by a profound sympathy for people in adversity. *Daijô no Tsuki* (*The Moon on the Tower*, 1962–63), an autobiographical novel about the author's relationship with Yokomitsu Riichi, is a quiet recollection of bygone years. *Shôan* (*Shôan*, 1963) has Akechi Mitsuhide, a general of the turbulent 16th century, as its hero. Nakayama depicts Mitsuhide, who is usually dismissed as a traitor, as a tragic figure who was faithful to his destiny as a general living in a turbulent age, and is successful in evoking the feeling of human sadness. Nakayama died in 1969 of cancer of the esophagus, but his struggling literary life is remembered affectionately by many people for its human warmth.

NAKAYAMA Gishu
Shôan *(Shôan)*
Published in *Gunzô*, January 1963–February 1964.

(Synopsis)

How often have I heard·
The Cuckoo singing
Among the trees of the forest?   (Shôan)

The leaves of the trees were deepening their green. It was at the beginning of summer when the long rain of early summer was about to start. In the sky above the wide field was nothing but gray rain cloud. A young warrior came running along in a great hurry. He wore black armor. He was carrying a head under his right arm, and he was holding a halberd in his left hand which shook violently as he ran. As he neared the tent of the general which was situated in an open place near a river, he shouted that he had killed the enemy general, Saitô Dôsan, and brought back his head.

When the head of Saitô Dôsan, the Governer of the Mino District, was displayed before the general Isshiki Noriyoshi, the attending officers and soldiers all gazed breathlessly at the pitiful sight. Dôsan was their former lord. The general, Isshiki Noriyoshi, who was Dôsan's son, said to the head, "You have only to blame yourself for this, you old dotard!", and kicked it. Looking at Akechi Mitsuhide's face, Noriyoshi said, "You are pale. You really look like a coward, Mitsuhide." Mitsuhide was then twenty-nine years old. He did not share the boldness and insensitivity of the tyrant Noriyoshi who had killed his two younger brothers and his father. Mitsuhide was later to became famous for his skill in shooting and was even reputed to be the best marksman in the country, and it was Dôsan who had taught Mitsuhide how to shoot. Mitsuhide was a sensitive man and he was really shocked by Dôsan's cruel death.

The will of Dôsan bequeathed the governership of the Mino District to Oda Nobunaga, and he was eagerly waiting for an opportunity to seize the Mino District. The members of the Akechi family were also very much concerned with the destiny of the Mino District, but Mitsuhide did not have enough military power to take any definite action. Three years passed. From Kyoto, Mitsuhide received the news that Matsunaga Danjô had killed the *shôgun* Ashikaga Yoshiteru, but Mitsuhide had gradually come to entertain a view of life which accepted such a thing as a matter of course.

Nobunaga twice invited Mitsuhide to enter his service but each time Mitsuhide declined his invitation. Nobunaga's intention was to use Mitsuhide, who belonged to an old clan in Toki, to get support from influential clans in the Mino District. In his third attempt to win Mitsuhide to his side, Nobunaga received voluntary help from an old man called Yamagishi who was a distant relative of Mitsuhide. Yamagishi visited Mitsuhide and tried to persuade him to accept Nobunaga's invitation. Mitsuhide was not against the idea at all; he had only been concerned with the idea of bringing something with him which would commend him in Nobunaga's eyes. He conceived a plan to act as a mediator between Nobunaga and Ashikaga Yoshiaki who was to become the fifteenth *shôgun* and who, having been driven away from Kyoto, was at the moment in Asakura. At Gifu, Mitsuhide met Nobunaga who was six years his junior. When Mitsuhide prostrated himself before him, Nobunaga said in a friendly manner, "I have been looking forward to seeing you. Please— no formality!", and granted Mitsuhide on the spot a fief in Yasuhachi-gun which would give him a revenue of 500 *kan*. When Mitsuhide suggested to him the idea of his winning Yoshiaki over to Nobunaga's side, Nobunaga replied in a good humour, "You have been thinking of commending yourself to me by that plan, have you? You are a sly person", and accepted his proposal. Mitsuhide was very much impressed by Nobunaga and was convinced that Nobunaga had the ability to unify Japan. At the same time he felt that it would not be an easy job to serve Nobunaga.

Mitsuhide distinguished himself by many military feats, was given a fief yielding 60,000 koku of rice, and held a castle in Sakamoto, Ômi (present Shiga Prefecture). Nobunaga thought very highly of Mitsuhide's administrative and diplomatic ability, and as Nobunaga's deputy, Mitsuhide acquired such importance that only Kinoshita Tôkichiro, who was Mitsuhide's senior, could compete with him in Nobunaga's eyes. Mitsuhide had only served Nobunaga for four years but had already made a spectacular rise in the world. Nobunaga was at that time regarded by many as the paramount power in the whole of Japan. He was subjugating one district after another. His principle was never to relent until he destroyed everybody in the clan which opposed him. He was really severe towards his enemies. He defeated the Asakura Clan, annihilated the revolting believers of the *Shin* sect, destroyed the Takada Clan, and decided to conquer the Môri Clan in the Chûgoku area next. Nobunaga's whole army was marching towards the Chûgoku area. Mitsuhide had also received an order to go and fight against the Môri Clan. Nobunaga himself went to Kyoto, accompanied by a few attendants, and was staying at the Honnô-ji temple. When Mitsuhide heard this, he received what he believed was a heavenly inspiration. Was this not a wonderful opportunity to seize power? Mitsuhide did not entertain any grudge againt Nobunaga, he even felt grateful towards Nobunaga; but Mitsuhide shared the dream of becoming the ruler of the whole of Japan with all the war lords of that turbulent age. It would be a shame if he who regarded himself as a good military strategist missed this opportunity. Mitsuhide summoned five of his trusted retainers and disclosed to them his plan of killing Nobunaga. The five retainers agreed to his plan, and the army under Mitsuhide's command killed Nobunaga at the Honnô-ji temple and, Nobutada, Nobunaga's son, at the Myôkaku-ji temple in the Nijô area. Mitsuhide seemed to have exhausted all his resources in successfully killing Nobunaga and Nobutada. He entered the Azuchi Castle (the castle of Nobunaga) and received a messenger from the Imperial court, which meant that he was recognized as the ruler of the country by the court, but to his disppointment, the war lords would not visit his camp. Before long Hideyoshi's army arrived like stormy waves to attack him. The decisive battle between Mitsuhide's army and Hideyoshi's army which took place at Yamasaki was quickly over. Mitsuhide's army was defeated, and he himself was killed by the spear of a peasant. Mitsuhide and Hideyoshi had been good friends. They were two equally excellent generals who had served Nobunaga. Each of them played a rôle alotted by Destiny: rôles which were quite suited to their character.

Niwa Fumio

Niwa Fumio was born in 1904 as the eldest son of a Buddhist priest in Yotsukaichi City, Mie Prefecture. His father's temple was called Sûken-ji temple, and it belonged to the Takado group of the *Shin* sect. His mother, who had been born into the family who had owned this temple for generations, deserted his father, who was the adopted son of her family, and began to live with another man. From this time on, Niwa had to learn how to endure this misfortune. From his childhood, he showed a tendency to devise means of escape from difficulty and pain, rather than to try to overcome them. This became his general attitude in life. He looked at life with a consciousness of sin, and his doubts about human existence lead him to take up literature. In 1923, he came to Tokyo to enter the First High School attached to Waseda University. In 1926, he entered the

Department of Japanese Literature in the Faculty of Literature of that university. He graduated in 1929. After his graduation, he went home and became a Buddhist priest. However, when his story, *Ayu* (*The Trout,* 1932) which he had sent from home to Nagai Tatsuo editor of *Bungei Shunjû* (*Literary Years*), was accepted and published in *Bungei Shunjû,* he returned to Tokyo. He gradually won recognition in the literary world by works such as *Shôkei-moji* (*Hieroglyphics,* 1934) and *Zeiniku* (*Indulgent Flesh,* 1934) but as fascist tendencies deepened in Japan, Niwa's writings came under censure on the ground that they were pornographic. From about 1935 onwards, he was virtually forbidden to write by the authorities.

After the war, he once again started writing vigorously. His postwar works are based on orthodox realism as before, but they attest to greater social concern on the part of the author. Among works which were published shortly after the war are *Iyagarase no Nenrei* (*The Age of Being a Nuisance,* 1947, translated by Morris, Ivan, *Modern Japanese Stories,* pp. 320–348, Tokyo, Tuttle, 1962), *Kokuheki* (*Wailing Wall,* 1947–8), *Tôsei Munezanyô* (*Calculation in the Present Age,* 1949) and *Hachûrui* (*The Reptile*). They are all fine literary efforts. After these, he wrote *Kôfuku e no Kyori* (*The Distance to Happiness,* 1951) and *Shadan-ki* (*The Crossing Gate,* 1952), both of which can be regarded as a literary experiments. In *Bodaiju* (*The Buddha Tree,* translated by Strong, Kenneth, London, Peter Owen, 1966), written during 1955 and 1956, Niwa uses his grandmother, father, and others as "models"; the novel is a revelation of his family background. *Ichiro* (*A Single Road*), which was published serially in *Gunzô* (*Group*) from 1962 to 1966, vividly depicts the hell which one woman makes of life through her lust.

One fundamental characteristic of Niwa's writings is that they clearly attest to the author's desire to communicate to his readers his understanding of the basic sinfulness of human nature. In his understanding, man is a being inextricably chained to carnal desire. Thus, in his works, all the characters are depicted as "sinful". On the other hand, Niwa believes that since human beings are weak pitiful creatures, they will be forgiven. Niwa published *Shinran* (the founder of the *Shin* sect) in the *Sankei Newspaper* from 1965 to 1969. *Rennyo* (a Buddhist priest of the *Shin* sect) has been published serially in *Chûô Kôron* (*Central Review*) since early 1971. Niwa is president of Nihon Bungeika Kyôkai (The Japan Writers' Association). He is also the editor and publisher of the magazine *Bungakusha* (*Men of Letters*) which offers new and aspiring writers an opportunity to publish their works.

NIWA Fumio
Ichiro *(A single road)*
Published serially in *Gunzô* from October 1962 to June 1966.
Published in book form by Kôdansha in August 1966.

(Synopsis) Kanako's father was the principal of a middle school. Thus, she was brought up in the home of a teacher. In Tan'ami City (a fictional provincial city invented by the author), there was a Japanese restaurant called Enparô. This restaurant was owned by a distant female relative of Kanako's family. When her father died, she became the head maid of this restaurant. Probably because she had learned Nô dances when she was fifteen and sixteen years old, she was a girl of fine carriage, and striking beauty. Because of her refinement and grace, she had a high reputation among the guests and geisha girls who came to the restaurant.

Consenting to a suggestion made by the mistress of the restaurant, she married Fushiki Kôdô, the chief priest of Shômyô-ji temple.

Kanako soon got used to the life of a Buddhist priest's wife. She also established good smooth relationships with the patrons of her husband's temple. After she had borne Kôdô two sons, he was sent, by order of the head temple, to Hokkaido for three years, to serve at a branch temple. It was an honour for a priest of a subordinate temple to receive such an order. It also meant that Kôdô would very likely in due time be promoted to a post in the head temple. While Kôdô was away in Hoddaido, Umemura Yûryô was hired as acting chief priest for Shômyô-ji temple. Kanako and Yûryô sat side by side in the main building of the temple and recited Buddhist sutras day after day. Their relationship gradually became intimate, until finally Kanako committed adultery.

World War II had already begun, and almost every night American B29 airplanes raided Tan'ami City. Listening to the drone of airplanes, Kanako again indulged in sexual intercourse with Yûryô. Finally she became pregnant. Yûryô was drafted into the army, but soon the war came to an end.

When Kôdô came back from Hokkaidô, Kanako confessed everything to him. He calmly listened to her, and tried his best to deal with the situation. He made Kanako have the baby in hospital. When a girl was born, he announced to the world that the baby had been born dead, and secretly asked a business-man called Senge, a patron of his temple, who had acted as a go-between when they married, to bring her up as his adopted daughter. Senge agreed, and thanks to the cooperation of Senge and his wife, no one ever discovered the secret of the child's birth. Kanako soon gave birth to Kôdô's third son. She seemed to be a person who soon forgot everything once it was over. This was probably because she was a woman of spirit.

When Yûryô was demobilized, he became the adopted son and heir of a priest who owned a temple in a town near Tan'ami City. Yûryô and Kanako started meeting secretly at a Japanese restaurant. They managed to avoid detection and indulged in secret pleasure.

Time passed, and Tokuyuki, the eldest son, became a priest like his father and got married. Satoshi, the second son graduated from a university in Tokyo, and entered a trading company there. On the way his office one day, he happened to meet Nobuko, Senge's daughter, in the street. She was a student of a women's college in Tokyo. They had met in Tan'ami City, but in their understanding, Satoshi was the son of the priest and Nobuko was merely the daughter of his patron. They did not know that they were brother and sister. By a whim of Fate, they soon fell in love with each other. They slept together in Satoshi's lodging, and Nobuko became pregnant. Satoshi wrote to his mother, Kanako, confessing everything and asking for permission to marry Nobuko. When she received this letter, Kanako became pale and trembled. She visited a gynaecologist of her acquaintance, at once, and asked him for a letter of introduction to a gynaecologist in Tokyo whom he knew. On that same day, she went to Tokyo and visited Satoshi's lodging. She told Satoshi that Nobuko was her child. Satoshi said that he could not stand to look upon her anymore, and rushed out into the midnight city. That night, Satoshi did not return to his lodgings.

The next morning, Kanako visited Nobuko at her college hall of residence. She took her out to Satoshi's lodgings, and recommended her to get an abortion. She did not have enough courage to confess that she was Nobuko's real mother, so she just said that if it became known that Nobuko, who was still a student had become pregrant, it would cause trouble to Senge as well as to the Shômyô-ji temple. "You've got to have an abortion!" she pleaded. Nobuko, who was made to believe that Satoshi had consented to this, accepted Kanako's entreaty and went to a hospital with her. The operation went smoothly, and Kanako returned to Tan'ami.

In five days, time, when Kanako was beginning to accept that everything had been well settled, she received news that Nobuko had committed suicide. Nobuko might have read a letter which Kanako had left at Satoshi's lodging house in Tokyo, warning him not to tell anything about the secret of her birth to Nobuko. Kanako was overcome by guilt, feeling that it was she who had killed Nobuko. She climbed the stairs to the main building of the temple and fell prostrate there. Kôdô heard his wife's groaning. He felt as if it was coming out of his own body. The idea rose in his mind, "If I cannot save this woman now, I have no right to remain a priest".

Nogami Yaeko

Nogami Yaeko was born in 1885 in Ôita Prefecture. Her real personal name is Yae. Her father was a rich brewer, and Nogami was his eldest daughter. She was awakened to literature by reading Japanese literary classics from her girlhood. She entered Meiji Girls' School in Tokyo. After graduation, she married Nogami Toyoichirô who was a pupil of Natsume Sôseki and who was also from Ôita Prefecture. She was introduced to Sôseki by her husband, and started writing novels as his pupil. At first she used the method of objective description and tried to give concrete expression to things as they are. She made her literary debut with works like *Enishi* (*Human Ties*, 1907), which she published in the *haikai* magazine *Hototogisu* (*Cuckoo*) through Sôseki's recommendation. Yaeko continued for a while to produce novels based on careful description, but as her consciousness as a wife and mother deepened, she liberated herself from the influences of plain descriptive writing, and established herself as a humanistic writer. *Kaijinmaru* (*The Neptune*, 1922, translated by Matsumoto Ryôzô, Tokyo, Kenkyûsha, 1957) which depicted people in starvation marked a turning-point in her development. She then published a series of novels which are commonly referred to as "Junzô novels" after the name of their hero. They are novels depicting a man involved in local politics, and are characterized by the clear intelligence of the author as well as by her healthy views of morals and society. *Machiko* which was published serially from 1928 to 1930 is a long novel dealing directly with problems of society. Through its heroine Machiko who cannot choose between a communist and a wealthy man who both court her, Nogami has expressed the idea that without establishing new morals on the private individual level, it is impossible to establish new higher morals on the social level or for the mankind at large. This novel attests to Nogami's deepened and enlarged social view.

Yaeko's works are characterized by a penetrating realistic touch and by fresh humanistic ideas. *Meiro* (*The Labyrinth*, completed in 1956) which took her more than twenty years to finish is an ambitious long novel which contains every single theme that she had been dealing with. It is written in an exquisite style and is permeated with the author's warm love of humanity. It is a product of a unique mature writer who has deep insights into society and man. *Hideyoshi to Rikyû* (*Hideyoshi and Rikyû*, 1962) is a very careful work and shows Yaeko at her best. Yaeko's literary career which extends over sixty years is by no means a showy one. Her works which appeal to human conscience, however, are in her old age still gaining in mellowness.

NOGAMI Yaeko
Hideyoshi to rikyu *(Hideyoshi and Rikyu)*
Published in *Chûô Kôron,* January 1962–September 1963.

(Synopsis) To sleep late into the morning was one of the things Rikyû had enjoyed at his house in Sakai. When he got up, the morning bath was always ready. It was a steam bath of brine, common in Sakai. After he came to live in Hideyoshi's palace, however, he could not lie leisurely in bed. A morning bath was, of course, out of the question. Hideyoshi would come in at any moment without notice. This was partly due to Hideyoshi's malicious intention to catch Rikyû unawares, but it was more to do with his impatience. Whenever he had some important business which he wanted to discuss with Rikyû, he impatiently sought to use Rikyû's tea-room which was suitable for secret talks. Rikyû was not only a tea master with an annual salary roughly equivalent to 15,000 bushels of rice, but also adviser to Hideyoshi, the Civil Dictator, even in political matters. This was well-known even to the feudal lords of distant fiefs. Rikyû was always conscious of Hideyoshi. When Hideyoshi talked to Rikyû, he used the Owari dialect freely as he had done when he had been Nobunaga's vassal and called Tôkichirô. This was one way of expressing his friendliness towards Rikyû. Rikyû, on the other hand, was always very formal. He was always trying to be attentive and responsive to everything Hideyoshi said or did. For Rikyû, to return to Sakai was an escape from the tension of serving Hideyoshi. It was a welcome relief.

Rikyû was a wholesale dealer of fish in Sakai, a free city of merchants. From the time he was a boy called Yoshirô, he had shown a profound interest in the tea ceremony. He had studied the tea ceremony under Dôchin, Jôô and Jukô and, by his devoted efforts, had finally mastered the mystery of the ceremony, and been given the name Sen no Sôeki. He established the concept of *wabizuki* (love of quiet taste). He served first Nobunaga and then Hideyoshi. He was a real master who was at home equally in a tea-room which was simplicity itself and in a gorgeous tea-room ornamented with gold. That both Nobunaga and Hideyoshi, who had become the rulers of Japan, cherished the tea ceremony more than anything else and esteemed Rikyû and other tea masters was partly because of their desire to win the cooperation of the merchants of Sakai who wielded financial power.

Hideyoshi loved Rikyû, and depended on him as his closest adviser. At the same time, Rikyû's perfect mastery of the tea ceremony and his authority as a tea master who said merely "Fairly good" to Hideyoshi when he made tea, induced Hideyoshi to entertain a certain hatred towards Rikyû. Hideyoshi had conquered the whole of Japan, and everything was as he wanted it to be. It was only Rikyû who gave him a sense of psychological oppression. Rikyû, on the other hand, was too conscious of Hideyoshi as an almighty political ruler. He felt that everything had to be done according to Hideyoshi's wish. Kisabuzô, Rikyû's youngest son, had ambivalent feelings towards his father who seemed to be complying with Hideyoshi's will too much. Sôji, Rikyû's uncompromising disciple, thought that this servility on Rikyû's part was causing the corruption of the tea ceremony. Sôji was banished from his residence, and was mercilessly killed by Hideyoshi at the time of the victory over the Hôjô clan at Odawara. After he had subjugated the whole country, Hideyoshi sent an expedition to Korea as the first step in the conquest of China, which had been his cherished dream for years. Hidenaga, the younger brother of Hideyoshi, died vomiting blood, and Rikyû lost his best supporter. Ishida Mitsunari, one of the influential lords of the time, who wanted to see politics conducted in an orderly fashion, had entertained hostility towards Rikyû for a long time because, though only a tea master, he had considerable political influence as a person close to Hideyoshi.

Rikyû casually said to Yahei, his brother-in-law, whom he trusted, that the conquest of China would not be so easy as defeating Akechi and his army. This reached the ears of Mitsunari and was reported to Hideyoshi

who had returned from Hakata. Rikyû was also denounced for the statue
of himself which he had had placed on the gates of the Daitoku-ji temple
at the request of his friend, Priest Kokei. This was censured as being dis-
respectful to the authorities. Hideyoshi interrogated Rikyû. He felt what
he thought was Rikyû's betrayal of him all the more sharply as he loved
him. Hideyoshi banished him to Sakai. Hideyoshi expected that Rikyû
would send an apology to him. When he realized that Rikyû had no intention of making an apology, he ordered him to commit harakiri. Hideyoshi was not really happy in ordering Rikyû to die. As for Rikyû, he was
convinced that by killing him, Hideyoshi would not be able to deprive
him of anything. What he had created for Hideyoshi, was in fact his own.
Hideyoshi would come to realize this more clearly after the other was
dead. Rikyû died believing this. Kisaburô, Rikyû's youngest son, who had
rebelled against his father and was wandering around the countryside,
received the news of the death of his father, who had been in a sense too
close to him, with mixed feelings.

Noma Hiroshi

Noma Hiroshi was born in Kôbe, Hyôgo Prefecture. His father, who
died when he was ten, was the head of a lay Buddhist order which adhered
to the teachings of Shinran. When he was a student at the Third Higher
School, he was attracted by symbolist literature. Later, he gradually came
to be interested in Marxism and Marxist movements. In 1935, he entered
the Department of French Literature at Kyôto University, and came to
know leading members of the leftist movements at Kyôto University, and
leaders of various labour movements. Upon his graduation, he found a
job in the social section of the Ôsaka Municipal Office, participated in
slum settlement activities, and worked to help people discriminated a-
gainst. In 1941, just before the outbreak of the Pacific War, Noma was
drafted into the army. In 1943, he was thrown into prison for his pacifist

convictions. He was released from prison within a few months, and continued to serve in the army under surveillance. In 1944, he was relieved from military service. After the war, he published *Kurai E* (*A Gloomy Picture*, 1946), *Hôkai Kankaku* (*Collapse*, 1948), *Seinen no Wa* (*The Circle of Youth*, 1949–70), *Shinkû Chitai* (*Zone of Emptiness*, 1952, translated by Frechtman, Bernard, Cleveland and New York, The World Publishing Co., 1956) and other novels, and came to be recognized as one of the most representative writers of the so-called "First Postwar Group". Noma continued to be very productive and published fine literary works like *Saikoro no Sora* (*The Sky of the Dice*, 1958–59) and *Waga Tô wa Soko ni Tatsu* (*My Tower Stands There*, 1961–62).

Waga Tô wa Soko ni Tatsu (*My Tower Stands There*) depicts the author's spiritual progress from his high-school days to his early university days, whereas *Kurai E* (*A Gloomy Picture*), published earlier, depicts his spiritual efforts during the latter half of his university life, which were spent in the midst of leftist movements and war.

The long novel, *Seinen no Wa* (*The Circle of Youth*) is an ambitious work. Its first part was published in 1949, but it was not until 1970, more than twenty years later, that it was completed. It depicts, comprehensively and from various angles, the spiritual development of intellectuals during the war.

NOMA Hiroshi
Waga tô wa soko ni tatsu (*My tower stands there*)
Published in *Gunzô,* November 1960–October 1961.

(Synopsis) Kaizuka Sôichi entered the Department of French Literature of Kyôto University in the spring of 1935. His father, Jitsuran, was a Buddhist teacher and was the head of a lay order related to the *Shin* sect (the True Pure Land sect) founded by Shinran, and Sôichi was designated by his father as his religious successor. This decision was made when Sôichi was in the second year of middle school. His father died shortly afterwards. At that time, he did not have any misgivings about the fact that he would be a Buddhist teacher as his father's successor, but when he entered the Third Higher School, and when his eyes were opened to art by his friend Yoshiba Shigesane, his choice of a religious career began to appear false in his eyes. Because of his doubts about religion, he founded a literary group magazine, and tried to free himself from the bonds of religion which had deeply influenced and fettered him since childhood. His religion was to him a dark secret, a burden which he had to bear by himself.

However hard he tried to escape from it, it continued to pull him back powerfully into the past. Sôichi's consciousness was split. After entering Kyôto University, almost every night he visited a temple in the suburbs of Kyôto where Hônen and Shinran, the founders of his religion, had pursued their search for truth, and looking at the tower of the temple, thought that he had to build a tower of his own for himself. He decided to disclose the secrets of his order to the tower and to try and rid himself completely of its influence. However, on his way to the temple at night to commit this act of defiance, he had a sort of hallucination which was caused by the heavy bondage of the religious community to which he belonged, and by his fear of hell which sprung from his sense of "original sin". Sôichi could not escape from the influence of his religion.

While he was thus being tormented by religious doubt, he received a letter from a member of the literary group magazine which had been giving Sôichi moral support in his struggle to free himself from the influence of his religion.

In this letter, his friend said that he was opposed to Sôichi's recent attitude towards art, and announced that he was going to break off their association. Sôichi began to feel that he would have to part with the literary group sooner or later. Sôichi's feeling, that his order was only offering people false salvation, led him to socialism which aims at changing the whole structure of current society. He started attending a discussion group on Marx's *Das Capital*. He found, however, a certain distance between him and the other members of the discussion group. Sôichi was very unstable. Apart from his mental torment, Takae, who was virtually his love, had been rejecting him after he had forcibly made love to her on the night of her sister's funeral. Since Sôichi was burdened by a sense of sin and shames he could not free himself from the pictures of hell depicted in Genshin', *Ôjô Yôshû* (*How to Get to Paradise*), a manual written in the 10th century which became the theological foundation stone of the Pure Land Sect, and which tells you how to enter Paradise by calling on the sacred name of Amida. He sold his copy of *Ôjô Yôshu* (*How to Get to Paradise*), a present from his late father, and visited a brothel with the money. But there he heard an hallucinatory voice counting the sins of human beings: coward-ice, lewdness, anger. He suffered from the memory of all the small lies and thefts he had committed since childhood.

Sôichi's mother, Satono, lived in Ôsaka, and was a veritable pillar of the sect. When he came home from Kyôto, he attended the funeral of a poor believer with her. Helping his mother, who was washing the dead body, while chanting the Buddhist scriptures, according to the rites of the order, Sôichi was desperately trying to resist the influence of the scriptures which some part of him insisted on chanting. Religion had an unexpectedly strong hold on him. Through attending this funeral, Sôichi was again brought face to face with the misery of lower class people. He felt that he could not desert the common people who clung to religion as their only support. At the same time, he felt disgusted by the complacency and ego-ism which their faith produced. Sôichi heard the rumor that Yoshima Kôkichi, the son of an influential believer, who had been his childhood rival, had been through a diligent course of training and was now aiming to be the next head of the order as a Buddhist teacher. Sôichi had been planning to put an end to the order by abandoning his religion when he became its head. If somebody else became the head, his plans would natu-rally be ruined. Sôichi made up his mind to confront Kôichi some day.

When Sôichi went back to Kyôto, he was finally rejected by Takae. To the other members of the literary group magazine, Sôichi announced that he was going to pursue literature from a Marxist point of view, and was severely criticized by them. In spiritual confusion, Sôichi visited Kôkichi who was training himself at a temple and began to criticize him. Kôkichi argued back tenaciously. Kôkichi pointed out that Sôichi could not ignore the "evil" within himself and that, accordingly, he could not help feeling interested in Shinran's idea that even a bad man can be saved. Sôichi criticized his order and said that it was trying to expand its influence by using the secular egoism of the common people.

On the 26th of May, wishing to understand himself, Sôichi attended an inter-university meeting sponsored by Marxist students. This meeting was stormed by the police. Pursued by the police, Sôichi, together with Tabata, one of the sponsoring students, took refuge at the Byôdô-in temple in Uji. There he talked with Tabata, who was the son of a priest of the *Jôdo* sect (the Pure Land Sect), and who had, in this respect, much in common with Sôichi. Tabata told him that he was trying to re-evaluate Shinran, who lived among poor people and did not recognize the privileged position of the emperor and aristocracy, from a Marxist point of view. Sôichi was very much impressed. Sôichi heard in his heart the voice of the poor believers of Ôsaka entreating: "Please don't desert us, Sôichi!" He decided to live, not for his order but for the people and with the people. Near at hand, a black tower made its presence felt against the dark sky.

Oe Kenzaburo

ÔE Kenzaburô started his career as a writer when he was only twenty-two years old. In this respect, he is quite unusual. His first work, *Kimyôna Shigoto* (*A Strange Job*, 1957), depicts a student who takes up a "strange" part-time job which consists of assisting in the killing of dogs kept at a hospital for medical experiments. A girl student is doing the same job with him. The hero, "I", sees in the harmless expression of the dogs, a fit symbol for the Japanese students who have lost their individuality and become vacant. In this work, we already find a prototype for Ôe's subsequent works which, often starting from images of weak animals, try persistently to depict the apathy of postwar Japan. The image of animals later overlaps with the image of masturbation. Sex is the connecting factor.

The hero of *Shisha no Ogori* (*Lavish are the Dead*, 1957), which was awarded the Akutagawa Prize, is also a student who takes up a part-time job at a medical school. His job is to help treat the corpses for dissection which are floating in alcohol in a tank in the dissection laboratory. In this novel, Ôe handles the relationship between the corpse which is dead matter, and conscious existence. Its other focal centre consists in showing how the state of lost freedom, which Ôe believes has become a general social disease, can be likened to the existence of a corpse. This novel is quite successful in depicting, in concrete language, the existential problems of death and loss of freedom.

Shiiku (*The Catch*, 1958, translated by John Bester, *Japan Quarterly*, Vol. VI, No. 1, 1959 and *The Shadow of Sunrise: Stories of Japan and the War*, Tokyo, Kodansha International, 1966) has a Japanese mountain village during the war as its setting. A Negro soldier who had to escape from his airplane by parachute is captured by the villagers. He is kept in confinement. In due course, however, he is granted a fair amount of freedom, and allowed to walk around the village. The curious village children surround him, but soon, a boy, the first person narrator of the novel, is taken by the soldier and kept as a hostage. Finally the Negro soldier is killed by the villagers and "I" is rescued. This novel depicts, using extremely vivid sensuous images, the children who "keep" the Negro soldier, against an idyllic village background which, however, contains the smell of blood. This work is a masterpiece which marks off the end of the first period of Ôe's development as a writer.

Me-mushiri Ko-uchi (*Tearing Buds and Shooting Children*, 1958) again has loss of freedom as its theme. Towards the end of World War II, the boys of a reformatory, who are evacuated to a mountain village, are left confined in the village: the villagers have left with the outbreak of an epidemic and all the traffic routes to the village have been cut off. In such a state of forced confinement, the boys create a world of their own which is quite free. They also establish a humanistic relationship with a discriminated Korean boy. However, all this comes to an end when the villagers come back. In this work, too, Ôe shows his unique talent for depicting a state of confinement.

Warera no Jidai (*Our Age,* 1959) again treats Ôe's favourite theme of confinement, and frustration, but by the stage in his development it is acquiring a greater political implication, since the confinement this novel handles is the self-imposed confinement of a postwar youth who is apathetic and cannot find any outlet for his frustration. Ôe depicts him as being impotent for psychological reasons. Although he is loved by a woman who is older than he is, he escapes from her feminine world. In this novel, Ôe uses images of erection and ejaculation to depict "death" obliquely as a tamed animal. In this novel, the hero's friendship with an Arab revolutionary is also depicted. Ôe's main intention is, however, to depict the world of postwar Japanese youth by using sexual images.

The idea of tamed death which occurs in *Warera no Jidai* (*Our Age*) is also the main motif in *Seventeen* (1961). It is reflected in the hero's violent longing for a selfless moment of fulfillment, in his longing to die for the Emperor.

Such an impatient desire to fulfil oneself is also a theme behind *Okuretekita Seinen* (*The Youth Who Arrived Late*). The hero was too young to fight as a soldier during the war. When the war is over, he appears as an apathetic, incompetent youth who missed a timely death. Ôe was born and brought up in a rural area. In this novel, he resorts to images of village life, and especially to pantheistic images prevailing in an agricultural area, to express the intense sense of alienation a man from a rural area feels in the great city, Tokyo, where he is not accepted. The hero of the novel, feeling lonely in the city, behaves as a sex-orientated man and masturbates. The sentence, "I am, after all, a barbarian outside the city-wall", gives expression to his sense of alienation.

Seiteki Ningen (*Obsessed,* 1963) depicts a man who molests women. Through this man's shuddering sense of excitement, Ôe depicts a longing for self-punishment by anti-social acts. This longing, Ôe thinks isw hat is hidden deep down in the subconsciousness of modern youths, who seem, on the surface, to be quite free.

The hero of *Kojintekina Taiken* (1964) (*A Personal Matter,* translated by Nathan, John, New York, Grove Press, 1968; Tokyo, Tuttle, 1969) is a man called Bird who becomes the father of a deformed child. The novel depicts the terror he feels at its birth and also his effort to regard his suffering as purgatorial and to give a more universal meaning to his personal suffering. In the end, he makes up his mind to hope and endure for the happiness of his child whom he once tried to kill, and thus resurrects himself from despair. In this novel, we find a desire for the solidarity of individuals who, while concerning themselves deeply with their own personal problems, still care to establish channels of communication with fellow human beings. *Man'en Gannen no Futto-bôru* (*Football Played in the First Year of Man'en*) depicts modern youths with frequent reference to a farmers' revolt which occurred in the first year of the Man'en period, 1860. The events described in the novel take place in a mountain village. Nedokoro Mitsusaburô and his brother, Nedokoro Takashi, come back to their home village. Takashi rouses the village youths with revolutionary ideas. He drills them and, with them, plunders the village supermarket, imitating a farmers' revolt of feudal times. However, this modern revolt suffers from internal disintegration. Takashi fails in his attempt to rape a village girl. In the end, he commits suicide, after having a love affair with his brother's wife. At the end of the novel, the story of his great-grandfather's younger brother is narrated: he was supposed to have been killed after taking part in a farmers' revolt, but, in fact, he hid himself in the cellar of a storehouse in order to punish himself. In this novel, the author has pursued the meaning of revolt in this age by making a double image of the past and present of a typical Japanese village surrounded by woods. However, even if the spiritual rebirth of Mitsusaburô and his wife is not arbitrary, his departure for Africa is a little abrupt. Also we doubt if the author's persistent reference to the Nedokoro (family) of a village in the wood has any relevance to our age. This novel was awarded the Tanizaki Jun'ichirô Prize.

Warera no Kyôki o Ikinobiru Michi o Oshieyo (*Outgrow Our Madness*, 1969) recommends hiding in the wood in order to escape from the dangers of this nuclear age, and is also an attempt to shed light on the inner deformity of modern life with the help of visionary power. It deals with two types of madness which are threatening us—madness within ourselves and madness in the world at large. A later work, *Kakujidai no Sôzôryoku*

(*Imagination in the Atomic Age,* 1970), a collection of essays, also shows pre-occupation with the same ideas; the images of hell in Genshin's *Ōjō Yōshū* (*How to Get to Paradise*), a product of the Japanese Middle Ages, are discussed at length. In this novel, Ōe has succeeded in grasping the spiritual condition of contemporary men by fully exerting his visionary power. Ōe seems to be trying to bridge the gulf between literature and politics by this imaginative power of vision.

Ohara Tomie

Ōhara Tomie was born in 1912 in Kōchi Prefecture. She entered Kōchi Prefectural Women's Normal School in 1927, and was particularly fond of literature. When she was sixteen years old, however, she suffered from tuberculosis of the lungs and had to leave the school. After fighting her illness, she went to Tokyo in 1941. She taught flower-arrangement at Nakano, Tokyo, and in her spare time started writing novels. First she became a member of the literary group magazine *Bungei Shuto* (*Literary Metropolis*) and published works like *Shuku Shussei* (*Celebration for Departure for the Front*). It was with the publication of *Wakaki Keikan* (*Young Valley,* 1943), a novel about production of raw materials for Tosa paper, that Ōhara became recognized. After that, she wrote works based on her everyday life, and expressed in a skilful style human lovableness. After the war her old tuberculosis of the lungs erupted again, and she had to live under medical treatment. *Sutomai Tsunbo* (*Deafness Caused by Streptomycin,* 1956) is a work whose material was collected during the period of her second illness. It consists of episodes imaginatively strung together, and its unique technique attracted attention. In a style born out of persistent self-examination, Ōhara depicts the spiritual antagonism between T.B. germs and "I" symbolically. There we find things belonging to different dimensions convincingly put together. This novel marked a big growth in Ōhara's stature as a writer. Ōhara had been collecting materials of *En to Iu*

Onna (Woman Called En) ever since about 1944, but it was as late as in 1960 that she actually wrote it. She had had to wait until a considerable deepening of her perception as a writer had taken place. In this novel Ôhara depicts a woman who spent forty years in confinement. She skilfully expresses the violent attachment to life on the part of the woman. This well-written novel makes one think once again about woman's life. *Seisai (Lawful Wife,* 1961) is in its theme closely related to *En to Iu Onna* (*A Woman Called En*), and depicts a samurai couple in the feudal society from the wife's point of view. It depicts in detail the unnatural human setup in which the position of a lawful wife is merely nominal.

When Ôhara depicts the loves and hates of women living fettered by conventions of the feudal age, she usually focuses her attention on their strong attachment to life. This is probably due to her own physical weakness.

Ôhara distinguishes herself by the neat style of her works, among which is *Kawa wa Ima mo Nagareru* (*The River still Flows,* 1962) and by raising important questions about women's life in her works. She is a writer who has a direct relevance to contemporary Japan, and is widely respected.

OHARA Tomie
En to iu onna *(A woman called En)*
Published in *Gunzô,* February 1960.

(Synopsis) Today the messenger arrived from the Andô family, and we received from the authorities a letter of release of our fief. After the messenger had gone, we—my mother who is over eighty, the nurse who is sixty-five years old, my sisters who are over forty, and I—embraced one another and cried. Seventy-five days ago, that is, on the 29th of June, my younger brother Sadashirô died, the last remaining male member of the Nonaka family perished. This is why we have been released from confinement. I became a prisoner when I was only four years old and could not understand what was going on around me. My younger brother was already a captive when he was only four months old. We were forbidden to go out of the gate. We were forbidden to marry. For forty years we were confined here. We were not allowed to *live;* we were just confined here. My father, Nonaka Kenzan, was an idealistic statesman. He studied the Confucianism of the new "Southern School" and became the chief minister of Tosa fief when he was only twenty-two years old. From that time, for twenty-seven years, he put into practical use his knowledge and his ideals which he had gained through study. He levelled hills, changed the direction of rivers, opened new rice fields, deepened ports and tried to create an ideal society in Tosa. He really made Tosa fief rich, but because of his power and his impatient severity, he created many enemies. He was forcefully removed from his post when he had not yet realized his vision, and died a lonely death in the same year.

After my father's death, his political enemies, as a posthumous punishment for him, confiscated our property and declared that our family was rendered extinct. The family was sent to a place called Sukumo to live there in confinement. Thus our family, twelve of us, began to live as prisoners. We did not see any human beings except ourselves. Day in and day out, we saw only ourselves. This way of life was really stifling. It was in such circumstances that I grew up, attained maturity as a woman in vain, and passed my prime. But my elder brothers taught me strictly. They taught me how to read and then opened my eyes to Chinese classics. I studied, among other books, Chu Hsi's commentaries on the Four Books of Confucianism, under their guidance. To learn Chinese characters, to read books and study—that was the only consolation of my life in confinement. But from time to time I was tormented by the cruel thought that learning in such circumstances was in vain since I would never have a chance to apply it to life. My eldest brother, Seishichi, died in the fifteenth year of confinement. My second brother, Chôroku, was driven insane by the frustration of his sexual instincts and died in the nineteenth year of our confinement. Kishirô, my third brother, whom I respected and loved so much, died in the thirty-fourth year of confinement. I was really astounded by the intensity and duration of hatred on the part of my father's political enemies, who would not rest until they had destroyed not only him but also his family. I could not help meditating on the nature of politics.

During all these years of confinement I ardently desired to meet people who were really alive and living. When I was twenty-six years old, a quiet miracle happened to us. A youth, who admired Kishirô's learning, came all the way from Kôchi, and sent in a message through the guard. He was called Tani Taizan. After that, I corresponded with him secretly. I built up a picture of him through his letters, and secretly longed for him. Even during my sleep, I dreamed about him. To think about him became the only support of my life.

After being set free, we walked in a world of freedom for the first time. How much we had longed for freedom! All our five senses were almost intolerably stimulated by the "free" world. We ran about in the fields and hills. I parted with my sisters and, accompanied by a former vassal of my father's, started for Kôchi with my mother. I was beginning to learn what life is at the age of forty-three. When I actually saw Tani Taizan, I found him much older than I had imagined. To my great disappointment I discovered that he had already a wife and children. This discovery was really a blow to me. Although I was over forty, my teeth were not stained black, and I looked like a young girl. I made a conspicuous sight in town. Attracting people's attention, I walked about in the castle town. It was a sort of revenge. Disguised as a man, I even walked about during the night. I came to be adored by a youth called Danshichi. My love for Taizan became more and more intense, but things did not go as I wished. He lost his position after a political change, was banished from Kôchi, and died in exile.

I have been earning my living by my knowledge of medicinal herbs which I acquired during the period of confinement. I am still a virgin. I am aging without having found fulfilment in life. It is nineteen years since I came out of confinement. I am now sixty-one years old. I am living here alone in such a dreary manner, and so it will be till I die.

Ooka Shohei

Ôoka Shôhei was born in Tokyo in 1909, the eldest son of a canvasser for a stockbrokers' company. His interest in literature was awakened when he entered the Middle School Department of Aoyama Gakuin College in 1921 and came under the influence of Christianity. As his faith cooled, his interest in literature deepened. When he was a student of Seijô Higher School, he became acquainted with Kobayashi Hideo, and through his influence he came to aspire to be a writer. Kobayashi Hideo, Nakahara Chûya and others awoke his interest in Valéry, Gide and Proust, and Ôoka entered the Department of French Literature of Kyôto University. He joined the literary group magazine *Hakuchi Gun (Group of Imbeciles)* and contributed to it a translation of Claudel's *Rimbaud* (1929) and so on. After graduating from Kyôto University, he worked for the Kokumin Newspaper Company and so on. In his spare time, however, he continued writing on literature, and deepened his understanding of Stendhal. From then until he published *Furyo Ki (Prisoner of War)* in 1948, he was mostly occupied by studying and translating Stendhal. He published critical essays on foreign literature. He was drafted into the army in 1944, and was sent to the Philippines. He became a prisoner of war in Mindoro Island and at the time of Japan's surrender was in the concentration camp on Leyte Island. *Furyo Ki (Prisoner of War)* is based on his experiences as a prisoner of war. When this novel appeared, it was highly praised in literary circles, and Ôoka suddenly came to be recognized as one of the important postwar writers. Ôoka then wrote sort of sequels to *Furyo Ki (Prisoner of War)* such as *San Hose Yasen Byôin (San José Field Hospital)* and *Reite no Ame (Rains in Leyte Island, 1948)*, and penetrated with unsentimental clarity into the psychology of captured soldiers and their distorted humanity. The technique of objectively analysing man (man, with his instinct to live, placed in an unbearably painful critical situation), was what he had learned from Stendhal. The sketching of a soldier's inner world through this scientific technique attained its culmination in *Nobi*

(*Fire on the Plain*, 1952, translated by Morris, Ivan, London, Secker and Warburg; New York, A. Knopf, 1957). Among Ôoka's other works are *Musashino Fujin* (*Madame Musashino*, 1950), a novel based on orthodox techniques of modern Western novels which depicts psychological complications caused by adultery, vanity and desire, and *Sanso* (*Oxygen*, 1952) which treats a similar theme on a larger social canvas. These works are bold literary experiments by the author who, through depicting prisoners of war, came to tackle increasingly the problem of human death. The work which reveals Ôoka's mature ideas about death is *Kaei* (*Shadows of Flowers*, 1961). This novel was said to be the first successful attempt to transplant the French psychological novel to Japan. Among Ôoka's other works is *Sakasasugi* (*Reversed Cryptomeria*, 1960).

ÔOKA Shôhei
Kaei (*Shadows of Flowers*)
Published in *Chûô Kôron*, August 1958–August 1959.

(**Synopsis**) Yôko had once worked at a bar called *Kurara* in Ginza but had been living in this flat as Matsuzaki's mistress for the past two years. Matsuzaki, who lived in Zushi would spend two nights a week here when he came to lecture on art history at a university in Tokyo. One day Matsuzaki said, "I am afraid that I won't be able to come to stay here for some time", and Yôko made up her mind to part with him and work at another bar in Ginza.

Yôko had a fairly pretty face with neat features but when you examined it more carefully, you found that her right and left eye were of different shapes. This defect, however, was compensated by the striking whiteness of her skin. From her childhood, she was called "cute" and "pretty". The children in her neighbourhood, however, shouted *shirokko* (white child) at her. Mr. Takashima told her that was Tokyo dialect and was a pun on *hiroikko* (a foundling). Takashima, a rich collector of art objects, had been one of Yôko's best patrons from prewar days. Yôko, who had lost her father, trusted Takashima like a father. She remained attached to him even after he became poor, and continued to ask for his advice whenever something difficult happened.

Yôko started working as one of the chief hostesses at a bar named Tonbo (Dragonfly) which Junko, her old colleague, had just opened. Although she was nearly forty, she was very lively in the bar, and charmed the customers. Yôko, who had been brought up by Tetsu, her step-mother, had worked in Ginza from her adolescence.

Yôko, with her red hair and white skin, was likened to Danielle Dalue at one bar and to Diana Durbin at another bar. She was admired and loved by many men. At one time, a rich iron factory owner sponsored her in the opening of her own bar. At another time, she cohabited with a novelist. She was a very good-natured person. When she got drunk, she was like an innocent child. She was loved by men and deceived by men. She did not save money, and so she could become neither the mistress of a bar nor the wife of a respectable person. It looked as if she had been born to be a bar hostess. Some time after she had started working at the bar Tonbo (Dragonfly), a man called Hata proposed to her. Hata was a man who had some influence in business circles and government offices, and he seemed to be some kind of a broker connected with tax and land transactions. Both Junko and Takashima encouraged her to marry him, but somehow Yôko was not very keen on this marriage, although she went so far as to visit Hata's house. One night, Yôko, while drunk, allowed Shimizu, a young TV producer who had accompanied her to her flat, to sleep with her. She had had similar experiences many times before.

Hata got drunk every night and was always ready to pick on a quarrel with Yôko. Hata's attitude acted as a catalyst to her relationship with Shimizu, and he came to stay at her flat quite often. Yôko was pleased to find that she could still attract a young man, and was obliging to him. Takashima teased Yôko by saying, "Isn't it true that every Jill has her Jack?" About that time, Takashima brought a man called Nokata to the bar Tonbo where Yôko was working. This man, who had once been Tôko's admirer, was now the president of a spinning mill. He came to visit the bar regularly, and asked Yôko if she would like to take charge of an inn in Yugawara which his father's mistress was running. Shimizu was angry because Yôko had become familiar with Nokata, and he left her. Yôko was very lively at night when she was drunk in the bar, but when she was in her flat during the day, everything was dull, and she felt melancholy. She thought it would be nice for her to live unobtrusively in a quiet place like Yugawara.

Unfortunately, because of Takashima's carelessness, Nokata became angry with Yôko, and Yôko's plans to accept Nokata's suggestion and live in Yugawara did not materialize. The bar *Tonbo* went bankrupt, and Yôko again became a hostess at *Kurara,* the bar where she used to work before. While she was working here Matsuzaki came to see her after a long interval. He was surprised to find that Yôko had aged suddenly. Yôko had decided that the time to die which she had been thinking about had come. Walking along an avenue of cherry trees with Matsuzaki, Yôko kept saying, "Aren't they beautiful!" She also said that she felt like eating cherry blossoms. Commenting on the fancy of a poet that under a cherry-tree lies a corpse, she said that it was a very pretty idea. They walked on, stepping on the faint shadows of cherry blossoms. Yôko had been ready to die for a long time. She wrote her will, and disposed of her personal belongings. One Sunday, she made a final sightseeing tour of Tokyo, and went to a public bath. For fear lest people became suspicious if she failed to turn off the lights, she took pills on Monday morning when it was already light after putting on her make-up. Feeling angry but at what she did not know, she swallowed the pills little by little, but quickly. Soon she began to feel dizzy, and the room began rotating around her. Outside the window children were calling in increasingly loud voices. They even peeped from the window and called *shirokko* (white child) many times. The voices sounded as if they were jeering. Then came darkness.

Ozaki Kazuo

Ozaki Kazuo was born in Ujiyamada, Mie Prefecture. His father was at that time a professor of Jingû Kôdôkan University which was the highest academic institution for *shinto* studies. His ancestors were for many generations *shinto* priests of the Sôga Shrine in Kanagawa Prefecture. When Ozaki was in primary school, his family returned to Shimosoga, their ancestral home. When he was in middle school, he read *Ôtsu Junkichi* by Shiga Naoya. Greatly moved by this work, Ozaki decided to become a writer. Despite his father's disapproval, he finally entered the Department of Japanese Literature of Waseda University, and visited Shiga Naoya. When Ozaki started writing, "Proletarian Literature" was flourishing. Ozaki remained unknown and lived in poverty for many years. It was through receiving the Akutagawa Prize in 1937 for *Nonki Megane (The Carefree Spectacles,* 1933) that Ozaki established himself as a writer. *Nonki Megane (The Carefree Spectacles), Fuso no Chi (Ancestral Place), Yume Arishi Hi (Hopeful Bygone Days,* 1940) and other novels which he wrote, are all characteristically Japanese "I" novels. Although the hero is haunted by poverty and illness, he does not see everything as black and desperate. He does not want to escape or rebel. Instead, with the help of his carefree wife, he lives energetically with humour and hope, and finds the seemingly hopeless life of poverty still worth living. These "I" novels are characterized by basic optimism. During and after the war, Ozaki became seriously ill, and for a long time it was hard to tell whether he was recovering or dying. *Koorogi (Crickets,* 1946) depicts this grave illness. *Mushi no Iro-iro (Various Kinds of Bugs,* 1948) is a work which depicts minutely and accurately the insects and bugs observed from a sickbed, the hero's mental state is expressed through his descriptions of them. *Utsukushii Bochi kara no Nagame (A View from a Beautiful Cemetery)* is another of his works written at about this time. These fine works are characterized by the auther's quiet resignation. He also published a series of humorous family novels which are called "the Yoshibei novels" from the name of one of the characters. The central figure of these novels is the wife. *Maboroshi no Ki (The Account of my Dreamlike Life)*, for which Ozaki received the Noma Literary Prize in 1961, is a work which expresses the beauty and richness of nature and life seen through the eyes of a person who constantly experiences the death of other people. Ozaki is regarded, together with Kanbayashi Akatsuki, as one of the two most genuine "I" novel writers of present-day Japan, and is highly esteemed. There is a spirit of resignation in his work, but Ozaki also likes to write about the cheerful aspects of life and of family life, or to express his mental state through his descriptions of nature, simply and humorously. Many of his recent works are works closely related to indigenous Japanese culture and are filled with action and humour, although they are written in natural and simple prose.

Ozaki Kazuo
Maboroshi no ki *(The account of my dreamlike life)*
Published in *Gunzô,* August 1961.

(Synopsis) While I was still lying in bed ill, somebody sent me a crateful of loquats. One of their stones which I had thrown out of the window put forth shoots the next year. The neighbours who saw that pulled faces and said "Pull it out". However, I decided to leave it like that. I thought that if I could eat the fruit of this young tree it would be interesting. Ten years passed, I was still alive, and ate the fruit of the loquat.

All kinds of things happen in a tiny village. It is sixteen years since I moved here. Since then there are very few houses in which nothing has happened. One person has died after another. Of course it is only natural that old men should die, but leaving that aside, there have been quite a few murders, suicides, and other unnatural deaths. In addition to this, many families have led a troubled life. A man who had lost his only son in the war, for instance, became a drunkard out of despair and often roughed the place up when he was drunk. When I look over things again it seems odd. Everyone looks so calm and normal, and yet, in fact in any household you care to mention, there is not one in which nothing has happened. When I think about it, it seems uncanny.

Shortly after the war the son of Mr. and Mrs. Shiina returned to his parents' house. At that time I was on friendly terms with Mr. Shiina. To my bewilderment, the return of her son did not seem to have cheered Mrs. Shiina. She looked rather gloomy. I wondered if something unpleasant had happened. Later I heard from Mrs. Shiina that her son had married. To his parents' disappointment, he had broken his former engagement, married another person, and settled down in Tokyo. Mr. Shiina died of a heart attack shortly afterwards. Half a year later, his widow was hospitalized for eye disease in Tokyo, and soon we ceased to hear from her, but before long we received an announcement of her death from her son. From time to time, we remember Mr. & Mrs. Shiina. They were a timid, modest couple and humbly resigned themselves to fate, yet unreasonable death snatched them away. I still cannot quite accept the fact that they are dead. I feel angry at the unreasonableness of fate. On New Year's Day, 1920, my father visited Ise Shrine. Unfortunately during this trip he caught a cold. It was the Spanish influenza then raging over almost the whole of the world. My father's influenza became serious and he died on the 10th of February. The next year (1921), I collapsed of pleurisy. Shortly afterwards, my elder sister became bedridden. In 1922 my younger sister died. She was twenty years old. I was induced to think that in this world there is something which callously refuses everything we desire or pray for.

When I was living in lodgings, I often spent time with a girl called S whom I had known from childhood. On the day when she announced that she was going to get married soon, we were quite naturally induced to sleep together for the first time. After that we were entangled deeper and deeper in this relationship, and neither of us could exert enough self-control to stop it running its unhappy course. After having a physical relationship with me for several months, S married her fiancé. She then gave birth to a child. I suppose that it must have been my child, but she pretended to everybody that it was her husband's child, which had been born prematurely. For a long time, I felt as if I could not look anybody in the eyes. Several years later, S gave birth to her second child. This time she did not recover after childbirth, and died. The baby also died. In a few years' time her husband also died. Already thirty years have passed since then.

I have so many things which I want to put in order. Everything is unsettled and scattered in my memory like driftwood on a beach. I do not know where to begin.

Sata Ineko

Sata Ineko was born in Yaoya-chô, Nagasaki City. She came to the world as the fruit of juvenile love between an eighteen year old middle-school boy and a fifteen year old schoolgirl. In the year she entered primary school, her young mother died. After this she was to lead a life full of painful struggles.

In 1915 her family moved to Tokyo. This migration to the capital which had been done without any plan was a cause of the family's subsequent impoverishment. Sata Ineko left school when she was in the fifth grade of the primary school, and worked at a caramel factory and at a Chinese noodle shop. Her first work *Kyarameru Kôjô Kara* (*From the Caramel Factory,* 1928) is based on her experiences of this time.

After that she worked at a knitting factory, was a maid at a Japanese restaurant, and finally found a job as a shop-girl at the haberdashery section of the Maruzen Bookstore. She impressed one of her superiors at the Maruzen Bookstore, and through his good offices, she got married to the heir of a wealthy family in 1924. Because of her husband's perverse personality, however, this marriage ended in failure within a year. This sad experience made her quite pessimistic. What saved her from nihilism was her association with young writers connected with the literary group magazine *Roba* (*Donkey*). Among them were Nakano Shigeharu, Kubokawa Tsurujirô and Hori Tatsuo. She married Kubokawa Tsurujirô in 1926.

Quite a few members of the magazine *Roba* (*Donkey*) came to play an important role in the Proletarian Literature movement. Through their influence, she began to read Marxist literature, and wrote works like *Kyarameru Kôjô Kara* (*From the Caramel Factory*) and *Restoran Rakuyô* (*Restaurant Rakuyô*, 1929). With these works she made an impressive "Début" as a woman writer.

From 1930 to 1934, she published the literary quintet, *Kanbu Jokô no Namida* (*The Tears of the Forewoman*), *Kitô* (*Prayer*), *Shô Kanbu* (*Little Leaders*), *Nani o Nasubeki ka* (*What is to be Done?*) and *Kyôfu* (*Fear*). In 1932 her husband was prosecuted. She had to become the pillar of the family economically, to bring up a boy and a girl. It was also in 1932 that she became a member of the Communist Party. Her experiences connected with the entry into the party are depicted in the long novel *Haguruma* (*A Cogwheel*) written after the war (1958–1959). Roughly from 1935, however, the change of times produced many instances of ideological conversion, and the outbreak of war further restricted personal freedom. Sata was also obliged to live like an ordinary woman without engaging in much political activity. Because of this, she entered into conflict with Kubokawa who had been released on bail. They were finally divorced in 1945.

The war ended in Japan's defeat, and this made her seriously tackle the problem of war cooperation and that of factional division in the Communist Party. Her short novels, *Kyogi* (*Untruth*, 1948), *Hômatsu no Kiroku* (*A Record of Bubbles*, 1948) and *Yoru no Kioku* (*The Memory of a Night*, 1955), reflect her painful mental struggles of this time.

What reward did Sata get who, without neglecting her role as a wife and a mother, had led more than thirty years of difficult existence as a revolutionary writer with utmost sincerity? Only divorce and expulsion from the Communist Party.

SATA Ineko
Mizu *(Water)*
Published in *Gunzô,* May 1962.

(Synopsis) Ikuyo had been crying for some time, squatting down by the side of the employees' room on the platform of Ueno Station. She knew that people were watching her suspiciously from the windows of the train above her head, but she could not stop crying, nor had she anywhere else to go.

It was on the previous morning that a telegram for her had arrived at the inn in Kanda where she was working. "Mother critically ill return immediately", it had said. Ikuyo's anxiety knew no end. However, when her employer said, "You had better wait for the next telegram. If she really is critically ill, even if you leave at once, you will not be in time anyway", Ikuyo could do nothing but obey and continue her hectic work in the kitchen.

It was the winter of two years ago, when Ikuyo, the daughter of a farming family in Toyama Prefecture, had come to work at this inn. The owner of the inn derived from the same area. This was how she had come to be employed at the inn as a scullery maid. Ikuyo had a rather short left leg, so she had been unable to get a job at the spinning factory in her neighbourhood. However, she had been quite content working at the inn. Her wages allowed her to send money to her mother every month. She was also saving money, although the amount of her savings was small. Ikuyo was hoping to send her mother for a hot-spring cure, when she had saved up enough money. When Ikuyo was a junior high school girl, her mother had gone for a hot-spring cure. When she came back, she had looked so much younger and refreshed. Since then, her mother had talked over and over again about the wonderful time she had had at the hot-spring resort; it became the favorite topic of Ikuyo's mother when she talked about happy memories. She used to say that because she had bathed in a hot-spring, her lifespan had been lengthened by at least three years. Apparently she could not forget either that she had seen plays performed by an itinerant troup for two consecutive evenings in the hall of the inn where she had stayed.

When Ikuyo had heard her mother say. "Your sister has sent money she earned working at the factory", she had decided that she would earn enough money to send her mother to a hot-spring resort when she became old enough to start working.

When Ikuyo was five years old her father had died. Ikuyo was the youngest child and was still sleeping in the same bed with her mother. In her sleep, sometimes, she searched for her mother's breasts. One night, several months after her father's death, Ikuyo had woken up, because her hand, which she had thrust into her mother's breasts, had been brushed away forcibly. When she obstinately tried to take hold of her mother's breasts, her mother had shuddered and again thrust her hands away. Of course, Ikuyo could not understand the delicate psychology of her mother who had lost her husband. Even after she had grown up, she remembered that event from time to time.

Ikuyo was, if not cheerful, quite gentle. She worked hard all day in the kitchen of the inn, and nobody noticed that she was physically a little handicapped. The head cook, as well as the owner, acknowledged her diligence. Therefore, when the telegram arrived, Ikuyo thought that she would be allowed to go at once.

Then the second telegram arrived. "Mother died. Are you coming?", it said. When Ikuyo read it, a faint cry: "Oh, Mummy!" escaped her, and she threw herself on the floor and wept. She no longer continued the work she had been doing. She walked out of the kitchen door of the inn with a canvas bag. Her hips were swinging more conspicuously than usual. Her mother's death meant that Ikuyo had lost the only reliable shelter she had ever known.

The train in front of which Ikuyo had been squatting was apparently about to depart, and the sound of a bell rang out over the platform. When she heard the bell Ikuyo stood up, and started walking with heavy steps. The tap on the station platform had been left running for some time. Ikuyo unwittingly turned off the tap, returned to the same place which looked brighter after the train had gone, squatted down and continued crying. The spring sun was shining on the place.

Sato Haruo

Satô Haruo was born in Shingû, Wakayama Prefecture. Shingû is situated at long. 136° E and lat. 33°40'N. and is in the southern part of Japan. Satô was a precocious boy, and already manifested his unusual talent in his middle school days. After entering the Faculty of Literature of Keiô University, he started publishing his poems.

The first collection of his poems was called *Junjô Shishû* (*A Collection of Sentimental Poems*) and was published in 1921. *Satô Haruo Shishû* (*The Collected Poems of Satô Haruo, 1926*) is also a collection of his early poetry. *Satô Haruo Zen-shishû* (*The Complete Poems of Satô Haruo*) was published in 1952. Satô Haruo was a very versatile person who produced besides poems, novels, critical works and paintings. As a novelist, he was first recognized for works like *Yameru Sôbi* (*Oh, Rose Thou Art Sick*, 1917). In 1918, the second part was added, and the enlarged revised version was published in 1918 under the title *Den'en no Yûutsu* (*Pastoral Melancholy*) and its companion volume, *Tokai no Yûutsu* (*The Melancholy of the City*, 1923), which depict in a lyrical, intellectual manner, the boredom of modern man and the anxiety, born away of life which is too subjective and introspective. His early novels showed a marked romantic tendency to pursue dreams and illusions as well as a strong tendency towards aestheticism. However, roughly from *Wabishi-sugiru* (*Too Lonely*, 1923) onwards, his works began to depict the joys and sorrows of life in a contemplative manner. Fresh vigorous intellect and intuition, however, characterize his works throughout. He also dealt with subjects related to social problems and produced works like *Baishôfu Mari* (*Mari, the Prostitute*, 1924). He was also interested in Freudian psychoanalysis, and produced works based on psychoanalytical techniques from an early date. The most representative of this type of work is probably *Kôseiki* (*Starting Afresh*, 1929). By 1930, the majority of his representative works had been written, and after that his works did not take any radical new direction. Fresh lyricism and vigorous critical spirit based on intuition characterized his works as before. He published, apart from novels, many works of literary criticism and biographies, and occupied a unique position in the literary world.

Aibyô Chibi no Shi (*The Death of Beloved Chibi*) was written shortly before the author died of a heart-attack. We wonder if we should call it a novel or an essay. It is a sort of elegy portending the author's death.

SATO Haruo
Aibyô chibi no shi *(The death of beloved chibi)*
Published in *Shinchô*, June 1964.

(Synopsis) My pet tom-cat, which I had been extremely fond of, and had affectionately called "Chibi", died in the midst of the chill of early spring this year. I had been looking after this cat for ten years. "Chibi", whom my son had brought home in his coat pocket, had spent the whole of his life at our place, and then died. When I saw that dead face it was unbearable and I wept. That must have been over a month ago, but I still feel unbearably sad. In my seventy years of life I have experienced the death of relatives and intimate friends so many times, and yet, strange to say, I never once became sentimental or emotional. This was because I knew that all living things must die, and that to meet was the first part of saying farewell. In spite of all this, why does this cat's death constantly move me to tears? Even I cannot answer.

I cannot help remembering bygone days with the cat. "Chibi" was not particularly beautiful, in fact, he looked rather like a grubby stray cat; but I could not help feeling that he seemed to be an extremely clever cat. When he was small I played with him; when he grew bigger I started to train him with some severity. When I first began this training he would flee from me, and observe me from the branch of one of the trees in the garden. He was good at catching mice, but usually got the worst of a quarrel and took cover in the house after being injured in a fight.

Cats are well-known gourmets, and Chibi was no exception. He would leave the food he had been given and, apparently thinking that my meal looked more appetizing, would approach the dining-table and wait for me to share my food with him. If it was something given him off my plate he would eat it with great relish, be it macaroni, bread, or anything else. He was good-natured to the point of being stupid, and even when the neighbourhood cats came and ate up his meal, he never showed any signs of anger. For that reason, all the cats in the neighbourhood used to gather at my house until the place looked like a veritable cat residence. They say that pets resemble their owners. In his sociability and dislike of taking a bath Chibi was the split image of me, but he had a peculiar habit all of his own. He would wander around quite freely without choosing a particular time or place, a thing which has certainly not been a habit of mine in recent years.

Chibi had no resistance to summer heat. Towards the end of last summer he began to look jaded, and all his teeth dropped out. I fed him with the food I had chewed up for him. Although he was getting weaker day by day, he was beaten in fights and came home hurt as usual. Even at the beginning of this year, a neighbourhood cat clawed his left eye to such an extent that he was almost in danger of going blind. From that time onwards he became enormously attached to people and would follow me about wherever I went. If there was anything that he could no longer do for himself, he tried to let me know what it was by gesturing, so that I could do it for him. When I watched these gestures, I thought that this is how things would be if I had a deaf and dumb child.

As things went on in this way, senile decay seems to have set in. His gums began to rot, and his hair to drop out, leaving his coat patchy. He had no appetite, and began to soil the inside of the house. I can still remember how crest-fallen and dejected he looked when I scolded him for this, feeling such unutterable pity.

A few day's before he died, I heard the most beautiful cat's wailing outside my room, and discovered that it was Chibi. It was a beautiful sound that I had never heard Chibi produce before. He came into the room and lay down at my side. After this he never ate again, and died four days later of heart failure. Chibi's coffin was a box. Was it my wife who placed two wreaths of garden flowers on top to cover him? There was no particular sign of suffering on that dead face, but when I saw those garden flowers I burst into tears. I know that it is not good to be so miserable on behalf of one cat but I cannot get rid of the ache of misery.

In order to rid myself of this sadness, I tried asking myself what the reason for it was. However intimate human beings may be, they always live in separate worlds of their own; the merest segment of the circle of their world may sometimes overlap with that of another—but that is all. However, the relationship between human beings and animals such as cats and dogs is that of two completely superimposed concentric circles. When we look at the life of a cat, more than the cat itself, we see our own selves, our own feelings. Chibi was ten years of my life, which I have lost. Is it not natural that I grieve at his death more than at the death of other human beings?

Satomi Ton

Satomi Ton, whose real name is Yamanouchi Hideo, was born in Yokohama in 1888. He is the younger brother of the famous writer Arishima Takeo and the painter Arishima Ikuma. He entered the Department of English Literature of Tokyo University in 1909, but he left it almost at once. When the humanitarian literary coterie magazine *Shirakaba* (*Silver Birch*) was started in 1910, he joined it from the beginning, and published novels under the pen name of Satomi Ton.

In his early works such as *Tegami* (*Letter,* 1912) we already find elements which were to reappear in later novels: elaborate psychological descriptions, and a hero who feels disgusted with himself, realizing that he is too weak to harmonize two conflicting tendencies within himself, namely the desire to indulge in the world of sensual pleasures and the ethical will to discipline himself.

In 1915, he published *Osoi Hatsukoi* (*Later First Love*) and established himself as a young writer. This work, together with *Natsu E* (*Summer Picture*, 1915) and *Tsuma o Kau Keiken* (*Experience of Buying a Wife*, 1917) form a youthful trilogy which depicts the circumstances leading from the author's first awakening of love to his marriage.

Zenshin Akushin (*Good Heart and Evil Heart*, 1916) is his attempt to depict the mental state of a truly free man who is liberated from external standards of good and evil, who is faithful to himself, who deepens his understanding of human life by experience, and who is not afraid of acting according to his convictions. Through this work Satomi wanted to establish a "philosophy of sincerity" within himself so that he himself could be such a free person. This work can be regarded as one of the peaks of his literary career. After this, he produced short story masterpieces which were distinguished by deep humane observations and technical competence. He attained great maturity as a short story writer.

In 1919, when the Japanese intellectual world was in a great turmoil, he left the *Shirakaba* (*Silver Birch*) group and founded in collaboration with others the magazine *Ningen* (*Man*). He showed a tendency towards aestheticism, and struck out a path of his own and pursued it. In works like *Chichioya* (*Father*, 1920) and *Jigoku* (*Hell*, 1920), he delved into the worlds of extreme human good and extreme human evil. In long novels, such as *Tajô Busshin* (*Fickle Feeling, Pious Heart*, 1922–23) and *Anjô-ke no Kyôdai* (*The Anjô Brothers*, 1927–30), he purported to show the validity of his philosophy of sincerity using his experience of love relationships as material. Although his aesthetic sense gained the upper hand over his ethical will in these novels, they have won a high reputation as his representative works.

Satomi throughout has been a man who, in his pursuit of true humanity and a true way of living, was very careful not to fall into any particular ideology. Neither during the prime of "Proletarian Literature", nor during the Second World War, was he influenced by the predominant ideology of the time. He followed his artistic conscience and wrote works which were peculiarly his. Among them were many fine short and medium-length novels.

After the end of World War II, he continued to be so productive that people forget how old he is. Among his postwar works are fine works like *Migotona Shûbun* (*The Admirable Scandal*, 1947) and *Gokuraku Tonbo* (*The Happy-go-lucky*, 1961). They are written in a beautifully polished style, and show the unfettered maturity of the author who enjoys his art.

Gokuraku Tonbo (*The Happy-go-lucky*), summarized above, depicts the history of a large business family throughout the Meiji, Taishô and Shôwa periods, choosing as its hero Shûzaburô, a good-natured prodigal son who is contemptuously nicknamed "Paradisal Dragonfly". The author puts all the "wisdom of life" he has gained from his rich experience into this work. It is his most representative postwar work.

Satomi Ton
Gokuraku tonbo (*The happy-go-lucky*)
Published in *Chûô Kôron*, January 1961.

(**Synopsis**) Yoshii Shûzaburô was born in 1885 the third son of Yoshii Ichizô, a businessman. He was a delicate child, and was spoiled by his parents. Thus he became a self-centred boy who behaved in a very self-willed manner. He became interested in sex when he was in the higher forms of primary school. He slept with a woman for the first time when he was fifteen years old. When he was in the third grade of middle school, he indulged in sexual intercourse with a girl called Hama, a daughter of his father's acquaintance who was under the care of the Yoshii family. This was discovered in private by the maid, and Shûzaburô was placed under the custody of a relative who lived in Kagoshima, Shûzaburô's father's native place. However, he still gave himself up to homosexual or heterosexual relationships. He failed his exams at school. Eventually his guardian,

Arimura, gave up trying to reform him. He was such a slovenly dissolute character, and yet there was something about him which endeared him to people. He was nicknamed "Paradisal Dragonfly" (a term of abuse directed at any frivolous carefree person) by his family and relatives, and they treated him with a mixture of contempt and affection. Shûzaburô, who had been abandoned by his guardian, Arimura, was rescued by Arimura's mother, and was appointed as her heir. After her death, Shûzaburô, who was then in the fifth year of middle school went to Tokyo, accompanied by his father who had been visiting his birthplace, Kagoshima. This time Shûzaburô returned to Tokyo triumphantly as the head of a family. He was transferred to the preparatory course of Keiô Gijuku (a private college in Tokyo), and again indulged in a life of debauchery with his school friends. However, fortunately, he was able to finish the preparatory course without failing the examinations. Then he made a big decision and went to the United States. He started working at "Wada's Shop" which an acquaintance of his eldest brother was running. However, his English was poor and he had little ability for the work he had been assigned. He was thus feeling quite depressed, when his former classmate at the preparatory course, Andô Kaaru, came to visit him at his lodgings. Andô came to live with him. Yoshii was involved in a homosexual scandal between Andô and a German person, and was injured. Mr. Wada, the owner of Wada's shop dismissed him, and he finally returned home. Using the 5,000 dollars which Andô had given him as funds, he founded the Yoshiyone Commercial Firm, a firm engaging in trade with the United States, with Yoneyama, a former playmate of preparatory school days. Although he was the president, he neglected to attend to business, and once again led a life of debauchery. When he visited the Andô family, taking Andô Kaaru's letter of introduction, he came to know Andô's elder sister, Yohana. They had an affair, and Yoshii hid himself with Yohana at Mt. Akagi. just then his father died, but he could not attend the funeral. The quarrel between Yohana's mother and Yoshii was settled when he married Yohana. He attended the Buddhist service for his father held on the seventh day after his death. He had been keeping very quiet in a corner of the room, but suddenly started crying loudly. He was pitied by his family and his relatives, since there was something in his personality which was somehow lovable. After his marriage, he started to work more diligently as the president of the Yoshiyone Commercial Firm, and became more responsible in his relationship with the rest of society. However, the great Tokyo earthquake of 1923 killed Yoneyama, his business partner. His house was also burnt down. He was helped by his younger brother who was running a flower garden, and built a new house, and secured a modest happiness. Then Andô Kaaru came back to Japan. Andô had become insane through opium poisoning, and when he came back to Japan, he strangled his mother to death. Shûzaburô took Andô to a mental hospital, and looked after him.

Shûzaburô continued to live on the legacies from his adoptive mother and his father. While he was spending his days in idleness with his younger sister, Yoshiko, he met his former mistress again and renewed his old relationship with her, and was absent even from the celebration of his mother's 77th birthday (an important celebration in Japan). When he came home one morning, he found that his wife, Yohana, had committed suicide by gassing herself. For some time, he lived in a state of abstraction, but was introduced to a teacher of *kouta* songs and started taking lessons from her. Within about three years, he became good enough to be awarded an "art name" by the teacher. Meanwhile, his eldest brother was killed, and his mother died. Andô Kaaru also died insane. Yoshii became famous in the artistic world for his skill as mediator. He indulged in a life of pleasure with his companions.

Then World War II broke out. He was chosen as the head of the town block association of his district and was also the head of the local civilian guards. As he was a good-natured person, he worked quite hard and with the best of intentions as the head of these associations. However, he overdid things, and people became hostile to him. Towards the end of the war, his area was burnt down during an air-raid. To divert himself from this ill fortune, Shûzaburô took to drinking at various bars. He met Kotomi, his former teacher of *kouta* songs and started to cohabit with her.

Fifteen years had passed since the end of the war. Seven of the brothers and sisters of the Yoshii family got together at the villa of the youngest brother, Shôgo, in Atami to have an evening of pleasant chat. They were already over seventy years old. Shûzaburô was not so eager to take part in games, but when he played with them, he became first, and got six hundred yen as the prize. The others said that he had all the luck, but he did not feel very lucky. He took a bath before going to bed, but because he was careless in handling the gas burners of the bath, he was finally killed by gas poisoning. His brothers and sisters held a wake over his body that night. They said that he was lucky to be surrounded by his family like this, since he himself had never attended similar occasions for his parents. At first glance, he was the sort of person who could never stick to anything; but from time to time he could be earnest enough about doing things to persist in them. People could not help remembering with warmth the life of Shûzaburô, the "Paradisal Dragonfly", who had been good-natured, light-footed and gay.

Setouchi Harumi

Setouchi Harumi was born in 1922 at Tokushima, Shikoku. She graduated from the Department of Japanese Literature of Tokyo Women's Christian College. She married immediately after graduation, went to China and lived in Peking. In 1946, the year after Japan's surrender, she returned to Tokyo. She got divorced in 1951.

She had been interested in literature from her girlhood. After the war, she started publishing studies, in the literary group magazine *Bungakusha* (*Literary Man*) whose chief editor was Niwa Fumio. She received the Shinchôsha Dôjin Zasshi Prize (a prize for outstanding work published in private-circulation magazines) in 1956. In 1957, she published *Kashin* (*The Heart of a Flower*) in the October number of *Shinchô*. This short story, which depicts women's life very realistically attracted considerable attention. In 1963, she was awarded the Women's Literary Prize for *Natsu no Owari* (*Summer's Ending*) and established herself as a writer. Apart from novels, she has also published biographies of various Japanese women writers. Among them are *Tamura Toshiko Den* (*The Life of Tamura Toshiko*) and *Kanoko Ryôran* (*The Life of Okamoto Kanoko*). In these biographies, she has depicted the life of women who rebelled against the traditions of Japan and asserted their will as women.

Among the main themes of Setouchi's works are entangled love affairs between men and women, and love for the children left behind at the house of a divorced husband. These works are based on the author's real experiences, and they vividly express women's attachment to life.

Natsu no Owari (*Summer's Ending*) also depicts the consciousness of a woman who is involved in a human relationship which breaks conventional ethical values. Behind it, we sense the author's rebellion as a woman against the rigid family system and traditional ethical standards of Japan.

SETOUCHI Harumi
Natsu no owari *(Summer's ending)*
Published in *Shinchô*, October 1962.

(Synopsis) It was in July that Tomoko returned from her journey to the U.S.S.R., a journey which had lasted for over a month. When the ship arrived at the Pier of Yokohama Port, she noticed that Shingo and Ryôta had come to meet her off the ship. Shingo was a rather unpopular novelist and was married and had children, but Shingo and Tomoko had been having an affair for eight years. Tomoko had been earning her living by dyeing cloth. That she was not imposing on Shingo financially was one source of Tomoko's self-confidence. This self-confidence and a unique philosophy of love protected her from having any guilty feelings towards Shingo's wife. Shingo's wife was also virtually allowing Shingo to continue his affair with Tomoko without interference.

Shingo divided his week neatly into two halves, and spent one half at his house in a seaside town and the other half in Tomoko's flat in Tokyo. Thus he had been travelling between the two places. Tomoko had a feeling of relief as though with a protective father when she was with Shingo, who was taciturn, unsociable, not good at earning money, and yet looked after Tomoko attentively. At the same time, she had a gentle feeling of love towards him and sympathized with his weakness. Thus outwardly there was a sort of balance and peace established between Shingo, his wife and Tomoko. But this "peace" was disturbed by the appearance of Ryôta. Ryôta was six years younger than Tomoko, and had once been her lover and occasioned her divorce from her former husband twelve years ago. However, the relationship between Tomoko and Ryôta had lasted less than half a year when they had separated. Tomoko had not met him since. After parting with Tomoko, Ryôta married another woman, but this marriage also ended in failure, and he returned to a bachelor life. Now he was working at a third-rate advertisement agency, and was living by himself. At the beginning of the year, when Shingo was at his house in the seaside town, Tomoko caught a bad cold. While she was ill in bed and feeling very lonely, Ryôta suddenly came to her flat. Their mutual loneliness united them, and their old relationship revived. Shingo had heard the story of her past from Tomoko, and thought that the love between Tomoko and Ryôta was a thing belonging to it, so, although Ryôta came to see Tomoko quite often, Shingo did not entertain any suspicion and treated Ryôta kindly as a guest. Tomoko felt sorry for her betrayal of Shingo. In order to punish herself, she wondered if she should not part with Shingo, which would be much more painful for her than to part with Ryôta. Ryôta, who was the youngest of the three, could not really be satisfied with such a triangular love affair, and his frustration came to the surface from time to time.

After Tomoko's return from the U.S.S.R. the same set-up continued. Ryôta told Tomoko that she, Shingo and his wife were a bunch of compromisers who were incapable of love. Tomoko replied that the person she really loved was Shingo and that her feeling towards Ryôta was merely that of pity. As for the triangular affair between Tomoko, Shingo and his wife, Tomoko said, she did not want to change the present set-up, because she knew that Shingo loved her more than his wife. Ryôta was deeply hurt by Tomoko's words. Tomoko was in danger of arousing desperate passion in Ryôta, who had been roughened by loneliness, but she would not consider bringing her relationship with Shingo to an end.

One day Tomoko found a letter inserted in one of Shingo's books. It was a letter Shingo's wife had written to him. Tomoko read it, and sensed in it a strong tie of love which had developed between the couple over years of everyday life together. That letter was in fact an old letter which had been written several years before, but Tomoko mistook it for a recent letter. She forgot herself in jealousy.

She rushed to Ryôta's dwelling and poured her feelings out to him. Disgusted by Tomoko's self-centredness and by her self-indulgent attitude, Ryôta left Tomoko in his room and went out by himself. Tomoko, who was left in the room alone, looked at her face in the mirror. It was an ugly face with eyelids swollen by crying. She was already thirty-eight years old, and her figure in the mirror unmistakenly showed signs of physical decline. When she went outside, she sensed coolness in the air. The summer was coming to an end.

The next day, Tomoko impulsively visited Shingo's house at the seaside town; she wanted Shingo to cure her of the hard blows she had received lately. His wife and children were out, and she sensed an empty roughened atmosphere in the house. Tomoko realized for the first time how much harm she had done to Shingo's wife, and felt sorry. In order to clear up the confused state of things that had existed up to that time, Tomoko confessed her relationship with Ryôta to Shingo, and asked him to tell his wife that she had come that day. Shingo agreed, but when Tomoko was getting on the bus to return to her flat, Shingo said to her "I will come to your flat the day after tomorrow" in that tone of voice to which she had been accustomed for eight years, and which seemed to indicate that nothing would change.

Shiina Rinzo

Shiina Rinzô was born in Hyôgo Prefecture in 1911. His real name is Ôtsubo Noboru. His home was in a complicated state from his childhood. When he was fifteen years old, he ran away from his family which had been ruined and led a difficult life. He worked consecutively as an assistant in a fruit shop, as a restaurant delivery boy, and as an apprentice cook. All the while he experienced considerable hardships. He studied in his spare time, and managed to pass the state examinations qualifying him as a high school graduate. However, he was beginning to turn somewhat nihilist. In 1928, he joined the Ujigawa Electric Railway Company and became a train conductor. He soon became interested in the labour movement and was active as a leader of the Japanese Communist Party unit formed in his company. He was arrested and imprisoned in 1931 when there was a wholesale arrest of members of the Communist Party. While he had been active in the labour movement, he had studied the works of Marx, Engels and Lenin. However, during his imprisonment he read Nietzsche, and gradually came to have doubts about his former self. He abandoned Communism. After his release from prison in 1933, he studied existential thinkers like Kierkegaard, Jaspers and Heidegger. He also read the Bible. In 1938, he read Dostoevsky, and his interest in literature deepened.

After the war, in 1947, he published two novels, *Shin'ya no Shuen* (*Banquet at Midnight*) and *Omoki Nagare no Naka ni* (*In the Middle of a Heavy Stream*). They depict heroes who, living in miserable surroundings dominated by poverty and hopeless ignorance, still search for the meaning of the world and the meaning of life, and endure the existential problems involved in this search. These novels won him recognition, and he made a hopeful start as an *après-guerre* writer. His novel *Eien naru Joshô* (*Eternal Prologue*, 1948) marks a turning point in his development as a writer. This novel whose theme is "freedom from death" attests to the author's growing affirmation of life. After bitter intellectual and spiritual struggles, he was finally baptized on Christmas, 1951. He overcame his former nihilism. Since then he has been exploring a unique world of ideas as a Protestant writer. His autobiographical novel *Jiyû no Kanata de* (*On the Other Side of Freedom*, 1953–54), *Utsukushii Onna* (*The Beautiful Woman*, 1955) and others show that he has become a mature artist.

Among his plays, *Daisan no Shôgen* (*The Third Testimony*, 1954), *Sasori o Kau Onna* (*The Woman Who Keeps a Scorpion*, 1959), *Yoru no Saiten* (*Night Festival*, 1961), and *Fuanna Kekkon* (*Uneasy Marriage*, 1963), are taken as his representative works. Recently (in 1970) he also published a dramatization of Dostoevsky's *The Possessed*. His plays use the commonplace everyday life of ordinary people as their material and show how the hidden bizarre side of human nature can come to the surface, when something unusual happens. Basically these plays are always attempts to depict existential aspects of the life of loneliness before God. Basically they are always asking the same questions, namely, "What is human life? What is freedom?"

SHIINA Rinzo

Nimotsu—a play in one act *(The parcel)*

by Shiina Rinzô

First performed by the theatre troupe Kumo in June 1970. Published in *Mitabungaku*, May 1970.

Place: A room in the flat where Fukuhara and his wife live.

Time: The present. One Sunday afternoon.

(Synopsis) Fukuhara Eiji is forty-two years old. He is now a senior clerk in a third class company. He is not getting on in the world at all. His wife, Nagako, is thirty-seven years old. It is fifteen years since they married. Their relationship is now indeed cold, and there is no longer any emotional or physical tie between them. Although they are living together, they are strangers.

Eiji, the husband, cannot find any reason for living in a society which seems to be full of contradictions and irrationalities. He wonders if a human being has any real purpose in life at all. "What is man?" he asks himself. Living with his wife whom he no longer loves, he has no hope or expectation from life. He has become a nihilist who loves only loneliness.

Nagako, his wife, is not satisfied with such a husband. Gradually she turns her attention to other things. She is now the vice-president of the Friends' Association, which has three thousand members, and is socially quite active. The election for the new president of the Friends' Association is near at hand, and she is regarded as the likeliest person to win this election. Since she earns a considerable amount of money by giving talks, her position economically speaking, is stronger than that of her husband, who is just a third class salaried man. In her eyes, her husband is of no importance. She does not pay him the slightest attention. Their relationship is so cold that divorce seems possible at any moment. The only thing which makes Nagako try to create the appearance of their being an ordinary married couple is the coming election for the presidency. She does not want to make herself unpopular through a divorce suit just now. They go on living together by the sheer force of inertia. The following is what happens one Sunday afternoon between this middle aged couple in such a critical relationship.

Nagako is winding into a ball red wool which she makes her husband hold around his wrists for her. The Friends' Association is going to donate woolen socks for the winter to various welfare institutions. She is irritated by Eiji who is not very cooperative. She starts accusing him of not having a feeling of social responsibility, and as usual a quarrel develops between them. Then a man from a forwarding agency with a parcel contained in a cardboard box roughly 47 centimeters square arrives. It is the parcel which Eiji has posted but which has been sent back marked "addressee unknown". Their quarrel further deepens over this parcel.

Ten days ago that parcel arrived from somewhere. In it, they found a bottle containing a foetus roughly in the fourth month of development preserved in formalin. Nagako had attacked Eiji, saying that a deserted partner of his had sent this to him in revenge. Eiji returned the same accusation to Nagako. Eiji sent back the parcel to the sender in an attempt to find out who had sent it, but it had just been sent back again.

When Eiji opens the parcel which the carrier has just brought back, they find a Japanese doll made of porcelain whose head has been chopped off. This package looks from the outside exactly like the one they received ten days ago, except that the content is different. At this discovery, both Eiji and Nagako are deeply relieved. At the same time, they start feeling remorse for their past sins, and confess to each other their secrets. Eiji says that he was always thinking of committing suicide, but that he did not have enough courage to die alone. He had thought of making a female clerk of his company his partner in suicide, and started to have a physical relationship with her. She became pregnant by him, but Eiji became tired of her and just deserted her. This was Eiji's confession. Nagako also confesses that she had an affair with the treasurer of the Friends' Association and that she had an abortion when she became pregnant. While they are talking, the carrier of the forwarding agency returns, and says that he has delivered the wrong parcel. He takes back the cardboard box with the Japanese doll in it, and leaves another parcel in a cardboard box which looks exactly similar. This is the package with the foetus in it which had been delivered ten days ago.

The relationship between Eiji and Nagako seems to have come to its final end. They have lost every kind of hope, and they are not spirited enough even for despair. Probably suicide is the only thing left for them. However, they resume the work of winding wool into a ball. Both of them are lonely mortals. Because they have become aware of the sins they have separately committed, they have discovered a tie between them as human beings helpless before God. As if to symbolize this newly discovered tie, the red woollen yarn unites Eiji and Nagako as they wind it into a ball together.

Shimao Toshio

Shimao Toshio was born in Yokohama, the second son of a trader of silk fabrics. His parents' home was in Sôma, Fukushima Prefecture in the northern part of Japan. On account of his father's business, Shimao's family moved to Kôbe when he was a fifth grade pupil of primary school. From his primary school days, he was introvert and masochistic, and started writing stories. He studied at Nagasaki Higher Commercial School and then entered Kyûshû University and specialized in Oriental History. He was temperamentally a wanderer, a solitary traveller. This is partly due to the fact that in his childhood and youth he moved from one port town to another. He was fascinated, for example, by the exotic atmosphere a White Russian girl carries with her. He was also enthusiastic about literature.

When World War II broke out, Shimao, still a student, became a reserve cadet in the Navy and received torpedo-boat training. He became the commander of a "special attack" unit, and with 183 men under his command was stationed in Kakeroma Island in the Amami Archipelago. This "special attack" unit was a real suicidal unit, and its members were to ride in a motor-boat in whose front part was placed an explosive, and to deliberately crash against the landing boats of the enemy force. Here Shimao lived with his soldiers for a year receiving military training and facing the prospect of a sure death. On 14th of August, 1945, Shimao's unit received the order for departure, but immediately before they started off on their mission, the war ended.

Shimao's experience could be compared with that of Dostoevsky who received a reprieve from the Czar immediately before his death sentence was carried out. Shimao's experience of imminent death which seemed absolutely unavoidable, and subsequent "resurrection", as well as his love for the daughter of the chief of the island in that exotic southern place, determined the course of his subsequent life. After the war he married this girl of the island who had pledged not to outlive him. Shimao returned with her to the main land of Japan, but their life was not easy. Struggling with harsh reality he wrote very unique *avant-garde* surrealistic works such as *Yume no Naka de no Nichijô* (*Daily Life in Dream*, 1948). They start from a description of harsh reality but then express the world of nightmare hidden in the subconsciousness of man. Shimao came to attract attention on account of these works. *Matenrô* (*Skyscraper*), *Kotô-mu* (*Dream in a Distant Island*), *Ôbasami* (*Big Scissors*), *Chinkonki* (*Requiem*), *Onihage, Shima e* (*To the Island*) and other works, which Shimao himself calls works of his dream series, are excellent *avant-garde* works, the like of which are not to be found in the whole of world literature. They express the essence of existence by using nightmares. I believe that in the direction of Shimao's works lies one of the fruitful roads for contemporary world literature to explore.

The life path of Shimao, who had been a member of a suicide squad, and who continued to be a solitary traveller in a metaphorical sense, was not an even one. His devoted wife whom a fateful love united with him, became insane when Shimao, driven by romantic fancy, fell in love with another woman. He nursed his sick wife devotedly, shared her mental torture, and became a Catholic. He depicted his relationship with his wife, which had been deprived of almost every illusion and mask due to her insanity with, prayer in the stories collected in *Shi no Toge* (*The Thorns of Death*).

Shimao now lives in Amami Ôshima of the Ryûkyû Islands, which is his wife's native place. As a most conscientious Japanese writer and as the best example of an *avant-garde* writer, Shimao is highly respected among Japanese writers and is exerting a considerable influence on their work. Although small in number, he has most enthusiastic readers. Recently, *The Collected Works of Shimao Toshio*, in five volumes, was published. His unique view of Japanese culture which tries to understand Japan, starting with the Ryûkyû Islands, as a part of the Pacific cultural sphere, is having a big influence on the Japanese intellectual world.

SHIMAO Toshio
Shi no toge *(The thorns of death)*
Published by Kôdansha in 1960.

The next day he suddenly realized that the alarm clock on his desk, long out of order, was going again. For the moment, he had nothing to do but hunt, as before, for editors who might ask him to write something. His wife knew it, but he could no longer expect her to behave as before, to worry herself about it, to think up ways of getting work, to scrape together money for their living expenses.

For a while he felt hunted; then he went out. The wife who for so long had been his unobtrusive companion was transformed now. From now on, he had begun to feel, he wanted to do this, to try that, anything to show himself as he was to his wife. During those three wretched days and nights he had discovered something in her that he wanted to hold on to and not let go. Yet he realized with annoyance and fear that one part of him still hankered after the ecstasies that for so long, neglecting his wife, he had sought elsewhere. And countless hidden things would come unexpectedly to the surface, like bubbles in the fetid water of a canal.

He set off back home, considerably later than he had told his wife. At each station left behind on the way the sense of apprehension that gnawed at his guts, threatening him with destruction, grew more and more unmistakable.

The gate, the front door, the glass sliding doors facing the garden, all stood open. Miho was not there.

Instantly, illogically, it occurred to him that his wife had taken the kitchen knife and gone to the woman's house; he could see her, brandishing the unfamiliar weapon and threatening to kill the other.

He rushed to that station out in the suburbs, dread and impatience chasing each other impotently in his brain. Fortunately, no disaster had occurred.

His wife came home after the last train had gone. "Today, I really am going to leave you," she said.

Neither of them slept a wink that night.

"I paid someone seventy thousand yen just to have her investigated," she said. "She's a terrible woman. Leave it to her, and she'll end up by killing you."

The cross-questioning went on day after day.

"I've caused you a lot of suffering. But from now on I'm not going to tell any lies, however small. So I want you to stop ferreting into the past and to think more about the future."

He dreaded the way any sign of questioning from his wife would agitate him and throw him off his balance. At such times, his whole body would begin to shake with hatred. His wife's fits increased in intensity. When work took him out, he could not be easy in his mind unless he took his wife and children with him.

He felt sorry for the children, who were already resigned to the wretched struggle between husband and wife, and referred to it as "trouble at home." He was appalled to hear his eldest son say one day, 'I'm fed up with you, Father—and that's the truth!" His wife remained obdurate, no sign of softening in her attitude. Everything he had experienced up to now seemed meaningless, his feelings became numbed, emptiness took over body and soul alike.

Shono Junzo

Shôno Junzô was born in Ôsaka in 1921, the third son of a middle class family. His father was a teacher. Thus he was brought up in the family of an intellectual, and his interest in literature was awakened naturally. At first, stimulated by the works of Itô Shizuo, a romantic poet, Shôno tried to write poems, and had no intention of trying a novel. He studied

Oriental History in the Faculty of Law and Literature of Kyûshû University. Among the students of the Department of Oriental History one year ahead of him was Shimao Toshio who was later to distinguish himself as an important writer of contemporary Japanese literature. Shôno became good friends with Shimao, and influenced by him, wrote a novel, *Yuki Hotaru* (*Snow Firefly*, 1943). In 1944 when he was still a student he was drafted into the army, and was stationed at a military base on the Izu Peninsula. After the war, he worked for a junior high school in Ôsaka, and published poems and novels written in his spare time. In 1949 he published *Aibu* (*Caresses*). Shôno's works in the manner of the "I" novel began to attract attention about this time. Shôno started to produce novels which reveal the nihilistic abyss of human life. When he left the junior high school, and started working for Asahi Broadcasting Company, this tendency deepened; he started depicting symbolically hidden unrest in the life of a lower middle class family. *Pûru Saido Shôkei* (*A Pool-side Scene*, 1954) focuses on the fact that a happy looking family resting at the side of a swimming-pool is in fact the family of an unemployed ex-salaried man who defalcated his company's money and was fired. This novel expresses in a concise symbolic style the uncanniness of human life. Shôno used a similar technique in writing *Seibutsu* (*Still Life*, 1960). His previous works tended to devote too much space to describing trivial details of the life of ordinary citizens without producing much effect. In this work Shôno has succeeded in relating everything organically to the central theme, the fragileness of family happiness, and in expressing it symbolically. By this work he acquired a literary method of his own, and opened a new path for his future development. He came to be regarded as one of the representative writers of present Japan. Shôno dealt with the theme of fragility of everyday life again in works like *Yûbe no Kumo* (*Evening Cloud*).

Shôno often uses suggestions and symbols. By depicting seemingly eventless life, he manages to evoke in the reader's mind thousands of things which are left unsaid, and makes him think about the problem of human happiness. This characteristic of Shôno is clearly shown also in *Itaria Fû* (*Italian Style*, 1958) and *Ganbia Taizai Ki* (*My Stay in Gambia*)

which are based on his experiences during his stay in the United States
which he visited at the invitation of the Rockefeller Foundation.

SHONO Junzo
Seibutsu—a short story *(Still life)*
Gunzo, June 1960.

"Do let's go to the fishing pond" the little boy who had just started
going to primary school begged his father. It was Sunday, and although
it was only the beginning of March, the weather that day made one feel
that spring had suddenly returned to the earth. It was a beautiful still day
without a breath of wind. "There's no point going fishing—you know
we won't catch a thing", his father answered. "You know that's not true
—even Masuko caught live fishes there". "What kind of fish?" "Gold-
fish". "Gold-fish . . . !" the father exclaimed, "What an anticlimax!" "If
we just went and tried, we might catch something, you know". This time
it was the little girl in the fifth year of primary school who spoke. "Hmm!
I suppose if you don't try, you never find out. You're quite right, my
girl". When her father was wavering, or worrying about something,
this little girl was brilliant at finding the right words to encourage him.
She was strangely wise for a child. "Off you go—and make sure you
work up good appetites", her mother put in. When the father left the
houses he suddenly felt in a good mood. "Ah! After all, it's really good
to be doing something like this!" he thought as he looked at the buckets
the children were carrying. What did it matter whether they caught anything or not? The important thing was to go out carrying your bucket!
For a start, it was no fun spending a holiday doing nothing but moon
about the house.

They seemed to be having no luck at all at the fishing pond. However,
when the father took his eyes off the line for a moment, the float moved
slightly; in some confusion, he raised the line out of the water and found
a tiny red thing stuck on the end of the hook. "A catch! A catch!" the

little boy started yelling. The catch was an amazingly small goldfish, about the same size as the bait. The new dwelling place of the catch was inside the glass bowl near the bay-window in the children's room, and it seemed to be happy as it swam about energetically. However, the glass bowl might at any moment be cracked by a flying ball, or knocked over by the children romping about. Surprisingly, however, this did not happen, although the father could not feel completely at ease about the fate of the precious fish. The mother was in the kitchen with the girl; they were making doughnuts, and seemed to be having quite a lively time.

After supper, the father read the newspaper to his family, gathered around the table. They started to talk about the article on eight-year old Susie, a girl who had come back to life in the coffin. The daughter tried to imitate Susie at the moment when she came back to life, and whispered "Mummy, I want some milk". "Stop speaking in that uncanny manner", her mother scolded her. The little boy went to have a bath with his father, and blew lots of soap bubbles and badgered his father for a story. His father told him a story he had heard from a hunter about a wild boar.

"Goodnight, Daddy", "Goodnight, Mummy", "Goodnight everyone", "Goo—oo—oo—dnight!" The children raced one another to be first into bed.

"The woman facing towards me, sleeping by my side—this is the woman who married me. For fifteen years I have been sleeping with this woman—in the same bed, every night". However, there was that time when they had slept in separate rooms. How long did it last? It must have been about three months. She had slept with their daughter who was just a year old then. One morning, after that had happened, his daughter had rolled out of the mattress into the corner of the room, although she was still clutching her knitted toy dog. She did yot know what had happened, but she looked like an orphan curled up in corner. When he tried to wake his wife up, she did not open her eyes. The little girl had been too young to know what had happened in her own family up to that time. What unknown hand had protected her from seeing her mother strangely sleeping on and on? However, it was soon over. They started sleeping in the same bed, as before; and that is the way they had continued, all these years. The book the father was reading slipped out of his hand; he picked it up and looked for the right page. "Ah, here it is! No, I seem to have read this before. Here? No, I seem to have a vague memory of this. Hmm! I don't know which . . . is what. . . ." The father's eyes closed. The book slipped out of his hand.

Sono Ayako

Sono Ayako was born in 1931 in Tokyo. While she was a senior high school girl at the Sacred Heart Girls' School, she became a member of the literary group, presided over by Nakagawa Yoichi, which produced the magazine *Ramancha*. *Susono* (*At the Foot of a Mountain*) which Sono published in 1951 was acclaimed by Usui Yoshimi, and in the autumn of 1951 Sono became a member of the literary group which produced the magazine, *Shinshichô* (*The New Tide,* the fifteenth magazine of that name). In 1953, she married Miura Shumon who was also a member of that group. In 1954, Sono graduated from the Department of English Literature of the Sacred Heart Women's University. With *Enrai no Kyakutachi* (*Visitors from Afar*), which she published in *Mitabungaku* (*Mita Literature*) in April of that year, she became the runner-up for the Akutagawa Prize, and this helped to establish her as a writer. This work depicts, from the point of view of a young female employee, the Americans who use a hotel reserved for the Occupation Forces. The various personalities of the Americans are clearly differentiated. Although the subject is a serious one, the style is not heavy. The atmosphere of the age is brilliantly evoked in this work. It was reprinted in *Bungei Shunjû* (*Literary Years*) in September of the same year. In 1954, Sono published *Babiron no Shojo Ichi* (*The Virgin Market of Babylon*) and *Garasu no Itazura* (*The Trick of the Glass*), and in 1956 she published *Reimei* (*Dawn*) and *Otoko-gari* (*Man-hunt*). Sono, together with Ariyoshi Sawako, became famous as a "talented woman".

She is the forerunner of the numerous women writers who have appeared during the postwar period. In 1956, Sono made a journey to South East Asia. After her return to Japan, she published *Yukiakari* (*Snow Light*, 1957), *Shisha no Umi* (*The Sea of the Dead*, 1958) and *Tamayura* (*For a Time*, 1959), all of which enjoyed a good reception. In 1959, she took part in a quick round-the-world flight. In 1960, she attended the P.E.N. club conference in Brazil. After that she published many works. Among them are *Nômen no Ie* (*The House of a Nô Mask*, 1960), *Rio Gurande* (*Rio Grande*, 1962) and *Gogo no Bishô* (*Afternoon Smile*, 1962).

Sono is, just like her husband Miura Shumon, a devout Catholic. She likes to handle large-scale subjects. She has a power of abstract thinking about life and human beings. She is also good at cynical intellectual observation. She is one of the representative writers of postwar Japanese literature.

The theme of *Yukiakari* (*Snow Light*), summarized above, is further developed in *Tamayura* (*For a Time*). In *Tamayura* (*For a Time*), Shizuko appears under the name of Keiko. Kiyohiko marries a woman who is neither Yayoi nor Keiko. This woman, however, immediately has an affair with another man, and divorces Kiyohiko. At the news of Kiyohiko's marriage, Yayoi becomes insane. Kiyohiko goes to Brazil on an inspection trip and is later reported missing. In *Tamayura* (*For a Time*), the women around Kiyohiko are depicted through the eyes of Keiko. *Yukiakari* (*Snow Light*) is a moving interesting short story told in a different manner from *Tamayura* (*For a Time*).

SONO Ayako
Yukiakari *(Snow light)*
Gunzô, February 1957.

(**Synopsis**)   It was about the beginning of December that Shizuko left Tokyo for Kanazawa with Yoshioka Kiyohiko. That they would make a journey together was kept secret from Yoshioka's mother, so Shizuko had to make the arrangements for the journey with Kiyohiko by always phoning him at his university research room. Kiyohiko's father had been an executive of a coal company, but he was already dead. The fortune of the Yoshioka family was on the decline. Kiyohiko's mother was left in the big old house with her son, and was living on memories of past glory alone. Shizuko's parents were both dead. She was a spinster over thirty years old, and was earning her living as a typist. It was in the house of her friend that she had met Kiyohiko for the first time. Kiyohiko, a senior of her friend's husband, had happened to be there, and had been introduced to her. Kiyohiko had graduated from the Faculty of Natural Science at his university, and had remained at the university. Shizuko's friend had made fun of Kiyohiko and Shizuko by saying, "Today we have two misogamists in the house." This accidental encounter had led to Kiyohiko and Shizuko going out together from time to time. Kiyohiko did not have any intention of marrying Shizuko right away; he could not leave his aged mother, who was very much attached to the old house, alone, and live separately with Shizuko. He was resigned to the fact that as long as his mother lived, the present state of things would have to continue. Shizuko knew this but still continued to go out with him. She felt that Kiyohiko was considerate and a nice prospective husband, but she did not have enough temerity to press Kiyohiko to marry her. On the other hand, she did not want to break away from him. When he invited her out, she was not reluctant to go.

When Kiyohiko and Shizuko arrived at an inn called Kagaya, not far away from Kanazawa's Saikawa River, to Shizuko's great surprise, two sisters called Yayoi and Kôko came out to welcome Kiyohiko. The sisters seemed to Shizuko to be competing with each other to monopolize Kiyohiko. Shizuko could not understand why on earth Kiyohiko had taken her to this inn when these two women were there. They were to stay there for a night, looked after by the two sisters, but Kiyohiko and Shizuko were allotted separate rooms. From her room, Shizuko could hear quiet voices and occasional gentle laughter from Kiyohiko's room, and in her mind's eye, Shizuko saw Kiyohiko being entertained by the sisters. Shizuko went to the window, and looked at the scenery outside.

The banks of the River Saikawa were silvered by moonlight, and she could see the white silhouette of a distant mountain range against the clear cold night sky. "That is probably the White Mountain", Shizuko thought, and somehow felt moved. The mountain looked sublime to her. From that instant, she felt at peace. She could laugh at her previous jealousy. Shizuko smiled to herself in the room illumined by the snow light. She felt as if she had been walking somewhere with her deceased mother on this moonlit night, and she vividly imagined that scene. She imagined that from that scene she had suddenly been transported to this room. Several decades would pass as in an instant, and the next time she watched such a moonlit winter sky, Kiyohiko would already be dead.

The next morning Yayoi said to Kiyohiko, "You will not visit us for some time, will you?" She seemed very sorry to part with him.

Shizuko and Kiyohiko returned to Tokyo. The New Year came. Shizuko had not heard from Kiyohiko for some time, when one day at the beginning of February, she received a telephone call from him. They arranged to meet at the bar where they had gone on their first date. It was a memorable place for Shizuko. Kiyohiko said to her, "Yayoi has written to tell me that she is engaged to be married." "Really?" For Shizuko, it was like a strange story of a distant land. "I thought Yayoi liked you", she said. "In a different sense, I am afraid she is marrying against her will. She must feel a silent pressure from her step-mother to marry. Besides, she is the sort of person who worries about other people. I am sure she is feeling a responsibility to marry soon for the sake of her younger sister." "I think she has decided to marry on her own accord. If she liked you, that would be a natural course of action in this case. A woman behaves like that", Shizuko said. Shizuko thought that Yayoi and she had only chosen different types of resignation towards Kiyohiko. "Aren't you going to Kanazawa to save Yayoi from this marriage?", she asked. "No, I can't do anything like that. The only thing I can do will be to send a congratulatory present", Kiyohiko said, smiling weakly. It was the harmless, helpless smile of a lazy man.

Takahashi Kazumi

Takahashi Kazumi was born in Ôsaka in 1931. His father was a technician who was running a small factory in Ôsaka. Takahashi was his second son. Under his father's influence, his interest in machines and in science was awakened early. He spent his childhood making tools for fun and reading science magazines avidly. He first wanted to study science. In 1945, the year of Japan's surrender, however, Takahashi was greatly shocked by the miserable state of Ôsaka which had been reduced to ashes by air-raids, and by the confusion of postwar society, and his interest in literature was awakened. In 1948 he entered Matsue Higher School, and was introduced to the study of Chinese classics by Komata Shinji, a professor of the school. In 1949 he entered the Faculty of Literature of Kyoto University. He chose Chinese Literature as his major subject and started treading the path of a future scholar. What was always on Takahashi's mind was his gloomy experience immediately after the war. The memory of those experiences had a decisive importance not only when he chose to be a scholar but also when he decided to be a writer. Takahashi was very much attracted by the works of Haniya Yutaka and Noma Hiroshi, and stimulated by them he started writing novels. Then he became good friends with Komatsu Sakyô who was later to distinguish himself as a writer of science fiction, and together they started the literary group magazine *Gendai Bungaku* (*Contemporary Literature*). Takahashi became ambitious about writing long novels. *Sutego Monogatari* (*The Tale of an Abandoned Child*) which he published at his own expense in 1958 is a work which depicts the nightmare of a boy abandoned in an alley of a slum area. Part of this work had first been published in the magazine *Gendai Bungaku* (*Contemporary Literature*). In order to pursue the path of a scholar and that of a writer harmoniously at the same time, Takahashi chose as the main theme of his writing the position of intellectuals in Japan. In 1959 he was appointed to a teaching post at Ritsumeikan University in

Kyoto. He joined a study group of literary theories, and started working energetically. He wrote essays on postwar Japanese intellectuals like Haniya Yutaka and Takeuchi Yoshimi. The long novel, Hi no Utsuwa (*Vessel of Sorrow*, 1962), is the first comprehensive literary expression of his intellectual ethical concern. This novel was received very warmly by the public partly because of its unique vigorous style based on Takahashi's solid knowledge of Chinese Literature and partly because the melancholy style of life of an intellectual depicted in it appealed to them. After the publication of this novel, Takahashi came to be regarded as one of the representative intellectual writers of present Japan.

He depicts the collapse of ideals in everyday life as the inevitable fateful mark of being human. His works hide denunciations of postwar Japanese society. Among his other works are *Yûutsunaru Tôha* (*Melancholic Faction*, 1965) and *Jashûmon* (*The Evil Faith*, 1966). In 1971 he died suddenly of cancer, at the early age of 39.

TAKAHASHI Kazumi
Hi no utsuwa *(Vessel of sorrow)*
Bungei, November 1962.

(Synopsis) It is unfortunately true that the quietness of my life has been broken by a single newspaper article. If nothing had come to light, I would still be an influential member of the judicial world and I would have no burden on my soul except that of daily intellectual labour as a university professor. The newspaper reported roughly as follows: "Masaki Tenzen (55 years old), professor of the Faculty of Law of X university, whose wife died of cancer of the larynx, has been living alone with his housekeeper for a long time. However it was decided through the good offices of his friend, Judge Okazaki of the Supreme Court, that he would marry Kuritani Kiyoko (27 years old), daughter of Dr. Kuritani Bunzô, professor emeritus of X University. Suddenly, however,

Yoneyama Miki, the 45 year old housekeeper, has sued him demanding compensation of 650,000 yen for a wrongful act". Below this was printed a photograph of Yoneyama Miki and her strong denunciation of me as a cruel man who violated her body and made a plaything of her. Three days later, the newspaper reported that I had sued Miki for libel, and for some time, the weekly magazines and the newspaper gossip columns were crowded with articles connected with this matter. I was particularly shaken by an article entitled "An Impeachment Letter Addressed to my Eldest Brother" which my youngest brother, Masaki Norisuke, a Catholic priest, had published in a widely circulating magazine. For it was I who had defended him, the eccentric of the family, before our somewhat tyrannical father who was a practitioner of Chinese medicine. My brother's letter, which denounced "my unpardonable sin" in strong language, made me recognise what I had really been looking for. From that time on my endless fall started, and I was forced into an endless war with an invisible enemy.

I hired Yoneyama Miki as housekeeper six years ago when Shizue, my wife, became hopelessly ill with cancer. Yoneyama was a war widow who had taught at a girls' school. Even a short business talk revealed her high intelligence. I do not remember exactly when our relationship started, but it was when a meeting of the criminal law society was just over. I was feeling suddenly relaxed after prolonged tension. I drank saké and suddenly I said to her that I wanted her. I did not force her by violence. At first she refused, but after a while, she came to my room and slept with me. My sick wife seemed to have sensed our relationship immediately. When I entered her room emitting an unusual smell from my body, she said, "I would like to die soon". My wife heard one of my youngest brother's sermons and committed suicide the day before an almost hopeless operation was to take place. My wife, Shizue, was the daughter of Professor Miyaji, my reverend teacher.

It was around 1935 that the police started putting pressure on the magazine *Kokka* (*State*) with which the talented pupils of Dr. Miyaji were connected. It was an age when the autonomy of universities was steadily being encroached upon. A contributor and the editor were arrested, but nobody knew the reason. That the cause was unknown made us even more panicky.

Ogino, assistant professor, Tomita, sub-assistant and myself, were summoned by Professor Miyaji and were asked to take over the running of the magazine *Kokka* (*State*). However, before long, Ogino, who had written the leading article for one edition, was arrested, and Tomita, who was in charge of editing, mysteriously disappeared. Students of public law were arrested one after another. I, who had escaped arrest, tried my best to defend the study of public law. I became an assistant professor, and married the daughter of my teacher. I became a public prosecutor in order to assume power enough to keep the magazine *Kokka* (*State*) out of trouble with the law. Ogino was detained in prison for a long time, was tortured and finally renounced his views. Tomita, who had written a genial thesis titled *Null and Void*, became an anarchist, and was arrested as the principal offender in a bank robbery. He went insane, and died in jail.

Life as a public prosecutor during the war meant being the puppet of the State and in that sense was a miserable job. On the other hand, at that time, only public prosecutors could openly study Marxism and so on with immunity. I established the Masaki Theory of conscientious objectors from the point of view of comparative jurisprudence. After a time my theory came to be highly esteemed, even in the U.S.S.R. During the war I endured everything for the sake of jurisprudence. Neither did I forget even for a day the fates of Ogino and Tomita, the two talented students.

After the war, I returned to the university as a professor and became the dean of the Faculty of Law. The students responded to my scandal immediately, and at one time boycotted my classes. I waited in the empty classroom until the fifteen minutes fixed by regulation had elapsed and I was free to leave. Just then the government tried to pass a bill through the diet regulating forcibly the performance of policemen's duties, and the students became too busy in opposing it to bother about the scandal. The chairman of the student body came to see me and tried to persuade me of the importance of joining the movement against the bill. As a jurist I could not agree with him. When a girl student called me a hound and traitor, I tried to call in the police and sue her for libel. I went to the diet to give my opinion as a reference. Although I was chosen for reference by the governmental party, I explained why I was, as a jurist, against the bill. The president of the university unexpectedly accepted my resignation which I had tendered just for formality's sake. When I visited the courthouse where I had worked as a public prosecutor, the judges and the public prosecutors, who were my juniors in school, tried to persuade me to drop my complaint against Yoneyama Miki. I refused. I had to part with my fiancée, Kuritani Kiyoko, who was the object of my longing and dreams, and who had loved me. When I saw Kiyoko as a witness on Yoneyama's side, I knew that all was over. And finally, I must admit, I have nothing to do with you gentle living folks.

Takami Jun

Takami Jun whose real name is Takama Yoshio was born in Mikuni, Fukui Prefecture. His real father, Sakamoto Sannosuke, was at that time the Governor of Fukui Prefecture. Takami, however, never saw his father in his life. He was an illegitimate child born of an affair between this politician who had been sent by the Central Government to govern the district and a native woman of the area. His illegitimacy was to be an important *motif* to Takami's writing for the whole of his life. The year after Takami's birth, his mother, as if driven out of the place, moved to Tokyo with his grandmother. They lived unobtrusively in a tenement in Azabu. The wish of his grandmother and his mother was to make Takami an honourable citizen and politician who would put his father to shame. To their satisfaction, he proceeded from the First Middle School to the First Higher School and then to Tokyo University, all top *élite* institutions of that time. He was a very brilliant student. However, although outwardly he was a good student and everything seemed to be all right with him, within his heart were hidden very complicated feelings, especially that of deep humiliation. At that time Communism was in great vogue in Japan. Studying at the First Higher School, and then at Tokyo University, Takami's interest in Literature deepened. At the same time he gradually came to be influenced by anarchistic and Marxist ideas. He knew that if he was won over by Marxism, it would disappoint his mother who had sent him to a university through her hard work. His poverty-stricken and painful background, however, disposed him all the more strongly to a sympathy for Marxism. Takami was not only a child 'born under a fateful star' but also a child of his age. After graduation he found a job in a record company. He became a member of the Japanese Proletarian Writers' League. He was arrested for his participation in a trade union movement. In the meantime he was deserted by his wife. From such experiences was born the long novel *Kokyû Wasure-ubeki* (*Should Auld Acquaintance be Forgot?*, 1935) which depicts the sufferings, perplexities and regrets of a conscientious intellectual of that time. In this novel Takami depicted with nausea the feelings of people who had once fought for their ideals but who now had to abandon them. This novel was warmly received by the intellectuals of that time who were themselves in a difficult predicament. Takami's voluble style, which ran counter to the existing mode of literary realism, his discontent with mere description and his urgent search for an adequate method of expression made him, together with Dazai Osamu, Itô Hitoshi and others, a pioneer of contemporary literature. He was one of the outstanding writers who dealt with the problems of Japanese intellectuals in the 1930's. Takami expressed, using the form of a confession, the disgracefulness and helplessness of human beings. In 1939 he wrote the long novel *Ikanaru Hoshi no Moto ni* (*Under What Star?*), an excellent novel of manners, which depicts the hero who finally finds his true self among the poor inhabitants of the city. During the war, he was drafted into the official reporters' unit of the army, and followed the army to the battlefields of Malay, Singapore and Burma. After the war he published *Waga Mune no Soko no Koko ni wa* (*Here at the Bottom of My Heart*, 1946–1951), an autobiographical novel of the author who grew up as an illegitimate child. He also wrote a novel which was a sort of self-criticism for allowing himself to be forced to cooperate with the Army during the war. Although he became a very popular writer after the war, he often behaved in a neurotic manner. *Seimei no Ki* (*The Tree of Life*, 1956–1958) is a novel which depicts a married middle-aged man who cannot resist the charms of a nymph-like girl. Takami tried to relate his personal problems and inner conflicts to those of his age by acquiring a comprehensive understanding of the Shôwa period through which he lived. The long novels, *Gekiryû* (*A Raging Torrent*, 1959–1963) and *Iyana Kanji* (*Disagreeable Feeling*, 1960–1963) were born out of such an effort. He conceived another ambitious series of novels in this direction, and was writing them, when he died of cancer of the esophagus.

He was a very energetic person. He published *Waga Maisô* (*My Burial*, 1953), a collection of poems on the theme of death; he also wrote powerful essays, and left behind him detailed diaries written during the war period; he also worked to found the Modern Japanese Literature Library, and was involved in many other enterprises. He was shy, but at the same time was capable of bold action. He was fond of confessions and was somewhat masochistic. As a true child of his age, he was born, lived, wrote and finally died in a most theatrical fashion. He was full of contradictions like the age he lived in. He was the very image of a writer.

TAKAMI Jun
Iyana kanji *(Disagreeable feeling)*
Published serially in *Bungakukai*, from January 1960 to May 1963. Published in book form by Bungei Shunjû Shinsha in July 1963.

(Synopsis) We stopped the taxi before a railway crossing. The place was dark. The young driver handed out the change and said, "You are going to have fun, aren't you?" He was smiling. "What are you talking about?" Sunauma Kôichi, my companion, snapped, snatching the change. The place was on the outskirts of Tokyo. Sunauma and I turned to the right into an alley. According to Sunauma, this was a first-class place, and there were many attractive women about. We had the money which we had earned that day through blackmailing. While we walked, women called to us from the small windows on both sides of the alley. All types of women were to be found here, and you could choose the type of woman you like. It was a time when the brothels were prospering.

I, Kashiba Shirô, am an anarchist. I was born as the second son of a small foundry owner at Shinohashi, Azabu. My father sent me to middle school, though with considerable difficulty. When I was in the fourth year, I read Kropotkin's *An Appeal to the Youth* translated by Ôsugi Sakae. I was so impressed by this book that I was converted to Socialism. In 1924, when I was nineteen years old, I joined the conspiracy to assassinate General Fukui. I escaped arrest, and was not executed. At the time of writing I was earning my living by blackmailing capitalists and getting money out of them.

Sunauma and I went to a privately owned brothel. Sunauma, however, tried to coerce several girls to sleep with him at the same time, and was thrown out of the place. Then we went to Yoshiwara. He was also unpopular there. However, at Akasaka, a certain geisha girl showed interest in him. As for me, I could not forget the sweet girl called Kurara whom I had noticed in the first brothel we had visited. She had said that it was her first day in the business. I left Sunauma in Akasaka and returned to the first brothel to see Kurara. I was completely charmed by her, and went to the brothel to see her many times after that. I wanted to ransom her and make her my wife. I was thinking of extorting a large sum of money by blackmailing to raise the ransom money.

I went to see Maruman who was keeping a street stall and who was organizing anarchists by giving advice about money matters. On this occasion I was introduced to a man called Saitô Kôdô, who had taken part in the Chinese revolution of 1911, being influenced by socialist ideas. According to Maruman, he was a great person.

Teruko (alias Kurara) seemed to love me, but a rather shady character kept visiting her. After confessing to me that she was the daughter of an adventurer working in China, she suddenly disappeared.

At Kôdô's house, I met a revolutionary officer called Lieutenant

Kitatsuki who was planning to start a revolution in which he aimed to use the Army. I was attracted by the calibre of Kôdô's character, and the sincerity of Lieutenant Kitatsuki, and joined their organization. I was a terrorist, and I could not resist the attraction of a revolution. Kitatsuki and his group were planning a *coup d'état*, and I consented to be in charge of terrorist activities. However, our *coup d'état* plans for March and October of 1931 were both detected beforehand and failed. They were made use of in a power struggle among high ranking officers of the army. I was very much angered by that. Receiving instructions from Lieutenant Kitatsuki and his group, I went to Seoul to assassinate General Ogaki. While I was waiting for a good opportunity, I was detected, and the military police investigated the inn where I was staying. I just managed to escape arrest, thanks to the presence of mind of Namiko, a maid at the inn. I returned to Japan with Namiko. I was gradually drawn into right-wing circles, and became involved in struggles among factions of the Army or of adventurers interested in China. I was caught in a trap by one such adventurer called Yashige and committed a senseless murder.

I married Namiko, who had accompanied me from Seoul. I hid myself in Nemuro at a place which an anarchist called Abiru had found for me. My wife worked at a crab cannery. We lived as ordinary citizens, and even had a daughter whom we called Shinako. However, my glorious past as a terrorist did not allow me to continue this peaceful existence in a remote part of Hokkaido. People who had been my fellow anarchists before had all become right-wingers and were making money on the continent by using the military authorities.

When I was just leaving for Tokyo to resume my activities, I coughed up blood, and had to stay at home to nurse my illness. I published poems under the pen name, Nonaka Tadashi, and gained a fair reputation as a poet. In the meantime, the *coup d'état* attempt of 1936 ("the February 26th incident") took place, and both Lieutenant Kitatsuki and their theoretical leader, Saitô Kôdô, were executed. I was extremely sorry that I had not been able to take part in the attempt at a *coup d'état*, and made up my mind to avenge the death of my comrades on those who had killed them. I left my family in Japan, and went to Shanghai alone, to operate as a terrorist. The war with China had started, and at that time, Shanghai was a really sinister place with so many assassins abroad.

Teruko, who had formerly been the prostitute called Kurara, had become the mistress of an adventurer called Shibata and was running a cabaret in Shanghai. I shot Roku, an assassin who had been trying to kill me, earned money by unscrupulous means, killed Shibata who had been maltreating Teruko, and was planning to kill Sunauma, who was making money by trading in opium, when I received the news that Shinako, my daughter, had fallen into a river at the back of our house and died. I went to the front. Probably I had become mad. A Chinese man was just about to be executed. I asked them to let me cut off his head. Probably I wanted to display myself for the last time, a pathetic figure, a terrorist from conviction who had deteriorated into a mere gangster. I borrowed a service-sword, and struck down as if I was chopping wood. A nauseating sensation ran through my body as my sword met the resistance of the man's neck. Nausea ran through me, when I saw that the man's head was hanging from his body connected only by the skin. From within me, an inexplicable fit of laughter burst out. I was crazy. I could not stop laughing. I stumbled into the hole for burying the man. Upon me was thrown the body with the hanging head.

Takeda Taijun

Takeda Taijun was born in 1912 at Hongo, Tokyo. His father was a Buddhist priest in charge of the Chôsen-ji temple. While he was a student at Urawa Higher School, he began to feel interested in Chinese Literature. Around that time, his contact with left-wing movements also began, and he once went to "normal schools" to distribute leaflets for the Anti-Imperialism League. He entered the Department of Chinese Literature of Tokyo University, but was soon arrested for distributing leaflets for the Anti-Imperialism League. He was detained in prison for roughly a month, and then was released. Takeda came to think that he was not well qualified as a champion of left-wing movements, and ceased to work for them. He also left the university within about half a year after being admitted, but he continued his studies of Chinese Literature. He was at that time suffering from misgivings about living in comfort on the donations of the believers as the priest of the temple. In 1937, he was drafted into the army, and was sent to Central China as a private soldier. Since he was assigned to clerical work, he found time to read Gide, Alain and other writers. Takeda said later, "The greatest benefit army life gave me was that it opened my eyes to human nature and to society for the first time". His previous experience of defection from left-wing movements, and his experience in the army really opened his eyes to man and society. The first fruit of this deepened understanding of man and society was Takeda's *Shibasen* (*Sze-ma Ts'ien*) which was published in 1943. According to Takeda, Sze-ma Ts'ien, the great historian of the Han period, tried to depict "political personalities who moved the world", in other words, "political personalities who had a certain indescribable extraordinariness about them" in his *History*. Since then, Takeda continued to depict extraordinary political personalities, free from the traditional schematic formal understanding of history, and tried to acquire a deeper understanding of man beyond the common sense division of moral and immoral, good and evil, beautiful and ugly. In 1944, he was appointed to a post in the Sino-Japanese Cultural Association in Shanghai. In 1946, he returned to Japan.

In the postwar period he became, together with Noma Hiroshi and Shiina Rinzô, one of the most representative of the "first postwar group" writers and produced many works. Among his main postwar works are *Mamushi no Sue* (*This Outcast Generation*, 1947, translated by Shibuya Yûzaburô, Tokyo, Tuttle, 1967), *Igyô no Mono* (*The Misshapen Ones*, 1950, translated by Seidensticker, E. G., *Japan Quarterly*, Vol. IV, No. 4, 1957), *Fûbaika* (*Anemophilous Flower*, 1952), *Hikarigoke* (*Luminous Moss*, 1954, translated by Goldstein, Sanford, Tokyo, Tuttle, 1967), *Mori to Mizuumi no Matsuri* (*The Grove and the Lake Festival*, 1955), *Shikon Shôsai* (*Samurai Spirit and Business Talent*, 1957), *Kizoku no Kaidan* (*Degrees of*

Aristocracy, 1959) and *Nisesatsu-tsukai no Shuki* (*The Autobiography of a Banknote Forgerer*, 1963). Takeda also wrote many critical works and essays.

Shikon Shôsai (*Samurai Spirit and Business Talent*), summarized below, depicts an extraordinary type of human being who contributed greatly to the development of Japanese capitalism and also the indigenous mental climate in which he worked. This novel is written with a fairly light touch. At the basis of this novel is the same understanding of history and man which Takeda expressed in *Shibasen* (*Sze-ma Ts'ien*).

TAKEDA Taijun
Shikon shôsai *(Samurai spirit and business talent)*
Bungakukai, January 1957.

(Synopsis) The thirteenth anniversary of the death of Ittoku Den'ichi, the founder of the Ittoku Transport Company, is being commemorated in a hotel room. Present executives of the company, influential personages in financial circles, high ranking officials of the Ministry of Transportation and the Ministry of Construction, chiefs of police stations, the bereaved family, and others have all gathered together here on this occasion. Now people are giving speeches in reminiscence of the late Mr. Ittoku. He was a bold man. There was no denying that he was vulgar, but he had great vitality. With such vitality and boldness, which even made him risk his life for a daring enterprise, he accumulated a great fortune within his lifetime. He was an unscrupulous concession hunter, but he was not without some discernment. His mentality was shown in that he was very proud of the hanging scroll on which an Army Minister had written *Shikon Shôsai* (samurai spirit and business talent) for him.

Since Den'ichi did not have any children, his nephew became his heir. Now Gen'ichi, the son of the nephew, is the head of the Ittoku family. Probably because Gen'ichi is not a direct descendant of Den'ichi, he is not at all like him. He is a nervous looking intellectual, and dislikes Den'ichi's roughness and vulgarity intensely. Gen'ichi even now is feeling worried lest the party does not finish quickly enough for him to be in time for the recital to be given by a famous violinist at present visiting Japan. Not knowing what is on Gen'ichi's mind, the guests are giving speeches one after another, and are talking about how Den'ichi got along in society.

Den'ichi came to Tokyo in the early years of the Meiji period. He came from Satsuma (Kagoshima). Taking advantage of the fact that there were a lot of people from Satsuma among the police personnel, he made money through his connections with them. When, after the Satsuma Rebellion of 1877, the people from Satsuma had lost their influence in the police force, Den'ichi changed his strategy, and approached the army. Getting the help of a military band for advertisement, he purchased at a low price the government securities which were given to samurai when they were deprived of their privileges. Den'ichi made a huge amount of money in this way. Establishing a connection with the prefectural office, he became its exclusive purveyor.

Gen'ichi, who has been listening to these episodes from the life of Den'-ichi, representing the worst aspects of modernization in the Meiji period, is feeling really bored, although he does not show it outwardly. Suddenly his beloved daughter Hanako who is at his side asks him in a loud voice, "Was my great grandpa a bad man or a good man?" Gen'ichi feels very much embarrassed. It is as if his daughter had seen what was going on in his mind. He takes her to the recreation room of the hotel and has her watch a children's programme on T.V.

The reminiscences of the speakers seem to have no end. They narrate how, after Japan's occupation of Taiwan, Den'ichi ran a brothel there for the sake of the country, that, with the help of the Mitsui company, Den'ichi built up the Ittoku Transport Company as it is today, that during its early years there were frequent fights with its rivals in which both sides enlisted the help of gangsters, but that Den'ichi, who had learned a bitter lesson from the first fight he had personally experienced, always disappeared from the office when such a fight was likely to take place. In this connection they also talk about Nakajima Tomekichi, who, as Den'ichi's right-hand man, risked his life for the sake of the company and even fought with the gangsters. Gen'ichi's graceful face is darkened by a frown as he listens to this story of Japanese capitalism burdened with the legacy of feudalism and bloody crime. Gen'ichi himself is deeply attracted by the refined culture of Europe, which he thinks is the very opposite of the feudalistic nature and bloodiness of Japanese capitalism. However, somehow, Gen'ichi appears slightly ridiculous despite all his culture. At last the party comes to an end. Gen'ichi hurries to the concert hall and is absorbed by the subtle sounds of the violin.

Nakajima Tomekichi is now about sixty years old, if he is still alive. In his twenties, he came to blows with Den'ichi over a woman, and has been missing ever since.

On the same day as the thirteenth anniversary of Den'ichi's death is being commemorated at a hotel in Tokyo, a strike by power-supply workers is just about to start at an electric power station whose equipment Den'ichi once had transported there and installed with considerable difficulty. Before the line of picketing young union members appears an old man, and he tries to break through the picket line. This is Nakajima Tomekichi who risked his life to construct this power station when he was young. He looks completely changed. Asked by the head of the power station who knows the past story of the place, he has come to break the strike singlehanded. The picketing youths feel at a loss how to deal with this old man. Taking advantage of an unguarded moment on their part, Tomekichi finally achieves his end. Tomekichi lectures the youths roughly as follows: He says he does not know whether Den'ichi was a good man or a bad man, but that he repaid Den'ichi's favour with treachery has been on his conscience for all these years, and this is the reason why he has defended the dynamo which Den'ichi took great trouble to have installed. In the course of the development of Japanese capitalism, such a master and servant relationship based on the ethics of *giri* (duty) and *on* (favour) has played an important part.

The next morning Nakajima Tomekichi appears at the huge green house of the Ittoku family. He meets Hanako, Gen'ichi's little daughter,

Hanako also asks Tomekichi whether Den'ichi was a good man or a bad man. Unable to answer her right away, Tomekichi remains silent for a while, when Hanako says that she dislikes Den'ichi. When Tomekichi hears this, he bursts into laughter, murmurs that children have unexpectedly good insight into things, and leaves. To be honest, even Tomekichi who has been feeling so much indebted to Den'ichi, does not really like him.

Tanaka Chikao

Tanaka Chikao, born in 1905 in Nagasaki, graduated from the French Literature Department of Keiô University. He had been interested in the theatre since the time he became a student, and had attended lectures given by Kishida Kunio, Iwata Toyoo, and others on the drama. He studied "psychological" plays of modern French dramatists, and was particularly interested in Vildrac by whom he was influenced. After graduation, he became a member of staff of the theatrical magazine *Gekisaku (Play-Writing)* and published his first play *Ofukuro (Mother)* in this magazine in 1933. This play was performed by the Tsukiji Za players and was a success. At once he was recognized as a promising new dramatist. *Ofukuro* is a one-act play which depicts the psychological conflicts between a mother and her children. It is distinguished by its fine structure and smooth flow of lively speeches.

During the Second World War, Tanaka returned to Tottori, his father's home, and wrote nothing. After Japan's defeat in the war, once more he started writing vigorously. *Kumo no Hatate (The Cloud Frontier, 1948)*, which depicts a young doctor who is troubled by the psychological scars of the war and the problem of sex, was highly prized as the first existential piece of literature in Japan.

After this, he wrote a series of plays such as, *Mezaru (A Female Monkey, 1948)*, *Kyôiku (Education, 1954)*, *Hizen Fudoki (The Hizen District, 1956)* and *Hino Yama* (*Volcano*) which are commonly called "misogynist plays". In these plays, Tanaka developed the dialectic of intense attachment to one's own ego, and the faith in God which lies above this. He succeeded in creating a unique dramatic world of his own.

He continued to produce fine literary works such as *Maria no Kubi* (*The Head of Mary*, 1959), *Chidori* (*Plover*, 1964), *Sasurai* (*Wandering*, 1964), *Shinri* (*Psychology*, 1967) and *Arai Hakuseki* (1968) in rapid succession. In these plays, not only themes developed in previous works, but also a great variety of new themes are explored: among these, for example, are the problem of pantheism in Japan, responsibility for the war, and the emperor system. In recent years, his plays have shown a tendency towards social satire and an imitation of various social "manners". He is also making use of the techniques of Japanese traditional drama in an attempt to create a new dramatic form which goes beyond the limitations of the present conventions of modern play-writing. At the same time, beneath all this, is the lonely human soul's persistent pursuit of salvation and freedom. In 1955, Tanaka was awarded the Yomiuri Literary Prize. In 1959, he was awarded the Kishida Theatrical Achievement Prize and in 1960, he was awarded the Education Minister's Prize for Artistic Achievement. He is still active as the leading dramatist of postwar Japan.

TANAKA Chikao
Chidori—a play in three acts (*Plover*)
Staged by the Haiyû Za in October 1959. Published in *Shingeki* in November 1959.

Place: The action takes place partly in a traditional Japanese-style room in the Saida family's house, also in their garden with its waterfall; and partly in the shaft of an abandoned mine which is in the hill at the back of their house. The Saida family is an old family of a village surrounded by mountains in Tottori Prefecture of the San'in District.
Time: Somewhere around 1956–1957

(Synopsis) (*Act I*) Saida Kônoshin is the 28th head of the Saida family which traces its ancestry back to the beginning of the 14th century. Until the end of World War II, he was a big landlord, and the highest taxed member in the House of Peers. However, because of the agricultural land reform after Japan's defeat in the war, most of his land has passed into the hands of his former tenant farmers. He has had to sell almost all his household effects, and is now on the brink of bankruptcy. His four children have left him, and only his wife, Rui, and his grand-daughter, Chidori, are living with him in his old age. They live in a quiet unobtrusive manner. But Kônoshin's heart is not at peace. He will neither recognize Chidori as his rightful grand-daughter nor have her name entered in the family register. He regards her as a child born of sin. On top of that, he has eye trouble, and is on the brink of losing his sight.

One evening, towards the end of August, he plays a piece called *Chidori* (*Plover*) on the *Shakuhachi* (a five-holed bamboo flute). The time of the *Bon* Festival (the festival of ancestors) is approaching, according to the old lunar calendar. Playing *Chidori,* he starts daydreaming. In his daydream, he starts talking with Yûzaburô, his third son, who was killed in the decisive battle at Guadalcanal during World War II. In Kônoshin's mind, the past and the present become indistinguishable. In his daydream, Yûzaburô says nice things to him to cheer him up. Yûzaburô also advises his father who loves no one except himself to "give up his obstinate pride and to open his heart". Kônoshin, who wants to restore his half-ruined family to former prosperity, is staking his last hope in mining the uranium which is buried in the hill at the back of his house. He will not listen to Yûzaburô who in his daydream says, "Father, give up your selfish desire and be at peace". Kônoshin travels back further in time. It is twenty-six years ago. Kônoshin's second daughter, Terumi, was a high school student at that time (around 1930). She fell in love with a university student called Mikage who had come to conduct a geological survey of the hill at the back. Mikage also loved her. Kônoshin was opposed to their relationship, but Terumi became pregnant. She also gave Mikage a secret map which showed the location of gold veins in the hill, a map which had been handed down in the family for ages. Angered by his daughter's treachery,

Kônoshin struck at Mikage with his sword while he was keeping a rendezvous with Terumi in the mine-shaft. Mikage, one arm cut off, ran away, leaving Terumi. Terumi was confined to the mine-shaft, and there gave birth to a girl. This girl was Chidori. Terumi sued her father for murder, and Kônoshin was arrested, but he was released on account of inadequate evidence. Terumi disappeared immediately afterwards. Kônoshin who had been betrayed by his beloved daughter, continued to bear strong hatred towards Mikage and was waiting for a chance to revenge himself. After Japan's defeat in the war, the allied occupation forces came to this distant village, and Mikage accompanied them as an interpreter. He also came to the house of Kônoshin, but Kônoshin who had weak eyes, did not recognize him.

(*Act II*) Kônoshin has come out of his daydream. He feels uneasy because his sight is gradually disappearing. This also makes him impatient. His wife, Rui, sorrowfully says, "This is a punishment for your arrogance and self-centredness". Kônoshin plans to send for his three children who have deserted him, and to distribute his fortune and nominate the next head of the family. He also plans to set his grand-daughter Chidori free from this gloomy-house. Just then, Mikage who has become an engineer of the Bureau of Development, comes to the village to investigate the uranium veins in the hill.

(*Act III*) Two days later, on the night of the *Bon* Festival, the three children who were surprised by the telegram from their father, hurriedly come home. They consist of Akemi, the eldest daughter, who lives in Kyôto and runs a small publishing company, Chiichirô, the eldest son, who is a judge in Tokyo, and Junjirô, the second son, who runs a department store in Kumamoto. When Kônoshin asks them to return to the village, take over the headship of the Saida family, and restore it to prosperity, none of them complies with his request. Chidori misses her mother and enters the mine-shaft where her mother had given birth to her. Mikage follows her and discloses to her that he is her father and that her mother (Terumi) died ten days ago. He gives her a rosary which her mother left, and asks her to leave the house and live with him. Chidori says that she cannot leave her lonely grandfather. At the time of the *Bon* Festival, girls dance with painted paper umbrellas. They also come to the house of Kônoshin. While they dance, Kônoshin and Mikage are reconciled by Chidori. Kônoshin hopes that Mikage will cooperate with him in developing a uranium mine, and again dreams of restoring the Saida family to its former prosperity. He is old, and now blind. He is weak, but still he refuses to give up the struggle, the struggle with an "invisible" enemy.

Tanizaki Jun'ichiro

Tanizaki Junichirô was born in 1886, and died in 1965. He was an unusually precocious wirter, and already wrote something resembling historical biographies at the age of fourteen or fifteen. He started his literary career in 1910. *Shisei (Tattoo,* 1910, translated by Morris, Ivan, in *Modern Japanese Stories,* pp. 90–100, Tokyo, Tuttle, 1962) which he published in the magazine *Shin-Shichô (New Trend)* that year made him famous overnight. After that, he wrote neat works with an affected imitation of European dandyism. He also wrote works reminiscent of the popular literature of the late Edo period. His *Chijin no Ai (A Fool's Love,* 1925) marked the end of a period in which he mainly wrote masochistic works characterized by diabolical aestheticism. After this, he produced works characterized by the traditional beauty of the Japanese language. First he depicted the love of a married woman in *Manji (The Buddhist Cross,* 1928). Then he published *Yoshinokuzu (Yoshino Arrowroot,* 1931), *Ashikari* (1932, translated by Humpherson, Roy & Okita, Hajime and published in *Ashikari and the Story of Shunkin,* Tokyo, Hokuseidô, 1936) and *Shunkinshô (A Portrait of Shunkin,* translated by Hibbett, Howard and published in *Seven Japanese Tales),* masterpieces of what is usually called Tanizaki's classical period. Tanizaki then translated *Genji Monogatari (The Tale of Genji)* into modern Japanese. Just before the war, he started writing his well-known novel, *Sasameyuki (The Makioka Sisters,* 1948, translated by Seidensticker, Edward, New York, A. Knopf, 1958; Tokyo, Tuttle, 1958). He completed it after the war. This novel, which depicts the fate of the four daughters of an old family of Senba, Ôsaka, was very highly praised upon its appearance. It attracted attention by depicting the charming traditions and climate of the Kansai District, which has moulded the beautiful language this novel uses. Then he published *Shôshô Shigemoto no Haha* (*The Mother of Captain Shigemoto*, 1950, translated by Seidensticker, E. G., *Modern Japanese Literature*, pp. 387–397, New York, Grove Press, 1956; Tokyo, Tuttle, 1957). The main works he published after that are *Kagi* (*The Key*, 1956, translated by Hibbett, Howard, New York, A. Knopf, 1961) and *Fûten Rôjin Nikki* (*Diary of a Mad Old Man*, 1962, translated by Hibbett, Howard, New York, A. Knopf, 1965). He died three years after the publication of the latter work. In this essay, which deals with the period after 1956, we shall concentrate on the two works just mentioned.

The hero of *Kagi* (*The Key*) is a fifty-six-year-old university teacher. His wife, Ikuko, is forty-five years old. They have a daughter, Toshiko. A young man called Kimura, who seeks Toshiko's hand in marriage, is the other main character of the novel. Although the hero is a university teacher, he is not bothered by the self-conscious scruples and doubts about himself quite common among intellectuals. His attention is wholly focused on how to satisfy his sexual desires. He wants to transform his wife into a sexually mature, passionate woman and enjoy love-making to the full. He jots this down in his diary. He deliberately drops the key of the drawer in which he has placed his diary in a conspicuous place so that his wife comes to read his diary. Ikuko, his wife, writes in her diary that she is willing to comply with her husband's wish. Each of them tacitly expects, that the other reads his or her diary, and so the novel progresses. Then the hero notices that Kimura is more attracted by his wife than by Toshiko, his daughter. He deliberately creates an opportunity for Kimura to be alone with his wife. This is because he wants to stimulate his own sexual appetite. His wife persuades herself that to comply with the tacit demand of her husband is the proper thing for an obedient wife to do, and she sleeps with Kimura. However, then she really comes to be charmed by Kimura. The hero's sexual excitement is heightened by this, until he finally dies of apoplexy. At the end of the novel the wife writes, "I admit that

I have inherited a lewd nature, but I did not know that a wicked heart which wished even the death of a husband had been hiding within me". She consoles herself by thinking that, since her adultery was committed out of obedience to her husband, he spent his life happily in the way he wanted.

In this novel, sex is depicted as something about which a human being cannot do anything, in other words, as a sort of karma which inevitably realizes itself. This shows one basic element in Tanizaki's understanding of human nature. The estimation of Tanizaki as "an artist without thought" made by Satô Haruo in 1924 is not entirely just. The problem of sex is also dealt with in *Fûten Rôjin Nikki* (*Diary of a Mad Old Man*), Tanizaki's last masterpiece.

The hero of *Fûten Rôjin Nikki* (*Diary of a Mad Old Man*) is an old man who is seventy-seven years old. He is living with his wife, his son and the wife of his son. He feels something like love towards Satsuko, his daughter-in-law. He buys her a ring which costs three million yen, but when his married daughter comes to borrow money from him, he casually dismisses her without committing himself to anything. The main part of the novel takes the form of this old man's diary, which is supplemented by the notes of his nurse, his doctor and his daughter-in-law covering the period during which he can no longer write. In *Kagi* (*The Key*), the diaries of the couple had the function of stimulating each other's sexual passion under a mutual tacit understanding. The old man's diary in this novel does not have such a function. It is simply the record of the old man's thoughts and feelings. From it, we find that, despite his age, he has a very lively sexual curiosity. He is quite absorbed in trying to get sexual satisfaction on a mental level. He is threatened by the shadow of death which cannot be so far away. His sexual longing makes him entertain the idea of making a rubbing of Satsuko's foot. When Satsuko asks him, "What is the rubbing of my foot supposed to do?", the old man says that using the rubbing he will engrave her footprint in stone, like the footprint of Buddha at Yakushi-ji temple in Nara, and that when he dies his bones will be buried under the stone. The sexual fancy of the old man, who has lost the physical ability to make love, leads him to fetishism, to the adoration of the foot of his daughter-in-law. This is more surprising in its extremeness than the death as the result of indulgence in sexual pleasure in Tanizaki's previous novel, *Kagi* (*The Key*). We notice that, in his last two novels, sex and death are closely connected, and that their union is the logical development of Tanizaki's sense of beauty. As Mr. Yamamoto Kenkichi has pointed out, it is significant in this connection that the old man's longing for the beautiful body of his daughter-in-law comes to the surface in his reminiscences of his mother. His yearning for his mother and his love for Satsuko become one in the short time he has left before death, and this creates a connection between sex and death. We are reminded here of Tanizaki's other works; for example, *Haha o Kouru Ki* (*Longing for Mother*, 1919), *Yoshinokuzu* (*Yoshino Arrowroot*), *Yume no Ukihashi* (*The Bridge of Dreams*, 1960, translated by Hibbett, Howard and published in *Seven Japanese Tales*, London, Secker and Warburg, 1964), in which the *motif* of love of one's young mother clearly appears. It is a sort of return to the maternal.

Tanizaki is not merely a sensuous writer—"an artist without thought"—as is commonly believed. Towards the end of his life, Tanizaki went beyond mere sensation and made sex and death the central issue of his thought. At any rate, Tanizaki, whose literary career from 1910 to 1965 was from the beginning to the end a productive one, is an exceptional writer, who continuously sought to extend his literary range and the depth of his treatments.

Tonomura Shigeru

Tonomura Shigeru was born in 1902 in Shiga Prefecture. He graduated from the Department of Economics of Tokyo University. He came from a rich merchant family, and after the death of his father, he took over the family business for a while. However, he soon realized that he was not suited to the job, and became a novelist as he had aspired to be from his student days.

At that time Proletarian Literature was on the ebb. He felt he did not share the ideas of the "Proletarian School", but he took up a *motif* of Proletarian Literature in his *U no Monogatari (The Cormorant Story, 1933)* and depicted the misery of a salesman who is exploited for the profit of the capitalists. However, the techniques he used in this novel were that of *Shinkô Geijutsu-ha* (The Neo-Artistic School) which was opposed to Proletarian Literature. Through this novel, he won recognition as a young writer dealing with social problems.

Then he completed a long novel called *Kusa Ikada (Grass Raft, 1935–39)* and this established him as a writer. This novel together with *Ikada (Raft, 1954–56)*, and *Hana Ikada (Flower Raft, 1957–58)*, form a lengthy trilogy which depicts the life of the Tonomura family through several generations. This trilogy is Tonomura's life work. It took him twenty-three years to complete it. These novels closely pursue the historical process of how a family of merchants becomes decadent as it rises in prosperity. The author shows an immediate concern for this process, because he himself is a descendant of such a family. At the same time, the novels have a social dimension, throwing light on the feudalistic structure of a family-owned shop with its inhumaneness and irrationality. The author is repelled by the ugliness of such an organization, and he longs for what is pure and beautiful. Such an attitude shows itself in his empathy or sympathy with women and children who are tyrannized and powerless within the rigid family system peculiar to the merchant class. His sympathy for them gives a lyrical atmosphere to these books.

From about the time he wrote *Kusa Ikada (Grass Raft, 1938)*, Tonomura showed a predominant interest in the exploration of his inner self. He gradually became a writer of typical "I" novels which deal with one's sexual passion or family life without relating them to social or economic conditions.

Miotsukushi (Waterway Signal, 1960), summarized below, is Tonomura's representative "I" novel which depicts the history of his love and sex life from his childhood to his later years. For Tonomura, sex was a subject which he could not avoid as long as he wanted to examine the source of human sinfulness. In this novel, he writes about the history of sex and love of a man straightforwardly and with decency. His novel *Nurenizo Nureshi* (*My Love Affairs*, 1961) deals with the same theme in a more detailed manner. However, shortly before its completion, he died of a tumor of the upper jaw at the age of fifty-nine. *Rakujitsu no Kôkei* (*View of the Setting Sun*, 1960) and *Hi o Itoshimu* (*I Love Sunrise*, 1961) written shortly before his death are beautiful "I" novels which impressively express religious resignation and the love of life of a man who faces death.

Tonomura is a peculiarly Japanese writer, who kept producing autobiographical novels about his family and his private life, using his experiences as raw material. At the root of Tonomura's work are his revolt against prevailing materialism, decadence and lasciviousness, and his moving longing for purity.

TONOMURA Shigeru
Miotsukushi *(Waterway signal)*
Published in *Gunzô*, July 1960.

(**Synopsis**) I, Shinmura Susumu, was born as the third son of Shinmura Ichitarô, a rich merchant of Gokashô-machi, Shiga Prefecture. I was a pale fragile child, and when I was very small, I was terribly afraid of ghosts, ogres and dead bodies. I saw a half naked woman in the drawing of the Buddhist hell in my neighbourhood temple. I became aware of female sexual power for the first time in this woman, and I was scared. I entered the primary school when I was eight years old. When I was in the second year of primary school, Kane, one of our maids, gave birth to a dead child in the shed. I was puzzled to see that my mother was scolding a male employee for this, and asked Toyo, another maid, why she did that. Toyo was embarrassed. I was aware of the fact of copulation because I had seen cocks and pigeons at it, but I could not imagine that human beings had anything to do with such a thing.

While Tatsu, our new maid, and I were playing together by tickling each other, I learned that to have physical contact with a woman was pleasant. I felt shame and sorrow, looking at the underwear of the maids hanging outside. Once I found that somebody had written on the wall that I was the special friend of a certain girl, and suddenly I became quite conscious of the girl. I grew up, feeling a certain longing and shyness towards women.

When I was fourteen years old, I entered Seze Middle School. My body gradually became masculine, but my inborn feminine passivity of character did not harmonize with my masculine body very well. I felt depressed. It was during these unhappy days that I learned to masturbate. When I was twenty years old, I entered the Third Higher School in Kyoto. I began to feel lonely. This was not so much because of the absence of a woman I could fall in love with, but because of my inner emptiness which did not give me the power to love another person. I diverted myself by drinking wine at a café and by joining the drama society at school. I also often talked with friends who loved literature as much as I did. I read many novels and plays. I was deeply impressed by Kurata Hyakuzô's play *Shukke to Sono Deshi* (*The Priest and his Disciples*). I also read *Tannishô* (a collection of Shinran's teachings) by Shinran (1173–1262) whom Kurata made the hero of his play, and I was very much attracted by Shinran's Buddhist thought which accepted men as they were with their inborn sinfulness, and preached religious salvation to them.

When I was twenty-two, I was examined for conscription. I was told that my sex organs were slightly abnormal, and felt deeply humiliated. In the summer of the same year, I took a trip to a mountain resort, and saw the naked bodies of young girls in the bathhouse of a mountain hotspring resort. I was fascinated by the beautiful soft lines of their bodies and by the beauty of their well-shaped symmetrical breasts. I felt deeply happy.

To get rid of my youthful depression, I frequented a café at Gionshita, Kyoto, with my friends. One day, a seventeen year old hostess of the café came to my lodgings after quarreling with the owner of the shop. I was obliged to sleep in the same room with her, but we did not go beyond taking each other's hand. I had already been feeling that my days in Kyoto were over, since I was soon entering Tokyo University.

In May of that year, I met Tokuko at a café in Roppongi, Tokyo, where she was working. I immediately felt that she was the woman for me. I took a trip with her. I kissed her in the midst of a thick mountain fog. When we came back to Tokyo, I slept with her at her place. After that we became man and wife in our eyes, and I loved Tokuko passionately. When I was twenty-five years old, she bore our eldest son. The next year my father died, and I took over his business. By the time I became thirty years old, Tokuko had given birth to two boys. On my 30th birthday, as a part of the celebrations, I entered Tokuko and our three children in the family register. After that, my fourth son and first daughter were born. However, when my wife became pregnant for the sixth time, she had to have an abortion on account of poor health. The war worsened, and not only our sexual life but our whole life became empty. In 1948, despite my affectionate nursing, my wife died of softening of the brain. She was forty years old.

The next year when I became forty-eight, I came to know Sadako who was thirty-nine, and I married her. I was still lamenting the loss of my first wife, and yet I found myself passionately loving my new wife. I felt the helplessness of man before the passion of love. I realized that everything in life was transient as Buddhism teaches. I felt the melancholy of love and wondered at Nature. Stimulated by Sadako's buxom body, my sexual appetite was roused again.

When I was fifty-six years old, I was hospitalized for a tumor of the upper jaw and received radiotherapy. My life was saved, but I became sexually impotent. Since I loved my wife, I felt sorry for her. When I was fifty-nine, she got breast cancer. It was fairly bad. She was to receive an operation at one hospital, and to receive radioactive cobalt therapy at another hospital. After my wife's operation, I saw the lamp of flesh which had been cut off from her breast. I thought that my sexual life had come to a final end. However, one morning, about the time my wife had just been moved to the other hospital, I woke up to find that my sexual ability had been restored.

Umezaki Haruo

Umezaki Haruo was born in 1915 in Fukuoka Prefecture. His father was a professional soldier and Umezaki was brought up in a strict family. He, however, read literary works from his childhood. He entered the Fifth Higher School in Kumamoto. Among his classmates was Shimota Shôji who was to be active as a leftwing writer in the postwar period. Stimulated by Shimota and others, Umezaki published poems in the alumni magazine, *Ryûnan,* and also published novels like *Asu* (*Tomorrow*) in a private circulation magazine *Roberisuku* (*L'obelisque*). He had, however, no intention of becoming a professional writer. He was thinking of becoming an ordinary salaried man. In 1936, at Shimota's suggestion, Umezaki entered the Department of Japanese Literature of Tokyo University, where he started the literary group magazine *Kikôchi* (*Port of Call*) and published *Chizu* (*Map,* 1936) in it. He did not change his original idea of becoming a salaried man. Obsessed by youthful gloomy ideas, he seldom went to classes. It was after publishing *Fûen* (*Feast of the Wind,* 1939), an attempt to get rid of neurotic ideas and to recover himself, that he began to aspire to be a writer. In this work, Umezaki made a detailed sketch of the psychology of decadent students. He had discovered his own subtle poetic method of depicting the abysses of human psychology. Then, unfortunately, the war broke out. He was drafted into military service, and stationed at various Navy bases in Kyûshû as a signal soldier. Immediately after the War, in 1945, Umezaki, who had received deep psychological scars during the war started writing novels again. In 1946 he published *Sakurajima* (*Sakurajima*). This novel depicts "I", a signal soldier, stationed at the communication base in Sakurajima. The psychology of "I" who feels the presence of death near him is very vividly described, and this work attracted attention. After publishing *Hi no Hate* (*The End of the Day,* 1947) and *Runeta no Shiminhei* (*The Civilian Soldiers of Luneta,* 1949), both of which deal with human psychology in a battle field, his high reputation was firmly established. He came to be regarded as a representative postwar writer who had created something new in war literature. He also published works dealing with the chaotic society of the postwar period. Among them are *Aru Tenmatsu* (*The Circumstances around a Certain Event*, 1947), *Ue no Kisetsu* (*Season of Hunger*, 1948), and *Boroya no Shunjû* (*Seasons in a Shack*, 1954) which skillfully caricatures the nothingness of human life. *Genka* (*Hallucination*, 1965), summarized below, is an ambitious work intended by the author as the culmination of his literary career. Umezaki's works are based on the techniques of the traditional Japanese "I" novel, and contain an intense nihilistic beauty. He died suddenly in 1965 at the early age of fifty leaving a great achievement behind him.

UMEZAKI Haruo
Genka *(Hallucination)*
Published in *Shinchô*, June 1965.

(**Synopsis**) When the retreating figure of Nio had finally disappeared, Gorô turned around, went to a wine-shop and bought a small bottle and paper cups. This was a precaution against a fit that might occur on the way. He felt that somebody was pursuing him. Before he had entered the hospital, he had always felt like that whenever he went out, and he would look back many times as he walked. This time, the feeling of being pursued was not so strong, but all the same it was there. Suddenly the field of his vision enlarged. Down below on the left side was the sea which was incredibly blue. A sweet sensation ran through Gorô's body. In the summer of twenty years ago, Gorô had walked from Bônotsu to Makurazaku. The Naval base at Bônotsu had been disbanded on about the 20th of August. Gorô was at that time only twenty-five years old, and he was vigorous and energetic. When he had arrived at this ridge, suddenly the sea had come into sight, and for the first time he had felt a strong sense of freedom as if his body was expanding infinitely. "How is it that I lost the memory of this place, and that experience of archetypal ecstasy? Perhaps I did not. It was simply at the bottom of my consciousness", he reflected. He had not decided to go to Bônotsu while drinking coffee that morning in the hospital on a sudden impulse. For a long time what was at the bottom of his consciousness had been inducing him to go. Now Gorô understood his unconscious, buried impulse. He finished the saké in the cup and started walking. He sang a war song in a low voice. It was a lance corporal called Fuku who had invented new satirical words for the song; he died a few days later.

Gorô saw a tree which looked like a tropical tree. He had forgotten its name, but he was sure that he had seen it before. Its flowers were drooping down, and they looked as if they were the flowers of Hades in the twilight.

He heard a voice. He noticed a woman standing with a fan in her hand. She appeared to be cooling herself. "What are you doing?", she asked. "Well, sort of sightseeing", Gorô answered. Gorô pointed in the direction of the bay, and asked, "What was the name of that rock?" "Sôkenseki", she answered. "Do you remember that there was a sailor who was drowned in this bay towards the end of the war?" Gorô explained that Fuku had got drunk with him here and had then tried to swim to the rock, Sôkenseki. "It was then that he was drowned", he continued. "Did you feel responsible?", the woman asked in a coquettish voice. "We are like passengers in the same train. Responsible? Well, no . . . although I have a feeling of solidarity with others. But to be honest, even that feeling of solidarity has been disappearing. . . . To forget the loneliness, I drank and gambled, but it was no good. At last I entered a hospital to get treatment. My body smells of medicine, doesn't it? I was in the hospital until this morning". So saying, Gorô drew the woman close and pressed her against his body with considerable force. "Now I want to cling to something", Gorô murmured. It was not wholly a lie. He pressed her harder against his body.

At the Mt. Aso terminal bus stop, he met Nio again. Nio smelt strongly of saké. (He had told Gorô that he had lost his wife and children in a traffic accident a month ago and had been drowning his sorrows in alcohol since then.) "So, we meet again!", Gorô greeted him. "Are you still alive?", Nio answered. Gorô felt like returning the same question to Nio, but he stopped. The crater-wall was very steep. In some places, it was almost vertical. The crater-basin was far down below and Gorô felt dizzy looking down into it. Since there was no wind, the white steam was rising straight upward. He could also see lava seething below. Nio said as if to himself, "This is an ideal place to commit suicide". Gorô kept silent. "Why is it that this man connects suicide with me?", he wondered. From the time they had boarded the plane at Haneda, Nio had been convinced that Gorô was going to commit suicide. Gorô had told him many times that it was a misunderstanding on Nio's part, but Nio would not believe him. "Let's bet!", Nio said suddenly. Nio wanted to bet whether Gorô would throw himself into the crater by the time Nio had completed walking around it. Nio started walking. His back became smaller and smaller. Gorô's heart started beating violently. Hastily he threw away his lunch packet and swallowed the saké in the small bottle. From the place Gorô stood, Nio was now a tiny dot. Suddenly he stopped. He seemed to be looking into the crater. He started walking again. In his heart, Gorô shouted: "Walk decently, you bastard!" Of course it did not reach Nio's ears. He stopped again, and looked into the crater. . . . He started walking again. . . .

Uno Chiyo

Uno Chiyo was born in 1897 in Yamaguchi Prefecture. Her family was an old family who had been brewers for generations. Uno was the eldest daughter. She lost her mother in her early childhood, and thus could not enjoy a happy family life. After graduation from Iwakuni Girls' High School, she started a life of wandering, earning her living as an assistant teacher and so on. Her interest in literature was deepened around 1917 when she became acquainted with Akutagawa Ryûnosuke and others during her wandering life. At that time she also started entering her works in the novel competition held by the Yorozu Newspaper Company. These novels are based on memories of her gloomy childhood. *Haka o Abaku*

(*Exhuming a Tomb*, 1922) depicts oppressed human beings, using Uno's own childhood family background. It brings out the author's sensitive girlhood in full relief. Her autobiographical "I" novel, *Tsuisô no Chichi* (*Reminiscences of my Father*, 1923) is one of her representative early works. Thus Uno started her literary career by writing naturalistic novels and autobiographical "I" novels. The tenor of her writing, however, changed gradually, and she came to depict mainly the mode of life of women around the 1930's, aiming to shed light on subtle nuances of the psychology of people in love. *Iro Zange* (*Confessions of an Amorous Life*, 1933) is the work which marked the turning point. It depicts in great detail the psychology of love and passion. It reflects Uno's own bold amorous experiences. After this, she gradually grasped the proper themes of her writings and appropriate techniques, and perfected her unique narrative novels. In her exquisite style she depicted different individualities three-dimensionally, and published works like *Koi no Tegami* (*A Love Letter*, 1938) and *Ningyôshi Tenguya Hisakichi* (*Tenguya Hisakichi, a Puppet-maker*, 1942). The work which shows probably Uno's highest attainment so far is *Ohan*, (translated by Donald Keene, *The Old Woman, the Wife, and the Archer*, pp. 51–118, New York, Viking, 1961), summarized below. This novel depicts, in a subtle narrative style reminiscent of 'jôruri' masterpieces, a man who is at the mercy of his own sexual desires.

Uno who has the memories of her gloomy childhood somewhere in the background, depicts the subtle psychology of women boldly, and brings out the weakness and wantonness of human beings in full relief. Her novels attain the level of delicate French psychological novels. Among her other works are *Sasu* (*Sting*, 1966) and *Kaze no Oto* (*Sound of the Winds*, 1969). At the age of seventy-four, she is still vigorously writing, and maintains the position of an active writer.

Uno Chiyo
Ohan *(Ohan)*
Published in *Chûô Kôron,* June–December 1950 and April–May, 1957.

(Synopsis) One evening when the *Bon* Festival was near at hand, I passed by a woman wearing a white bathrobe on Garyû Bridge. It was my former wife, Ohan. "Isn't it Ohan? How are you? It's a long while since we saw each other last", I said. Ohan was not a particularly attractive woman, but she had a fine complexion. I asked her about my child. It was a boy called Satoru, and Ohan was with him when we had to separate. I just did not want to offend her, so I said, "Why don't come to see me sometime?" without reflecting on its possible consequences. After that, for a while, I was secretly looking forward to seeing Ohan. The summer festival at Gion was over, but Ohan had not yet come. It looked as if she had decided not to. At that time I was still living with Okayo in her house. Okayo was running a geisha house. During the day I ran a shop under the eaves of a certain house and sold secondhand articles. One evening I asked Okayo, "Don't you feel any remorse for depriving a woman of her husband to live with me?" Okayo nonchalantly answered, "No, not at all." One afternoon, roughly two weeks later, I noticed that Ohan was standing behind the stone-lantern in front of my shop. "Ohan! Isn't it Ohan?", I called to her. She looked as if she would run away at any moment. I asked her to come into the house behind the shop. In the semi-darkness of the room, Ohan's face looked conspicuously white. As I remembered how we had separated seven years before, both of us in tears, I felt tenderness for her again and unawares took her hand. I embraced her chubby body. Ohan protested only faintly, and started crying. After that, Ohan would come to the shop at least once every ten days. As we repeated our secret rendezvous, I became loath to lose her. One day, a little boy came to the shop and said, "Uncle, don't you have any balls?" When I answered that I didn't, the boy, looking a little shy, ran away. His figure somehow moved me deeply. I wondered if he was not my son whom I had not seen for seven years, although we were living in the same town. When Ohan came, I told her the event of the day. She said that it must be him, and wept. The next day, I bought a ball and gave it to Satoru in a casual manner. After that, without knowing that I was his father, Satoru would often come to the shop and announce, "Uncle, I have come." Okayo wanted to adopt her sister's daughter, Osen. I was, however, bursting with the desire to hear the word "Father!" from my own child. One day, I hastily said to Ohan, hugging her shoulder, "I have made up my mind to marry you again." "What did you say?", Ohan said in surprise, and suddenly started crying, pressing her head against my chest. But while yet the words were fresh from my mouth, I found myself making love to Okayo. One day shortly afterwards, Okayo came back with Osen, her sister's daughter. Osen called me "Father" without any hesitation. After promising Ohan to marry her again, I had been still living with Okayo for four months before I found a suitable house to start a new life with Ohan. It was the day after the Festival of the Weaver. Ohan said, "I am so glad", and wet the sleeves of her *kimono* with tears. That evening I made love to Ohan secretly in that house. "Did Okayo really consent to your moving here to live with me?", Ohan asked. "Yes, she did", I answered firmly in spite of myself. After that, however, torn between two women I made myself a shameful spectacle every day. One day when there was a shower Satoru came, naked and completely wet. He said to me, "Uncle, you are a big liar. You have promised to come to fetch us soon, but you haven't." His words pierced my heart. I said, "I am going to decide on which day we are moving to the new house now" and took out a calendar. I decided to move on the 13th of September. When I announced this, Satoru looked very pleased, and went back. And that was the last time I saw him alive. On the day we moved to the new house, it rained heavily, and Satoru slipped on the bank of Ryûkô River, fell into it and died. It was as if I had chosen that day of heavy rain as the day of moving to kill this child. I felt aghast. Ohan disappeared, leaving a letter saying, "I am the happiest woman in the world." I became more than ever dependent on Osen's childlike voice and on Okayo's warm body.

Yamakawa Masao

Yamakawa Masao was born on the 25th of February, 1930. His real name is Yamakawa Yoshimi. After graduating from the Department of French Literature of Keiô University, he became editor of the magazine *Mita Bungaku* (*Mita Literature*). He also wrote novels, and published two collections of short novels, *Kaigan Kôen* (*Seaside Park*, 1961) and *Ai no Gotoku* (*Like Love*, 1965). He experienced the war when he was entering adolescence, a stage when his personality was still being formed. With a penetrating nihilism, characteristic of a person who has come to feel the weight of death in human life while still quite young, and with a concise style, he expresses his experiences and thoughts in short novels which indicate his sensitivity and lyrical predilection.

Yamakawa calls the blue summer sky which he saw on the day of Japan's surrender "the beautiful transparent blue sky". Yamakawa continued, "Our ideals are dead; that blue sky is now the grave of my old self". That he connected the image of a blue sky with the grave shows the obsession of his generation with death. In Yamakawa's *Saisho no Aki* (*The First Autumn*, 1964), the hero, "I", says that he is no longer young. From his words we sense premature aging or tiredness on the part of the author. The words we find in his *Ai no Gotoku* (*Like Love*) express a similar sentiment: ',There is no longer love, madness or children's season. Neither is there any dream nor any stability. . . . What is left is only an eventless routine of lonely life and the same family responsibility—a mediocre windy dusty path full of humiliation and anger". We can also understand the clear-headed regretful realization of the hero "I", of *Tenbôdai no Aru Shima* (*An Island with an Observation Platform*), that love which he has been trying to avoid is already born, in a similar light. Such sentiment is not Yamakawa's monopoly. It may be shared by all the writers of his generation. In any case, Yamakawa is a writer who has persistently tried to evaluate his boyhood experience of war. During the war, boys, including

Yamakawa, were taught how to die rather than how to live. The spiritual vacuum they experienced at the surrender of Japan was like a momentary death of their souls. It took time before they could make up their minds to live again. These young people who had already experienced death in anticipation very often showed a premature aging and tiredness with life. Yamakawa Masao managed in his short life of thirty-five years to express this experience of his generotion [in refined lyrical works full of purified sorrow. In his works we find every aspect of youth. However, behind them, is a clear awareness rather than the confused consciousness characteristic of youth. We can see in this the peculiarity and misfortune of Yamakawa who was not allowed to enjoy his youth. Yamakawa was killed in a traffic accident on the 20th of February 1965.

YAMAKAWA Masao
Tenbôdai no aru shima
(An island with an observation platform)
Published in *Shinchô*, February 1965.

(Synopsis) One autumn afternoon I visited Shônan Coast with my fiancée. After going to an aquarium, we crossed a concrete bridge and went to an island. The island formed a fairly high rocky hill. We used an escalator, and went to the observation platform on the top of the hill. Because it was not summer, the place was empty. We cast our eyes in the direction of the coast from there. The Ninomiya Coast where I had once lived as an evacuee was visible. When we married, we would live there. Standing on the observation platform, I felt as if I were watching my past and future from there. It seemed to me that we two were standing on time present which was cut off and isolated from time past as well as from time future. I felt that love which I had carefully avoided had been born.

We walked down the rocky hill. I noticed that my fiancée looked tired. I suddenly realized that I was also tired. Solicited by a barker, we entered an old inn. I had not even kissed my fiancée. It was my principle not to do such a thing until we married. Before I realized it, however, I was holding her in my arms and was kissing her passionately. Through a glass door, the dark evening sea was visible. On the glass door was reflected the image of us embracing each other. Usually such an image would have disgusted me. But somehow I thought then that my figure mirrored on the glass door was beautiful. Roughly in two hours' time, we left the inn. After crossing over the bridge, I looked around. A round moon was shining over the island, and a big peculiar-shaped cloud, which fishermen believe augurs a good catch of sardines, was floating slowly in the night sky. The dark silhouette of the island loomed beyond the bridge illuminated by street-lamps, and only lights from souvenir-shops and neon signs of inns were shining on the dark island.

Yashiro Seiichi

Yashiro Seiichi was born in 1927 in Ginza, Tokyo. He graduated from the Department of French Literature of Waseda University in 1950. While he was a student, he joined the Haiyû Za (Actor's Theatre) Troupe as a member of its literary department. His original intention was to be a producer. He started, however, to publish his dramatic studies in the magazine *Kindai Bungaku* (*Modern Literature*) and also to translate plays by Anouilh and others. At the end of 1949, he left the Haiyû Za (Actor's Theatre) Troupe and joined the Bungaku Za Troupe. In 1950, after publishing *Hataraki-bachi* (*A Worker Bee*), he caught a chest disease and had to spend more than a year in the hospital. In December 1952 his play *Kitsunetsuki* (*Possessed by a Fox*), which took its theme from a novel by Nakajima Atsushi, was staged. This was the first time that a play of his had been staged. His next work *Shiro* (*Castle*, 1954) won him a reputation as a talented playwright.

Around that time, the possibility of verse drama in Japanese was being debated enthusiastically. Yashiro's *Shiro* (*Castle*) and *Uta* (*Songs*), which were inspired by the plays of Giraudoux and Anouilh, had a rich poetic imagery and wild imaginativeness which was greatly appreciated. Yashiro's "verse drama" was welcomed and he was praised for the solidness of the speeches in his plays. However, his most successful plays have probably been those which use a traditional play or popular legend as their basic and express the feelings of young postwar intellectuals. *Esugata Nyôbô* (*Portrait of Wife*) and *Kokusenya* (the name of the son of a Chinese refugee to Japan who tried to restore the Ming Dynasty) are two examples of this type of play. They were written between 1955 and 1959 and staged by the Seinen Za Troupe. The former is based on a folk-tale called *Zô to Kanzashi* (*The Elephant and the Hairpin*) and parodies *Tenpô Rokkasen* (a story written by Shôrin Hakuen, 1831–1905).

Yashiro next wrote a nostalgic play called *Kiiro to Momoiro no Yûgata* (*Pink and Yellow Evenings*), again influenced by Anouilh. His *Chizu no Nai Tabi* (*A Journey without a Map*) is a cynical comedy. In *Kuro no Higeki* (*Black Tragedy*) Yashiro depicted a story of friendship and betrayal during the war and postwar periods, and described the postwar intellectual climate as one in which real spiritual freedom is not achieved. After writing such deep plays, he wrote *Yûkai* (*Kidnaping,* 1965), a cheerful and entertaining play. *Yoake ni Kieta* (*Gone with the Dawn*), summarized below, imitates the form of a biblical drama, and deals with the theme of discovery of one's faith and the meaning of life. About this time Yashiro also wrote *Miyagino* (*Miyagino Field*) and *Ten'ichibô Shichijû Ban* (*Ten'ichibô, the Impostor*) and expressed his belief in the importance of everyday sincerity through the absolute love prostitutes and farmers' sons have towards their childhood.

YASHIRO Seiichi
Yoake ni kieta *(Gone with the dawn)*
Published in *Shingeki,* September 1968.

(Synopsis) When the curtain rises, the producer comes onto the stage and says that a friend of his nicknamed 'Beanpole' suddenly disappeared one day. He says that Beanpole was a promising young couturier and designer who had returned from the interior of Manchuria after the war and who had been to the same primary school as himself.

Then a fashion model comes on stage. He says that Mr. Beanpole had many affairs with women, liked gambling and was a great drinker. He adds that several days before his disappearance, he stated that he had eaten human flesh during the war. The producer says that Beanpole has recently sent a drama to him and that at the end of the drama was written "At Jerusalem". Then on the stage this drama of Beanpole is produced, interspersed with scenes in which the producer does some investigations into the life and thought of Beanpole.

The play is set in a cave in Mt. Olive near the Dead Sea, and deals with a period of several years, after the crucifixion of Christ. Coward and his sister, Miser, are in the cave. They are robbers. Laggard, the daughter of a commander under Pilate, arrives. She is followed by Bear, a despised slave from an outcast community. Then Lark, a prostitute, and Beanpole, a dandy, also arrive. Laggard, who is a pious Christian, has been told by God to marry a man she meets in this cave. Following what she believes in God's will, Laggard marries the nihilist Beanpole, the stray sheep in the flock of a hundred, who is said to have eaten human flesh.

In due course, Laggard gives birth to a baby by Beanpole, but this baby is thrown into the river and drowned by a girl, who has been raped by Beanpole. She has done this out of revenge. Laggard laments the baby's death, but Beanpole is unmoved. He tells Laggard that he intensely dislikes her pious looks. He also says that the reason why he has married Laggard is that he wanted to live idly and in luxury under the protection of Pilate. Laggard never attacks Beanpole. Bear, however, is indignant with him, and says that Christians are suffering a lot because of him. Laggard tells Bear that she has heard that people from an outcast community have defiled themselves by drinking the live blood of poisonous snakes and that if other people touch them they will also be defiled and their bodies will rot. She adds that she does not believe it at all, and says that Bear can hug her as proof. Bear is very pleased, and hugs her, but soon she thrusts him away. Bear feels really hurt. He renounces his faith, and betrays Christians to the authorities of Rome.

Many Christians have been burnt to death. It becomes beautiful Laggard's turn to be burnt. She has behaved very nobly and has been encouraging others to pray, but when she is placed above the burning wood, she soon starts screaming, "Stop! Help!". Hearing her voice, Bear triumphs. Beanpole, who has been watching the scene without knowing what to do, says that Laggard's body has not been wounded so much as her soul. He also says, "Since God is omnipotent and omniscient, he will save Laggard. I am now becoming meek. If I become a Christian, the others will laugh at me". He leaves.

Beanpole meets a blind haggard old woman at the place of the recent martyrdom of Christians. Upon her request, he reads, as a substitute for Laggard, a passage from the gospels. The passage is that in which Jesus tells Peter in the courtyard that he will deny him three times before the cocks crow. Beanpole murmurs, "Why do I like this story so much?"

Bear has become a man who finds his meaning in life in persecuting Christians. He holds a feast with Miser and Lark. He invites Beanpole to this feast, and tells him that Coward is dying and that he is hoping to go to paradise. Bear asks Beanpole if he can visit Coward and tell him about God. This is just to catch Beanpole out, but Coward has already been approached by a woman in rags who looks like an aged beggar. She will not leave Coward alone, recommending him to be a real Christian.

The woman is Laggard. Although Beanpole cannot recognize her at first, Bear notices it immediately and says that Laggard has not given up her faith. Then Bear congratulates Beanpole, saying that he is a lucky man. Beanpole says that he is really lucky. Laggard tells Beanpole that she loves him. She also wants him to continue his earthly existence without faith rather than be caught as a Christian by Bear and die a martyr's death. Beanpole says that when a little one or a baby is about to be killed before your eyes, you come to face the Absolute. "Lord, damn me, who am without love, to hell so that people may see the importance of love," He carries Laggard on his back, and as Bear commands, he walks with Laggard into the sea in the dawn and disappears. Here the play within a play ends.

As a hymn is sung gently, the producer appears on the stage and says that although Beanpole and his wife, Laggard, are in actual life still missing, he is no longer so worried about them.

Yasuoka Shotaro

Yasuoka Shôtarô is one of the writers making up the "daisan no shinjin" (Third New Generation) group, a group of writers comprising Yoshiyuki Junnosuke, Kojima Nobuo, Shôno Junzô, Endô Shûsaku and others who established themselves as writers around 1955. Yasuoka was born in 1920, and was old enough to be drafted into the army during the war. He was sent to North Manchuria. However, he became ill and returned to Japan. In Japan, he started writing novels on his sick-bed, afflicted by poverty and illness. In 1953, he was awarded the Akutagawa Prize for *Inkina Tanoshimi* (*Gloomy Pastime*) and *Warui Nakama* (*Evil Companions*). Yasuoka's generation was too young to be influenced by Marxism or other ideologies of the prewar period. This made the "daisan no shinjin" ("Third New Generation") writers different from many of the "dai-ichiji sengo-ha" ("First Postwar Group"), writers and critics who had been influenced by Marxism in the prewar period. People like Yasuoka wanted to live realistically, relying on their common-sense, during the hard days of the postwar period. They all dislike "ideologies" and "uniforms". On the other hand, no matter how hard-pressed by harsh circumstances, and despite their nihilistic outlook, they are not easily defeated, unlike Dazai Osamu who committed suicide. Although they are masochistic, they show resilience to an unexpected extent. At the same time, behind Yasuoka's works is an inferiority complex, and he regards himself as a social misfit.

Tonsô (*Flight*) reflects Yasuoka's experience in the army. The hero of *Tonsô* is a man called Yasugi Kasuke. The story depicts, with humour and with some masochism, his way of living in the army and in the hospital.

Unlike Noma Hiroshi's *Shinkû-Chitai* (*Vacuum Zone*), a voice of protest is not raised against the inhumanity of army life. Even one's own sufferings are looked at, somewhat masochistically, in a detached manner. The author sees in such physiological phenomena as appetite and diarrhoea, fit symbols for the way a man like Yasugi lives.

The hero of *Shitadashi-tenshi* (*An Angel Who Sticks out Her Tongue*) is a translator, of suicidal disposition. He lives at the house of his elder brother as a dependent, and has an affair with his sister-in-law. He is also cornered by a show of deep affection from a woman older than himself. He tries to run away but is caught by her. After such experiences, he comes to love Yôko, a young bar hostess working in Ginza. However, he is tormented by self-disgust, thinking that he is a useless man. He feels that only an abysmal despair lies in store for him. Yôko does not love him as much as he loves her. Burdened by debt, and leading a chaotic life, finally he climbs Mt. Yatsugatake and dies in the snow. This novel is said to have been inspired by one of Yasuoka's friends, a talented critic who committed suicide; however, this could not have been more than one of the many impetuses which drove Yasuoka to write this novel. The novel is a logical development of Yasuoka's sense of being a social failure.

Kaihen no Kôkei (*View of the Bay*, 1959, translated by Ackroyd, Joyce and Hiramatsu, Mikio, in *Hemisphere*, Vol. 8, No. 6, June, 1964, pp. 17–19, Australia) is probably the best work Yasuoka has produced so far. It is far from shallow. The hero of the novel, "I", together with his father, goes to see his mother at a sea-side mental hospital facing Kôchi Bay. She is suffering from dementia senilis. The novel depicts the events of the nine days which "I" spends there, nursing his mother. "I" reflects on his past relationship with his mother, and his recollections are interspersed with memories of the dire poverty of the postwar days. Sometimes he had been aware of his mother's "femininity". He also remembers that he came to understand himself better because of his mother's bullying attitude. He is moved by the recollection that he once found his own image in his mother, who was, in a sense, nothing but an ugly animal. In the intervals between these recollections, life in the hospital is depicted. His mother finally dies. He feels that the nine days nursing has been an act of recompense to his mother. At the same time, he wonders if the very fact that he had been her son was not already enough recompense. In the hospital ward, which is always exposed to the afternoon sun, "death became as something seen, or palpable, as if he had grasped it in his own hands". He is moved by the mysterious correspondence between Nature and Man: a human life has gone out with the ebbing tide. The author has succeeded not only in depicting the death of a particular mother who, though disliked, still clings to her son, but also in raising the universal question of human fate and death, and the effect of death on human relationships. The author's sharp powers of observation are what make this novel a masterpiece. The novel was awarded the Noma Literary Prize. *Shichiya no Nyôbô* (*The Pawnbroker's Wife,* 1960, translated by Seidensticker, E.G., in *Japan Quarterly,* Vol. VIII, No. 2, p.188 ff.) is a short story, narrated in the first person, with a student as its hero. He is a bad student who visits his friends at their lodgings or goes to brothels at Yoshiwara, without attending lectures. One day he goes to a pawnbroker's shop with his coat, and meets the pawnbroker's rather attractive wife. As he repeats his visits to the pawnbroker's shop, he comes to know her more and more intimately, until finally he makes love to her. However, when he returns to his lodginghouse, he finds a conscription order from the army. He has to leave within a week. The night before the day for joining his regiment, the pawnbroker's wife comes to see him, and gives him the coat which he had pawned, as a farewell present. The story ends here. This story depicts in a detached, light manner a student who is somewhat of a social misfit. It is slightly pathetic, but, at the time, in it we feel the presence of the author's masochistic spirit of making fun of oneself. It is a well-constructed story. *Hanamatsuri* (*Buddha's Birthday Festival,* 1962) shows how a middle school student ("I" in the novel) has experienced the awakening of erotic desire. He is under the custody of a buddhist priest, and lives in the temple. Such puritanic surroundings stimulate his imagination all the more strongly, and, in his daydreams, he has a love affair with the priest's wife, with Katsuko, the maid, and with a young girl called Fusae. All these remain merely imagined things, except that he once kisses Katsuko. However, even in this he does not cut a very gallant figure as he is a very backward pupil. On top of that, a friend of his called Inoue, who was his playmate, dies through drinking mercury. In the temple, children are singing songs for the Buddha's birthday.

In this novel, the author depicts the subtle psychology of an adolescent boy, with his purity and his awkwardness. It is unfortunate, however, that the novel somewhat lacks in concentrated power.

The hero of *Maku ga Orite kara* (*After the Curtain Falls*, 1967) is an illustrator called Hirano. The novel describes two days out of a ten-year period since the end of the war, and depicts the poverty and harshness of postwar life, as experienced by Hirano's family, and a painter called Okada, and his wife, who share the same house with the Hiranos. The pessimistic view of human relationships expressed in this novel is similar to that of *Kaihen no Kôkei* (*View of the Bay*). However, this work is rather diffuse, whereas *Kaihen no Kôkei* (*View of the Bay*) is more concentrated and has a clear focus on the mother's death. In these works, Yasuoka seems to be trying to go beyond the limitations of the "I" novel and to deal with themes having a universal appeal.

Yoshiyuki Junnosuke

Yoshiyuki Junnosuke was born in Okayama. His father, Yoshiyuki Eisuke, was a modernistic writer who was active around 1930. His mother, Yoshiyuki Aguri, was famous as the first western-style beautician in Japan. Yoshiyuki was their eldest son. When he was three years old, his family moved to Kôjimachi, Tokyo. He began to be interested in literature when he was a student of Shizuoka High School. It was also during his high school days that he began to suffer from asthma. Because of bad health, he was exempted from military service, but he lost many of his good friends on account of the War. His war experiences made him nihilistic, and although he had been a good student up to this time, he chose to live as a superfluous good-for-nothing on society. When he was a student of the Department of English Literature of Tokyo University, he became a member of such longstanding and famous group magazines as *Shinshichô* (*New Tide of Thought*) and *Sedai* (*Generation*), but while the other members were absorbed by progressive political ideas, Yoshiyuki consciously chose to visit prostitutes and lead a decadent life. He left Tokyo University without completing his course. He became a journalist working for a popular magazine, and tried to write novels in his spare time. In 1950 Yoshiyuki published his first novel, *Bara Hanbainin* (*The Seller of Roses*). In 1954 he received the Akutagawa Prize for *Shûu* (*Shower*). He was regarded as a member of the so-called "Third New Generation", which was comprised of writers such as Yasuoka Shôtarô, Kojima Nobuo, Miura Shumon and Shôno Junzô. Yoshiyuki attracted attention as a young writer of the aesthetic type. *Shûu* (*Shower*), *Tadayou Heya* (*The Floating Room*, 1955), *Genshoku no Machi* (*Primary Colors Street*, 1956) and *Shôfu no Heya* (*A Prostitute's Room*, 1958) all deal with the theme that the hero can regain his humanity only by submerging himself in the world of prostitutes who are excluded from ordinary society. Despite their subject-matter, these works are intellectual and give a surprising impression of purity. Yoshiyuki also wrote *Honoo no Naka* (*In the Flames*, 1956) which depicts a youth spent during the war with the frequent air-raids, and a number of other short stories which are reminiscences of his childhood. These stories are written in a lyrical but intellectual manner free from sentimentality. In his recent works he has been dealing mainly with the problems of sex. Among them are *Yami no Naka no Shukusai* (*Festival in the Dark*, 1961) which depicts the triangle of the hero, his wife and his mistress, and tries to understand what the man-and-wife relationship and "home" essentially are, *Suna no Ue no Shokubutsugun* (*A Group of Plants on the Sand*, 1963) which was inspired by a painting by Klee, *Hoshi to Tsuki to wa Ten no Ana* (*Stars and the Moon are Heaven's Holes*, 1966) and *Anshitsu* (*The Dark Room*, 1969). Through depicting various types of sexual experience, he has been trying to find out the "essence" of sex. Yoshiyuki's aim is not so much to expose the perverted sexuality hidden in an ordinary human being, but to grasp something behind the sexual phenomena, the naked essence of human existence revealed there. Yoshiyuki has become increasingly interested in caverns or closed rooms containing only a man and a woman, and his works have shown an increasingly strong nihilistic tendency. Yoshiyuki's writings, however, are products of refined urbanity, and in depicting sex, Yoshiyuki does not lose intellectual restraint. Yoshiyuki, who describes human existence in his works in a delicately sensuous fashion, is one of the most highly valued writers of present-day Japan. He is a master of short and medium-length novels. We may say that his works are based on the traditional aesthetic concepts of *yatsushi* (deliberate degrading of oneself) and *iki* (*chic*). In a sense Yoshiyuki is a writer who is following in the footsteps of Kawabata Yasunari.

YOSHIYUKI Junnosuke
Anshitsu (*The dark room*)
Published in *Gunzô,* January–December 1969.

(Synopsis) Recently I have so often been reminded of the past. For example, I received a telephone call from Tsunoki Tôru. We were friends, but I had not heard from him for ten years. He invited me to go with him to an "interesting" bar he knew.

Twenty years ago, we were about twenty-three years old. It was immediately after the war; everything was in confusion. Tsunoki and I were both members of a certain literary group magazine. I was a mere journalist working for a third-rate magazine company, whereas he was recognized as a promising young writer. He was called a genius or a prodigy. He was by nature an amorous man, and his high reputation as a writer was making him even bolder in his relationships with women. Once he came to my house when I was out, and wooed my wife. However, Tsunoki gave up writing novels before long. Now I am earning my living by writing novels.

The bar Tsunoki took me to seemed to be a bar for homosexuals, and I found it boring. However, I did manage to caress the breasts of two women guests who were sitting on seats near mine. I also kissed them, and made an appointment with one of them, a girl called Maki, to meet at this place the next evening. She turned up the next evening as she had promised. She pointed out that both Tsunoki and I looked like victims of something, which showed her sharp power of observation. She also told me that I was the first man who had touched her breasts without nauseating her.

For ten years since my wife's death I had been enjoying freedom as a bachelor. When I wanted a woman, I would phone either Takako or Natsue and we met at an inn for intimate couples. When both of them could not find time, I would sleep with a prostitute. One snowy night, since both of them were busy, which was rather rare, I went to the bar again for a change and sent for Maki. Maki induced me to come to an inn with her. She said that she wanted to know why my touch was not nauseating. As I had expected, Maki's body gave me an impression of slightness when I slept with her. She shook her head violently from side to side, and when intercourse was over, said, "At last I have made it with a man, haven't I?" She had been a lesbian. I traveled around the San'in District with her. After that I slept with her once more. Then Maki, who had become pregnant, went to New York.

Takako was a teacher of flower arrangement. My relationship with her continued for several years. She was shy in the first stage of love making, and then became really wild. That was the peculiarity of her sexual behaviour. I did not allow her to come to my house. When we met, I said very little, for my sole purpose was to sleep with her. However, she was devoted to me, and probably she was secretly hoping to marry me. One day, she suddenly said that she was going to marry someone else. I did not try to stop her. I phoned her after her wedding, but she sounded as if she had become a different woman. I sensed her secret revenge on me.

Now I had only Natsue left. I was aging, but the thought that only death would be waiting for me if I stopped making love to a woman induced me to phone Natsue. I had become acquainted with her at a supermarket. She had given me the impression that she was somehow like me, and we became close. She had a lover, but she parted with him, and now her sole meaning in life was to be embraced by me. She had got rid of every superfluity, and was living only for sensuous pleasure. My heart gradually opened up to her. Natsue wore cloth around her neck, wrists and ankles, and behaved like my slave. She enjoyed being whipped by me.

During my student days, when I had been on the verge of a nervous breakdown, I had escaped into the countryside near my old home to rest and cure myself. I lived as a lodger with a family. The landlord and his wife treated me kindly. I soon discovered that there were an idiot girl and an idiot boy in the dark attic of the main building, and that Uchiyama Torao, who confined himself in the attic of the annexe for the most of his time and studied, was the brother of these crawling idiots. Uchiyama, who was a talented scientist, is now an influential person in the academic world. I hear that this Dr. Uchiyama who married the daughter of a university professor refused to have children for fear that they might be born mentally retarded. On my face I have a mole which signifies that I will be troubled by women, but have no children. All sorts of ideas occur to my depressed mind.

The only thing which is certain is that today I will again go to the dark room in which Natsue lives. When I enter the building I will sense her faint smell in the air. The smell will become increasingly strong and overwhelming, until I stand in front of Natsue's door. I will grasp the knob of the door. On the other side of the door the dark room waits.

APPENDIX

Below a number of works are listed for each author included in this volume. A single asterisk (*) indicates that an English translation is available and that the English version which follows in parentheses has been taken from the translated volume. The publisher of the English volume is given at the end of the entry. Two asterisks (**) indicate that an English synopsis of the entry is available in Volume II of this series or the periodical *Japan Pen News*. The precise location is given in parentheses at the end of the entry.

ABE KÔBÔ

Owarishi michi no shirube ni (As a signpost for the road I have come), *Kosei*, Feb., 1948.

Akai mayu (Red cocoon), *Ningen*, Dec., 1950. Translated by John Nathan, *Japan Quarterly*, Vol. 13, No. 2, 1966, pp. 217–219.

Kabe (The wall), Getsuyô Shobô, 1951.

Chinnyûsha (Intruders), *Shinchô*, Feb., 1952.

Kiga-dômei (Starvation league), Kôdansha, 1954.

Kemonotachi wa kokyô o mezasu (Animals are heading their home), *Gunzô*, Jan.–Apr., 1957.

Bô ni natta otoko (Stick), *Shin Nihon bungaku*, Jan., 1958. Translated by John Nathan, *Japan Quarterly*, Vol. 13, No. 2, 1966, pp. 214–217.

*Daishi kanpyô-ki (Inter ice age 4), Kôdansha, 1959. Translated by E. Dale Saunders, Alfred A. Knopf, New York, 1970; Tuttle, Tokyo, 1970.

**Suna no onna (The woman in the dunes), Shinchôsha, 1962. Translated by E. Dale Saunders, New York, Knopf, 1964, 241pp. *PEN*, No. 2, pp. 10–12.

Mukankei na shi (Irrelevant death), Shinchôsha, 1964.

*Tanin no kao (The face of another), Kôdansha, 1964. Translated by E. Dale Saunders, New York, Knopf, 1966; Tokyo, Tuttle, 1967.

Tomodachi (Friends), *Bungei,* Mar., 1967. Translated by Donald Keene, N.Y., Grove press, 1969; Tokyo, Tuttle, 1970, 94pp.
*Moetsukita chizu (The ruined map), Shinchôsha, 1967. Translated by E. Dale Saunders, Tokyo, Tuttle, 1969.

AGAWA HIROYUKI

Nennen-saisai (Year after year), *Sekai,* Sept., 1946.
Rei sandai (Three deceased), *Shinchô,* Sept., 1946.
Haru no shiro (A castle in spring), Shinchôsha, 1952.
*Ma no isan (Devil's heritage), *Shinchô,* Aug.–Dec., 1953. Translated by John M. Maki, Tokyo, Hokuseidô, 1957. 247pp.
Kumo no bohyô (Gravemarker of clouds), *Shinchô,* Jan.–Dec., 1955.
Yoru no namioto (The sound of waves at night), *Shinchô,* May, 1957.
Saka no ôi machi (The town of many hills), *Bungakukai,* Sept., 1957.
Karuforuniya (California), Shinchôsha, 1959.
Aoba no kageri (The shade of leaves), *Gunzô,* Nov., 1960.
Yamamoto Isoroku (Yamamoto Isoroku), *Bungei Asahi,* Oct., 1964–Sept., 1965.
Gentô (Side lights of a ship), *Gunzô,* May, 1966.

AKIMOTO MATSUYO

Reifuku (Full dress), first performed by Haiyûza, 1949.
Mono iwanu onna tachi (The silent women), first performed by Mingei, 1955.
Maruoka Iheiji den (The life of Maruoka Iheiji), first performed by Gekidan Nakama, 1960.
Kasabuta shikibu kô (An investigation on lady scab). *Bungei,* June, 1969.
Hitachibô Kaison (Hitachibô Kaison), Bokuyôsha, 1964.

AMINO KIKU

Mitsuko (Mitsuko), *Chûô kôron,* Feb., 1926.
Kisha no naka de (On the train), Shun'yôdô, 1940.
Kin no kan (Golden coffin), *Sekai,* May, 1947.
Sakura no hana (Cherry blossoms), Shinchôsha, 1961.

Yureru ashi (Trembling reed), *Bungei*, Dec., 1962.
Ichigo ichie (Once in a lifetime), *Gunzô*, Nov., 1966.

ARIYOSHI SAWAKO

Jiuta (Jiuta ballad), *Bungakukai*, Jan., 1956.
Masshiroke-no-ke (Pure white), *Bungei*, Oct., 1956.
Shiroi uchiwa (White fan), *Kingu*, June, 1957.
Kinokawa (The River Kinokawa), *Fujin gahô*, Jan.–May, 1960.
Kôge (Incense and flowers), Chûô Kôronsha, 1962.
Sukezaemon yondai ki (The four generations of Sukezaemon), Bungei Shunjû Shinsha, 1963.
Aritagawa (The River Aritagawa), *Nihon*, Jan.–Dec., 1963.
Hidakagawa (The River Hidakagawa), *Shûkan bunshun*, Jan.–Oct., 1965.
Hi-shoku (Non-coloured), Chûô Kôronsha, 1966.
Hanaoka Seishû no tsuma (The wife of Hanaoka Seishû), *Shinchô*, Nov., 1966.
Izumo no Okuni (Okuni of Izumo district), *Fujin kôron*, Jan., 1967–Dec., 1969.

ENDÔ SHÛSAKU

Furansu no daigakusei (Students in France, 1951–52), Hayakawa Shobô, 1953.
Aden made (Till Aden), *Mita bungaku*, Nov., 1954.
Shiroi hito, kiiroi hito (White people, yellow people), *Kindai bungaku*, May–June, 1955.
Aoi chiisana budô (Green little grapes), *Bungakukai*, Jan.–June, 1956.
**Umi to dokuyaku (The sea and poison), Bungei Shunjû Shinsha, 1958. *PEN*, No. 2, p. 2.
Obaka-san (Blockhead), *Asahi shinbun*, Apr.–Aug., 1959.
Otoko to kyûkanchô (Three men and a starling), *Bungakukai*, Jan., 1963.
*Fuda no Tsuji (Fuda no Tsuji), *Shinchô*, Nov., 1963. Translated by Frank Hoff and James Kircap, *PEN*, No. 14, pp. 1–9.
Nanji mo mata (You, too), *Bungakukai*, Feb., 1964–Feb., 1965.
Ryûgaku (Studying abroad), *Gunzô*, Mar., 1965.
Ryûgakusei (A student abroad), Bungei Shunjû Shinsha, 1965.
Rûan no natsu (Summer in Rouan), Bungei Shunjû Shinsha, 1965.

*Chinmoku (Silence), Shinchôsha, 1966. Translated by William Johnston, Tokyo, Sophia University, 1969; Tokyo, Tuttle, 1969; London, Prentice Hall, 1970, 306pp.

*Ôgon no kuni (The golden country), *Bungei,* May, 1966. Translated by Francis Mathy, Tokyo, Tuttle, 1970.

Bara no yakata (A house surrounded by roses), *Bungakukai,* Sept., 1969.

ENJI FUMIKO

Banshun sôya (A noisy night in late spring), *Nyonin geijutsu,* Oct., 1928.

Shu o ubau mono (The vermilion pilferer), *Bungei,* Aug., 1955–June, 1956.

*Yô (Enchantress), *Chûô kôron,* Sept., 1956. Translated by John Bester, *Japan quarterly,* Vol. V, No. 3, 1958, pp. 339–357.; *Modern Japanese short stories,* Tokyo, Japan Pub.C Trading Co., 1960, pp. 90–117.

*Onna-zaka (The female slope), *Shôsetsu shinchô,* Feb. & Nov., 1953; Apr., 1954; Jan. 1957. Kadokawa Shoten, 1957. *The waiting years,* translated by John Bester, Tokyo, Kôdansha, 1971, 203pp. *Synopses II,* pp. 192–196. *PEN,* No. 2, p. 2.

Nisei no en shûi (The two worlds, gleanings), *Bungakukai,* Jan., 1957.

Onna-omote (A woman's mask), *Gunzô,* Apr.–June, 1958.

Futa-omote (Two matching faces), *Gunzô,* July, 1959.

Namamiko monogatari (Tale of an enchantress), Chûô Kôronsha, 1965.

FUJIEDA SHIZUO

Iperitto gan (Mustard gas and eye disease), *Kindai bungaku,* Mar., 1949.

Inu no chi (Blood of a dog), *Bungei shunjû,* Mar., 1957.

Kyôto Tsuda Sanzô (Tsuda Sanzô, the assasin), *Gunzô,* Feb., 1961.

Kûki atama (Air brain), Kôdansha, 1967.

Gongu jôdo (Seeking to enter paradise), *Gunzô,* Apr., 1968.

Michi (Road), *Kindai bungaku,* Sept., 1947.

FUKAZAWA SHICHIRÔ

*Narayamabushi-kô (The oak mountain song), *Chûô kôron,* Nov., 1956. Translated by John Bester, *Japan quarterly,* Vol. IV, No. 2, 1957, pp. 200–

233. "The songs of oak mountain", translated by Donald Keene, *Three modern Japanese short novels*, N.Y., Viking, 1966, pp. 3–50.
Tôhoku no zunmutachi (A tale from Tôhoku), *Chûô kôron*, Jan., 1957.
Fuefuki-gawa (The River Fuefuki), Chûô Kôronsha, 1958.
Fûryû mutan (An elegant fantasy), *Chûô kôron*, Nov., 1960.
Yôjutsuteki kako (The magical past), *Gunzô*, Mar., 1968.
Shomin retsuden (The biographies of common people), *Shinchô*, June, 1962.

FUKUDA TSUNEARI

Saigo no kirifuda (The last trump), *Jigen*, Jan., 1948.
Susono (The base of the mountain), *Bessatsu bungei shunjû*, Dec., 1947–Aug., 1950.
**Kitty taifû (Typhoon Kitty), *Ningen*, Jan., 1950. *Synopses II*, pp. 167–170.
Ryû o nadeta otoko (The man who stroked a dragon), *Engeki*, Jan., 1952.
Gendai no eiyû (A hero of modern time), *Gunzô*, July, 1952.
Meian (Light and darkness), *Bungakukai*, Jan., 1956.
Akechi Mitsuhide (Akechi Mitsuhide), *Bungei*, Mar., 1957.
Arima Ôji (Prince Arima), *Bungakukai*, Oct., 1961.
Okumanchôja fujin (The millionairess), *Tenbô*, Mar., 1967.
Wakatte tamaruka! (You can't understant it!), Shinchôsha, 1968.
Sôtô imada shisezu (Hitler is still alive), Shinchôsha, 1970.

FUKUNAGA TAKEHIKO

Tô (Tower), *Kôgen*, Aug., 1946.
Bôdorêru no sekai (The world of Baudelaire), Yashiro Shoten, 1947.
Bungakuteki kôsatsu (Literary observations of the year), Shinzenbisha, 1947.
Fûdo (Climate), *Bungaku '51*, May–Sept., 1951.
Meifu (Hades), *Gunzô*, Apr. & Sept., 1954.
Kusa no hana (Flower of grass), Shinchôsha, 1954.
Yoru no jikan (Hours of the night), *Bungei*, May–June, 1955.
Sekai no owari (The end of the world), *Bungakukai*, Apr., 1959.
Haishi (Abandoned town), *Fujin no tomo*, July–Sept., 1959.
Gôgyan no sekai (The world of Gauguin), Shinchôsha, 1961.
Kokubetsu (Farewell), *Gunzô*, Jan., 1962.

**Bôkyaku no kawa (River of forgetfulness), Shinchôsha, 1964. *PEN*, No. 18, pp. 12–14.
Kaishi (Mirage), Shinchôsha, 1968.

FUNABASHI SEIICHI

Daivingu (Diving), *Kôdô*, Oct., 1934.
**Bokuseki (Miss Dry-as-dust), *Bungakukai*, Oct., 1938. *Synopses II*, pp. 73–74.
Shikkaiya Kôkichi (Kôkichi the dyed-cloth salesman), Sôgensha, 1945.
*Gamô (Thistile down), *Bungakukai*, July–Oct., 1947. Translated by Edward G. Seidensticker, *Japan quarterly*, Vol. VIII, No. 4, 1961, pp. 431–459.
Yuki Fujin ezu (Life scenes of Lady Yuki), *Shôsetsu shinchô*, Jan., 1948–Feb., 1950.
Aru onna no enkei (A distant view of a woman), *Gunzô*, May, 1961.
Suki na onna no munekazari (The brooch of the beloved woman), *Gunzô*, Nov., 1967.
Kagee nyonin (Portrait of a lady), *Chûô kôron*, Sept., 1961–Nov., 1963.

HANIYA YUTAKA

Shiryô (Ghosts), *Kindai bungaku*, Jan., 1946–Nov., 1949.
Shin'en (Abyss), *Gunzô*, Oct., 1957.
Fugôri yueni ware shinzu (I believe because it is absurd to believe—Credo, quia absurdum—), Gendai Shichôsha, 1961.
Yami no naka no kuroi uma (A black horse in the darkness), *Bungei*, Dec., 1963.

HOTTA YOSHIE

Sokoku sôshitsu (Fatherland lost), *Gunzô*, May, 1950.
Haguruma (Cogwheel), *Bungaku*, May, 1951.
**Hiroba no kodoku (Solitude in the plaza), *Chûô kôron—bungei tokushû*, Sept., 1951. Translated by Horo Shirakawa, *Review*, Otaru Univ., of Commerce, No. 10, 1955, pp. 1–62; No. 12, 1956, pp. 199–226. *Synopses II*, pp. 188–189.
Jikan (Time), *Sekai*, Feb., 1953.

Yoru no mori (Forest at night), *Gunzô*, Jan., 1954.
Kinenhi (Monument), *Chûô kôron*, May–Aug., 1955.
Kibukijima (Kibuki Island), *Gunzô*, Feb., 1956.
**Kawa (Rivers), *Chûô kôron—bungei-tokushû*, Jan., 1959. *PEN*, No. 6, pp. 5–6.
Uminari no soko kara (From the bottom of the rumbling sea), *Asahi journal*,
 Sept. 1960–Sept. 1961.
Shinpan (Judgement), *Sekai*, Jan. 1960–Mar., 1963.

IBUSE MASUJI

Aogashima taigaiki (Aogashima tragedy), *Chûô kôron*, Mar., 1934.
*John Manjirô hyôryûki (John Manjirô, the castaway, his life and adventures),
 Kawade Shobô, 1937. Translated by Kaneko Hirokazu, Tokyo, Hoku-
 seidô, 1940.
Gojinka (The sacred fire), *Kodomo asahi*, June–Aug., 1943.
Honjitsu kyûshin (No consultations today), *Bessatsu bungei shunjû*, Aug. &
 Dec., 1949, Mar. & May, 1950. Translated by Edward G. Seidensticker,
 Japan Quarterly, Vol. 8, No. 1, 1961, pp. 50–79; *No consultations today*,
 Tokyo, Hara Shobô, 1964, pp. 8–123.
*Yôhai taichô (A far-worshipping commander), *Tenbô*, Feb., 1950. Translated
 by Glenn Shaw, *Japan quarterly*, Vol. I, No. 1, 1954, pp. 53–73; *No consulta-*
 tions today, op. cit. pp. 126–213; *The Shadow of sunrise*, Tokyo, Kôdansha,
 1966; London, Ward Lock, 1966, pp. 157–186. "Lieutenant Lookeast,"
 translated by John Bester, *Lieutenant Lookeast and other stories*, Tokyo,
 Kôdansha, 1971, pp. 23–51. *Synopses II*, pp. 170–172.
**Hyômin Usaburô (Usaburô the castaway), *Gunzô*, Apr., 1954–Dec., 1955.
 PEN, No. 1, p. 1.
Chinpindô shujin (The curio dealer), *Chûô kôron*, Jan., 1959.
Mei no kekkon (The niece's marriage), *Shinchô*, June, 1965–Sept., 1966.
*Kuroi ame (Black rain), Shinchôsha, 1966. Translated by John Bester, *Japan*
 quarterly, Vol. XIV, Nos. 2–4, 1967, Vol. XV, Nos. 1–3, 1968 in 6 parts;
 Tokyo, Kôdansha, 1969; London, Secker and Warburg, 1971, 300 pp.

IIZAWA TADASU

Fujiwara Kakka no enbi-fuku (The swallow-tailed coat of His Excellency
 Fujiwara), *Gekisaku*, Sept., 1931.

Pekin no Yûrei (The ghosts of Peking), *Engeki*, Feb., 1943.
Chôjû gassen (The battle of birds and beasts), *Butai*, Dec., 1947.
Sukiyabashi no shinkirô (The mirage at Sukiyabashi), *Nihon Engeki*, Mar., 1950.
Konronzan no hitobito (People at Mt. Konron), *Higeki kigeki*, Sept., 1950.
Nigô (The mistress), *Shingeki*, Jan., 1955.
Yashi to onna (Coconuts and a woman), first performed by Bungakuza, June, 1956.
Mugaina dokuyaku (Harmless poison), *Shingeki*, Feb., 1965.
Gonin no Moyono (Five people called Moyono), *Higeki kigeki*, Aug., 1967.
Akushu·akushu·akushu (Yet another handshake), *Higeki kigeki*, Oct., 1969.
Mô hitori no hito (One more emperor), *Bungei*, Mar., 1970.

INOUE MITSUHARU

Kakarezaru isshô (An unwritten chapter), *Shin Nihon bungaku*, July, 1950.
Yameru bubun (The sickened part), *Shin Nihon bungaku*, Aug., 1951.
Sôtô no washi (Two-headed eagle), *Kindai bungaku*, Feb., 1952.
Nagagutsu-jima (Boot-shaped island), *Shin Nihon bungaku*, June, 1953.
Hoshi (Stars), *Bungakukai*, Apr., 1954.
Gadarukanaru senshi shû (War poetry of Guadalcanal), *Shin Nihon bungaku*, May, 1958.
Shisha no toki (The time of the dead), *Shin Nihon bungaku*, Jan., 1959–Sept., 1960.
Kyokô no kurên (Fictitious crane), Miraisha, 1960.
Chi no mure (The crowd of the ground), *Bungei*, July, 1963.

INOUE YASUSHI

Tsuya no kyaku (Guests at the wake), *Bessatsu bungei shunjû*, Dec., 1949.
*Ryôjû (The hunting gun), *Bungakukai*, Oct., 1949. Translated by Yokoo Sadamichi and Sanford Goldstein, Tokyo, Tuttle, 1961; London, Prentice-Hall, 1961, 74p.; "Shotgun", translated by George Saitô, *Modern Japanese stories*, London, Spottiswoode, 1961; Tokyo, Tuttle, 1962, pp. 416–451.
Tôgyû (Bullfight), *Bungakukai*, Dec., 1949.
*Hira no shakunage (The azaleas of Hira), *Bungakukai*, Mar., 1950. Translated by Edward G. Seidensticker, *Japan quarterly*, Vol. II, No. 3, 1955, pp. 322–

348; *Modern Japanese short stories,* Tokyo, Japan Pub. Trad. Co., 1960, pp. 141–177; *Lou-lan,* Tokyo, Hara Shobo, 1964, pp. 129–229.

Kuroi ushio (Dark tide), *Bungei shunjû,* July–Oct., 1950.

Aru gisakusha no shôgai (The counterfeiter), *Shinchô,* Oct., 1951. Translated by Leon Picon, *The counterfeiter and other stories,* Tokyo, Tuttle, 1965; London, Prentice-Hall, 1965, pp. 15–69.

Fûrin kazan (Wind, forest, fire, mountain), *Shôsetsu shinchô,* Oct., 1953– Dec., 1954.

**Kuroi chô (Black butterfly), Shinchôsha, 1954. *Synopses II,* pp. 214–217.

Shatei (Firing range), *Shinchô,* Jan.–Dec., 1956.

Hyôheki (Wall of ice), Shinchôsha, 1957.

Tenpyô no iraka (The tiled roofs of Tenpyô), *Chûô kôron,* Mar.–Oct., 1957 *PEN,* No. 1, pp. 1–2.

*Rôran (Lou-lan), *Bungei shunjû,* July, 1958. Translated by E. G. Seidensticker, Tokyo, Hara Shobô, 1964, pp. 129–229. *Japan quarterly,* Vol. VI, No. 4, 1959, pp. 460–489.

Tonkô (Tun-huang), *Gunzô,* Jan.–May, 1959.

*Kôzui (Flood), *Koe,* July, 1959. Translated by John Bester, *PEN,* No. 4, pp. 1–4.; *Flood,* Tokyo, Hara Shobô, 1964, pp. 8–75.

*Aru rakujitsu (Splendid sunset), Kadokawa Shoten, 1959. Translated by Uramatsu Fuki, *The Yomiuri,* Apr. 16–Aug. 9, 1960.

Aoki ôkami (Blue wolf), *Bungei shunjû,* Oct., 1959–July, 1960.

Yodo-dono nikki (The diary of Lady Yodo), Bungei Shunjû Shinsha, 1961.

Fûtô (The wind and the waves), *Gunzô,* July & Oct., 1963.

Oroshiyakoku suimu-tan (Castaway in Russia), *Bungei shunjû,* May, 1968.

Tsuki no hikari (Moonlight), Gunzô, Aug., 1969.

ISHIHARA SHINTARÔ

Haiiro no kyôshitsu (Gray classroom), *Ikkyô bungei,* Dec., 1954.

*Taiyô no kisetsu (Season of violence), *Bungakukai,* July, 1955. Translated by John G. Mills, Toshie Takahama, and Ken Tremayne, Tokyo, Tuttle, 1966; London, Prentice-Hall, 1966, pp. 13–57.

Shokei no heya (The punishment room), *Shinchô,* Mar., 1956. *Season of Violence, op. cit.,* pp. 61–107.

Kiretsu (The crack), *Bungakukai,* Nov., 1956–Sept., 1957.

Kanzennaru yûgi (Perfect play), *Shinchô,* Oct., 1957.

Funky jump, *Bungakukai*, Aug., 1959.
Chôsen (Challenge), *Shinchô*, Nov., 1959–June, 1960.
Ôkami ikiro buta wa shine (Live, wolves! Die pigs!), *Chûô kôron*, May, 1960.
Shi no hakubutsu shi (Natural history of death), Shinchôsha, 1963.
Kôi to shi (Action and death), *Bungei*, Feb., 1964.

ISHIKAWA JUN

Kajin (Fair lady), *Sakuhin*, May, 1935.
Hinkyû mondô (Dialogue on poverty), *Sakuhin*, Aug., 1935.
**Fugen (The merciful Bodhisattva), *Sakuhin*, June–Sept., 1936. *Synopses II*,
　　pp. 41–43.
Ôgon densetsu (The golden legend), *Chûô kôron*, Mar., 1946.
Taka (Falcon), *Gunzô*, Mar., 1953.
*Shion monogatari (Asters), *Chûô kôron*, July, 1956. Translated by Donald
　　Keene, *Three Modern Japanese short novels*, N.Y., Viking, 1961, pp. 119–172.
Hakutô-gin (Lays of the white-haired), *Chûô kôron*, Apr.–Oct., 1957.
**Yakeato no Iesu (Jesus among the ashes), Shinchôsha, 1957. *PEN*, No. 8,
　　pp. 7–9.
Shura (Asura), *Chûô kôron*, July, 1958.
Kitsune no ikigimo (The fox's liver), *Shinchô*, May, 1959.
Omae no teki wa omae da (Your enemy is yourself), *Gunzô*, Sept., 1961.
Aratama (Violent soul), *Shinchô*, Jan. 1963–May 1964.
Shifuku sennen (Millennium), *Sekai*, Jan., 1965–Oct., 1966.
Tenma fu (Ode on a heavenly horse), *Umi*, July–Sept., 1969.

ISHIKAWA TATSUZÔ

Sôbô (People), *Seiza*, Apr., 1935.
Ikiteiru heitai (Living soldiers), *Chûô kôron*, Mar., 1938
Nozominaki ni arazu (Not without hope), Yomiuri Shinbunsha, 1947.
Doro ni mamirete (Soiled by the mud), *Home*, Nov., 1948.
*Shijû-hassai no teikô (Resistance at forty-eight), *Yomiuri shinbun*, Nov., 1955–
　　Apr., 1956. Translated by Kazuma Nakayama, Tokyo, Hokuseidô, 1960.

ITÔ HITOSHI

Yukiakari no michi (Snow-lighted path), Shiinokisha, 1926.

Kanjô saibô no danmen (A phase of emotional life), *Bungei review*, May, 1930.
Seibutsu sai (The festival of the living), *Shin bungei jidai*, Jan., 1932.
Yûki no machi (The street of demons), *Bungei*, Aug., 1937.
**Machi to mura (Town and village), Daiichi Shobô, 1939. *Synopses II*, pp. 56–59.
Tokunô Gorô no seikatsu to iken (The life and opinions of Tokunô Gorô), *Chisei*, Aug., 1940–Feb., 1941.
Narumi Senkichi, Hosokawa Shoten, 1950.
Shôsetsu no hôhô (The methods of writing fiction), Kawade Shobô, 1948.
Hi no tori (Fire-bird), *Bungei shunjû*, Aug., 1952.
Nihon bundan shi (A history of the Japanese literary world), *Gunzô*, Jan., 1952–June, 1969.
Shôsetsu no ninshiki (Understanding novels), Kawade Shobô, 1955.
**Hanran (Overflow), *Shinchô*, Nov., 1956–July, 1958. *PEN*, No. 3, pp. 8–9.
Hakkutsu (Excavation), *Shinchô*, Jan. 1962–Oct., 1964.
Hen'yô (Transformation), *Sekai*, Jan., 1967–May, 1968.

KAIKÔ KEN

Panikku (Panic), *Shin Nihon bungaku*, Aug., 1957.
Hadaka no ôsama (Naked king), *Bungakukai*, Dec., 1957.
Ryûbôki (Account of wandering), *Chûô kôron bungei tokushugô*, Jan., 1958.
**Nihon sanmon opera (Threepenny opera of Japan), *Bungakukai*, Jan.–July, 1959. *PEN*, No. 5, pp. 8–9.
Robinson no matsuei (Robinson's descendants), *Chûô kôron*, May–Nov., 1960.
Mita, yureta, warawareta (I saw, I vibrated, and was laughed at), Chikuma Shobô, 1963.
Betonamu senki (Vietnam war), Asahi Shinbunsha, 1965.
Kagayakeru yami (Shining darkness), Shinchôsha, 1968.

KANBAYASHI AKATSUKI

**Sei Yohane Byôin nite (At St. John's Hospital), *Ningen*, June, 1946. *Synopses II*, pp. 100–103.
*Haru no saka (Vision in spring), *Bungei shunjû*, Dec., 1957. Translated by John Bester, *PEN*, No, 3, 1959. pp. 1–7.

Onme no shizuku (Tears from your eyes), *Gunzô*, Jan., 1959.
*Shiroi yakatabune (A stately white barge), *Shinchô*, Aug., 1963. Translated by
Warren Carlisle, *PEN*, No. 17, 1966, pp. 8–13.

KAWABATA YASUNARI

*Izu no odoriko (The Izu dancer), *Bungei jidai*, Jan.–Feb., 1924. Translated
by Edward G. Seidensticker, *Atlantic monthly* 195, 1955, pp. 108–114;
The Izu Dancer, Tokyo, Hara Shobô, 1963, pp. 7–68.
Jûrokusai no nikki (Diary of a sixteen-year-old), *Bungei shunjû*, Aug.–Sept.,
1925.
Bungakuteki jijoden (Literary autobiography), *Shinchô*, May, 1934.
*Hokuro no tegami (The mole), *Fujin kôron*, Mar., 1940. Translated by E. G.
Seidensticker, *Modern Japanese literature*, N.Y. Grove Press, 1956; Tokyo,
Tuttle, 1957, pp. 366–374; *Modern Japanese short stories*, Tokyo, Japan
Pub. Trad. Co., 1960, pp. 190–200; *The Izu Dancer*, Tokyo Hara Shobô,
1963, pp. 133–162; *Japan quarterly*, Vol. II, No. 6, pp. 86–93.
*Saikai (Rediscovery), *Sekai*, Feb., 1946. Translated by Leon Picon, *Orient/
West*, Vol. VIII, No. 4, 1963, pp. 37–47; *The Japanese Image*, Tokyo
Orient/West, 1965, pp. 197–211: "Reencounter" translated by Leon Picon,
The Izu Dancer, Tokyo, Hara Shobô, 1963, pp. 69–132.
*Yukiguni (The snow country), Sôgensha, 1948. Translated by E. G. Seiden-
sticker, New York, A. Knopf, 1957, 175 pp.; Tokyo, Tuttle, 1957;
London, Secker and Warburg, 1957, 188 pp; *Snow country and thousand
cranes*, N.Y. Knopf, 1969, pp. 1–175.
*Senba-zuru (A thousand cranes), *Bessatsu yomimono jiji*, May, 1949–Oct.,
1951. Translated by E. G. Seidensticker, New York, A. Knopf, 1958,
147 pp; London, Secker and Warburg, 1959, 144 pp.; Tokyo, Tuttle,
1960, 147 pp.; N.Y. Barkley Pub., 1958; *Snow country and thousand cranes*,
N.Y. Knopf, 1969, pp. 1–147.
*Suigetsu (The Moon in the water), *Bungei shunjû*, Nov., 1953. Translated by
George Saito, *United Asia*, Vol. VIII, No. 4, 1956, pp. 260–264; *Diliman
review*, Vol. VI, Nos. 2–4, 1958, pp. 460–472. *Modern Japanese stories*,
London, Spottiswoode, 1961; Tokyo, Tuttle, 1962, pp. 245–257; *The
Izu Dancer*, Tokyo, Hara Shobô, 1963, pp. 163–199.
*Yama no oto (The sound of the mountain), *Kaizô bungei*, Sept., 1949–Apr.,

1954. Translated by E. G. Seidensticker, *Japan quarterly*, Vol. II, No. 3, 1964, pp. 309–330; Vol. II, No. 4, 1964, pp. 446–467; N.Y., Knopf, 1970; London, Peter Owen, 1970; Tokyo, Tuttle, 1970; London, Secker and Warburg, 1971, 276 pp.

*Nemureru bijo (House of the sleeping beauties), *Shinchô*, Jan.–June, 1961; Jan.–Feb., 1962. Translated by E. G. Seidensticker, *House of the sleeping beauties and other stories*, Tokyo, Kôdansha International, 1969, pp. 13–99; London, Quadriga Press, 1969; London, Shere, 1971; N.Y., Ballantine Books, 1970; "The sleeping beauty", translated by J. I. Ackroyd and Mukai Hiro, *Eastern horizon*, Vol. IV, 1965, pp. 53–64.

Koto (The ancient capital), *Asahi shinbun*, Oct., 1961–Mar., 1962.

*Kataude (One arm), Kôdansha, 1969. Translated by E. G. Seidensticker, *Japan quarterly*, Vol. XIV, No. 1, 1967, pp. 60–71.; *House of the sleeping beauties and other stories, op. cit*, pp. 103–124.

Kami wa nagaku (Long hair), *Shinchô*, Apr., 1970.

KINOSHITA JUNJI

Nijûniya machi (Twenty-two nights of waiting), *Shôtenchi*, Aug., 1946.

Hikoichi banashi (The tale of Hikoichi), *Shôtenchi*, Nov., 1946.

Akai jinbaori (The warrior's red coat), *Bessatsu bungei shunjû*, Feb., 1947.

Fûrô (Wind and waves), *Ningen*, Mar., 1947.

*Yûzuru (Twilight crane), *Fujin kôron*, Jan., 1949. Translated by A. C. Scott, *Five plays for a new theatre*, N.Y., New Directions, 1956, pp. 129–159; *Twilight of a crane*, translated by Takeshi Kurahashi, Tokyo, Miraisha, 1952, 51pp.

Yamanami (Mountain range), *Bessatsu geijutsu*, Mar., 1949.

Kawazu shôten (The ascension of the frogs), *Sekai*, May & June, 1951.

Onnyoro seisuiki (The rise and fall of Onnyoro), *Gunzô*, May, 1957.

Higashi no kuni nite (In the east country), first performed by Budô no kai, Oct., 1959.

Ottô to yobareru Nihonjin (The Japanese called Otto), *Sekai*, July & Aug., 1959.

Shinpan (Judgements)—Part I of *Kami to hito to no aida* (Between men and Gods)—*Gunzô*, Oct., 1970.

KITA MORIO

Hyakugafu (A hundred moths), *Bungei shuto*, Apr., 1950.
Yûrei (Ghosts), Private edition, 1954. Chûô Kôronsha, 1960.
*Iwaone nite (On the rock ridge), *Kindai bungaku*, Jan., 1956. Translated by
Clifton Royston, *Japan quarterly*, Vol. XVI, No. 4, 1969, pp. 423–430.
*Haari no iru oka (A hillock of winged ants), *Kindai bungaku*, Mar., 1960;
New Orient, Vol. VII, June 1968, pp. 103–106.
Dokutoru Manbô kôkaiki (The voyage of Dr. Manbô), Chûô Kôronsha,
1960.
Yoru to kiri no sumi de (In the corner of night and mist), *Shinchô*, May, 1960.
Dokutoru Manbô konchuki (Insects), Chûô Kôronsha, 1961.
**Nire-ke no hitobito (People of the house of Nire), *Shinchô*, Jan.–Dec., 1962.
PEN, No. 22, pp. 1–4.
Bokushin no gogo (The afternoon of a Faun), Tôjusha, 1965.
Shiroki taoyakana mine (Graceful white peak), Shinchôsha, 1966.
Dokutoru Manbô seishunki (Youth), Chûô Kôronsha, 1968.

KIYAMA SHÔHEI

No (Field), *Bungei puraningu*, 1929.
Mekura to chinba (The blind and the lame), private edition, 1931.
Jinzô no haru (The spring for Jinzô), *Waseda bungaku*, Aug., 1935.
Kôhone (A candock), *Bungakusha*, Feb., 1940.
Ujigami-sama (The guardian god), *Bungei*, Mar., 1943.
Tairiku no hosomichi (The narrow road of Asia), *Sunao*, Dec., 1947.
Mimigakumon (A smattering of knowledge), *Bungei shunjû*, Oct., 1956.

KÔ HARUTO

Kô Haruto shishû (The collected poems of Kô Haruto), private edition, 1930.
Suichû no kuwa (A mulberry in water), private edition, 1938.
Kage no tochi (Shaded ground), *Bungakukai*, July, 1939.
Shimon (Fingerprint), *Bungakukai*, Aug., 1948.
Akegata no kyaku (A visitor at daybreak), *Tanchô*, Nov., 1948.

Shijin Senke Motomaro (The poet Senke Motomaro), Bijutsu Shuppansha, 1957.
Ushinawareta sokoku (Lost fatherland), Kôdansha, 1960.
Furo-oke (Bathtub), *Shin Nihon bungaku,* Feb., 1966.

KOJIMA NOBUO

Shôjû (A rifle), *Shinchô,* Dec., 1952.
**Kitsuon gakuin (School for stammerers), *Bungakukai,* Aug., 1953. *Synopses II,* pp. 202–204.
American school, *Bungakukai,* Sept., 1954.
Kami (God), *Bungakukai,* Dec., 1954.
Shima (Island), *Gunzô,* Aug.–Dec., 1955.
Ai no kanketsu (The end of love), *Bungakukai,* Dec., 1957.
Hiru to yoru no kusari (Chain of day and night), *Gunzô,* May–Aug., 1959.
Henshô (Reflections), *Gunzô,* May, 1964.
**Hôyô kazoku (Keep the family united), *Gunzô,* July, 1965. *PEN,* No. 18, pp. 7–9.
Onoborisan (Guests from the country), *Shinchô,* Jan., 1970.

KÔNO TAEKO

Yôji-gari (Boy-hunting), *Shinchô,* Dec., 1961.
Hei no naka (Within the walls), *Bungakusha,* Jan., 1962.
Kani (Crabs), *Bungei shunjû,* Aug., 1963.
Fui no koe (Unexpected voice), *Gunzô,* Jan., 1968.
Kusaikire (Steaming grass), *Bungakukai,* Oct., 1967–Apr., 1969.
Kaiten-tobira (Revolving door), Shinchôsha, 1970.
Saigo no toki (Time of death), *Bungei,* Apr., 1966.

KURAHASHI YUMIKO

*Parutai (Communist party), *Bungakukai,* Mar., 1960. "Partei", translated by Haneda Saburô, *The Reeds,* 7, 1961, pp. 87–108.
Hinin (Outcast), *Bungakukai,* May 1960.
Hebi (Snake) *Bungakukai,* June., 1960.
Kon'yaku (Betrothal), *Shinchô,* Aug., 1960.

Dokonimo nai basho (Not of this world), *Shinchô*, Jan., 1961.
Ningen no nai kami (God without man), Kadokawa Shoten, 1961.
Kurai tabi (Gloomy journey), Tôto Shobô, 1961.
Sasoritachi (Scorpions), *Shôsetsu chûô kôron*, Jan., 1963.
Yôjo no yôni (Like a witch), *Bungei*, Dec., 1964.
Seishôjo (Holy girl), Shinchôsha, 1965.
Suikyô nite (In a drunken state), *Bungei*, May, 1969.
Shiroi kami no dôjo (The little girl with grey hair), *Bungei*, Dec., 1969.
Sumiyakisuto Q no bôken (Adventures of Q, the Sumiyakist), Kôdansha, 1960.
Yume no ukihashi (The bridge of dreams), *Umi*, July–Oct., 1970.
Kakô nite (At the mouth of a river), *Bungei*, May, 1970.

MARUOKA AKIRA

Madamu Marutan no namida (Madame Martin's tears), *Mita bungaku*, Feb., 1930.
Kôkan kyôju (Exchange lessons), *Mita bungaku*, Apr., 1930.
Ikimono no kiroku (The records of living things), *Mita bungaku*, Oct., 1935.
Dôjidai ni ikiru hito (My contemporaries), *Gunzô*, Mar., 1953.
Yônen jidai (Childhood), Kadokawa Shoten, 1954.
Nise Kiristo (False Christ), *Gunzô*, Nov., 1956.
*Barairo no kiri (Rose-colored mist), *Gunzô*, Mar., 1963. Translated by Warren Carlisle, *PEN*, No. 17, pp. 14–22.
Shizuka na kage-e (Tranquil shadow picture), Kôdansha, 1965.

MARUYA SAIICHI

Ehoba no kao o sakete (To flee the face of Jehovah), Kawade Shobô Shinsha, 1960.
Okurimono (A present), *Fûkei*, Oct., 1966.
**Sasamakura (Pillow of grass), Kawade Shobô Shinsha, 1966. *PEN*, No. 23, pp. 25–28.
Nigiyaka na machi de (On the thriving street), *Bungei*, Mar., 1967.
Himitsu (A secret), *Bungakukai*, Sept., 1967.
Toshi no nokori (Life's remaining year), *Bungakukai*, Mar., 1968.

Shisô to mushisô no aida (Between thought and its absence), *Bungei,* May, 1968.

Nashi no tsubute (Have heard nothing from them), Sôbunsha, 1966.

MASAMUNE HAKUCHÔ

Sekibaku (Loneliness), *Shin shôsetsu,* Nov., 1904.

*Jin'ai (Dust), *Shumi,* Feb., 1907. Translated by Robert Rolf, *Monumenta Nipponica,* Vol. XXV, No. 3–4, 1970, pp. 407–414.

Shinjû misui (Attempted double suicide), *Chûô kôron,* Jan., 1913.

Azuchi no haru (The spring in Azuchi), *Chûô kôron,* Feb., 1926.

**Sensaisha no kanashimi (Sorrow of a war victim), *Shinsei,* Jan., 1946. *Synopses II,* pp. 92–95.

**Kotoshi no aki (This autumn), *Chûô kôron,* Jan., 1959. *PEN,* No. 5, pp. 11–13.

MISHIMA YUKIO

Hanazakari no mori (Flowering forest), Shichijô Shoin, 1944.

Tabako (Tobacco), *Ningen,* June, 1946.

*Kamen no kokuhaku (The confessions of a mask), Kawade Shobô, 1949. Translated by Meredith Weatherby, N.Y., New Directions, 1958; London,, Peter Owen, 1964; Tokyo, Tuttle, 1970, 255 pp.

Ao no jidai (The age of blue), *Shinchô,* Aug.–Dec., 1950.

*Kinjiki (Forbidden lust), *Gunzô,* Jan.–Oct., 1941. Translated by Alfred H, Marks, N.Y., Knopf, 1968; London, Secker and Warburg, 1968; Tokyo. Tuttle, 1969, 403 pp.; Harmondsworth, Penguin Books, 1961, 429 pp.

*Sotôba Komachi (A modern Noh play: Sotôba Komachi), *Gunzô,* Jan., 1952. Translated by Donald Keene, *Virginia quarterly review,* Spring, 1959, pp. 270–288.

*Yoru no himawari (Twilight sunflower), *Gunzô,* Apr., 1953. Translated by Shinozaki Shigeho & Virgil A. Warren, Tokyo, Hokuseidô, 1958, 143 pp.

*Shiosai (The sound of waves), Shinchôsha, 1954. Translated by Meredith Weatherby, N.Y., Knopf, 1956; Tokyo, Tuttle, 1956; London, Secker and Warburg, 1957, 182 pp.

*Shigadera Shônin no koi (The priest and his love), *Bungei shunjû,* Oct., 1954. Translated by Ivan Morris, *Modern Japanese stories,* London, Spottiswoode, 1961; Tokyo, Tuttle, 1962, pp. 481–501; "The priest of Shiga temple and his love", translated by Ivan Morris, *Death in midsummer and other stories*, N. Y., New Directions, 1966; Secker and Warburg, 1967; pp. 59–75; Harmondsworth, Penguin Books, 1971.

*Hanjo, *Shinchô*, Jan. 1955. Translated by Donald Keene, *Encounter*, Vol. VIII, No. 1, 1957, pp. 45–51.

Shizumeru taki (The submerged waterfalls), *Chûô kôron*, Jan.–Apr., 1955.

*Kindai hôgaku shû (Five modern Noh plays), Shinchôsha, 1956. Translated by Donald Keene, N.Y., Knopf, 1956.

*Kinkakuji (The temple of the golden pavilion), Shinchôsha, 1956. Translated by Ivan Morris, N.Y., Knopf, 1958; Tokyo, Tuttle, 1959; London, Secker and Warburg, 1959, 262 pp.

Rokumeikan (Rokumei Reception Hall), *Bungakukai*, Dec., 1956.

Bitoku no yoromeki (Wavering virtues), *Gunzô*, Apr.–June, 1957.

Kyôko no ie (Kyôko's house), Shinchôsha, 1959.

*Utage no ato (After the banquet), *Chûô kôron*, Jan.–Oct., 1960. Translated by Donald Keene, N.Y., Knopf, 1963, 270 pp.; Tokyo, Tuttle, 1963; London, Secker and Warburg, 1963, 271 pp.

*Hyakuman-en senbei (Three million yen), *Shinchô*, Sept. 1960. Translated by E. G. Seidensticker, *Japan quarterly*, Vol. IX, No. 2, 1962, pp. 190–200; *Death in midsummer and other stories*, N.Y., New Directions, 1966; Secker and Warburg, 1967, Harmondsworth, Penguin Books, 1971, pp. 30–42.

*Yûkoku (Patriotism), *Shôsetsu chûô kôron*, Dec., 1960. Translated by Geoffrey W. Sargent. *Death in midsummer and other stories*, N.Y., New Directions, 1966; London, Secker and Warburg, 1967, pp. 93–118; Harmondsworth, Penguin Books, 1971.

*Mahôbin (Thermos bottle), *Bungei shunjû*, Jan., 1962. Translated by E. G. Seidensticker. *Japan quarterly*, Vol. IX, No. 2, 1962, pp. 201–214; *Death in midsummer and other stories*, N.Y., New Directions, 1966; London, Secker and Warburg, 1967, pp. 43–58; Harmondsworth Penguin Books, 1971.

Utsukushii hoshi (A beautiful star), *Shinchô*, Jan.–Feb., 1962.

Yorokobi no koto (The joyful harp), *Bungei*, Feb., 1964.

Kinu to meisatsu (Silk and insight), *Gunzô*, Jan.–Oct., 1964.

Mikumano-môde (A visit to the three Kumano shrines), *Shinchô*, Jan., 1965.

Eirei no koe (Voices of the dead), *Bungei*, June, 1966.

Suzakuke no metsubô (Downfall of the Suzaku family), *Bungei*, Oct., 1967.

Hôjô no umi (The sea of plenitude), *Shinchô*, Sept., 1965–1971.

MIURA SHUMON

Gaki (An inspired painter), *Shinshichô*, Apr., 1951.
Meifu sansui zu (Landscape of hades), *Tenbô*, Sept., 1951.
Ono to batei (An axe and a groom), *Bungakukai*, Feb., 1952.
Semiramisu no sono (The garden of Semiramis), *Tsukue*, Apr., 1952.
Yasei no yagi (Wild goat), *Gunzô*, Dec., 1954.
Ponape-tô (Ponape Island), *Gunzô*, Feb., 1956.
Seruroido no tô (A celluloid tower), Bungei Shunjû Shinsha, 1960.
Jisshi (One's real child), Shinchôsha, 1961.
Tomo enpô yori kitaru (A friend comes from afar), *Bungakukai*, Feb., 1961.
Shinwa (Myth), *Gunzô*, Nov., 1963.
Tsume no kai (Society of nails), *Gunzô*, Mar., 1966.
Hakoniwa (Miniature garden), *Bungakukai*, Feb.–Mar., 1967.
Oshie no niwa (School), *Gunzô*, Sept., 1968.
Michi no nakaba ni (Halfway along the road), *Bungakukai*, Dec., 1967–Dec., 1968.

MIURA TETSURÔ

Punpe to yunohana(A pump and sulphur mud), *Hijô*, Feb., 1955.
Jûgo-sai no shûi (The surroundings of a fifteen-year-old), *Shinchô*, Dec., 1955.
Shinobugawa, *Shinchô*, Oct., 1960.
Haji no fu (Genealogy of shame), *Shinchô*, Mar., 1961.
Roba (A donkey), *Bungakukai*, Aug., 1961.
Shoya (The wedding night), *Shinchô*, Oct., 1961.
Kikyô (Home-coming), *Shinchô*, Feb., 1962.
Danran (Happy home), *Shinchô*, Apr., 1963.
Yoru no e (A night picture), *Shinchô*, Mar., 1964.
Umi no michi (A road along the sea), *Bungakukai*, Jan., 1967–Oct., 1969.
Sankaku bôshi (A three-cornered hat), *Bessatsu bungei shunjû*, June, 1968.

MORI MARI

Chichi no bôshi (Father's hat), Shinchôsha, Oct., 1957.

Kutsu no oto (The sound of footsteps), Shinchôsha, 1958.
Zeitaku binbô (Luxurious poverty), Shinchô, June, 1960.
Bocchicheri no tobira (Botticelli's door), Gunzô, Jan., 1961.
Koibitotachi no mori (Forest of lovers), Shinchô, Aug., 1961.
Kareha no nedoko (Bed of withered leaves), Shinchô, June, 1962.

MURÔ SAISEI

Jojô shôkyoku shû (Lyrical melodies), Kanjôshisha, 1918.
Ai no shishû (A collection of love songs), Kanjôshisha, 1918.
Yônen jidai (Childhood), Chûô kôron, Aug., 1919.
Sei ni mezameru koro (Awakening to sex), Chûô kôron, Oct., 1919.
Aojiroki sôkutsu (Pale haunt), Yûben, Mar., 1920.
Utsukushiki hyôga (The beautiful glacier), Chûô kôron, June, 1915.
Kurogane shû (Iron), Shiinokisha, 1932.
*Ani imôto (Brother and sister), Bungei shunjû, Jan., 1934. Translated by
    Edward G. Seidensticker, Modern Japanese stories, London, Spottiswoode,
    1961; Tokyo, Tuttle, 1962, pp. 145–161.
Kamigami no hedo (The vomit of the gods), Yamamoto Shoten, 1935.
Onna no zu (Portrait of a woman), Takemura Shobô, 1935.
**Fukushû (Revenge), Takemura Shobô, 1935. Synopses II, pp. 27–29.
Onnahito (Women), Shinchô, Jan.–June, 1955.
Anzukko, Shinchôsha, 1957.
Tômegane no haru (Spring through a telescope), Shinchô, Aug., 1957.
Waga aisuru shijin no denki (The life of my favorite poet), Fujin kôron,
    Jan.–Dec., 1958.
Kagerô no nikki ibun (The women of Kagerô diary), Fujin no tomo, July,
    1958–June, 1959.
Mitsu no aware (Moving sweetness), Shinchôsha, 1959.
Ware wa utaedo yabure-kabure (I sing, but in a devil-may-care mood),
    Shinchô, Feb., 1962.

NAGAI TATSUO

Kappanya no hanashi (The story of a printer), San'esu, Sept., 1920.
Kuroi gohan (Black boiled rice), Bungei shunjû, July, 1923.
Ehon (A picture book), Bungaku jidai, Feb., 1930.

Tebukuro no katappo (An odd glove), *Bungakukai,* Apr., 1943.
Kurumiwari (Nutcracker), *Gakusei,* Oct., 1948.
*Asagiri (Morning mist), *Bungakukai,* Aug., 1949. Translated by Edward G,
Seidensticker, *Modern Japanese stories,* London, Spottiswoode, 1961; Tokyo.
Tuttle, 1962, pp. 302–319.
Kaze futatabi (The returning wind), Asahi Shinbunsha, 1951.
*Shiroi saku (The white fence), *Bungei shunjû,* Jan., 1952. Translated by
William L. Clark, *Various kinds of bugs and other stories from present-day
Japan,* Tokyo, Kenkyûsha, 1958. pp. 55–71.
*Ikko (One), *Shinchô,* Aug., 1959. Translated by E. G. Seindensticker, *Japan
quarterly,* Vol. VII, No. 2, 1960, pp. 211–217.
Ikko sonota (One, and other stories), Bungei Shunjû Shinsha, 1965.
Aotsuyu (The blue rainy season), *Shinchô,* Sept., 1965.

NAKAMURA MITSUO

Fûzoku shôsetsu ron (On the novel of manners), *Bungei,* Feb.–May, 1950.
Hito to ôkami (Man and wolves), *Chûô kôron,* Dec., 1957.
Futabatei Shimei den (The life of Futabatei Shimei), *Gunzô,* Jan., 1957–
June, 1958.
Pari hanjô ki (A record of flourishing Paris), *Koe,* July & Oct., 1960.
Waga sei no hakusho (White paper of my sexual experience), *Gunzô,* Oct.,
1963.

NAKAMURA SHIN'ICHIRÔ

**Shi no kage no moto ni (Under the shadow of death), Shinzenbisha, 1947.
Synopses II, pp. 111–113.
Shion no musumetachi (Maidens of Sion), Kawade Shobô, 1948.
Aijin to shishin to (The god of love and the god of death), *Bungei,* Nov.,
1948–June, 1949.
Tamashii no yoru no naka o (Through the night of the soul), Kawade Shobô,
1951.
Nagai tabi no owari (Journey's end), Kawade Shobô, 1952.
Tsumetai tenshi (A cold angel), Dai Nihon Yûbenkai Kôdansha, 1955.
Yahanraku (Music at midnight), Shinchôsha, 1954.
Koi no izumi (Fountain of love), Shinchôsha, 1962.

Ishi no inori (Prayer of a stone), *Gunzô*, Mar., 1969.

NAKANO SHIGEHARU

Dai isshô (The first chapter), *Chûô kôron*, Jan., 1935.
Hitotsu no chiisana kiroku (One tiny document), *Chûô kôron*, Jan., 1936.
Shôsetsu no kakenu shôsetsuka (A novelist who cannot write novels), Take-mura Shobô, 1937.
Uta no wakare (Farewell to song), *Kakushin*, Apr.–Aug., 1939.
**Muragimo (The heart), *Gunzô*, Jan.–July, 1954. *Synopses II*, pp. 205–208.
Hagi no monkakiya (The crest painter of Hagi), *Gunzô*, Oct., 1956.
Nashi no Hana (Pear Blossoms), *Shinchô*, Jan., 1957–Dec., 1958.
Kô otsu hei tei (A, B, C, and D), *Gunzô*, Jan., 1965–Sept., 1969.

NAKAYAMA GISHU

Ishibumi (Stone monument), *Bungei shunjû*, June, 1939.
Teniyan no matsujitsu (The last days of Tinian), *Shinchô*, Sept., 1948.
Sôrenka (The pilgrimage of a woman) *Bessatsu bungei shunjû*, Feb., 1952.
**Atsumonozaki (The thick-petalled chrysanthemum), *Bungakukai*, Apr., 1952. *Synopses II*, pp. 67–70.
Daijô no tsuki (The moon on the tower), *Shôsetsu shinchô*, Jan., 1962–Feb., 1963.
Shôan (Shôan), *Gunzô*, Jan., 1963–Feb., 1964.

NIWA FUMIO

Ayu (The trout), *Bungei shunjû*, Apr., 1932.
Shôkei-moji (Hieroglyphics), *Kaizô*, Apr., 1934.
Zeiniku (Indulgent flesh), *Chûô kôron*, July, 1934. Translated by Richard Foster, *The hateful age*, Tokyo, Hara Shobô, 1965, pp. 139–245.
**Iyagarase no nenrei (The hateful years), *Kaizô*, Feb., 1947. Translated by William L. Clark, *Various kinds of bugs and other stories from present-day Japan*, Tokyo, Kenkyûsha, 1958, pp. 97–175. "The hateful age," translated by Ivan Morris, *Japan quarterly*, Vol. III, No. 1, 1956, pp. 54–78, *Modern Japanese stories*, London, Spottiswoode, 1961; Tokyo, Tuttle, 1962, pp. 321–348. *Synopses II*, pp. 114–116.

Kokuheki (Wailing wall), *Gunzô*, Oct., 1947.
Tôsei munazan'yo (Calculation in the present age), *Chûô kôron*, Sept.–Dec., 1949.
Hachûrui (The reptile), *Bungei shunjû*, Jan.–June, 1950.
Kôfuku e no kyori (The distance to happiness), *Gunzô*, Oct., 1951.
Shadan-ki (The crossing gate), *Shinchô*, Nov., 1952.
Bodaiju (The Buddha tree), *Shûkan yomiuri*, Jan. 1955–Mar., 1956. Translated by Kenneth Strong, London, Peter Owen, 1966; Tokyo, Tuttle, 1968, 380 pp.
Ichiro (A single road), *Gunzô*, Oct., 1962–June, 1966.
Shinran (The founder of the *Shin* sect), *Sankei shinbun*, Sept., 1965–Mar., 1969.
Rennyo (A Buddhist priest of the *Shin* sect), *Chûô kôron*, Jan., 1971—.

NOGAMI YAEKO

*Kaijinmaru (The Neptune), *Chûô kôron*, Sept., 1922. Translated by Matsumoto Ryôzô, *The foxes*, Tokyo, Kenkyûsha, 1957; *Japanese literature new and old*, Tokyo, Hokuseidô, 1961, pp. 119–176.
**Meiro (The labyrinth), *Chûô kôron, Sekai*, 1936–1956. *Synopses II*, pp. 48–51.
**Hideyoshi to Rikyû (Hideyoshi and Rikyû), *Chûô kôron*, Jan., 1962–Sept., 1963. *PEN*, No. 15, pp. 12–14.
Enishi (Human ties), *Hototogisu*, Feb., 1907.

NOMA HIROSHI

Kurai e (A gloomy picture), *Kibachi*, Apr., 1946.
Hôkai kankaku (Collapse), *Sekai hyôron*, Jan.–Mar., 1948.
Seinen no wa (The circle of youth), Kawade Shobô, 1949–1971.
*Shinkû chitai (Zone of emptiness), Kawade Shobô, 1952. Translated by Bernard Frechtman, Cleveland, World Pub. Co., 1956. 319pp. "Vacuum zone", *Synopses II*, pp. 201–204.
Saikoro no sora (The sky of the dice), *Bungakukai*, Feb., 1958–Nov., 1959.
Waga tô wa soko ni tatsu (My tower stands there), *Gunzô*, Nov., 1960–Oct., 1961.

ÔE KENZABURÔ

Kimyôna shigoto (A strange job), *Tokyo Daigaku shinbun,* May 22, 1957.
Shisha no ogori (Lavish are the dead), *Bungakukai,* Aug., 1957. Translated by
John Nathan, *Japan quarterly* Vol. XII, No. 2, 1965, pp. 193–211.
Shiiku (The catch), *Bungakukai,* Jan., 1958. Translated by John Bester, *Japan
quarterly,* Vol. VI, No. 1, 1959, pp. 69–94; *The shadow of sunrise,* Tokyo,
Kôdansha, 1966; London, Ward Lock, 1966, pp. 15–60.
Me-mushiri ko-uchi (Tearing buds and shooting children), *Gunzô,* June,
1958.
Warera no jidai (Our age), Chûô Kôronsha, 1959.
Seinen no omei (Bad name of a youth), *Bungakukai,* Aug., 1959–Mar., 1960.
Seventeen, *Bungakukai,* Jan. (Part I) & Mar. (Part II), 1961.
Okuretekita seinen (The youth who arrived late), *Shinchô,* Sept., 1960–Feb.,
1962.
Sakebi-goe (Cries), *Gunzô,* Nov., 1962.
Seiteki ningen (Obsessed), Shinchôsha, 1963.
Nichijô seikatsu no bôken (Adventure in everyday life), *Bungakukai,* Feb.,
1963–Feb., 1964.
*Kojintekina taiken (A personal matter), Shinchôsha, 1964. Translated by
John Nathan, N.Y., Grove Press, 1968. 214 pp.; Tokyo, Tuttle, 1969.
Man'en gannen no futto-bôru (Football played in the first year of Man'en),
Gunzô, Jan.–July, 1967.
Warera no kyôki o ikinobiru michi o oshieyo (Outgrow our madness),
Shinchô, Feb., 1969.
Kakujidai no sôzôryoku (Imagination in the atomic age), Shinchôsha, 1970.

ÔHARA TOMIE

Shuku shussei (Celebration for departure for the front), *Bungei shuto,* Mar.,
1938.
Wakaki keikan (Young valley), *Kaizô,* Aug., 1943.
Sutomai tsunbo (Deafness caused by streptomycin), *Bungei,* Sept., 1956.
**En to iu onna (Woman called En), Kôdansha, 1959. *PEN,* No. 5, pp. 10–11.
Seisai (Lawful wife), *Gunzô,* Mar., 1961.
Kawa wa ima mo nagareru (The river still flows), *Gunzô,* July, 1962,

ÔOKA SHÔHEI

Furyo ki (Prisoner of war), *Bungakukai,* Feb., 1948. Translated by Sakuko Matsui, *Solidarity,* Vol. II, No. 7, 1967, pp. 54–84.

San Hose Yasen Byôin (San José Field Hospital), *Chûô kôron,* Apr., 1948.

Reite no ame (Rains in Leyte Island), *Sakuhin,* Aug., 1948.

Musashino fujin (Madame Musashino), *Gunzô,* Jan.–Sept., 1950.

**Nobi (Fire on the plain), *Tenbô,* Jan.–Aug., 1951. Translated by Ivan Morris, London, Secker and Warburg, 212 pp.; New York, A. Knopf, 1957, 246 pp.; Tokyo, Tuttle, 1967, 246 pp.; London, Transworld, 1959, 191 pp.; London, Panther, 1968, 204 pp.; Harmondsworth, Penguin Books, 1969. *Synopses II,* pp. 147–150.

Sanso (Oxygen), *Bungakukai,* Jan., 1952–July, 1953.

Kaei (Shadows of flowers), Chûô Kôronsha, 1961.

Sakasasugi (Reversed cryptomeria), *Gunzô,* Jan., 1960.

Reite senki (An account of battles in Leyte Island), *Chûô kôron,* Jan., 1967–July, 1969.

Mindoro Tô futatabi (Mindoro Island again), *Umi,* Aug., 1969.

OZAKI KAZUO

Fuso no chi (Ancestral place), *Waseda bungaku,* June, 1935.

Nonki megane (The carefree spectacles), Sunagoya Shobô, 1937.

Yume arishi hi (Hopeful bygone days), Sunagoya Shobô, 1940.

Kôrogi (Crickets), *Shinchô,* Sept., 1946.

*Mushi no iroiro (Various kinds of bugs), *Shinchô,* Jan., 1948. *"Insects of various kinds,"* translated by Mukai Hiroo, *Pacific spectator* Vol. V, Fall, 1951. *Various kinds of bugs and other stories,* translated by William L. Clark, Tokyo, Kenkyûsha, 1958, pp. 73–96.

Utsukushii bochi kara no nagame (A view from a beautiful cemetery), *Gunzô,* June, 1948.

*Yaseta ondori (The thin rooster), *Bungaku kaigi,* Jan., 1949. Translated by E. G. Seidensticker, *Japan quarterly,* Vol. II, No. 2, 1955.

**Maboroshi no ki (The account of my dreamlike life), *Gunzô,* Aug., 1961. *PEN,* No. 11, pp. 9–10.

SATA INEKO

Kyarameru kôjô kara (From the caramel factory), *Puroretaria geijutsu*, Feb., 1928.
Restoran Rakuyô (Restaurant Rakuyô), *Bungei shunjû*, Feb., 1928.
Kanbu jokô no namida (The tears of the forewomen), *Kaizô*, Jan., 1931.
Shô kanbu (Little leaders), *Bungei shunjû*, Aug., 1931.
Kitô (Prayer), *Chûô kôron*, Oct. 1931.
Nani o nasubeki ka (What is to be done?), *Chûô kôron*, Mar., 1932.
Kyôfu (Fear), *Bungaku hyôron*, May, 1934.
Kyogi (Untruth), *Ningen*, June, 1948.
Hômatsu no kiroku (A record of bubbles), *Hikari*, Sept., 1948.
Yoru no kioku (The memory of a night), *Sekai*, June, 1955.
Haguruma (A cogwheel), *Akahata*, Oct., 1958–Apr., 1959.
Mizu (Water), *Gunzô*, May, 1961.

SATÔ HARUO

*Supein-inu no ie (The house of a Spanish dog), *Seiza*, Jan., 1917. Translated by George Saitô, *Modern Japanese stories*, London, Spottiswoode, 1961; Tokyo, Tuttle, 1962, pp. 162–172.
Yameru sôbi (Oh, rose thou art sick), *Kuroshio*, June, 1917.
Den'en no yûutsu (Pastoral melancholy), Shinchosha, 1919.
Junjô shishu (A collection of sentimental poems), Shinchôsha, 1921.
Tokai no yûutsu (The melancholy of the city), *Fujin kôron*, Jan.–Dec., 1922.
Wabishi-sugiru (Too lonely), *Chûô kôron*, July, 1923.
Baishôfu Mari (Mari, the prostitute), *Kaizô*, July, 1923.
*Jokaisen kidan (The tale of the bridal fan), *Josei*, May, 1925. Translated by Edward G. Seidensticker, *Japan quarterly*, Vol. IX, No. 3, 1962, pp. 310–336.
Satô Haruo shishû (The collected poems of Satô Haruo), Daiichi Shobô, 1926.
Kôseiki (Starting afresh), *Fukuoka nichinichi shinbun*, May–Oct., 1929.
**Kikusui monogatari (Tale of the chrysanthemum crest), *Tokyo nichinichi shinbun*, June–Sept., 1935. *Synopses II*, pp. 20–22.

Satô Haruo zen-shishû (The complete poems of Satô Haruo), Sôgensha, 1952.
Aibyô Chibi no shi (The death of beloved Chibi), Shinchô, June, 1964.

SATOMI TON

Tegami (Letter), Shirakaba, Dec., 1912.
Osoi hatsukoi (Later first love), Chûô kôron, Apr., 1915.
Natsu e (Summer picture), Shin shôsetsu, Nov., 1915.
Zenshin akushin (Good heart and evil heart), Chûô kôron, July, 1916.
Tsuma o kau keiken (Experience of buying a wife), Bunshô sekai, Jan., 1917.
Jigoku (Hell), Ningen, Jan., 1921.
Tajô busshin (Fickle feeling, pious heart), Jiji shinpô, Dec., 1922–Dec., 1923.
Chichioya (Father), Ningen, June, 1923.
*Tsubaki (The camellia), Kaizô, Nov., 1923. Translated by Edward G. Sei-
densticker, Modern Japanese stories, London, Spottiswoode, 1961; Tokyo,
Tuttle, 1962, pp. 138–143.
Anjô-ke no kyôdai (The Anjô brothers), Chûô Kôronsha, 1931.
**Migotona shûbun (The admirable scandal), Kaizô, Jan., 1947. Synopses II,
pp. 114–116.
**Higan bana (Daughter's marriage), Kadokawa Shoten, 1958. PEN, No. 3,
pp. 10.
Gokuraku tonbo (The happy-go-lucky), Chûô kôron, Jan., 1961.

SETOUCHI HARUMI

Tamura Toshiko den (The life of Tamura Toshiko), Bungei Shunjû Shinsha,
1961.
Kanoko ryôran (The life of Okamoto Kanoko), Fujin gahô, July, 1962–June,
1964.
Natsu no owari (Summer's ending), Shinchô, Oct., 1962.
Kashin (The heart of a flower), Tôhôsha, 1964.

SHIINA RINZÔ

**Shin'ya no shuen (Banquet at midnight), Tenbô, Feb., 1947. Synopses II, pp.
119–122.

Omoi nagare no naka ni (In the middle of a heavy stream), *Tenbô,* June, 1947
Eien naru joshô (Eternal prologue), Kawade Shobô, 1948.
Jiyû no kanata de (On the other side of freedom), *Shinchô,* May–Sept., 1953.
Daisan no shôgen (The third testimony), *Teatoro,* Dec., 1960.
*Ai no shôgen (The flowers are fallen), *Shinjoen,* Jan.–Dec., 1955. Translated
   by Sydney Giffard, London, Heinemann, 1961, 208 pp.
**Utsukushii onna (The beautiful woman), *Chûô kôron,* May–Sept., 1955. *PEN,*
   No. 1, pp. 3.
Sasori o kau onna (The woman who keeps a scorpion), *Shin Nihon bungaku,*
   Feb., 1960.
Yoru no saiten (Night festival), *Shingeki,* Oct., 1961.
Fuanna kekkon (Uneasy marriage), *Shingeki,* May, 1963.

SHIMAO TOSHIO

Kotô-mu (Dream in a distant island), *Kôyô,* Apr., 1946.
Matenrô (Skyscraper), Shinzenbisha, 1948.
Yume no naka de no nichijô (Daily life in dream), *Sôgô bunka,* May, 1948,.
Chinkonka (Requiem), *Gunzô,* Sept., 1949.
Shutsu kotô ki (Account of the departure from the solitary island), *Bungei,*
   Nov., 1949.
Onihage, *Gendai hyôron,* June, 1954.
**Shi no toge (The thorns of death), *Gunzô,* Sept., 1960. *PEN,* No. 7, pp. 6–7.
Shima e (To the island), *Bungakukai,* Jan., 1962.
Shuppatsu wa tsui ni otozurezu (Departure never came), *Gunzô,* Sept., 1962.
Ôbasami (Big scissors).

SHÔNO JUNZÔ

Yuki hotaru (Snow firefly), *Mahoroba,* Apr., 1944.
Aibu (Caresses), *Shin bungaku,* Apr., 1949.
Pûru saido shôkei (A pool-side scene), *Gunzô,* Dec., 1954.
Itaria fû (Italian style), *Bungakukai,* Dec., 1958.
**Ganbia taizai ki (My stay in Gambia), Chûô Kôronsha, 1959. *PEN,* No.7
   pp. 7–9.
**Seibutsu (Still life), *Gunzô,* June, 1960. Extract. Translated by Ted Takaya,
   PEN, No. 17, pp. 22–25,.

Yûbe no kumo (Evening cloud), Kôdansha, 1965.
Akikaze to futari no otoko (Autumn wind and two men), Gunzô, Nov., 1965.

SONO AYAKO

Susono (At the foot of a mountain), Ramancha, May, 1951.
Enrai no kyakutachi (Visitors from afar), Mita bungaku, Apr., 1954.
Babiron no shojo ichi (The virgin market of Babylon), Bungakukai, Oct., 1954.
Garasu no itazura (The trick of the glasses), Shinchô, Nov., 1954.
Reimei (Dawn), Kôdansha, 1957.
Yukiakari (Snow light), Gunzô, Feb., 1957.
Otoko-gari (Man-hunt), Bungei shunjû, July, 1957.
Shisha no umi (The sea of the dead), Chikuma Shobô, 1958.
Tamayura (For a time), Gunzô, Oct., 1959.
Nômen no ie (The house of a Nô mask), Chûô Kôronsha, 1960.
Rio Grande, Bungakukai, June & July, 1961.
Gogo no bishô (Afternoon smile), Mainichi Shinbunsha, 1962.

TAKAHASHI KAZUMI

Sutego monogatari (The tale of an abandoned child), Adachi Shobô, 1958.
Hi no utsuwa (Vessel of sorrow), Bungei, Nov., 1962.
Yûutsu naru tôha (Melancholic faction), Kawade Shobô Shinsha, 1965.
Jashûmon (The evil faith), Asahi journal, Jan., 1965–May, 1966.

TAKAMI JUN

**Kokyû wasure-ubeki (Should auld acquaintance be forgot?), Nichireki, Feb.–July, 1935. Synopses II, pp. 14–17.
Ikanaru hoshi no moto ni (Under what star?), Bungei, Jan., 1939–Mar., 1940.
**Seimei no ki (The tree of life), Gunzô, Sept.–Dec., 1956; Dec., 1957–Nov., 1958. PEN, No. 5, pp. 5–6.
Waga mune no soko no koko niwa (Here at the bottom of my heart), Bungei, Jan.–Feb., 1957.

Gekiryû (A raging torrent), *Sekai,* Jan., 1959–Nov., 1961.
Iyana kanji (Disagreeable feeling), *Bungakukai,* Jan., 1960–May, 1963.
Waga maisô (My burial), Shichôsha, 1963.

TAKEDA TAIJUN

Shibasen (Sze-ma Ts'ien), Nihon Hyôronsha, 1943.
*Mamushi no sue (This outcast generation), *Shinchô,* Aug.–Oct., 1947. Translated by Shibuya Yusaburô and Sanford Goldstein, *This outcast generation and Luminous moss,* Tokyo, Tuttle, 1967. pp. 21–89.
*Igyô no mono (The misshapen ones), *Tenbô,* Apr., 1950. Translated by E. G. Seidensticker, *Japan quarterly,* Vol. IV, No. 4, 1957, pp. 472–498; *Modern Japanese stories,* Tokyo, Japan Publications Trading Co., 1960, pp. 52–89.
Fûbaika (Anemophilous flower), *Gunzô,* Jan.–Nov., 1952.
**Hikarigoke (Luminous moss), *Shinchô,* Mar., 1954. Translated by Shibuya Yusaburô and Sanford Goldstein, *op. cit.,* pp. 93–145. *Synopses II,* pp. 208–211.
Shikon shôsai (Samurai spirit and business talent), *Bungakukai,* Jan., 1957.
**Mori to mizuumi no matsuri (The grove and the lake festival), *Sekai,* Jan., Aug., 1955–May, 1958. *PEN,* No. 2, p. 1.
Kizoku no kaidan (Degrees of aristocracy), *Chûô kôron,* Jan.–May, 1959.
Nisesatsu-tsukai no shuki (The autobiography of a banknote forger), *Gunzô,* June, 1963.

TANAKA CHIKAO

Ofukuro (Mother), *Gekisaku,* March, 1933.
Kumo no hatate (The cloud frontier), *Gekisaku,* Aug., 1947.
Mezaru (A female monkey), *Bungakukai,* Sept., 1948.
Kyôiku (Education), *Shingeki,* July, 1954.
Hizen fudoki (The Hizen district), *Shingeki,* Oct., 1956.
Hime yama (Volcano), *Shingeki,* Aug., 1957.
Maria no kubi (The head of Mary), *Shingeki,* Sept., 1959.
Chidori (Plover), first performed by Haiyûza, Oct., 1959.
Sasurai (Wandering), *Shingeki,* Nov., 1964.
Shinri (Psychology), first performed by Haiyûza Shôgekijô, June, 1967.
Arai Hakuseki, *Tenbô,* Oct., 1968.

TANIZAKI JUN'ICHIRÔ

*Shisei (The Tattooer), *Shinshichô,* Nov., 1910. Translated by Howard Hibbett, *Seven Japanese tales,* N.Y., Knopf, 1963; London, Secker and Warbug, 1964; Tokyo, Tuttle, 1963, pp. 160–169. "The young tattooer" translated by Miyamori Asataro, *Representative tales of Japan,* Sanko Shoin, 1917, pp. 1–19. "Tattoo" Translated by Matsumoto Ryôzô, *Japanese literature new and old,* Tokyo, Hokuseido, 1961, pp. 105–118. "Tatoo" Translated by Ivan Morris. *Modern Japanese stories,* London, Spottiswoode, 1961; Tokyo, Tuttle, 1962, pp. 92–100.

Haha o kouru ki (The house where I was born), *Osaka mainichi shinbun, Tokyo nichinichi shinbun,* Jan., 1919. Translated by S. G. Brikeley, *The writing of idiomatic English,* Tokyo, Kenkyûsha, 1951, pp. 118–129.

Chijin no ai (A fool's love), *Osaka asahi shinbun* (Part I), Mar.–June, 1924, *Josei* (Part II), Nov., 1924–July, 1925.

Manji (The buddhist cross), *Kaizô,* Mar.–May, 1928.

Yoshinokuzu (Yoshino arrowroot), *Chûô kôron,* Jan.–Feb., 1931.

*Ashikari (Ashikari), *Kaizô,* Nov.–Dec., 1932. Translated by Roy Humpherson and Okita Hajime, *Ashikari and the story of Shunkin,* Tokyo, Hokuseidô, 1936.

*Shunkin-shô (A portrait of Shunkin), *Chûô kôron,* June, 1933. Howard Hibbett (tr.), *op. cit.,* pp. 3–84. Roy Humpherson and Hajime Okita (tr.), *op. cit.*

*Sasameyuki (The Makioka sisters), *Fujin kôron,* Mar., 1947–Oct., 1948. Translated by E. G. Seidensticker, New York, Knopf, 1957, 530 pp.; Tokyo, Tuttle, 1958.

**Shôshô Shigemoto no haha (The mother of captain Shigemoto), *Mainichi shinbun,* Dec., 1949–Mar., 1950. Translated by E. G. Seidensticker, *Modern Japanese literature,* N.Y., Grove Press, 1956; Tokyo, Tuttle, 1957, pp. 387–397. *Synopses II,* pp. 162–164.

*Kagi (The key), *Chûô kôron,* Jan.–Dec., 1956. Translated by Howard Hibbett, N.Y., Knopf, 1961, 183 pp.; London, Secker and Warbug, 1961; Tokyo, Tuttle, 1962.

*Yume no ukihashi (The bridge of dreams), *Chûô kôron,* Oct., 1959. Translated by Howard Hibbett, *Seven Japanese tales,* N.Y., Knopf, 1963; London, Secker and Warbug, 1964, pp. 95–159; Tokyo, Tuttle, 1963, pp. 95–159.

*Fûten rôjin nikki (Diary of a mad old man), *Chûô kôron,* Nov., 1961–May, 1962. Translated by Howard Hibbett, N.Y., Knopf, 1965, 203 pp.; London, Secker and Warbug, 1966; Tokyo, Tuttle, 1967, 177 pp.

TONOMURA SHIGERU

U no monogatari (The Cormorant story), *Kirin,* Sept., 1933.
**Kusa ikada (Grass raft), Sunagawa Shobô, 1938. *PEN,* No. 3, p. 8.
**Mugen hôei (Transient image), *Bungei shunjû,* Apr., 1949. *Synopses II,* pp. 157–159.
Ikada (Raft), *Bungei nihon,* Nov., 1954–Mar., 1955.
Hana ikada (Flower raft), Mikasa Shobô, 1958.
Miotsukushi (Waterway signal), *Gunzô,* July, 1960.
Rakujitsu no kôkei (View of the setting sun), *Shinchô,* Aug., 1960.
Hi o itoshimu (I love sunrise), *Gunzô,* Jan., 1961.
Nurenizo nureshi (My love affairs), *Shûkan gendai,* Feb., 1961.

UMEZAKI HARUO

Asu (Tomorrow), *L'obélisque,* No. 1, Feb., 1934.
Chizu (Map), *Kikôchi,* June, 1936.
**Genka (Hallucination), *Shinchô,* June & Aug., 1965. *PEN,* No. 19, pp. 5–7.
Ue no kisetsu (Season of hunger), *Bundan,* Jan., 1948.
**Kurui dako (Crazy kite), Kôdansha, 1963. *PEN,* No. 15. pp. 14–17.
Fûen (Feast of the wind), *Waseda bungaku,* Aug., 1939.
*Sakurajima, *Sunao,* Sept., 1946. Translated by D. E. Mills. *The shadow of sunrise,* Tokyo, Kôdansha, 1966; London, Ward Lock, 1966, pp. 63–117. *Synopses II,* pp. 106–108.
*Sora no shita (under the sky), *Shinchô,* Aug., 1951. Translated by Shioya Sakae, Univ. of Utah, *Western humanities review,* Spring, 1952, pp. 119–128.
Hi no hate (The end of the day), *Shisaku,* Sept., 1947.
Runeta no shiminhei (The civilian soldiers of Luneta), *Bungei shunjû,* Aug., 1949.
Boroya no shunjû (Seasons in a shack), *Shinchô,* Aug., 1954.
Aru tenmatsu (The circumstances around a certain event), *Bungei,* Oct., 1947.

UNO CHIYO

Haka o abaku (Exhuming a tomb), *Chûô kôron,* May, 1922.
Tsuioku no chichi (Reminiscences of my father), *Chûô kôron,* Mar., 1923.
Iro zange (Confessions of an amorous life), *Chûô kôron,* Sept., 1933–Mar., 1935.
Koi no tegami (A love letter), *Chûô kôron,* Nov., 1938.
Ningyôshi Tenguya Hisakichi (Tenguya Hisakichi, a puppet-maker), *Chûô kôron,* Nov.–Dec., 1942.
*Ohan, *Chûô kôron,* June–Dec., 1950; Apr.–May, 1952. Translated by Donald Keene, *Three modern Japanese short novels,* New York, Viking, 1961, pp. 51–118.
**Sasu (Sting), *Shinchô,* Jan. 1963–Jan., 1966. *PEN,* No. 19, pp. 7–10.
Kaze no oto (Sound of the winds), *Umi,* June, 1969.

YAMAKAWA MASAO

Hibi no shi (Daily death), *Mita bungaku,* Jan., 1957.
Kaigan kôen (Seaside park), *Shinchô,* May, 1961.
Ai no gotoku (Like love), *Shinchô,* Apr., 1964.
Entotsu (Chimney), *Bungakukai,* Nov., 1964.
Saisho no aki (The first autumn), *Shinchô,* Nov., 1964.
Tenbôdai no aru shima (An island with an observation platform), *Shinchô,* Feb., 1965.

YASHIRO SEIICHI

Hataraki-bachi (A worker bee), *Kindai bungaku,* (in one vol.), Mar. & Apr., 1950.
Kitsunetsuki (Possessed by a fox), Hakusuisha (Gikyoku daihyôsaku senshû), 1953.
Shiro (Castle), *Shingeki,* Apr., 1954.
Uta (Songs), *Mita bungaku,* Oct., 1954.
Esugata Nyôbô (Portrait of wife), *Shingeki,* Apr., 1955.
Kokusenya, *Shingeki,* May, 1957.

APPENDIX

Kiiro to momoiro no yûgata (Pink and yellow evenings), *Shingeki,* Oct., 1959.
Chizu no nai tabi (A journey without a map), *Shingeki,* Jan., 1961.
Kuro no higeki (Black tragedy), *Shingeki,* Sept., 1962.
Yûkai (Kidnaping), *Shingeki,* Apr., 1965.
Miyagino (Miyagino field), *Higeki kigeki,* Dec., 1966.
Yoake ni kieta (Gone with the dawn), *Shingeki,* Sept., 1968.
Ten'ichibô shichijû ban (Ten' ichibô, the impostor), *Shingeki,* Dec., 1969.

YASUOKA SHÔTARÔ

Garasu no kutsu (Glass shoes), *Mita bungaku,* June, 1951. Translated by Edward Seidensticker. *Japan quarterly,* Vol. VIII, No. 2, 1961, pp. 195–206.
Aigan (Pet), *Bungakukai,* Nov., 1952.
Inki na tanoshimi (Gloomy pastime), *Shinchô,* Apr., 1953.
Warui nakama (Evil companions), *Gunzô,* June, 1953.
Shitadashi-tenshi (An angel who sticks out her tongue), *Gunzô,* Apr., 1958.
**Kaihen no kôkei (View of the bay), *Gunzô,* Nov.–Dec., 1959. Translated by Joyce Ackoyd and Hiramatsu Mikio, *Hemisphere,* Vol. VIII, No. 6, 1964, pp. 17–19. *PEN,* No. 5, pp. 9–10.
*Shichiya no nyôbô (The pawnbroker's wife), *Bungei Shunjû,* May, 1960. Translated by E. G. Seindensticker, *Japan quarterly,* Vol. VIII, No. 2, 1961, pp. 188–195.
Hanamatsuri (Buddha's birthday festival), Shinchôsha, 1962.
Maku ga oritekara (After the curtain falls), *Gunzô,* Mar., 1967.

YOSHIYUKI JUNNOSUKE

Bara hanbainin (The seller of roses), *Shinjitsu,* Jan., 1950.
Genshoku no machi (Primary colors street), *Sedai,* Jan., 1952.
Shûu (Shower), *Bungakukai,* Jan., 1954.
Tadayou heya (The floating room), *Bungei,* Nov., 1955.
Honoo no naka (In the flames), Shinchôsha, 1956.
Shôfu no heya (A prostitute's room), *Chûô kôron,* Oct., 1958.
Yami no naka no shukusai (Festival in the dark), *Gunzô,* Nov., 1961.
Suna no ue no shokubutsugun (A group of plants on the sand), *Bungakukai,* Jan.–Dec., 1963.

Hoshi to tsuki to wa ten no ana (Stars and the Moon are heaven's holes), *Gunzô*, Jan., 1966.

(After having compiled this list, the editor was informed of the publication of a more comprehensive bibliography, *Modern Japanese Literature in Western Translations,* published in May 1972 by the International House of Japan in Tokyo. The compiler, Mr. Fujimoto Yukio, modestly states in the preface that exhaustiveness could not be claimed, yet this bibliography may be the most up-to-date catalogue which covers the books published from 1868 to this date. The title index appended to the end of this bibliography and classified according to each language group indicates the amount of works translated in the respective language areas, including Soviet Union. This volume is a valuable contribution to the study of Japanese literature overseas.)